PENGUIN BOOKS

THE MERRY HEART

The son of a journalist, Robertson Davies was born in Thamesville, Ontario, and educated at Queen's University and at Oxford. He had three successive careers: first as an actor with the Old Vic Company in England; then as a publisher of the Peterborough *Examiner;* and finally as a university professor and the first Master of Massey College at the University of Toronto.

It is as a fiction writer that Davies gained international recognition. His work includes three critically acclaimed trilogies: the Salterton trilogy, composed of *Tempest-Tost, Leaven of Malice* and *A Mixture of Frailties;* the Deptford trilogy of *Fifth Business, The Manticore* and *World of Wonders;* and the Cornish trilogy, *The Rebel Angels, What's Bred in the Bone* and *The Lyre of Orpheus.* He also wrote *Murther & Walking Spirits* and *The Cunning Man,* both available as Penguin paperbacks.

D0863345

THE
MERRY HEART

SELECTIONS 1980–1995

Robertson Davies

Penguin Books

PENGUIN BOOKS
Published by the Penguin Group
Penguin Books Canada Ltd, 10 Alcorn Avenue, Toronto, Ontario, Canada M4V 3B2
Penguin Books Ltd, 27 Wrights Lane, London W8 5TZ, England
Penguin Books USA Inc., 375 Hudson Street, New York, New York 10014, U.S.A.
Penguin Books Australia Ltd, Ringwood, Victoria, Australia
Penguin Books (NZ) Ltd, cnr Rosedale and Airborne Roads, Albany, Auckland 1310
New Zealand

Penguin Books Ltd, Registered Offices: Harmondsworth, Middlesex, England

First published as a Douglas Gibson Book by McClelland and Stewart Inc., 1996
Published in Penguin Books, 1998
10 8 6 4 2 1 3 5 7 9

Copyright © Pendragon Ink, 1996
Introductions © Douglas M. Gibson, 1996

All rights reserved.

Manufactured in Canada.

Canadian Cataloguing in Publication Data

Davies, Robertson, 1913–1995
The merry heart: selections 1980–1995

ISBN 0-14-026577-5

I. Title.

PS8507.A67A6 1997   C818'.5408   C96-932039-6
PR9199.3.D38A6 1997

Except in the United States of America, this book is sold subject to the condition that it shall not, by way of trade or otherwise, be lent, re-sold, hired out, or otherwise circulated without the publisher's prior consent in any form of binding or cover other than that in which it is published and without a similar condition including this condition being imposed on the subsequent purchaser.

The following chapters appear by permission of those noted below:
2. Upper Canada College *Old Times*; 3. The excerpts from Douglas LePan's poetry appear courtesy of the author and of McClelland & Stewart; 5. *Johns Hopkins Magazine*; 6. *Compass, A Jesuit Journal*; 7. Reprinted from the 1989-90 Wiegand Foundation Lecture with the permission of the Faculty of Arts and Science, University of Toronto, and the Wiegand Foundation; 11. *First Things*, New York; 13, 14. The University of Utah Press; 18. Selections from *The Papers of Samuel Marchbanks*, published by Irwin Publishing, Toronto, 1985, reprinted with the permission of Stoddart Publishing Co. Limited, North York, Ontario; 22. Penguin Books Ltd., U.K.

Visit Penguin Canada's web site at **www.penguin.ca**

A merry heart doeth good like a medicine:
but a broken spirit drieth the bones.

Proverbs 17:22

CONTENTS

INTRODUCTION

When Robertson Davies died on December 2, 1995, the sad news circled the globe, inspiring obituaries in a dozen countries. All of the writers—and readers too many to count—mourned the fact that a unique, utterly distinctive voice had been stilled.

It is true that the world will never see another novel by Robertson Davies. Our sense of loss is all the greater because even after he had passed his eightieth year, there was no sense of decline in his work. He was writing at the top of his form until his final, short illness. It is notable that *The Cunning Man,* one of his most accomplished and successful novels, was completed in the spring of 1994, when he was eighty years old. But while he researched and prepared for the novel that would follow it—to make up what might have become known in time as "The Toronto Trilogy"—he went on writing, producing speeches, book reviews, even a libretto.

Fortunately, because of his prodigious energy and discipline (he believed that the writer's craft was like a muscle, and needed constant exercising), we are able to celebrate a new book by Robertson Davies.

In the last months of his life, as his publisher I had started to lay plans with him for the publication of such a work. There was a happy precedent. In 1977 we had worked together to bring out a selection of his speeches, entitled *One Half of Robertson Davies,* which was published to a warm reception. The new plan was to use that book as a model, but to range a little more widely, including not only his speeches but other writing such as book reviews, articles, and other occasional pieces. He would put the selection together with a general preface, and would provide additional introductions to each of the chosen pieces.

My letter confirming these arrangements and planning for publication in Canada in the fall of 1996 lay on his desk unopened at the time of his death.

Some weeks later his widow, Brenda Davies, and their second daughter, Jennifer Surridge, contacted me. They had decided to create a literary enterprise—Pendragon Ink—to look after his works, published and unpublished. As the first order of business, they had decided to carry forward the plans for the selection.

What their researches revealed was extraordinary. The fresh, unpublished material that existed in his files was so extensive that even after secondary material had been set aside, the first-class pieces would clearly fill not one but two books. After further editorial consultations it was decided that one book should be devoted to Robertson Davies on the performing arts: on his great love, the theatre, on opera and on music. The title for that selection would be *Happy Alchemy*.

The other book—to be published first, and which you now hold in your hand—would deal with the world of books. More specifically, it would deal with writing, and reading, and other authors, and even with fragments of never-written books. It would, in short, be a cheerful mixture of ingredients with something for all true book-lovers.

What should such a book be called?

Brenda Davies had the answer. Her husband, she knew, had always wanted to call one of his novels *The Merry Heart*, an idea taken from the old saying: "A merry heart doeth good like a medicine." This was ideal. The title was appropriate, since the book was indeed uplifting, full of keen interest in and relish for life. There seemed no better source for a title than Robertson Davies himself. And, above all, it was pleasing to be able to fulfil a long-held hope of his at this late date.

Sadly, that very lateness means that the selection here lacks some of the central contributions by Robertson Davies we had originally planned. First, the final selection is not his. Second, in the place of the individual introductions to the pieces he planned to provide, we have used his own words from diaries and letters, along with further details about the occasion and the setting that often draw on Judith Skelton Grant's 1994 biography, *Robertson Davies: Man of Myth.* And third, although the alert reader will find several themes, and even specific examples, re-emerging in these pieces, we have allowed some elements of repetition to stand rather than leave the reader wondering what editorial excision followed the traditional tantalizing editorial marks. . . .

For the same reasons, in the following pieces that were originally delivered as speeches, we have kept the introductory "ritual paragraph." Here we know we act with Robertson Davies' endorsement. In *One Half of Robertson Davies* he wrote:

Because these pieces are, in the main, speeches, I decided not to cut out those passages at the beginning of each in which I have, so to speak, made my bow to the audience, paid it a few compliments, and thanked the Chairman. These are necessary decorums of public speaking, and to leave them out would be to do precisely what I am determined not to do—that is, to pretend that I am offering you something to read, rather than something to hear. And, to let you in on a speaker's secret, it is in such passages that he tries out his voice (because he is always fearful that it may have deserted him during the Chairman's introduction) and winds up his courage to a point which makes it possible for him to speak at all. Because, you see, the poor wretch is nervous.

Speakers' nerves affect them in various ways. Some tremble, some become frenzied. I lose all confidence, and suffer from a leaden oppression that makes me wonder why I ever agreed to speak at all; the Tomb and the Conqueror Worm seem preferable to delivering the stupid and piffling speech I have so carefully prepared. But there is no escape; speak I must, and I need a ritual paragraph in which to ease myself into the job.

Before he eases himself into this job, let me add a brief word about the order of the pieces. The primary organizing principle is to allow the variety of Davies' interests and concerns to enjoy free rein. For that reason no attempt has been made to corral the pieces into tight little subject groups. Instead the roughly chronological order is shuffled on occasion to allow a short book review, for example, to punctuate two lengthy lectures. The arrangement is designed to allow the reader the pleasure of browsing through Robertson Davies' well-stocked mind; of being, in the felicitous phrase of the first essay, "a rake at reading."

Most, but not all, of the pieces appear in print here for the first time. Some, as the copyright page reveals, have appeared in magazines; others have graced newspapers such as the *New York Times*. "Reading" and "Writing" have made up in a slim volume sold under that joint title, and "A Christmas Carol Re-harmonized" has appeared elsewhere.

For the rest, only a roomful of admirers lucky enough to be present have had the pleasure of hearing these words delivered from a podium in the distinctive voice of Robertson Davies. Now that voice, mourned across the world at the time of his passing, rings out unmistakably from every piece in the book, loud and clear.

Listen to it now, remembering Davies' own advice that "the ear— even when it is the mind's ear—is a surer judge of prose than the scampering, skipping eye." And share in the very personal pleasures of *The Merry Heart*.

Douglas Gibson
Toronto, April 1996

THE
MERRY HEART

I

A RAKE AT READING

Robertson Davies' interesting account of a lifetime's encounter with books—ranging in sophistication from *The Little Red Hen* to *Ulysses*—encompasses his philosophy of reading before moving on to the provocative assertion that "we who are committed readers may appear to choose our books, but in an equally true sense our books choose us."

Davies chose the University of Manitoba in Winnipeg to deliver these thoughts as the 1980 Warhaft Memorial Lecture. The event had initially been arranged for October 16, 1980, but Davies came down with flu and the lecture was rescheduled for November 20. In his diary he deals frankly not only with the reaction to his talk, but also with his own reaction to hearty prairie fare at the residence breakfast table. The diary records: *Then my lecture at University College to over 500 people: hall full. Goes extremely well and lots of people want to talk afterward. I like the pretty girls who say "Oh, you're wonderful!"—Vain old ass that I am, but what one could not attain in youth one savours in age.*

The next day: Get some breakfast this morning, but ate Shredded Wheat as apparently the students eat three fried sausages partnered with three great stovelids of wheatcakes, drenched in maple syrup: my soul yearned after this dish, but I knew that my senile gut would never put up with it. . . .

"People say that life is the thing, but I prefer reading." Did I say that? No, Logan Pearsall Smith said it, but I have thought it so many times that sometimes I mistake it for my own. However, as you will know by the time I have done, that is not my final, most carefully considered opinion. All my life long, reading has been my great refuge and solace, and in those words I have given myself away. What, you are thinking, does he not read for information, for enrichment, in order to acquaint himself with the best which has been thought and said in the world? Is he admitting that he reads for escape?

Alas, though necessity has driven me to read much that even Matthew Arnold would have approved, and a mountain of rubbish that nobody could approve—I mean mediocre journalism, government publications, the essays of students, and all that sort of thing—when I read for my own satisfaction, I read just as I please. That is why I have called this address "A Rake at Reading." The phrase comes from a letter written to a friend by Lady Mary Wortley Montagu: "I have been a rake at reading," says she. The word rake, in the middle of the eighteenth century when Lady Mary made her confession to the Countess of Bute, still meant to roam or stray, but I think she also meant it to have a hint of what was dissolute and irresponsible. So— I confess I have been a rake at reading. I have read those things which I ought not to have read, and I have not read those things which I ought to have read, and there is no health in me—if by health you mean an inclusive and coherent knowledge of any body of great literature. I can only protest, like all rakes in their shameful senescence, that I have had a good time.

It occurred to me on my last birthday that I have been reading for sixty years. Before that time people read to me. My parents chose books they supposed would be good for me. My father read from Kingsley's *The Heroes* and Hawthorne's *Tanglewood Tales,* and these adventures into classic myth frightened me out of my wits and marked me forever as a lover, and victim, of myth. My mother read Ruskin's *The King of the Golden River* and Grimm's Fairy Tales, and I have been devoted to both ever since. But my brothers read to me, as well. On the sly, they read the comics for me—in those days we called them the Funny Papers—and I had a powerful urge to live in the exciting, slangy, violent world of Mutt and Jeff and Mr. and Mrs. Jiggs. Like so many small children I longed to impress myself on the adult world—that world of gods, ogres, monsters, and inexplicable forces. I should have liked to possess one of those weapons that every hero of the mythic past called his own—a great bow or a magic sword—but I would have been just as much thrilled by the power to throw spittoons and rolling pins with the deadly accuracy displayed in the Funny Paper world. You see I had no taste, no discrimination. I have developed a little of those qualities since then, but vulgarity and rough stuff still have a strong appeal for me.

Best of all, perhaps, were what may be called Family Stories—reminiscences by my parents of their own life in childhood. My mother recalled visits to her native city by Sir John A. Macdonald, when children whose parents were not of Sir John's political colour danced along the streets beside his carriage, singing –

I wish I were in the land of cotton
Sticking pins in Old John's bottom.

My father, who was born in North Wales, spent his childhood in a town dominated by a Castle, inhabited by a real Earl and his beautiful Countess, and these were figures of fable. But even more fascinating were the characters from Welsh low-life—his nurse Liz Duckett and her husband, John Jones, known in Welsh fashion as Jack the Jockey—to distinguish him from Jack the Skinner, who was also a Jones. These inherited memories peopled my world of fantasy, where the Earl of Powys was a hero as authentic as Hercules, and Sir John A. was a monster in no way less terrifying than the Minotaur. Thus narrative and fable entered my life much earlier than education, or reading. And so I think it must be for all lucky children.

I did not learn to read until I was six, which I believe is considered rather late. But with people ready to read to me, what inducement had I to learn? I must have had a queer notion of what reading involved, for I remember that the first day I went to school, I returned home, took a volume of the encyclopaedia from the shelf, opened it, and waited for it to tell me something. I knew that reading was a skill that came of going to school, and I was humiliated to find that it involved a tedious encounter with a creature called the Little Red Hen.

Have you ever met the Little Red Hen? Hers was the first story in the *Ontario Primer*, and it was printed not in the Latin alphabet, but in the debased calligraphy which was taught to children at that time, ruining their handwriting forever. Why it was thought that children could read this script more easily than print, I do not know. In the pictures illustrating the story, the Little Red Hen was larger than the cat, the dog, and the pig with whom she shared the farmyard. Much later in life, when I became interested in the ikons of the Orthodox church, I discovered the reasoning behind this apparent absurdity; the Little Red Hen was morally bigger than the cat, the dog, and the pig, so she was drawn larger, just as saints in ikons are drawn larger than pagans or people of mere ordinary virtue.

The story was that the Little Red Hen found some wheat; she called on the cat, the dog, and the pig to help her plant, reap, grind, and make bread from the wheat, but they refused. But when the Little Red Hen said, "Who will help me eat the bread?" they were eager for a share. This was the Little Red Hen's finest hour. She declared: "You would not plant the wheat, you would not cut the wheat, you would not grind the wheat, you would not bake the bread; you shall not eat the bread. My little chicks shall eat the bread." And they did.

This is unexceptionable doctrine. Not Karl Marx, not Chairman Mao at his finest, not even Mrs. Thatcher could have improved on the political doctrine of the Little Red Hen. Yet—somehow I did not like it. During my life I have met a great many Little Red Hens, and they are quick to point out that they are the salt of the earth; they are always working for the good of somebody else. They are morally superior; they know best. It never occurred to the Little Red Hen that the dog had been guarding the farmyard for her; that she had been free to enjoy the physical beauty and music of the cat; that barnyard culture owed an immeasurable debt to the philosophy and general dignity of the pig; no, in the conduct of her life she was confined within the world-view of a hen, and she asked no more.

Once out of the toils of the Little Red Hen things got better in the Primer. That group of little pigs who went to market, stayed at home, had roast beef, went hungry, and said "Wee, wee" (and what child ever failed to put his whole heart into reading "Wee, wee"?) came next, then Humpty Dumpty, then Jack and Jill, and then—wonder of wonders—Christina Rossetti's poem *Who Has Seen the Wind?* which was our first glimpse of poetic beauty, and to meet it at the age of six, and to be able to read it for oneself, was an adventure. Of course I did not know that it was a fine lyric, but I felt its grace, and I knew it came from a source very far away from the Little Red Hen.

Here I should like to speak in praise of the committee, as I suppose it must have been, who chose the material for those old Ontario School Readers. These were graded to meet the reading ability of children between six and twelve, but they were not confined to somebody's notion of what children at that time of life might most easily understand. The Readers contained a good deal of what was commonplace, and much that was of a narrowly moral tendency, because in the course of time the Little Red Hen changed her name to Benjamin Franklin, and we were confronted with samples of his cautious, cynical, mean-spirited attitude toward life—the boy who was warned against adults who wanted him to turn the grindstone, and the boy who paid too much for his whistle—as if the price of a really fine, heart-lifting whistle could be estimated in money. This was in the vein of the Little Red Hen, whose influence is strong. It is not commonly known that two of her chicks went into the Reader business for themselves, under the names of Dick and Jane. But there were splendid, life-enhancing things, as well. There was Aesop, whose fables were gold, whereas the Little Red Hen and Benjamin Franklin were gilded tin. There was somebody of whom I know nothing, called F.W. Bourdillon, who, when we were eight, told us that—

The night has a thousand eyes,
And the day but one;
Yet the light of the bright world dies
With the dying sun.

The mind has a thousand eyes,
And the heart but one;
Yet the light of a whole life dies
When love is done.

There's a mind-stretcher for children! There is what I think of as an educational time-bomb, for it reaches its target, and explodes later. I suppose it was fifteen years after I read that poem in school before I really understood what it meant, but when I needed it, there it was, ready to mind.

Who put these time-bombs in those Readers? Some unknown teacher who would not have agreed with the later educational psychologists who were so earnest in their desire that a child should not be confronted with anything it could not fully comprehend, and who were astonishingly sure that they knew what children could comprehend, and who never understood how warmly intelligent children respond to what they partly comprehend. Another of these time-bombs for me was this—

It is not growing like a tree
In bulk, doth make man better be;
Or standing long an oak, three hundred year,
To fall a log at last, dry, bald and sere:
A lily of a day
Is fairer far in May,
Although it fall and die that night;
It was the plant and flower of light.
In small proportions we just beauty see;
And in short measures life may perfect be.

Nobody told us that was a Pindaric, and a great one. Nobody said anything about the author, Ben Jonson. They simply said that it meant that you could lead a good life even as a child. That was enough for us at the time. But the splendour of expression is for a lifetime.

Of course the Readers did not always move on that high level. There was much in them that was commonplace, much that would now be hopelessly out of fashion, telling of heroic deeds and impossible aspirations, but there was very little downright trash. Even the trash had a romantic glow about it, like a bad lobster in a dark cellar. An example is a dreadful story which told how Beethoven, walking through the streets of Bonn one night, heard someone playing his Sonata in F; he investigated and found that the player was a blind girl, poor and despairing because she wanted to go to Cologne to hear the great master play in person. Rushing in, Beethoven cried, "I am a musician; I will improvise a Sonata to the Moonlight," and he did, then and there, and rushed off at once to write down the Moonlight Sonata while he could still remember it. This did not impress me, because my family was musical and I knew that composers didn't work like that; I also knew that Beethoven had been about as kindly and charitable as a bear with a thorn in its paw. Nevertheless, the romance of the story appealed to me. Not so much, however, as the romance of Don Quixote's fight with the windmills, which was in the same Third Reader.

I must not detain you over these Readers of my Ontario childhood, but I think they are worth some time as evidence of what was offered, not in a school for advanced children, or children from wealthy homes, but to all the children of the province, in its public schools. Nowadays such selections would probably be condemned as élitist, for they gave children hard nuts to crack, and it is certain that not every child cracked them. But I think that behind the selection there stood a fine ideal, which was nothing less than to create, on however modest a scale, a coherent body of literary knowledge in which everybody could share, so that in future every citizen of Ontario would know who Don Quixote was, and who Mr. Pickwick was, and Ali Baba and his Old Man of the Sea, and that Sir Walter Scott and R.L. Stevenson

8 THE MERRY HEART

had written stirring ballads and romances, and that we had in Canada
writers whose work was fit to stand in this distinguished company.
There is an idea prevalent today that Canadian writing was scorned
and neglected until quite recently, but that is not true. The Readers
contained Canadian poems and tales of historic adventure, and
although the bias was certainly toward English writers, and then
toward American writers, with Longfellow, Lowell, and Whittier well
to the fore, Canadian writers, and especially Canadian poets, were not
neglected.

Later, in high school, we used a fine anthology compiled by Professor W.J. Alexander of the University of Toronto, called simply
Shorter Poems, divided into four parts for use over four years; each part
contained a generous selection of Canadian verse, and to encounter
Wilfred Campbell's *How One Winter Came in the Lake Region*—

> That night I felt the winter in my veins,
> A joyous tremor of the icy glow;
> And woke to hear the north's wild vibrant strains,
> While far and wide, by withered woods and plains,
> Fast fell the driving snow.

—that was literary adventure, for there was our own weather and our
own landscape transformed into poetry.

I spoke of élitism a few minutes ago; Professor Alexander seems to
have been an élitist, for in his preface he writes: "Here are to be found
some poems of very slight poetic merit; because something in them—
their dash, their fun, even their didactic content or moralizing vein
—may give them a hold upon those whose imaginative and aesthetic
sensibilities are dull or undeveloped." You see, he did not expect every
pupil to understand everything in his anthology at the same level of
intensity. Or was he not simply a realist? I often wonder if the élitists
are not those who, like the Little Red Hen, assert their judgements
on the basis of what they themselves think best, relying on some
inborn grace, rather than an acquaintance with a broad culture.

Permit me to refer just once more to the school Readers of my childhood, for there was a selection in the Fourth Reader, which I suppose I encountered at the age of eleven or twelve; it has remained with me through the years, not because of its romance or richness of style, but because of the chill it cast upon me then and which it casts to this day. If you wanted something for children of that age, would it occur to you to choose the 159th number of Addison's *Spectator?* It is called *The Vision of Mirzah,* and its tells of an Eastern sage who climbs into the mountains above Baghdad, and there meets the Genius of the Rocks, who shows him a vision: far in the valley below he sees a great sea, and the Genius tells him that it is the Vale of Misery, and that the water is the great Tide of Eternity. At both ends of the water is mist, and between stretches the bridge of human life; the bridge has seven entire arches, and after that a few broken arches, and over this bridge, which is beset with many perils, Mirzah sees the procession of mankind making its stumbling way until, worn out with the journey, each figure falls into the waters below. When Mirzah grieves that the fate of man should be so wretched, the Genius dispels some of the mist at the further end of the bridge and shows him the islands where the blessed ones find peace; but the fate of those who are not among the blessed the Genius refuses to reveal. As Mirzah eagerly seeks to gain the secret of time and eternity, the Genius vanishes and the allegory of life vanishes as well, and Mirzah sees only Baghdad in the valley below.

Now, isn't that a dainty dish to set before a child of eleven? There is a good deal of Biblical material in the Readers as a whole, but this is a cold blast from the eighteenth century, and none the worse for that. When I meet contemporaries today I sometimes ask them: Do you remember the *Vision of Mirzah?* The best of them do. They are not the ones with cosy minds.

Perhaps you are wondering what was rakish about reading what I was obliged to read in school. Nothing at all; the rakishness began at home. My parents were keen readers, and had a lot of books, but they were also readers of a kind rarer in our day than it was in the early twenties. They read a lot of periodicals: the *Atlantic Monthly* and *Scribner's* came into our house, and these, with the *Saturday Evening*

Post, which was a great fiction magazine at that time, were our contributions from below the border. From England came the *Strand* and *Pearson's,* as well as *Punch,* but so far as I was concerned *Punch* meant pictures. Thus a great many short stories were available to me every month, at a time when the short story engaged some of the best writers of the day. P.G. Wodehouse was a favourite, and innocent; but Somerset Maugham was not, and I devoured his supposedly cynical tales of adultery with a powerful appetite, because, although I was not sure what adultery was, I knew it was wicked. There were, even at that late date, new stories about Sherlock Holmes by Conan Doyle, and the funny stories about sailors and poachers by W.W. Jacobs.

I spoke of the readiness of children to welcome what they cannot wholly understand; I well recall my puzzled fascination with Kipling's story "Dayspring Mishandled," which I first met in one of these English magazines of fiction.

Sometimes there was a serious article on a hot topic, and I especially remember one by a bishop headed "Is Nudity Salacious?" (The bishop thought it need not be, if encountered in the proper spirit, but he gave a lot of enlightening examples of conditions under which it might be, in his word, "inflammatory." There wasn't much nudity in our neck of the woods, and I enjoyed that article tremendously.) There were many stories with backgrounds of high life and society, which I suppose would be thought unsuitable for a child. I was not supposed to read these magazines, but as nobody supervised my reading very carefully, I read them on the sly. A magazine was taken especially for me; it was called *The Youth's Companion;* it came from Boston and was of a morally improving tendency, containing stories about remorselessly grammatical boys and girls who were helpful to their parents and generally admirable. I read all the stories about girls, hoping to penetrate their secrets; I knew girls had secrets because all the girls I met were great whisperers and gigglers.

Much more fun, for a boy like me, was the bound volume I received each Christmas, of an English boys' magazine called *Chums.* It was about Anarchic Boys, who put their schools on the rocks and drove their masters to the brink of madness by their ingenious pranks;

there were also Daring Boys, who had adventures with mountains, the sea, and criminal foreigners. (Foreigners were sharply divided between Good Foreigners, who might be Dutch or noble-minded East Indians, and Bad Foreigners, who were German, or Russian, or evil-minded Easterners who were usually described as "rascally Lascars"). There were boys who saved the Honour of the School by sporting feats. And of course there were boys who lived in past ages of history, and did marvels at Trafalgar, or Waterloo, or even at Crecy and Agincourt.

The one thing all these boys had in common was that they were not Canadians. I did not question this; it seemed natural enough that everything interesting happened somewhere else. Many years later I was told by a reader for a great London theatrical producing company, to which I was trying to sell some of my plays—"Nobody is interested in Canada." This opinion is still strong in England, though it seems to be losing its grip elsewhere.—But I am mistaken. I had one book of Canadian adventures by William Kingston called *Snowshoes and Canoes,* and a thrilling book it was.

There was nothing rakish about these publications that were aimed at children, but I read other things, not in magazines. I read a lot of Dickens, and though there are still people who think Dickens innocuous for children, I can tell them they are wrong. I did not know quite why Quilp was pursuing Little Nell, but I sensed that it was for no good purpose. I was strongly aware of Evil, even if I could not pin it down. I was told not to read *Tess of the D'Urbervilles,* as it was, in my parents' phrase, "beyond me," and I suppose it was, because so far as I could discover Tess fell asleep under a tree in the company of the wicked Alec D'Urberville, and shortly afterward had a baby, about which there was an unholy fuss, considering what tedious creatures babies were. As you see, I was sexually uninformed. On my mother's strong recommendation I read Victor Hugo's *Nôtre Dame de Paris,* and it won an allegiance that I have not relinquished to this day; I must have read it five or six times. But I didn't know why the wicked priest was trying to get the beautiful Esmeralda into his alchemist's cell in Nôtre Dame; my interest was all in the grotesque Quasimodo, who also wanted Esmeralda, whom he presumably meant to keep as a pet.

I knew about Love, of course; Somerset Maugham had made it clear that Love was dangerous and fascinating. Sex was to come later.

If there was to be any Sex, I wanted it with style and magic. And sure enough, when I was about fifteen, along came just the right book; it was *Mademoiselle de Maupin* in the Powys Mathers translation, and I read it at boarding school, after lights-out, with the aid of a flashlight. Here was the thing I wanted; the language was splendid, the story entrancing, and the descriptions of sexual encounters exquisitely managed, being at once intense and delicate in their atmosphere. The lovers were sophisticated adventurers but they were neither coarse nor yet cripplingly innocent, like Tess, who must have been, I decided, a dumb-bell, as well as a Pure Woman, and I did not like the combination. Here, you see, rakishness is at last apparent; I was not impressed by conventional literary judgements. Is there a serious student of literature, I wonder, who would rank Theophile Gautier above Thomas Hardy? I was not a serious student of literature. Never was, and doubtless never will be. But I had a taste of my own, which is not a luxury every serious student of literature permits himself.

From *Mademoiselle de Maupin* I never looked back, and my next rung on the ladder of literary rakishness was Aldous Huxley. Since his death, he has been enskied and sainted by people who put heavy emphasis on his later, serious books, but when I met him he was thought to be a dangerously cynical and sophisticated fellow, and the girls I knew were all forbidden to read him. His very title-pages were thought to be seminal.

What appealed to me about *Antic Hay*, which was the first of his novels to come my way, was not that it was funny—though it is very funny indeed—but that it looked at life, so to speak, through the wrong end of the binoculars, giving it a wonderful clarity, while at the same time putting it at a distance, so that compassion became an irrelevance. I had, by that time, had enough compassion in literature to last me for several years, and a holiday in the intellect, with emotion temporarily removed from the scene, was just what I needed. But Huxley was only one of the authors who won me a reputation as a rake at reading. Probably the greatest was Bernard Shaw, whose plays and prefaces I consumed by the dim illumination of my flashlight, when I should have been asleep. The father of one of my friends, having heard me speak with enthusiasm of Shaw, forbade my friend ever to ask me to the house again. I was obviously in training to become an anarchist. But I was unimpressed by this sort of disdain. I went beyond Shaw and Huxley and read Havelock Ellis.

This was in my first year at Queen's, and I had to get the book from the sulphurous region beyond the Librarian's office where the Special Collection was housed. I have never met anyone else who has read the whole of *Studies in the Psychology of Sex;* I believe they are now condemned as wrong-headed by modern psychologists, but they were admirably written, and the case histories they contained gave me an idea of the infinite variability of mankind for which I am profoundly grateful. Ellis was not obtrusively compassionate, but he was accepting of human variety, and at a time when it is fashionable to rate him rather low, I still think him a great man.

From Ellis it was an easy leap to Freud, whose major works I gobbled with a greedy appetite. The vision of life Freud presented was bleak, but the Ontario Readers had given me enough high-mindedness and aspiration to make a heavy dosage of bleakness very acceptable. Freud is tough chewing, and while I was reading him I had not time or inclination to read many other things that bulked large in the reading of my contemporaries. I never read much Hemingway. Under the urging of a friend who had read *Farewell to Arms* five times I read it once, and told him I thought it a sentimental account of an uninteresting adultery between uninteresting people. He was furious; this was blasphemy. But I spoke sincerely; under the spell of Shaw and Huxley I could find nothing of interest in Hemingway's tongue-tied, hard-breathing lovers.

Nor did I get on any better with Thomas Wolfe, whom I thought insufferably tedious. Scott Fitzgerald I considered to be attempting to do what Evelyn Waugh splendidly achieved. My friends said I could see no good in any writer who was not English. Not so. Sinclair Lewis was one of my heroes, a taste encouraged by my mother, who once told me that whenever she felt herself feeling tenderly toward the clergy she hastened to correct it by a rereading of *Elmer Gantry*. Another American writer whom I read with avidity was H.L. Mencken, and although now I can hardly bear anything of his except the great books on the American Language, I owe him a debt of gratitude for some rough eye-openers in my youth.

Not very rakish yet, you may say. Nothing really offbeat in any of this. But in 1933 I discovered an author, by no means widely popular yet, though I think him one of the giants of our century, and so do some other critics whom I respect. I speak of John Cowper Powys. It was in that year that *A Glastonbury Romance* appeared; it was just what I wanted and I read its 1,174 pages with wonderment, sometimes with bafflement, but eventually with breathtaking illumination. I had found one of my great men. He was not English, nor was he American; he declared himself to be Welsh, though he was not by any reckoning as Welsh as I was myself. Very often he described his best fictions, which I hastened to read, as romances, which is a better name for them than novels, for they break every rule that the high priests of the novel have devised. He was as great a master as Joyce—in my view greater—but he did not try to extend the confines of language as Joyce did; instead he attempted, with variable success (for he is not one of your fine-tuned writers, not a great stylist) to extend the boundaries of what language can do in evoking rare and unusual modes of feeling. His books are romances in the old Celtic sense, for in them the point of view changes whenever he pleases, the prevailing mood varies and bypaths are pursued with what is sometimes maddening caprice. But they enlarge the reader's concept of what may be comprised within a single consciousness in a way that many masters of the novel, like Henry James, cannot achieve. Yet he was not describable as romantic; sometimes he is a realist, sometimes a cynic. He is, to put it as simply as possible, a very great man of a Blake-like breadth of perception. If I had no time for Hemingway or Faulkner or D.H. Lawrence, it was because I was greatly occupied elsewhere.

At the same time I found my bonnet giving shelter to a very fine bee. Consider this: from the age of seventeen onward I devoted a great deal of time to greedy reading of the drama of the nineteenth century.

Why, I shall not explain. There is an explanation, but it belongs to another portion of my autobiography. Wedged in among Freud and Powys I was reading anything I could get my hands on of the social drama, the costume drama, the farce, and the melodrama of the period between 1800 and 1880. Of course I read Ibsen, to see what had supplanted the theatre of my favoured period, and I fell under the spell of that magnificent psychologist and have remained his devoted admirer ever since. I did not read nineteenth-century plays to jeer at them, but for the enjoyment they brought me. I never scorned them: these were plays, I reminded myself, that Dickens, Thackeray, George Eliot, and a score of other great ones had seen, and while they condemned the worst, they applauded the best; therefore there must be something in them. Our forefathers did not leave their brains at the door when they went to the theatre.

Where did I find such plays? The fine collections of Michael Booth and George Rowell were far in the future, and I had to rummage in the outside barrows of bookshops on Tottenham Court Road on my occasional visits to England, and pick up shabby copies for sixpence apiece. I have now, I may say, about twelve hundred of those forgotten, scorned plays in their original form, and I smile when university librarians enquire, with the utmost casualness, where I intend to bestow them when I can read them no more. In my own reading, and in my university courses, I had thrust myself deep into the drama that the academic world at that time considered worthy of study. I knew the Elizabethans and the Augustans, and the playwrights who were admired during the last of the nineteenth century and the first thirty years of this one. But in between I had fitted the plays that came between Sheridan—the last English dramatist endurable to the academic mind—and Shaw.

Why did I do it? Was it perversity or eccentricity? No, it was curiosity, and a conviction that those plays—superficially false and rhetorical in their language and mechanical in their plots—must have some content that had once given them life. I think I found what I was looking for. The language in some of them is of remarkable vivacity and strength, and modern productions of Boucicault and O'Keeffe have shown it again in its special gloss. No less a critic than Hazlitt called O'Keeffe "the English Molière." At the heart of so many of them is the ideal of Poetic Justice, which appealed so powerfully to an age where great social upheavals and their inevitable injustices were the stuff of daily experience. I even went so far as to decide that melodrama is as valid a mode of synthesizing human experience as tragedy or comedy, and that whereas few of us are so happy as to live our lives in terms of comedy, and fewer still move in the terrible world of tragedy, most of us live out our existence in that combination of cheerfulness, despair, coincidence, poetry, low comedy, and slapdash improvisation that is the shimmering fabric of melodrama.

One of the astounding successes of the recent theatrical season in London is a nine-hour dramatic presentation of Dickens's *Nicholas Nickleby;* Dickens, who longed for success on the stage, has it at last, and it is made manifest in the theatre that his work is in the melodramatic mode at its greatest, and that at its greatest it is a profoundly revealing vision of man's existence.

Every September I smile inwardly when a group of students assembles at my university to begin a seminar with me in the study of these plays which were so utterly neglected when I was their age. I am proud that I have had some part of putting those plays into perspective. And when I begin by saying that it is not necessary for a play to have obvious literary worth in order to reach far into the spirit of man, I seem to hear at my shoulder the gasps of my professors of forty-five years ago who would have burned their gowns rather than admit any such thing.

As a young man, I spent several years working as a book-reviewer. There is little chance for rakishness there, because a reviewer has to do his best with what comes to his desk, and inevitably the popular books that everybody wants to hear about make first demands on him. But when I worked on *Saturday Night*—which I did, all told, for several years—I was able to give attention to some of the best books Canadian writers have produced, and I am proud to say that I welcomed the best with enthusiasm.

It was a principle with me to review, so far as possible, only what

I could honestly praise; I have never seen much use, or found much satisfaction, in knocking a book. Praising the best of these Canadian books was easy and delightful work. Hugh MacLennan's *The Watch that Ends the Night,* Sinclair Ross's *As for Me and My House,* and Gabrielle Roy's *Where Nests the Water Hen,* to name only three that came my way, were fine books by international standards. I was particularly pleased to have the opportunity to praise the books of reminiscences that were published, late in her life, by Emily Carr. Canada has had more than enough of gaseous, self-justifying political reminiscence and biography; the distilled thoughts of an artist of fine and strongly individual perception have a value far beyond such non-sense, and I still think Emily Carr one of the finest writers this country has ever produced, although her great fame is as a painter.

A book reviewer has to read a great deal, and he is lucky if he is a fast reader. I have not that gift. I rank only slightly above those who move their lips and follow the lines with a careful finger. I read most of each day in an inner office, without daylight, in a constrained posture and heavily sedated by a pipe or a Dutch cigar. Did it take a heavy toll of my health? As you may see, I am not of a noticeably feeble frame, and my eyesight is decidedly better than it was when I was twenty-one. The Little Red Hen would not approve, but these are the facts.

Not only did I read most of each day, but I did some of my reading for review at night, and when I was tired of that I read for pleasure. What did I read? An incoherent mass of books, as I had done, and continue to do. I am one of those obsessed creatures who must read any print that comes within my range. I have told you that as a child I read anything and everything. When I visited my grandmother I read my grandmother's books, and that is how I came to be one of the few people I have met who have read *Lavender and Old Lace.* It was at my grandmother's that I made the acquaintance of an author nobody seems to read now, Charles Lever, whose *Charles O'Malley* and *Harry Lorrequer* exactly suited my romantic and melodramatic taste. I have read a lot of Charles Reade, Wilkie Collins, and Harrison Ainsworth. If some of you are saying, So have I, let me ask you this: How much have you read of Henry Cockton? I do not urge him upon you, for he is not third-rate, he is thirty-third rate, but he provides a special insight into the nineteenth century, because he was once a best-seller, and he is a startling example of what people will read by an author who has a reputation for being funny. It has long been a principle of mine that to understand the writing of any age, one must read not only the best, but what was most popular at the time. In Thomas Hardy's words—

> If way to the better there be
> It exacts a full look at the worst.

Cockton, a comic novelist, was part of the worst of nineteenth-century writing.

What any age thinks funny is a special key to its nature. That is what has led me, in my time, to read a great many old Jest Books. It is a salutary experience to read Jest Books from the seventeenth century, for they reveal what the ordinary man of that era thought uproariously funny, while the comedies of Farquhar, Vanbrugh, and Congreve were amusing the intelligentsia. A clerical friend of mine used to say that nothing is so dead as the last generation's books of theology: I dispute that—dead humour is not merely dead, but rotten, and only a literary ghoul like myself can feed on it with pleasure.

Do you ask for an example? Consider this from *The Pickwick Treasury of Wit,* the date of which is 1845—almost yesterday: "It having been proved on a trial at Guildhall that a man's name was really *Inch* who pretended it was *Linch,* I see said the judge, the old proverb is verified in this man, if we allow him an *Inch* he will take an L." Or do you prefer this: "A tailor who lived near a church yard in a large town, used to count the number of funerals by putting a stone into a pot, hung up in his shop for that purpose. On his death taking place, his house was shut; and on enquiry, it was observed by a next door neighbour, that the tailor himself was *gone to pot.*"

In the course of time I became a writer myself, and of course that had a strong effect on my reading. In what way? I quickly found out that there was no advice better than that of Sir Walter Scott, who said that when he was writing, he read avidly, anything and everything, so long as it had no bearing on the subject of his book. A writer reads to distract the surface of his consciousness, while below the surface it is busy composing. He must be careful that he does not absorb, and unwittingly repeat, something that has been written by somebody else. With him, more than with most people, reading is a drug.

You might suppose that what is called "light reading" would be just the thing under these circumstances. I never found that to be the case. I have never been able to read detective stories with any satisfaction; they are puzzles, written, it seems to me, by people who are not in the least interested in the well-springs of criminal thought and behaviour. I do not like travel books, because I have a poor visual imagination, and descriptions of foreign scenes baffle me. All my life I have refused to read any book whatever that attempts to explain politics or economics.

So, when I am writing—which is virtually all the time, nowadays—what do I read? Dickens, the great melodramatist, I have read and reread many times, and the more I read the more I find. I have often said that if you hope to come seriously to grips with a book, you should read it when you are at least the age the author was when he wrote it. Alas, I am now considerably older than Dickens was when he died, but he still has secrets for me. But one must read Dickens as a whale takes in its food, in vast gulps. The broad effect is everything, though many of the details are exquisite. But unless you attack the books as melodramas, they will not yield their splendid savour to you.

Too much unrelieved Dickens is bad for you, and as an antidote I recommend Anthony Trollope, one of the greatest of realistic novelists, though, as with all realism, his has, with the passing of years, taken on a romantic glow. Trollope called Dickens "Mr. Popular Sentiment," and it is true that Dickens would do extraordinary things, and sometimes unworthy things, to catch the crowd. But not even Trollope could be as realistic as he knew how; read his *Autobiography* and learn how much he had to falsify the love scenes in his novels to make them palatable to an age that dearly loved a long, eloquent, agonized proposal uttered by a young man to a girl who fully intended to accept him and would have been a fool if she had done otherwise. Of course, neither Dickens nor Trollope, nor any of their English or American contemporaries, was free to write what they knew about the sexual involvements of their characters.

If you want to know what they knew but dared not tell, you must read Balzac. There is a writer who fills me with extravagant delight, for he seems to deny himself nothing. If he wants to tell you in detail how the printing trade worked in the early nineteenth century he does so, because he knew a lot about printing and thought it interesting. We could do with less of this, but his enthusiasm is so great that he carries us along, protesting but yielding. About sex he knew everything, and whatever he knew, he wrote into a novel. There are sophistications of sexual involvement in Balzac that are beyond the range of any but a handful of writers. I particularly enjoy his descriptions of those very rich bourgeois who had to maintain a mistress because it was owing to their financial importance; furthermore, the mistress must be of transporting beauty and wit (by which was meant a gross and abusive impudence toward her protector) and she must have horses, carriages, and apartments equal to the finest in Paris. In return her protector was permitted to visit her often, if he gave sufficient notice that he was coming, and he was allowed to talk with her, be petted a little by her, and cheered by her slangy, guttersnipe conversation. He might sleep with her now and again, but this was a rare indulgence, and apparently it was not necessarily his right; indeed, he was jeered at so harshly that he might not feel like attempting it. But the final turn of the dagger in the wound was that he had to maintain her real, youthful lover, as well as the girl, give him an allowance and pay his debts. An unenviable bargain, one might think, but fashion has its dreadful exactions, like any other addiction.

Balzac knew obsession as no other writer of my experience knew it. I mean obsession with money, and also with objects, as well as people. If you wish to know what the collector's mania can do to a man, read *Cousin Pons,* which is at once one of the funniest and most pathetic books known to me.

Balzac, however, writes of bourgeois life and I sometimes have a taste for a dash of high life, and I find that in Proust. The world is full of people who talk about *À la recherche du temps perdu,* but they are more numerous than those who have read its full twelve volumes. Much of it is tough chewing, but it is enormously rewarding. It is a book within which one may live, and I have known people who seemed, for years at a time, to be subsumed in it. It has been described in many ways, but to me it is romantic and melodramatic. Perhaps those are qualities I bring to it, but certainly I find what I am looking for in its pages.

Proust's aristocrats are gold and silver plate, and Proust collects them as Cousin Pons collected objects of art. Real aristocrats are to be found in the novels of Tolstoy, that immense, dismaying genius. Here we find people who are not obsessed by society, which they do not notice any more than the air they breathe. I am not convinced by Tolstoy's peasants; he never knew them as, for instance, Thomas Hardy knew them. But his aristocrats ring true, and they are to Proust's people as the krugerrand is to those chocolate coins wrapped in gilt foil that children used to be given at Christmas. I called Tolstoy dismaying, because as I read him I cannot help but compare his people with the people I know, and the sort of person I am myself, and the comparison is not a comfortable one. Tolstoy is full of compassion, but I mistrust it because he has no humour, and I believe humour and compassion to be inseparable.

Not all these novelists who move on the heights put us to shame. I am happy, at any time, to enter into the world of Thomas Mann, labyrinthine though it often is. But with Mann there is always a saving irony; he has an extraordinary sense of humour that does not shake one with laughter, but possesses one with a mirth too deep for noisy expression. If you do not believe me, reread the passage in *Joseph and His Brothers* in which Joseph is set upon by Potiphar's wife. If you do not find it splendidly comic, I think you have missed the point. Mann is serious but he is not drowned in his own seriousness, as is, for instance, Dostoyevsky. In reading Dostoyevsky it is often useful to remind oneself that he considered himself a pupil of Dickens; he has the Dickensian eye, and the Dickensian instinct for the revealing detail, but the pull of his spirit is toward tragedy. What is really Dickensian about him is his revelation of the absurdity, the hilarity that stands so close to much tragedy, including the tragedy of Dostoyevsky's own life.

Don't you read anything but novels, I hear you say. I wish I could say that I really read novels. There are libraries full of novelists who are thought great whose work I have not read, or cannot read. I know some of Henry James, but not much, because I would rather read Powys. With the best will in the world I have never been able to get beyond the first few pages of *Moby Dick*. Of the novels of Virginia Woolf I forbear to speak, because although I have read them, nothing can make me read them again; too much acute sensibility affects me as if I were a deep-sea diver—I get the bends. And I have to keep my mouth shut about D.H. Lawrence. I do not deny these delights to those who are able to appreciate them, but I am too old to pretend that they are for me.

It was Oscar Wilde, I believe, who said that nobody appreciated all periods of art equally except an auctioneer. I am suspicious of people who love all the fashionable writers with an undiscriminating zeal, and talk about them all with equal enthusiasm.

To return to the question, however, I read a great deal outside the huge world of the novel. I read a great deal of poetry, old and new, but I mistrust my judgement of the new, so I do not consider myself a judge of poetry. I read many plays, old and new, but we have not the time to talk about that, for it is another address, and quite a different one. There, I am prepared to back my own judgement against anyone. But in the time that is left, I should like to comment on seven books that I read and reread—books that I do not read from cover to cover, but into which I dip for refreshment and reassurance. They are an odd jumble, but if you attempted some such assemblage of the books that really mean much to you and which have done much to shape your life, you might arrive at an even odder list.

First comes a conventional choice, for it is the Bible, with which I link the Apocrypha and the Anglican Prayer Book. For many years I never read the Bible at all. I had too much of it in childhood, and it is not a child's book, and the children who appear in it are not attractive. My parents were drenched in the Bible, and I heard it quoted from my birth. Unhappily, my parents too had had too much Bible in youth, and their quotations were often of the kind that Bibliolaters would rather forget. I early became acquainted with the vomit quotations: "He hath swallowed down riches, and he shall vomit them up again: God shall cast them out of his belly." (That's from Job.) "As a dog returneth to his vomit, so a fool returneth to his folly." (That's Proverbs.) This dog was a close friend of the sow that was washed and returned to her wallowing in the mire. (That's Second Peter.) I knew about the Philistines who were smitten with "poignant emerods in their secret parts," and in my own battles with the Philistines I have often longed for the power to serve them in the same way. My parents had a deep loathing for anything they considered sanctimonious, and in their experience the Bible was often the weapon of the sanctimonious. So it took me some time to discover the book as a repository not only of salty, hardbitten wisdom, but as a never-failing book of wonders and inspiration that are timeless, and in the Prayer Book I discovered how much, for me at any rate, religious feeling is dependent on invocation, on splendour of language. The people who are always monkeying with these great books to make them fully comprehensive have no friend in me, for in their realm the fully comprehensible is not worth comprehending. It is to be felt, not worried and interpreted like a Blue Book. Poetry will carry us nearer to God than the unleavened bread of painstaking translation, for some things are beyond full comprehension but are not for that reason unapproachable.

About the religious approach of the Bible—because, despite its immense variety, it has a prevailing attitude—there is something rebuking, and there are often times when I want something nearer to my own frailty than that. I have said nothing about my long involvement with the work and thought of C.G. Jung, which I have studied and puzzled over for something like thirty years. I spoke earlier of my careful reading of Freud, and although I still reverence him as one of history's great liberators of the human spirit, I disagree with his idea that the human spirit is completed in each of us by the age, roughly speaking, of forty, and that after that we run downhill. Jung's insistence that intellectual and spiritual development continues as long as life lasts, and the convincing proof he provides in his own life, have won my allegiance. But it is not easy to follow Jung and be a strictly orthodox Christian; in much of Christianity there is a considerable measure of the spirit of the Little Red Hen, and indifference to the vagarious nature of the human soul. I determined, when composing this address, to be as honest with you as I could, and so I confess that there are times when I wonder whether polytheism has not a great deal to be said for it. And that is what leads me to frequent readings and browsings in a very great book from the pagan past; it is *The Golden Asse* by Apuleius. It reminds me of another great work that is often misunderstood—Mozart's opera, *The Magic Flute*—which blind people see simply as a splendid pantomime, but which contains enough wisdom to shape a life.

As you see, I am a great man for marvels, and I dearly love to read books that had a greater importance in the past than they have now, because they are a port of entry not merely to an age that has gone, but to the human mind, which changes its fashions, but not its body. So I frequently dip into *The Golden Legend* by Jacobus de Voráginé. This thirteenth-century compost heap of legend and belief has been described by the greatest of modern hagiologists, Hippolyte Delehaye, as a compilation not of careful, historically based lives of saints, but rather of legends which contain what people wanted to believe about the saints, at a time when saints were as near as, in our time, world figures in politics, or rock stars, or great athletes, about whom extraordinary accretions of legend deposit. What people greatly desire to believe is quite as interesting as truth, and generally it is more immediately influential. *The Golden Legend* is rich feeding for the reader whose mind has a Jungian bias. But this sort of thing needs a corrective.

I find my corrective in three books written by men who thought of themselves as clear-sighted, perhaps even as realists. Two were great humorists—among the greatest in literature. One is François Rabelais, and the other is James Joyce. Great humorists, certainly, and great humanists as well. Neither one, to me at any rate, is a man to be read from cover to cover every time one picks up *Gargantua and Pantagruel,* or *Ulysses*. I confess that though I wrestle with *Finnegans Wake* from time to time, I am not of the elect who exult over it. But dearer to me than Rabelais or Joyce is a man who never meant to be a humorist, but who has written a magnificent work of humanistic learning and reflection; I speak of Robert Burton and his *Anatomy of Melancholy*. He wrote the book, he said, to dispel his own melancholy, and since his day it has worked the same healing and lenitive art on thousands of others, among whom I count myself.

The last of these books to which I turn for refreshment when others fail may seem to you a surprising choice. It was once popular and ran through countless editions, but you do not find it now in many private libraries. It is *The Ingoldsby Legends, or Mirth and Marvels,* written, in the character of Thomas Ingoldsby, by a clergyman of the nineteenth century, the Rev. Richard Harris Barham. It is, in its way, a sort of parody of *The Golden Legend,* and it is a reprehensibly prejudiced work by an Anglican parson, who wrote much of it in mockery of the revival of interest in saints and ritualism that troubled his church during the first part of the nineteenth century. I do not read it for the satire, which is absurd and often rooted in ignorance; I read it for its irrepressible gaiety of spirit and the magnificently ingenious comic verse in which most of it is couched. But I confess it is a cult-book, and you might not like it. It seizes upon some people, and not long before he died the American critic Edmund Wilson confessed in an article in *The New Yorker* that he never felt happy in any house in which he lived, if there were not an Ingoldsby on the shelves. This is precisely my own situation; I loved it as a boy, and now I find I have nine copies. I wrote to Mr. Wilson to say so, and received from him a letter in which he said that he knew of only one other addict, and he was the Bishop of Texas. I am sure there are others, but God forbid that we should ever form an association, and publish a newsletter, as is the modern trend.

I realize now how foolish and hopeful I was to embark on an address about the reading I have done in my lifetime. It sounds as if

I were recommending books to you, which is quite the contrary of what I intend. No: I want you to find your own books. Which is another way of saying that I want your own books to find you.

That is not the tedious excursion into whimsicality that it might appear. If you were to question me now, you might reasonably ask: If you had your life to live again, would you read in the same way—wanderingly, capriciously, following your own nose? And I should reply, Certainly I should do so, without in the least expecting that I would read the same books. Another life means other reading. You might ask: Have the books you have read done anything to make you whatever it is you are? Of course they have, but that cuts two ways, because when you read a book, you are at least half of the totality of that experience; the reader makes something fresh of whatever it is he reads. A book is renewed every time it finds a perceptive reader, and no book is the same to every reader. If the books I have talked of have made me, in part, whatever I brought to them made something individual of them. Logan Pearsall Smith was wrong; reading is not a substitute for life, because it is indivisible from life. Indeed, it is a reflection of the spirit of the reader, and I am truly convinced that we who are committed readers may appear to choose our books, but in an equally true sense our books choose us. By an agency that is not coincidence, but something much more powerful that Jungians call synchronicity, we find, and are found by, the books we need to enlarge and complete us. Reading is not escape, something done at random; it is directed unerringly toward the inner target. It is truly a turning inward. It is exploration, extension, and reflection of one's innermost self. If I have been a rake at reading, the caprice has been to the outward eye alone. The inward spirit, I am convinced, knew very well what it was doing.

2

A CHAPTER OF AUTOBIOGRAPHY

Sadly, we will never see an autobiography by Robertson Davies, although the fragments that exist show that the world has lost a great book. Yet for his admirers there is much to be learned from what exists; from Judith Skelton Grant's 1994 biography, *Robertson Davies: Man of Myth;* from the scenes in his novels that clearly draw on his experience of life—this, after all, is the man who states later in this book that "to ask an author who hopes to be a serious writer if his work is autobiographical is like asking a spider where he buys his thread"; from the talks or essays in this book and elsewhere that resonate with the voice of the man; and, perhaps most directly, from the autobiographical fragments that tell us about how he recalled aspects of his life, recollected in tranquillity.

Davies attended Upper Canada College in Toronto from 1928 until 1932. The distinguished private school's founder Sir John Colborne, whose statue stands at the current school's core, gave Davies the perfect name for its close fictional equivalent, Colborne College. There Dunstan Ramsay taught, and three boys who were to play important roles in *The Cunning Man*—Brochwel Gilmartin, Charles Iredale, and Jonathan Hullah—met and became friends.

Davies' account of his schooldays, published in the school's alumni magazine *Old Times* in 1979, is vivid and requires little explanation. The Headmaster, W. L. "Choppy" Grant, was the son of a legendary Principal of Queen's University in Kingston (the Salterton of Davies' young manhood and early novels) and a member of a family that continues to contribute much to Canadian life and letters. By contrast, the mysterious initials "OISE" represent the Ontario Institute for Studies in Education, an establishment founded in the 1960s that continues to attract the scorn of traditionalists like Davies.

Convocation Hall, mentioned here as the setting for the *St. Matthew Passion,* is the great hall at the centre of the University of Toronto. It was there that the public Celebration of the Life and Work of Robertson Davies was held in the week after his death. The speakers included other writers such as Margaret Atwood, Timothy Findley, John Kenneth Galbraith, Rohinton Mistry, and Jane Urquhart. All of the platform party—unaware of the entrance's significance for the young Davies seventy years before—came in by "The Artist's Door."

He wrote in his diary: *September 11: Make start on my piece for UCC, which is more serious in tone than I had foreseen. September 13: Work most of the morning on the UCC piece and finish it except for rounding-off paragraph. Have tried to be honest, and neither to knock the place nor pretend it was what it was not.*

It has long been fashionable for writers of autobiography to abuse their boarding-schools, at which they declare they were unhappy, misunderstood, bored, and ill-used. Only fools expect to be happy all the time. Only people of primitive perceptions think that youth is a time for unalloyed enjoyment. Occasionally I meet people who assure me that their school days were the happiest time of their lives, and I pity them; I wonder what they have been doing with the years that have passed since they left school forever.

My earliest days at the school were clouded by several rebuffs. Not more than three days had passed before I was summoned to the Headmaster's office, and I recall still exactly what he said to me: "Davies, I think you ought to know that you won that scholarship for which you competed, but I decided to award it to Blank instead of you; his mother, as you perhaps know, is a clergyman's widow, and your father can well afford to send you here." My contribution to the conversation was "Yes, sir," but I wished afterward (and I wish still) that I had the courage to say, "Why not give Blank the money and award me the scholarship?" I should greatly have liked to be a scholarship boy, and I think it would have made a difference to my school years, because UCC respected brains, and I thought I had enough to take my place with others who bore the scholarship mark.

Perhaps it was this rebuff which led me to make a stupid mistake a few days later. New boys were given an intelligence test that now seems to me to have been of a primitive and arbitrary kind—but intelligence tests were then in their infancy. It consisted of a number of problems in mathematics, in which I knew I should fail dismally, but its other side was a series of word tests, in which I was confident I could do well. One of them, I recall, was a short story in which candidates were asked to fill in the missing words in a paragraph which begins rather like this: "One fine————, Little Red————was walking through a deep, dark————, carrying a————of————to her————." Aha, I thought, here's where I show 'em! And I filled in the missing words in such a way as to give the story a wholly new meaning.

I had reckoned without the sort of mind that delights in intelligence tests. I was put in the lowest form, IIIB, and the master in charge of the test called me in and told me in sorrowing tones that I had failed abysmally. How badly, I asked. He would not assign a numerical mark, but said, "The result shows that if you entered the Army as a private, you could never hope to be promoted to corporal." This was a heavy blow, and although in a week or two I was pushed up to the Lower Fifth, where I more or less belonged, I never quite recovered, and there were a few masters who persisted for a year or so in regarding me as a cretin. Fortunately there were others who understood that I had simply not acquired the knack of doing the expected, which was at that time—and is still, to some extent—the secret of passing tests.

Membership in the College Rifle Battalion was obligatory, and as I had some musical training I tried to get into the band. No buglers were needed, but there were openings for drummers. I could not drum; stiff wrists. So out I went to the parade ground with an old and impotent rifle, where I was a painful spectacle because I tend to become confused when shouted at.

Add to this that I was put to share a room with Blank, the son of the needy widow, who had been given my scholarship. He was an uneasy companion. He walked in his sleep, and twice took my clothes while in the trance and put them in a room on a lower floor, so that I had to trace them in the morning. Nor was that all. Somnambulism—which he attributed to disturbed nerves—upset his digestion, and while sleeping he vomited in the washstand basin. Every night. This sounds like grossly farcical invention, but I swear by all I hold sacred that it is strict truth. I asked the housemaster to move me, and told him why, and he took pity on my wretchedness.

Blank further distinguished himself that first autumn term when the school doctor gave the boarders two lectures about sex, in the Prayer Hall after classes. The doctor was not a gifted lecturer, his subject embarrassed him, and he was afflicted with an opacity of vocabulary that made it hard for us to know what he was talking about, much of the time. But he did manage to say that self-abuse was a grave matter, attended by dire consequences, and that he was personally able to tell a boy given to this enormity simply by looking at him. At that moment Blank fainted, to the doctor's dismay, and the extravagant delight of all the rest of us.

It gives me keen pleasure to add that Blank was expelled before the end of his first year. I think it was because of gambling, on which the School cast a cold eye. He was last seen by me driving down the avenue in a taxi, smoking a large cigar. This was educational: I have never trusted the son of a deserving widow since, nor has this principle ever failed me.

Perhaps my worst handicap was that I had no cousins. UCC seemed to me at that time to be peopled entirely by WASPS whose interrelationships were more complicated than those of the gods of Olympus.

I had no known relatives, my family was not notably rich, and instead of being a WASP I was rather obviously a Celt. But so was the Head-master, thank God.

Quite soon I acquired a reputation for eccentricity. This was not surprising, for if you tell a boy he is odd, he is likely to become odd, even if only to be obliging.

These things, and the total lack of privacy which was a dominating factor in school life, made my first year a difficult one. It was wholly out of the question for a boy to be alone, and when once we had left our living-quarters in the morning, we were forbidden to return to them, even for a book or a handkerchief, until the end of the school day, when we went up to change for sports. One never knew the luxury of a moment's silence or solitude. I took refuge in music lessons; when one is practising the piano one can be pretty sure of being left to oneself. It was possible to practise scales while reading a book.

The school building was a curiosity, and even I could see that it had not been built to house a school; a school was imposed upon a building which had formerly been, I believe, a military hospital. It had the air of jerry-building and gimcrackery which one associates with buildings put up under government contract; it was a congeries of unexpected draughts, unaccountable noises, and inconvenience. In winter heat was sporadic; at about five in the afternoon the radiators were boiling, and this was the time when many boys dried their sweaty long underwear, worn for football or hockey, on the coils, so that the frequent icy blasts through the loose window casements were a relief. Heat ceased at nine, when the boarders went to prayers and the smaller boys went to bed; the older boys who had another hour's study, and went to bed at eleven, often sat with rugs over their knees at their desks, before creeping into beds under the mattresses of which they had put a thick layer of newspaper, for warmth. The rule was that at night every window must be open as wide as it would go; more than once I have wakened with snow on my bed.

The washing arrangements were old-fashioned; every room, in which two or three boys lived and slept, had a washstand, with a white crockery basin and a jug, in which hot water could be fetched from a tap up the hall. Bathing was a public affair, and the water closets were in booths which had no doors. There were not enough tubs—showers were unknown—so that there was a schedule to arrange bathing-times for everybody, and the schedule was subject to constant and elaborate change. It was not, I suppose, worse than Rugby in Doctor Arnold's day.

In high winds the school tower moved perceptibly. It was inhabited by junior masters, and on windy nights they were all extremely cold and some were noticeably nervous.

I was told that the food at UCC now is good. In my day it was not. It depended heavily on starchy dishes, like macaroni and cheese, tapioca, rice, and a variety of hashes. There were two high moments in the year; the first was in autumn, when an Old Boy sent venison to the school, and we feasted royally, and the other was late in the Spring term, when the cook provided extraordinary quantities of asparagus. At night, before going to bed, we could, if we wished, have milk, and some boys mixed it with a powder distantly related to chocolate, called Toddy. There was a boy from the West Indies who made himself late-night tea, out of tea-leaves sodden in hot water from the tap. In the cold weather I suffered frequently from neuralgia, and perhaps at this late date I may confess that I treated it by going to the music room, where the music master kept a bottle of Scotch hidden (as he supposed) behind a chair. I have had a fondness for a snort of neat Scotch ever since.

No account of UCC fifty years ago would be complete without reference to the code of behaviour to which we were expected to conform. Masters must invariably be addressed as Sir, and it was said—not quite truthfully—that no Master should ever see a boy seated, except in classroom or assembly. We leapt to our feet as if galvanized whenever a Master appeared, and stood with hands at our sides—*never* in pockets. The Headmaster, who had a keen zest for etiquette, lectured us about this, and gave vivid imitations of boys who lounged, who chewed gum, who were all the things a UCC boy must never be. He insisted that when we met our seniors in the streets we must raise our hats (for we all wore hats, and, except for games, caps were anathema) and we must raise them high enough for him to see a patch of sky under the hat. I do this to the present day, sometimes to the amazement of my juniors, who know nothing of hats. We must converse in sentences and paragraphs, and slang was the mark of a low and vulgar contempt for language.

It was a black day for the Headmaster when there was a brief craze for a thing called a Whoopee Hat, which was a hat in the Fedora style, but of cherry red or canary yellow. Boys with a sense of the vogue began to wear these things to school, until a ban was placed upon them, as it was placed on the use of cars. We were reminded sharply and often that we were expected to be gentlemen, and precisely what a gentleman was formed the basis of at least one talk in Assembly every week.

A gentleman, as defined by Dr. W.L. Grant, was one who claimed his place in the world by devotion to high standards of honesty and courtesy, and maintained his claim by unrelenting hard work for some aspect of the public weal. We were told, in the plainest possible words, that we were a privileged group, and every crumb of privilege had to be paid for in the coin of public service. And simply to pay for one's place in the world was the least that was expected; we must strive to do better than that and leave the world a better place than we found it. Good manners were merely the external sign of the inward man; fine manners unaccompanied by fine principles were worse than unenlightened bad manners, because they were a fraud.

This, as you see, was the "character moulding" against which there has been so much protest in recent years. Dr. Grant was the son of the great Grant of Queen's, and his father-in-law was Sir George Parkin, first secretary of the Rhodes Trust, so the apostolic line as it came to us was as unclouded as it could well be.

All three were men of admirable character and distinguished mind, worthy of imitation. But this line of thinking could lead to absurdities. Strenuosity, for its own sake, may be counter-productive, and the best efforts of a fool result only in more folly. I recall my housemaster, William Mowbray, assuring us that we harmed our characters irreparably if we wore our slippers to breakfast, because Sir George Parkin had said that a man who did so revealed a sad lack of moral stamina. Later I was to learn from one of Sir George's grand-daughters that he could hardly have said anything of the kind, because he was himself a committed slipper-wearer, and had to be kept up to a suitable standard of dress on public occasions by the efforts of his wife and daughters. The doctrine as expounded to us was pure Mowbray, disguised as Parkin. But there were more sinewy adjurations to live well. I recall a Sunday evening service of prayers where Dr. Grant startled some of us by shouting the great cry of Luther: "Live in the large: avoid sin if you can, but if you must sin, *sin nobly!*" Life was never dull when Choppy Grant was near to charge it with his extraordinary enthusiasm and pedagogic zeal.

He was the source of energy for the School. Sometimes he was wrong-headed and occasionally he was silly, but most of the time he was a vivid and inspiring element in our daily life. He was an admirable teacher and sometimes in the winter months when so many masters were ill that classes were without teachers, he would fill in, teaching with a richness of reference and personal knowledge that made languages splendid, history a revelation of human greatness or depravity, and any literature a key to the mysteries of the human spirit; exact subjects—maths and sciences—were not within his range, but anything that could be illuminated by a far-ranging mind was his by right.

As a disciplinarian and administrator he was capricious—not meanly capricious, but whimsical; we never knew what he would decree. I think that there is much to be said for such an attitude; even-handed justice is for democracies, and UCC under his rule was undemocratic, in that a stupid offence by a boy who obviously knew better might be severely punished, whereas the same breach by an oaf who knew no better could be treated lightly. He was charitable towards what he called, in the term of Catholic theology, "invincible ignorance." Dr. Grant backed his own judgement of boys, and so far as I could observe, he had uncanny instinct, most of the time.

He treated us as men, as so did those who worked with him. I recall an occasion when a master, goaded beyond endurance by a boy whom we all knew was not merely third-rate but thirty-third rate, called the boy a shit—in private rebuke, not in class. The boy made a self-righteous fuss to William Mowbray, who was acting as Head-master during Dr. Grant's absence. Mowbray, a notably just but not a humorous man, pondered the complaint briefly, then said: "Considering the matter in fairness, do you think the word was ill-chosen?" As a way of dealing with boys who are supposed to be intel-ligent, I think that goes to the root of the matter in a way undreamed of by Student Grievance Committees or Staff-Student Disciplinary Boards, or any of the other elaborate means of avoiding the point devised by recent educational theorists.

Discipline could be rough. Boys had their hair pulled and their heads smacked when direct action seemed called for. One Master, Mr. Darnill, kept a boxing-glove filled with some heavy material on his desk, attached to a leather thong; when a boy was stupid or impu-dent, Darnill threw the glove at him, and never missed; he then retrieved it, hand over hand, amid applause from the class. I was once hit in the face with a banana skin, flung by a master who thought I was not so well up in my Latin translation as I ought to have been. I bear him no grudge; his action was direct and made its point.

Boys are variable creatures, sensitive about some things and bar-barous about others. I recall a very young master, woefully ill-suited to the teaching profession, which has its mystical link with lion-tam-ing. The rumour in the school was that he had to be given a job because he was a relative of the Governor-General—at that time Lord Bessborough—and the G.G. was our patron. Poor Mr. Ponsonby's classes were Chaos and Old Night; now and then the uproar was so dreadful that the Headmaster would have to send someone to cope. He grew tired of doing it himself, and he could not always send another master, so he took the fearful course of dispatching a prefect to do the job, literally sending a boy to do a man's work. I suspect that he was sick of poor Ponsonby. Once I was given the task. The order was plain: "Go to Mr. Ponsonby's class and restore order." It was not difficult. Poor Ponsonby was in a corner looking like an aristocrat (which he was) under threat of a Paris mob, and when I appeared the mob fell silent. I gave Mr. Ponsonby some trumped-up message from the Headmaster about a special Assembly the following day, and left, signalling to the class by my glance that if they did not let up on poor Ponsonby the Head would wash them in steep-down gulfs of liquid fire. They were no more brutish than most boys, but they could not resist torturing a helpless creature.

Corporal punishment, though not frequent, was always a possibility. We had a system of Punishment Drills, and a boy who piled up too big a number of these was Gated—that is to say, he could not have weekend leave and must spend the time in study, under supervision; day-boys had to come to school on Saturday for this punishment. But a grave offence could bring a caning, usually of six strokes. Impudence amounting to serious ill-manners was the commonest cause. If this seems a trivial reason for a punishment that is now regarded with horror by many apparently sane people, reflect on the nature of the School: nobody was compelled to go there and the parents of those who went paid substantial fees to have their sons taught as well as possible, and trained in the code which the Headmaster urged upon us in his talks at morning prayers. A boy who rebelled against some school custom would be given a hearing, but a boy who was simply a bloody-minded nuisance and disturber of the peace was beaten. No obloquy clung to him; he had wiped out his offence and he was in good standing afterward. He was not a hero to the other boys; he was simply someone who had incurred a debt and paid it.

At the root of the punishment system lay the principle that boys were not treated as adults unless they showed adult responsibility. We were being trained for maturity; it was not assumed that we brought it with us in our trunks.

Now and then we were given surprising adult treatment. I remember one afternoon, when I was walking in the grounds, the Headmaster met me, and said, "Walk with me, and I'll tell you what I remember about the downfall and trials of Oscar Wilde." Which he did, laying true schoolmasterly stress on the objectionable character of the Marquess of Queensbury, who was a bad speller and wrote a note to Wilde calling him a "somdomite." What astonished me was that he had compassion for Wilde and thought he had been hardly used. I felt that I had been invited into the adult world, just as I did when the music master, Richard Tattersall, asked me to come to a Sunday rehearsal of the *St. Matthew Passion* at Convocation Hall, saying, "Come in by the Artist's Door; I think it's time you did." I grew several inches in the instant. The masters at UCC knew how to treat boys, when to rebuke and when to offer them the Keys of the Kingdom. They were men of character, old warriors, ripe scholars, men who knew not OISE and its fashionable follies.

I was grateful to many of these men, and one I hated. He taught mathematics, and for two years his daily litany of contemptuous abuse, directed at my stupid head, was worse than anything I have had to endure since—and writers become acquainted with bitter criticism. At last the Headmaster excused me from maths, on the grounds of "invincible ignorance." (I can now, by the way, do simple reckoning far better than most bank clerks.)

Of the many who taught me well, I can pay a tribute only to Mr. Wright (I never knew his first name) who taught English and demanded of me that I read Browning's *The Ring and the Book,* which was not required by the curriculum but which he thought was my cup of tea. It was my bottle of brandy, for it revealed to me that between great poetry and depth psychology there is no division but that determined by the presence, or lack, of imagination, for imagination is not dream-spinning, but insight.

It was such men as these I bore in mind when I was describing the character of Dunstan Ramsay in my Deptford Trilogy.

My time at the School coincided with the worst days of the Depression, and we felt something of its chill, for many parents were hard hit; and I now know what we were not supposed to know then, which was that many parents were in default for fees, and the School bore the default bravely. Several masters who had considerable sums of money in the fairy gold of Stocks Purchased on Margin discovered that the gold had turned to withered leaves.

Although I am not certain that market troubles were the whole

cause, one of the housemasters committed suicide, and a suicide in a
school must be tactfully handled. Two prefects had heard the shot, and
rushed to his study to find him already dead; they were sworn to
secrecy, and I believe they did indeed keep their mouths shut, but
matters of that kind have a way of making themselves known. I
remember his funeral clearly, because on a Saturday morning I was
detailed to carry funeral wreaths to the Prayer Hall as they arrived,
and after an hour or two I was to be seen mounting the stairs, laden
with flowers and weeping uncontrollably. It was not grief, for I had
not known the man; it was rose-fever, to which I am a victim still.

More cheerful occasions marked the celebration of the School's
Centenary. Prize Day that year was of a special magnificence, for the
Governor-General was present; he was Lord Willingdon, a figure of
impressive distinction and splendour of dress. But splendid dress was
not confined to him alone; the procession of masters to the dais was
notable for the variety of morning dress that appeared under the silk
gowns and the gaudy hoods. One or two masters had no degrees, and
I recall Commander J.N.B.P. de Marbois in splendid naval kit; it was
like UCC at that time that geography should be taught by a sailor, who
had actually visited the strange lands he talked about and who had, it
was said, eaten human flesh among the savages of Tierra del Fuego.

Most of the masters wore heavy bands of war decorations, and some
of them—Mr. Parlee, Mr. Potter—bore graver evidence of service in
a war we were never allowed to forget.

We were not unaccustomed to Governors-General. I recall a later
visit from Lord Bessborough, to whom we paid scant attention
because he was accompanied by his beautiful French wife, who gave
the prizes to the boys of the Prep and kissed each one. There were
many seniors, and I was among them, who wished for the first time
on that occasion that we were younger.

No great celebration passes without some element of farce, and our
Centenary was marked by a football song, composed by one of the
junior masters and sung to the tune of "John Brown's Body." It went
thus:

St. Andrews, welcome here today
You've come to meet your doom;
For UCC, with no delay
Will leave you little room,
To harbour doubt about the play
We'll fill you full of gloom
In our CEN-TEN-A-RY!
Charge team, and hit them with your HEADS low!
Play fair and square until they ALL know
U.C.College fights just like a TRUE foe,
In her CEN-TEN-A-RY!

I shall not reveal the name of the writer of these lines, for he later attained to academic distinction, and I do not wish to shame him. Many of the boys, who believed they had some taste in verse, were aware that this was not simply doggerel; in Stephen Leacock's words it sank even lower, and was describable only as chickerel, or possibly piggerel. We roared it with ironic delight on every conceivable occasion, knowing full well that the School could not very well condemn literary criticism as ordinary impudence.

Such reminiscences as these, however, are not sufficient to sum up the atmosphere and quality of the School as I knew it. Its dominating characteristic was that the relationship between the masters and the boys was that of adepts to aspirants, not that of retailer to consumer, or employer to unionized worker, which sometimes seems to be the ideal of our state schools. The authority they had was maintained by their superiority of learning, experience, and intellect; whatever rights we achieved we had to earn by showing our fitness to use them wisely. And the influence of the Headmaster, that learned, enthusiastic, vivid, mercurial man, set the tone for everything. We were encouraged to live in the large, and some of us had a shot at it.

3

LITERATURE IN A COUNTRY
WITHOUT MYTHOLOGY

Strong transplanted Scottish (or, in the usual Canadian usage, "Scotch") characters abound in the fiction of Robertson Davies, from Dunstan Ramsay's fierce mother in *Fifth Business,* who might never have left her Dumfries home, to the philosophical journalist Hugh McWearie in *Murther & Walking Spirits* and *The Cunning Man,* whose view of human nature is formed by his background as the son of an Edinburgh policeman, not to mention the advantage of an education at the University of St. Andrews. In *What's Bred in the Bone* the key fact about the town of Blairlogie is that "the best of the town's money and business was firmly in the hands of the Scots, as was only right and proper."

In his own everyday life Davies did not minimize his own "fine confusion of Scottish blood," his winter headgear being adorned with a pin reproducing the McKay family crest. So it was no surprise that he relished the invitation to give the lecture named after the Scottish novelist Neil Gunn (1891–1973), in the capital city of Edinburgh. The May 27, 1988, lecture gave him the opportunity to speak to an understanding audience about the difficulties of maintaining a distinctive national culture in the face of an overwhelming neighbour to the south. He speaks very directly about the then-current debate about the Free Trade deal with the United States and specifically about his fears concerning its long-term effect on Canada's culture, "turning the link into a shackle."

In his diary he writes very enthusiastically about this trip to Scotland and about Walter Cairns, who was the head of the Scottish Arts Council at the time, and who had invited him to speak. In a piece written in August 1995 called "Remembering Walter Cairns" he tells the following story of his visit to the other great city of Scotland, and an emergency that called for the powers of a Magnus Eisengrim:

Walter joins us later in the day, in time for tohubohu and brouhaha at our Glasgow hotel, where, when we go to our room, we find the housekeeper, the manageress, a maid, and a boy with a ladder and a flapping towel attempting to cope with two alarmed pigeons, who swoop and dive alarmingly, and have become copiously incontinent with fright. This circus goes on for quite a while, the manageress grieving "Oh, what must you think of us?" as the housekeeper dashes at the birds with an umbrella which she opens and shuts rapidly; it was Walter, I believe, who suggested that the boy's towel might better be used to trap the birds, and that if the housekeeper would stop gunning with her umbrella, the birds might come to rest. This is the plan that works: the boy creeps upon the pigeons like a poacher, traps them and thrusts them out into the great world of Glasgow. We retire, while the room is put in order—no small task.

Does anyone, I wonder, ever begin a lecture like this without being overwhelmed by misgiving that he has totally mistaken his subject and based his remarks on assumptions that are groundless? I do not know what you expect of me, but because you have asked me to come from Canada to fill this distinguished lectureship this year I assume that you want me to speak as a Canadian, and that you want me to say at least something about my own work. It is by no means visitor's flattery when I say what pleasure it gives me to be here, for, like so many Canadians, I carry in me a fine confusion of Scottish blood—mostly, I may say, from the Highlands—and a number of my forbears received their education in the famous university of this city. But in Edinburgh you have no lack of Robertsons or Mackays, so it is as a Canadian I shall speak. I shall even attempt the daunting task of saying what a Canadian is. And though I hope that what I may say will have some wider application to literature, I shall set off from a Canadian point of view.

These are days when literature and writers are much in the news, because there are so many countries where free expression is forbidden, and writers—who are a rebellious lot, as a usual thing—are forced to take political stands, espouse causes and stand by principles which are often only slightly associated with their real work. This worries me because, though I admire the courage that is demanded of writers in, for instance, South Africa and in many parts of South America, I cannot persuade myself that such political action is a writer's first duty, and I fear that the increasing emphasis on the Author As Hero may be harmful to the greater task of the Author As Fabulist, Moralist and Visionary. Sometimes, when I am talking to students, they ask me what I think a writer is. I know that often they want me to speak of the author as he leaps upon the barricades carrying the red flag of freedom, because young people understand and admire action—would, indeed, rather act than think. But I say to them: the author today is the descendant of the storyteller who went into the market-place, sat himself down upon his mat, and beat upon his collection bowl, crying, "Give me a copper coin and I will tell you a golden tale!" That is what I truly believe. All honour to the Author As Hero, when firm necessity demands that he be a hero or lose his honour. But let us not, in the heat of these troubled times, assume that a Hero is what an author must be or he is no author. It may seem harsh to say so, but the golden tale may save a thousand lives when the heroic death has been forgotten.

In Canada we are, upon the whole, free from grave political trouble of the kind I have mentioned. Oh, we have a lunatic group in Parliament who want to impose an absurd Censorship Bill on art of all kinds in the country, but we can mock them into silence, I think. The prudery of the half-educated is always with us in Canada, but no worse than it is anywhere else. Indeed, until quite recently, Canadian writers were so little heeded that they could have written almost anything they pleased, without official interference. Our censors were so sure that all evil would enter Canada through the Customs that they never thought of looking for the home-grown variety. The myth of our innocence and purity was very widely believed.

I have spoken of a myth, and the title of my address is "Literature in a Country Without a Mythology." That is a Canadian paradox, and it is the title of a poem by one of our finest living poets, my old friend Douglas LePan. In his poem he writes of a lone adventurer travelling in his canoe along the West Coast of Canada, where the only traces of human life to be seen are the occasional aboriginal villages. The poem concludes:

> ... not a sign, not an emblem in the sky,
> Or boughs to friend him as he goes: for who
> Will stop where, clumsily constructed, daubed
> With war-paint, teeters some lust-red manitou?

It is a poem that speaks of the sense of isolation felt by the Canadian of today, at most only a few generations from Europe, in a land which still declares itself to be strange, and if not unfriendly, certainly reserved and only partly comprehensible. It is a land where there is no easily accessible guide to the past, no widely accepted tale of our beginnings, no friendly jumble of things that are taken for granted. A country, in fact, without a mythology.

What is a mythology, after all? A body of ill-assembled religious belief, a cosmology, a muddle of superstition and folk-belief? It may be these things to people of crudely rational mind, but if we look deeper we see that a mythology looks very much like the unconscious mind of a people, that area which is accessible only in dreams and visions, and where extraordinary energy resides. It is what a people calls on when rationality seems exhausted, and it does not fail those who call. The word soul has a bad savour to many people today, but it is hard to avoid it when we talk of these matters. A mythology is one of the evidences of the soul of a people. Can it really be that Canada has no such thing? No soul?

Oh yes, Canada has a soul right enough, but it has until recently been exceedingly cautious about letting it show. Nor was this simply because Canada was shy, though reticence is a national characteristic; it was because Canada was spiritually lazy, and was perfectly happy to borrow soul, if it might be needed, from Britain or the United States. Noble, haughty Britain: vigorous, freedom-loving United States. Who needed to bother about a soul when these two countries had so much, and were so ready to let their souls hang out, and to let Canada make do with whatever slopped over from their vast, intoxicating tubs of emotion? But those days of dependency are over. We have come to the time in our history when we must find and possess our own soul. And how are we going to do that?

Are we indeed a country without a mythology? The phrase is a provocative one, but it talks of an impossibility. The base and ground of all mythologies is human experience, which does not vary immeasurably from one people to another; mythology is the way in which a particular people has chosen to state its experience, not to impress other people but in the hope of understanding itself. Mythologies are not coherent structures, except when they are regularized for children's reading. Mythologies are huge cairns of anything and everything that helps to explain a people to itself; some of the rocks in the cairn are ugly boulders and others may be quite smooth pebbles. It doesn't matter so long as the cairn rises above the level ground and serves, in some way, as a home of the gods. Canada has a mythology, but it is only now, after about four hundred years of history, forced to decide what it is going to do about it.

The pressure comes from outside. Canada was for long a British colony, never the favourite colony because it is a land that has never appealed powerfully to the European imagination. The French have never thought well of it. The early explorer Jacques Cartier wrote quite seriously that it was "the land God gave to Cain." Voltaire called it a few acres of snow. Napoleon, when he was reduced to giving advice from his seclusion on St. Helena, said that England would be better off without it. British administrators who were sent there tended to regard it as a place of exile. Things have not got better. It is asserted that our name comes from the remark of a Spanish explorer, "Aca nada"—nothing there. Kingsley Amis nominates *Canadian Wit and Humour* as one of the world's shortest books. I could go on for a long time in this strain, for Canada may say with Falstaff: "Men of all sorts take a pride to gird at me." But whatever outsiders may say to the detriment of Canada, we say much worse things ourselves. Indeed, in an early play of mine, I once said that Canada was not a country one loved, but a country one worried about, and to my dismay I now find that remark enshrined in a book of quotations.

And yet, somehow, by sheer weight of geography, and the passage of time, and a slow accumulation of national wealth, we seem to be forcing ourselves upon the attention of the world, and we are now in the uncomfortable position of having to discover, and in some measure to define, our national soul.

Are we late in the day? Not really. I suppose if we were to assign sizes to national souls, as we do to shoes or hats, we might agree that the largest, most powerfully defined national soul in all of history— the unquestioned Number Nine—would be Russia, but it was not until the nineteenth century that anybody began to talk about the Russian Soul. We are a little bit slow in getting off the mark, but we have begun, and the talk of the Canadian soul has begun for us, as it began for Russia, with our writers.

Talk about the Russian soul was not utterly rejected by the Russian people, because a great many of them assumed that the national soul was in the care of the Orthodox Church. Of course Orthodoxy was not the whole of what the Russian writers were talking about. Not even Dostoyevsky thought that all that made Russia Russian was to be found in the Church. In Canada we have no such generally accepted caretaker for the national soul, and consequently talking about it is hard work. Telling Canada that she has a soul used to be rather like telling a stupid and unsophisticated girl that she was beautiful; she laughed coarsely, and kicked you on the shins. A great deal of persuasion was needed before she would pay attention to what you were saying, and stop calling you a fool. But during the last year or so something has happened which has made the stupid girl listen a little more seriously.

I will not bore you with detail: simply, it is the desire of the present Canadian Government, and particularly its leader and our Prime Minister, to enter into a Free Trade agreement with the United States. The Government, and the world of big business that supports it, insists that such an agreement would enormously enlarge Canada's national wealth, create a great many new jobs, and open up the country to the sort of development that would bring in American capital.

As I have said, the business community is, in the main, delighted by this idea and supports it as big business usually does—by laughing at its opponents as people who do not understand how the world wags, and who should be content to trust their betters in such supremely important matters as money and trade. But there is substantial opposition to the Free Trade proposal on both sides of the border for a variety of complex reasons, but in Canada by a strong misgiving that a Free Trade agreement would threaten and eventually wipe out any indigenous Canadian culture. Loud and clear, a lot of Canadians are saying that there are things in our national life that are more important than money and trade, and the word culture is being used on the street, so to speak, in a new sense.

The new sense confuses the tycoons, because they think they know what culture is. For them it is art galleries and ballet companies and opera companies, and theatre companies, to which some of them contribute quite generously. But they still live in a world where pictures and ballet and opera and theatre are heavily dependent on imported goods, and they do not really understand that the fostering and production of such things within Canada could mean anything very much, or employ any important number of people. They are determined that the worth of an activity is related to the number of jobs it creates.

The Canadians who resist them know better. These cultural activities which the tycoons understand, now have a local habitation in Canada, and the people they employ are important to the country in a way the tycoons have not yet comprehended. When we send a symphony orchestra or a ballet company abroad, they make Canada known in an international world that is of the highest importance because it shows that we are part of the *internationale* of cultivated people, and that, insofar as international cultural exchange favours a climate of world peace, we are doing not at all badly. Furthermore, we are submitting ourselves to the judgement of the world on a level that asks for no favours, and is not directly hitched to the world of business.

It is a matter of history, of an inherited governmental system, and of a national psychology. The questions of the governmental system may be dealt with most easily. What virtually all Americans, and too many Canadians who deal in the international world of money, fail utterly to understand, is that Canada is that political oddity, a socialist monarchy. We have created an elaborate and very successful welfare state under a monarchical set-up which is itself a declaration that there are things of national importance that are above politics and above simple matters of finance. The U.S., for historical reasons, mistrusts the concept of a welfare state, and this mistrust shows itself nakedly under present U.S. government, which commits uncounted billions of the national wealth to what it calls defence, and is closefisted in giving money to plans which would ameliorate the grinding poverty of a great part of its people. Quite simply, in Canada you could not get away with that. We have been accused of being halfhearted in our defence system, and although we blush slightly under such accusations we know in our hearts that our gigantic country—the second largest in the world in land mass—is wholly indefensible, and so we would rather compromise and debate than get into wars we know we could not win. Is this want of national pride? No, it is want of a bellicose spirit that would seek to impose its ideals on any other people. We have other fish to fry, and they are fish we catch in our own waters.

That's enough about our governmental system and whatever it implies and includes. What about our history?

Canadian history is supposed to be dull. I would rather say that until the present century it has been such a sad story that we remember it, but do not choose to dwell on it.

Who are we? The naked fact is that virtually all of us are descended from people who never wanted to go to Canada, and who did so under the lash of grim necessity. Our first European settlers, the French, came to Canada more than four hundred years ago, because life at home was hard and without hope; there were adventurers, and traders, but the farmers and tradesmen knew they were exchanging a bad way of life for another which they hoped, by determination, to make less bad. The vigour and intransigence of their spirit is still a powerful factor in our national politics.

The French are not a majority. What about the others? I know a good deal about them, not from the history books, but because I feel it very deep in my bones. Some of them had to leave the British Isles—many were Scots, but many also were Irish—because the cruelties of history made it impossible to stay in their homelands. I do not have to tell their story here; it is part of your history. Harsh landowners, having displaced them from their bits of land, sold them aboard emigrant ships at about a guinea a head, and they found themselves in a country of which they knew nothing, but where the choice was survival or death. Their sufferings were pathetic in the highest degree. Some of them—usually men from the British armies—had been given grants of land by gentlemen in Whitehall who had utterly inadequate maps, and when the settlers arrived they found that their new holdings were either masses of rock, or unproductive muskeg, or were even under water. For a time I lived in a community whose earliest settlers were Irish peasants from the city of Cork who had been transported to Upper Canada to be farmers. They knew nothing of farming, and pathetic tales were still told of wretched men and women hanging about the doors of taverns, offering to dance a jig for a penny. The ability to dance a jig was all they had brought with them.

My mother's father was descended from a Scottish group for whom I have a special sympathy. Their origin was the uttermost northern part of Scotland, and so the gentlemen who arranged for their transport to Canada assumed that they would be best suited at a latitude comparable to the homes they left behind them. So these wretches were deposited on the shore of James Bay, and if you do not happen to know where it is, I can assure you that it is a brutal place even for people from Sutherland. A great many of them died, of course, but some managed the long trek to more southerly Canada, and survived. But when I look at photographs of my grandfather today, I think I can see something of the desolation of those early settlers in his face still, a century later.

But the immigration from Scotland and Ireland is not our only hard-luck story. After the American Revolution Canada received many thousands of political refugees from the new republic. When I say refugees I use the word in its fullest sense, for they had been deprived of civil rights, of land and money, their children were driven from the schools, and they were subject to all the harassment of the losers in any war. They got to Canada as best they could, sometimes on foot, sometimes by the waterways, often assisted by Americans who felt some sympathy for these outlaws who were given and gladly received the name of Loyalists. Many of them were people who had been prosperous in the American Colonies before the Revolution, and in Canada they were tireless in their labours to re-establish the economy, the education, and the religious institutions that they had been forced to leave behind in the land of the free and the home of the brave.

To this day they have not forgotten that they had to make a run for it, in the post-Revolutionary days, and though they are unfailingly polite to Americans, they do not look southward with any particular warmth.

Does it seem to you that I am talking about a nation of losers, of exiles and refugees? Modern Canada is a prosperous country, but the miseries of its earliest white inhabitants is bred in the bone, and cannot, even now, be rooted out of the flesh.

Which brings me to the third element of which I spoke earlier, which is the psychology of Canada. Is it fanciful to ascribe a psychological character to a country? If that were so, how would we know the French to be French, and Germans to be Germans—and the Scots to be Scots? These people, of course, exhibit obvious and sometimes even farcical national characteristics, but such things are not what give them individuality. In Canada we have nothing that marks us outwardly as what we are, but the inward character is something very clear, when you know what you are looking for.

In psychological terms Canada is very much an introverted country, and it lives cheek by jowl with the most extraverted country in the world, and indeed the most extraverted country known to history. Let me explain the terms. In personal psychology, the extravert is one who derives his energy from his contacts with the external world; for him, everything lies outside and he moves outward toward it, often without much sensitivity to the response of that toward which he moves. The introvert, on the other hand, finds his energy within himself, and his concern with the outside world is a matter of what approach the outside world makes to him. It is absurd to say that one psychological orientation is superior to the other. Both have their value, but difficulties arise when they fail to understand one another.

The extraversion of the United States is easy to see. It assumes that it must dominate, that its political and moral views are superior to all others, and that it is justified in interference with countries it thinks undemocratic, meaning unlike itself. It has also the unhappy extravert characteristic of seeing all evil as exterior to itself, and resistance to that evil as a primary national duty. This is what makes so much trouble between the United States and the U.S.S.R.; the fact that the U.S.S.R. is, and has been all through its history, a strongly introverted state makes for continuous trouble and ill will, and assertions of moral superiority on both sides.

Canada, the introverted country, feels no impulse to spread its domination beyond its own boundaries, and has shown itself generous and sometimes absurdly permissive in its acceptance of the behaviour and customs of the numberless refugees that seek our shores. We are prepared to put up with almost anything to avoid trouble. This looks like weakness, and sometimes it is. But it also brings the introvert trait of selfishness. Americans are generous to a fault: we sometimes behave as though it were a fault to be generous, and we are used to being rapped over the knuckles because we do not give enough to have-not countries of the Third World. We wonder, deep in our hearts, how they are ever to make a place in the world if they are always on the take. That was not the way we had to do it. Deep in our hearts we are what you might choose to call a thrawn people. Such a description is not wholly justified, but it is not without some grounds. Now, suddenly, we are faced by a desire on the part of our Government and our powerful and vocal business community, with the likelihood of what many of us see as, eventually, a take-over not immediately political, but cultural and indeed spiritual. We have built up our arts by means not approved in the States; a lot of public money goes into the support of, for instance, our national broadcasting company, which is one of the things that knits together a vast land still sparsely populated. We have a flourishing National Film Board. Music, opera, ballet, and theatre receive public support in a measure which is not adequate—when have artistic people ever considered any degree of support adequate?—but which recognizes their significance in our national life. Although the performing arts are important and are easily seen to be important, it is by our literature that we have made our deepest impression, and I do not need to tell this audience that the state cannot beget a literature, and can do very little to support it, except for grants-in-aid to writers who are thought to be promising. But grants cannot ensure public acceptance, and the acceptance Canadian literature now enjoys all over the world rests simply on the quality of the work—quality and individuality.

How gratifying this is to Canadian writers I cannot begin to express. A couple of years ago I was asked to attend a conference on Canadian literature in Vienna, and I went, though I am not temperamentally a conference-going sort of man. At the opening dinner I sat next to a Hungarian scholar who proceeded to quote to me from the poems of my old friend Douglas LePan, of whom I spoke earlier. I was abashed to find that he knew my friend's work with a completeness and depth of penetration far beyond my own. Nor was this an isolated instance. I have travelled a good deal in Europe during the past five years, and everywhere I go I am astonished and somewhat breathless to find how much we mean to friends abroad of whom we know nothing. My own work has been pretty widely translated, and I am always surprised to hear from readers in South America—a world utterly unknown to me. The last news I had of a translation of my work came from Israel. Not ungratefully, I assure you, but in utter amazement I wonder what people in Israel would find to engage them in my work. Now, if I were to hear that some things of mine were to appear in Arabic, I would be convinced that I was indeed internationally recognized. I have never appeared in Chinese but English editions of my work are pirated in Hong Kong, and that is, I suppose, a compliment in the Oriental manner. Canada, through its writers, has suddenly come under international literary scrutiny.

You may ask why I suppose that a Free Trade agreement with the United States, and all that it implies, would alter or endanger this situation. But I can remember, and many other Canadian authors can remember, being offered publication in the United States on the condition that we would make a few alterations in our text that would transfer the scene of our novel to the U.S.A. To this day that is virtually a condition of having a moving-picture made of a Canadian novel. We have a Canadian film industry, and our films are much respected at international festivals. But we cannot get distribution for them in the U.S. because they are seen as a form of competition with Hollywood, and Hollywood is not the most generous or culturally conscious part of the great Republic, and doesn't like any sort of competition. All the film distribution of the North American continent has been in American hands, and a Free Trade agreement is not going to change that.

May I interrupt the thread of what I am saying for a moment to tell you a story that gives great delight in Canada? Because it is cheaper to make films in Canada, many U.S. companies come north to make portions of their films, and last year a group appeared who wanted to film some scenes in a street. But there was a problem: our Canadian streets are much cleaner than American city streets, so the property people were sent off to get some suitable dirt and rubbish with which to Americanize our Toronto street. When the trash had been distributed to the liking of the director, the crew broke for lunch. While they were away, some of our street cleaners appeared and were greatly affronted. What a dirty street! So they cleaned it up, and when the film crew returned all their splendidly atmospheric dirt had been carted away, and they were furious. That sounds like a Swiss story, but I assure you it is Canadian.

Nor is a Free Trade agreement going to be friendly toward our publishing industry, which is a substantial one, and has had to maintain its position by adroit manoeuvring and some government assistance of an indirect kind. Such governmental assistance would undoubtedly be protested by American publishers as a restraint on their freedom of trade, and unfair competition.

Would it matter? Yes, it would. Not long ago a popular Canadian writer, Pierre Berton, wrote a history of Canada's involvement in one of the great battles of the First World War—the Battle of Vimy Ridge. The book sold 70,000 copies in hardcovers, and another 100,000 in paperback, and for Canadian publishing that is a triumph. Would any American publisher have produced such a book? Of what interest would the Canadians at Vimy be for U.S. readers? But that book is a solid contribution to Canadian pride and nationhood, and we don't want to throw such things away for the satisfaction of car manufacturers, and other forms of Big Business. Canada is waking up. Canada, where Biblical references are still understood by quite a few people, sees itself suddenly as Naboth's Vineyard. You remember that the great King of Samaria coveted Naboth's vineyard, and made him an offer for it. Naboth replied, "The Lord forbid it me that I should give the inheritance of my fathers unto thee." Poor Naboth lost the fight, and was traduced and stoned to death. But those of us who have Canada's newly found nationalism and national culture near to our hearts have hopes of reversing that nasty story, and keeping our vineyard for ourselves and our children.

This dispute is a particularly difficult one because one of the parties to the difference does not see that there is any dispute at all. An American tycoon, commenting on the Free Trade proposal, said, as if he were disposing of a trivial objection, "It's all business, isn't it?" But that is precisely what it is not, and why it is not so is extraordinarily hard to make clear to what may be called the extraverted Front Office Mentality. A couple of months ago a friend of mine, an important Canadian publisher, spoke on this theme to an influential group in New York called The American Society. The members, who were all important figures in business, are worried because Canadian investment in the U.S. is becoming a factor in their economy which they regard, probably quite rightly, as a threat. Within the last two years the largest single holding of Manhattan property has passed into the hands of a Canadian company; the largest moving-picture distribution complex has become Canadian-owned; the largest association of retail stores in the U.S.A., of which Bloomingdale's is the best known, now is owned by a Canadian entrepreneur. To the business mind, this is almost the equivalent of a Russian invasion. My friend the publisher was trying to explain why a distinctively Canadian culture was important and why we were determined to preserve it. After she had done her best she was astonished to be asked by the wife of an American publisher: "I don't get it. You keep talking about *Canadians*. Aren't you all Americans, too?"

Americans are precisely what we are not, and what we don't want to be. And the Americans, charming, extraverted, certain of their acceptance everywhere, simply cannot understand it. And of course it is a problem. A Canadian historian, Arthur Lower, said once that we Canadians love England but don't like Englishmen, and that we love Americans but can't stand the United States. I have been trying to explain to you why this is so. There was an embarrassing war in 1812, which Americans tend to ignore, because it was the first occasion when their armed forces were defeated, and they were defeated by Canada. The Americans, urged by their friends the French, attempted to invade Canada, in order to create a diversion and draw some British troops away from Napoleon's difficulties on the Continent. Being Americans, they had to have a high-toned reason for their invasion, and they let it be known that they were going to free Canada from the hateful British yoke. To their incredulous dismay, they found that, although Canada was not abjectly devoted to the hateful British yoke, we preferred it infinitely to the flabby American yoke, and we fought fiercely to repel the invasion, and were indeed so successful that we made a sally into the States and burned the city of Washington. We had the good sense, of course, to return to where we belonged, but we made our point. Several of my forbears fought in that war, and some died in it, a fact in which I take a good deal of pride.

Why are we so obstinate in this matter? What are we defending? In part it is our land, so much of which is a part of that Great Laurentian Shield that extends across the Atlantic and rises again in Northern Europe. I believe strongly that the land upon which one lives influences one's character, and our land has given us qualities that are more akin to the Scandinavian countries than any part of the U.S. except the New England States. I have spoken of our national introversion, and I see sympathies in our national feeling that attach more strongly to the lands of Ibsen and Strindberg than to anything to the south of us. And as our land makes us what we are, it of course gives its quality to the best of our literature. The poet I have already quoted, Douglas LePan, speaks in one of his poems of the Canadian as

Wild Hamlet, with the features of Horatio.

It is a striking figure, and one I have pursued in my own work.

I should like to speak to you now about my own work, because it is characteristically Canadian, and I assume that you expect something personal from me, or you would not have asked me to be here today. I could certainly talk of the work of several other Canadian writers, but I feel that might be to refine modesty to a point of needless scrupulosity.

I have been a writer all my life, not because I ever felt any overmastering urge to be one, but because I was born to the trade. My parents and brothers were writers, usually as journalists, but as literary craftsmen as well. I assumed that writing was something that everybody did, and I think I was at least twelve years old before I realized that not everybody does write, that there are people who find writing insuperably difficult, and that there are people who aspire powerfully to be writers but don't know how to begin. I am frequently

asked for advice by young people who are in this latter quandary, and
all I can honestly tell them is that if they don't know how to begin
they had better reconsider their ambition to write. Beginning is simple. You write at the top of the page: "Once upon a time." If nothing
comes to mind to follow that introduction you are not a writer. A
critic, perhaps, but not a writer.

I have no belief in the power of anyone to teach someone else how
to write, and although I am aware that universities everywhere now
offer instruction in what is called Creative Writing, I have no idea how
they go about it, nor have I observed any astonishing flow of brilliance
from those who undergo such instruction. Being a writer is somewhat
like being double-jointed. Either you have it or you don't. Of course
you can work upon what nature has given you, and perhaps become a
Boneless Wonder, or Indiarubber Man of literature, but without the
initial endowment you are not likely to do it. If you are very, very lucky,
you may be born a very good writer—perhaps a poet—but there is a
disagreeable corollary to that piece of good fortune; you may die young,
while the roses in your chaplet are still fresh. Or, even less desirable,
you may live on, without any perceptible development of your powers, and the rose-leaves in your chaplet fall off, with your hair. Lucky
writers get better as they grow older, like wine, and die rich in fruiti-
ness and delicious aftertaste, so that their works survive them.

My work was not very warmly received in Canada during my early
days. I was criticized as being unCanadian. I think now that what
bothered critics was that it was simply not Canadian as they conceived
Canadianness to be. I began writing during a rather gloomy period in
Canadian literature. As one of our best writers, Margaret Atwood, has
said, Canadian literature has a strong pull toward what is sombre and
negative. It is allowable to be a humorist, a relentlessly funny writer,
who writes the kind of book you take to people in hospital, but the
idea of humour as an element inseparable from writing even on serious subjects, of humour as the light that plays on a writer's mind, was
not understood and was rebuked in my early work. But it was out of
the question for me to change. I was born very much under the influence of the planet Mercury, and my outlook on life is mercurial. Not,

I assure you, frivolous, or trivial; not jeering or contemptuous; but most assuredly not solemn for the sake of solemnity—a quality which critics are apt to confuse with seriousness. I was indeed serious, but not solemn.

In time the critics became used to me. And at last, when I was fifty-seven years old, I wrote a book that made even the most reluctant decide that I was a serious writer, however regrettably flawed by humour, and that my subject was indeed Canada. Not Canada simply as a geographical expression, but as a climate of being, an ambience, an inescapable psychological fact.

The book in which I made my serious intentions so clear that it could not be misunderstood even by the most perfunctory reviewer, was called *Fifth Business*. I did not write it, I assure you, to prove anything or demonstrate any thesis, and I shall speak of that later. But I was surprised and pleased many years afterward to read some remarks made by Eugene O'Neill, the American playwright, and this is what he said:

> The playwright of today must dig at the roots of the sickness of today as he feels it—the death of the old God and the failure of science and materialism to give any satisfying new one for the surviving primitive religious instinct to find a meaning for life in, and to comfort its fears of death with. It seems to me that anyone trying to do big work nowadays must have this big subject behind all the little ones of his plays or novels, or he is simply scribbling around the surface of things and has no more real status than a parlour entertainer.

That is what I was trying to do in my book: to look at what O'Neill—not a notably cheerful man—called the sickness of today, but which I would rather call the spiritual predicament of today. But I was not, I assure you, attempting any such thing consciously. I was simply writing a book that demanded to be written. I wrote "Once upon a time," and there it was.

Does that sound grandiose? Was I visited by some Muse who urged me on? No, but I was certainly impelled to write that book because I was troubled and haunted by an image. Doubtless you know how these things happen. When we are unoccupied, and perhaps somewhat tired, pictures arise in our minds which we would be troubled to explain. In my mind, for several years during which I was much occupied with other work—I was setting a new college going in the University of Toronto—I was troubled by such an image. It was a simple one: in a village street, at about six o'clock on a winter's night— the night of Boxing Day, I was sure—two boys appeared who had quarrelled while playing; one boy was walking some distance in front, and the other boy threw a snowball at him, and I knew that concealed in that snowball was a stone and that if it hit the boy it might hurt him badly. And that was all the picture told me.

This happened so often that I became aware that I must investigate that image if I was ever to have any peace. This is what I did, and the novel *Fifth Business* was the result.

I shall not give a long account of what the book is about. Briefly, the stone-laden snowball did not hit the boy it was meant for, but hit a woman who was out walking with her husband, and it affected her so badly that she miscarried the child she bore, and never regained her reason—as the world of that village understood reason. She became the local madwoman, and did a number of things that the village could not endure. As for the child who was born prematurely, he became a neglected and pitiable but unusually self-reliant and surviving sort of man who later achieved a good deal of celebrity as a conjuror, and illusionist, and psychologically a trickster.

But the first boy, whose name was Dunstan Ramsay, was plagued by overwhelming guilt, because he was convinced that the woman had suffered in order that he might survive. In her seemingly mad behaviour he saw saintliness, and his life was dominated by an absurd problem: could such a woman be a saint in the true sense of the word? Indeed, what *was* the true sense of the word? Heroic virtue? Miracles? As a Presbyterian he had no experience of saints, but his obsession drove him to become a well-known expert on saints, a hagiologist, and when the madwoman was without friends in the world he made himself responsible for her care. His profession—for being a hagiologist is not a paying task—was that of a schoolmaster, and to the world in which he lived he seemed no more than a somewhat eccentric teacher in a boys' school. But after many years, he contrived a meeting—not a confrontation, simply an encounter—between the boy who had thrown the fatal snowball, and who had become a very rich and influential industrialist, and the famous illusionist. Neither was known to the other, and when Ramsay made it plain how they were involved, they were cool and polite. But when, shortly afterward, the great industrialist was found in his car at the bottom of Toronto harbour, with a stone in his mouth, it was Ramsay, who had preserved that stone for fifty years, who knew what had really happened, and indeed who had killed Boy Staunton. Was it the magician? No: not really.

As I worked on that book I became aware that one book was not enough to explore the story as it demanded to be explored. So in the course of the next five years I wrote two other books: one was the story of the rich industrialist, and the effect his character had exerted on everybody around him, and particularly his unhappy son. The rich industrialist was not what the world calls a bad man, but he was very much an extravert, and he had edited out of his memory anything that might be damaging to his idea of himself. That was his self-image until he ended up in the harbour with the stone in his mouth.

The third book was, of course, the tale of the illusionist, whose life had been one of dreadful privation and servitude until, by lucky chance, he met the woman who transformed his destiny, and who in time lifted the load of Presbyterian guilt from the heart of Dunstan Ramsay.

As I told you, in the beginning this story was not warmly received in Canada. But when it gained very warm commendation in the United States and elsewhere, Canada changed its opinion. Many Canadians began to see in the tale of Dunstan Ramsay some relevance to themselves and to their country. Began, indeed, to think that perhaps the Canadian is Fifth Business in the affairs of the world.

And what is Fifth Business? It is an expression from the world of the theatre, and especially of opera. This is how it was defined for

Ramsay by the woman who at last brought him to a sense of what he really was:

"Who are you? Where do you fit into poetry and myth? Do you know who I think you are, Ramsay? I think you are Fifth Business.

"You don't know who that is? Well, in opera in a permanent company of the kind we keep up in Europe you must have a *prima donna*—always a soprano, always the heroine, often a fool; and a tenor who always plays the lover to her; and then you must have a contralto, who is a rival to the soprano, or a sorceress or something; and a basso, who is the villain or the rival or whatever threatens the tenor.

"So far, so good. But you cannot make a plot work without another man, and he is usually a baritone, and he is called in the profession Fifth Business because he is the odd man out, the person who has no opposite of the other sex. And you must have Fifth Business because he is the one who knows the secret of the hero's birth, or comes to the assistance of the heroine when she thinks all is lost, or keeps the hermitess in her cell, or may even be the cause of somebody's death if that is part of the plot. The *prima donna* and the tenor, the contralto and the basso get all the best music and do all the spectacular things, but you cannot manage the plot without Fifth Business! It is not spectacular, but it is a good line of work, I can tell you, and those who play it sometimes have a career that outlasts the golden voices. Are you Fifth Business? You had better find out."

I spoke earlier of what Eugene O'Neill said about the necessity for the writer to explore the malaise of our time—the changed conception of what God is and how God is encountered in the life of man, in our day. It is not easy work to present that malaise to the modern reader in a way he will accept. My novel *Fifth Business* is written in the form of an extended letter from Ramsay to his Headmaster, apparently to explain why he is not such a dull dog as the world at large thinks him. It is vital to the understanding of the book to recognize, as the story proceeds, who this Headmaster is. Do you know that not once since that book was published in 1970, and has been the subject of a great number of critical essays and considerations by academic critics of the most impeccable qualifications for being critical, has any critic recognized who the Headmaster is? Quite simply, and to me obviously, the Headmaster is God, to whom Ramsay is saying—this is what my life has been, what my destiny has made of me, where your hints and nudges have taken me. Judge me, for I am your creature. Ramsay has lived his whole imperfect and eccentric life in the constant awareness of God, and in the end he knows, like a true introvert, that God is within him and not external to him, and that in that consciousness he is saved or damned—to use the Presbyterian terms familiar to him from childhood. In the end he knows that he is saved, which is to say that he has come to terms with his destiny as honestly as he knows how. And he recognizes that the means by which he has been saved are not those that had ever been made known to him by the religion of the past. The knowledge of God must begin with self-knowledge; where it goes after that is every man's task to find out.

I thought I had said that as clearly as anyone could, without being rudely and inexcusably didactic—without hitting the reader over the head with that most objectionable of literary appurtenances—a Message. I hate books with Messages. Though I am beguiled by the magnificent style of *Pilgrim's Progress* I can never really like the book because Bunyan was obsessed by his Message. I have never liked *Robinson Crusoe,* despite its enviably plain style, because Defoe could not hold his peace, and must always be preaching and nudging his reader to accept his Message. Tolstoy, that splendid barbaric giant, almost discredits himself by the frequency, the simple-mindedness, and the remorseless nagging of his Messages. The real author, in my view, is the one who approaches his hearers with a Golden Tale.

Real readers can understand what a book is saying without having it spooned into them like brimstone and treacle. Of course, not all readers are real. My books are frequently recommended to students in Canadian schools, and from time to time students come to see me, to talk about them. Often this is an experience agreeable to them and to me. The ones who try my patience are those who, when I have explained some point in a book, look me in the eye with all the confidence of youth and say, "What you're *really* trying to say is—" To that I have a well-worn reply, and it is this: "My dear young friend, I am not *trying* to say anything: I am *saying* it as clearly as careful consideration and my not wholly inconsiderable art permit me to do. Your job is to understand it." But I have many readers who do understand, and the letters they write me are one of the foremost satisfactions of authorship.

A country's literature is a crystal ball into which its people may look to understand their past and their present, and to find some foretaste of their future. The pictures are never simple, never wholly clear, and certainly never didactic. They need interpretation; not the interpretation of the literary critic, unless the critic is a person of gifts comparable to the writer, but the interpretation of the heart, the sympathy and understanding that are the partners of insight. Canada has, over the years, produced such a literature, and during the past quarter of a century that literature has grown to an extraordinary maturity. It has done so with the encouragement of a growing body of readers who want to hear what their writers have to say, and make it part of their national consciousness. I avoid the term "national culture" because it has been abused by people who think of culture as a commodity, separable from the rest of the national life. Culture is an ambience, a part of the air we breathe. That special ozone is now to be breathed in Canada, because it arises from the land itself—not a few acres of snow, but a country of immensely varied beauty of landscape and of season, including our lovely and dangerous winters. It arises from our history, not dull, but covered, sombre in palette but with wonderful flashes of brilliance. It arises from our psychology, which takes its colour from the land and the history. The fear that it might be lost if we entered into a closer financial link with our southern neighbour is, I think, exaggerated, for the land and the history and the psychological direction cannot be wholly changed by anything so superficial. You, in Scotland, know that political unity with a more aggressive and powerful country is not the death of the essence of your own country. But such a link could be dangerous and in some respects depleting, and I hope we have the self-preservative good sense to declare against it. A strong link already exists, and it is sufficient without turning the link into a shackle.

As I said at the beginning, I have no idea of what you expected or wanted me to say. But I have given you what our grandparents called "a piece of my mind"—not, I hope, too disagreeably. I have attempted to show you something of the wild Hamlet who lurks behind the features of Horatio.

4

PAINTING, FICTION, AND FAKING

∼༼ව༽∽

Many readers of his novels are enchanted by the arcane knowledge that flows so effortlessly from Davies' pen. Clearly, his mind was unusually well-stocked, but in many cases that encyclopedic knowledge was hard-won. He researched many of these topics tirelessly, expending great effort to give the proper effect of ease.

For example, *What's Bred in the Bone* (published in 1985) involves Francis Cornish in the mysteries of art restoration and art faking. As Judith Skelton Grant puts it in her invaluable biography, *Robertson Davies: Man of Myth,* it was not that the author knew nothing of art, but that his knowledge of painting fell "far short of his grasp of music, literature or drama, and so he did a great deal of research to underpin what he did know and to avoid errors." Before writing the book Davies made himself thoroughly conversant with art fakery both through wide reading and direct consultation with authorities in the art world, including his brother-in-law Sir Russell Drysdale, the well-known Australian artist.

Three years after *What's Bred in the Bone* appeared, Davies was invited to speak at the Metropolitan Museum of Art, on April 17, 1988, and he made good use of the wide knowledge he had gained. One point he did not make when describing Bronzino's *Allegory of Love* to the New York audience is worth noting here. Judith Skelton Grant points out that Davies hung a reproduction of this painting in his rooms at Oxford in 1935. Exactly fifty years later when visiting the original in London he recalled an unhappy youthful love affair. His diary notes: *Impressed as always by the facial resemblance of the figure of Fraude with a girl I loved when I first met her when she was seventeen. And Fraude she was to me, with the honeycomb and the sting.*

Dealing with the speech at the Metropolitan and its agreeable aftermath, his description of his performance ("not too bad") is quintessentially Canadian: *The auditorium where I speak is big—750 seats—and sold out; pretty good speaking arrangements but as so often the lectern is not the right height, so I have to hold my manuscript above it, or disappear below it. But I do my best, though not as good as I wish, not too bad, and the reception is very friendly and prolonged. As the reception was so good I cut the text hardly at all and it ran 1 hour and 10 minutes. Went to the Lures' apartment after the speech. A wonderful supper—I was reminded of the late-night suppers in Balzac and other 19th century writers—and the kind of conversation one so much wants and so rarely gets—sophisticated but not sharp-edged, informed but not pedantic, witty but not wise-cracking—and we enjoyed it hugely.*

It would have been of inestimable help to me when I was preparing this address if I had known who you would be—you who are gathered here tonight to hear me talk about Painting, Fiction, and Faking. Are you a group of connoisseurs of art? If so, what could I say that might interest you? Is it the word Fiction that draws you? I may claim to know a little bit about fiction, especially in its primary meaning of "the action or product of fashioning or imitating"; fiction, looked at in that light, has a strong underground link with painting. As for Faking, are we not all fascinated by it? Are we not at once drawn and repelled by those people who produce works of art—sometimes very fine ones—and pass them off as the work of someone the world has agreed to think of as a man far greater than the faker? At the name of Rembrandt every knee shall bow. But at the name of Tom Keating, who, during a career of twenty-five years, produced over 2,000 fakes, and successfully passed them off as Rembrandts, Paul Potters, Fragonards, Bouchers, Goyas, Degas, Renoirs, and Turners, our knees do not actually bow, but certainly they shake, partly in awe of his astonishing effrontery, and partly with laughter. I confess to a fascination with fakers. They carry into the world of art the spirit of the god Mercury, who was the special protector of both artists and thieves, and to whose heart both Rembrandt and Tom Keating must have been dear. Without the intervention of Mercury in human affairs, what pompous asses we should surely be!

I do not say that I know nothing about art, but I approach painting simply for refreshment of spirit, and not with any aesthetic theory to help me. All my life I have been a gallery visitor—this gallery, among many others. I have favourite paintings, to which I return again and again; one—an obvious choice—is Vermeer's *The Painter in his Studio;* but another, not so obvious, is Bronzino's *An Allegory of Love*— you have doubtless seen it in the National Gallery in London—about which I have puzzled my head for over sixty years, and I never visit it without having some new idea about it. I like Mannerist painting, and I think my wife and I must be among the few people whose kitchen walls are hung with full-size reproductions of Arcimboldi's refreshing and evocative picture of The Seasons. Do we collect? Yes, we have some very good Novgorod School ikons, which we bought before they became so popular as they are now. We have some of the work of my brother-in-law, an Australian painter of great attainment. And we have an extensive collection of pictures—paintings, prints, and odd things done in tinsel, which illustrate the theatre of the eighteenth and nineteenth centuries in all its immensely energetic variety. We have this ill-assorted assembly of things for a reason that would surely bring a frown to the face of the art expert, and a patronizing smirk to the face of a dealer.

I am not going to say we have them because we like them. That is what everybody, including some of the most informed and wealthy collectors, say. Of course we *like* them—but why? Because they speak to us of enormous energy and spiritual insight. The theatre things tell of the dreams and ideals of a past age, to whom the theatre meant something that it means no longer. And the theatre, I need not remind you, is the very home and temple of illusion, in which some of the most important truths known to man are given form and body by means of the most elaborate and sophisticated arts of—fakery. The ikons speak resonantly and without illusion of faith and the shackles of the flesh, and the nobility that triumphs over death. So, you see, we have the world of illusion and the word of truth constantly before us.

When we lived in university surroundings, students who came to our house would say, "It must be like living in a museum." But it isn't. It is living in a place where everything on the walls has something important to say. Suppose for an instant that I am at home, and I am looking at a watercolour of a very pretty girl dressed in green velvet; she has decorated her charming face with a saucy little moustache and a tiny beard; she is showing rather a lot of leg. To you it might not call for a second glance, but to me it is the beautiful Miss Louisa Fairbrother, dressed to play the part of Little John in a pantomime about Robin Hood. The time? Oh, about 1845. I know a lot about her, including the surprising fact that she became the morganatic wife of one of the sons of King George III, and that she lived a long and very respectable life under the name of Mrs. Fitzgeorge. You smile the superior smile of the art-lover; this information has nothing to do with the artistic quality of the picture. Ah, but when I look at Miss Fairbrother's beautiful eyes, I know that those eyes once rested on this picture, and obviously approved of it. I know what a lot of pleasure Miss Fairbrother gave when she appeared in that guise on the stage. I know also that she lived long and died rich, and was loved by a duke and respected by a fashionable circle, thereby giving the lie to the notion that all such girls died in poverty and of the pox. Indeed, you understand, I am *reading* the picture; I am not admiring its planes, and its composition and its coloration—though they are all there. And when I look at our ikon of St. Paraskeva I am reminded of a life of noble renunciation and purity of spirit. It is a very good ikon, but to me it is first and foremost a saint.

This is not, you see, the art expert's approach. But it is very much the approach of the man whose life is preoccupied with fiction and whose desire is not merely to look *at,* but *through,* objects and situations. The question is not: "What is this object that I see before me and how does it conform to the aesthetic principles I have made my own?" No, the question is: "What does this *say* to me?" That may not be the most artistically pure approach to a picture, but I venture to think that it is the approach of a very great number of people, by no means all of whom are simple-minded.

It is the question that is asked by the public of every new school of art as it presents itself, and until the question is answered the new school is greeted with rejection and often with mockery. This is as true today as it ever was, and perhaps the mockery is uglier than it has been in the past, because so much new art is deeply confusing.

All art, I think we may agree, is created in the hope that it will say something to interested people. The purpose of all art is to give delight, whether it be painting or sculpture or music or literature. The special problem of the modern artist, who offers us arrangements of colour and form, is that he has—along with the rest of the world—abandoned the language which every cultivated person used to understand, and which has now become almost a dead language. I speak of the language of faith and mythology; to great numbers of people, even when the language is carefully translated, it carries little conviction. In the jargon of our time, it has ceased to be "relevant."

I want to speak of that language for a while, because we cannot walk through any great gallery and not be aware of it, even when it says little to us. It is a language that tells us a great deal about what painters are saying. I do not for a moment suggest that the great painters of the past were simply illustrators, offering us scenes of the Old and New Testaments, or from the Lives of the Saints, or from Classical Mythology. Not at all. But it was through such subjects that they spoke to us of what was most significant to themselves, because all art of the highest quality rises from the depths of the artist's personal perception of the great mysteries of the spirit, which may not have a great deal to do, directly, with religion or mythology, but which could be made known to the world through those means.

Let us consider a picture which has recently been acquired by the

Detroit Institute of Arts; it is called *Madonna and Child with St. John the Baptist* and it was painted in 1540 by a painter whom I particularly admire, Agnolo Bronzino. I choose it because it is not extremely familiar, and it is not the work of an artist who is put in the very first rank by most experts, though he is an admired Old Master. Therefore no overwhelming mystique attaches to it; we are not hypnotized by the reputation of the artist or by centuries of admiring description by literary artists like, for instance, Ruskin, who could make you believe that a kitten playing with a ball of string had extraordinary spiritual resonance. Allow me to quote to you some words in which one of the experts in Detroit describes it:

> The painting illustrates many features characteristic of Bronzino's mature style and of Florentine mannerism in general. The figures are placed close to the foreground plane and occupy much of the surface of the picture; their features are highly refined, conforming to a preconceived, formal, and even abstract idea of beauty, rather than deriving from the observation of real individuals. The serenely perfect and delicate features of the Madonna reflect an ideal of divine beauty, while the infant Christ and John the Baptist seem more like angelic than human types. The Virgin's head is proportionally small compared with her body while her torso appears unnaturally elongated. Such features conform precisely to the highly artificial mannerist ideal of beauty, which emphasized extremely attenuated proportions and anatomically difficult yet apparently effortless and graceful poses. In the twisting postures of both the Virgin and the Christ Child, the mannerist love of complicated and contorted but nonetheless elegant movement is expressed. Complex torsions are harmoniously resolved and all sense of strain or struggle has been drained from the figures.

Excellent. Not a thing wrong with that. But is that what you think when you look at the picture? If you are a trained critic and art historian these things are apparent at a glance, but I do not think that is why Bronzino painted it. After all, there are innumerable pictures of the Virgin with Christ and St. John, and if the painter had wanted to exemplify what the critic calls "his typically mannerist, flame-like posture of the Madonna" he could have painted something else. But he painted this subject. Why?

As I have told you, I am particularly interested in Bronzino, and among other reasons it is because he has so much to say about women. Art critics tend to be patronizing in their references to him. They speak of "elegant posturing, empty of religious feeling," and of "a secular, court style," of "icy fascination" and "insolent assurance." Of course I am respectful of these learned men, but I am sceptical of their pretensions to be experts about depth of religious feeling. That cannot be confined to the peasant Christs and Apostles of Rembrandt. Certainly Bronzino conveys a kind of religious feeling that has much to say to me, and in the Detroit picture he paints an idealized Madonna, who is indeed idealized womanhood, just as the Christ and St. John are idealized children. The love in the face of all three figures is perhaps cool, but none the less real for that. What I see in this picture is a thrilling realization of two great archetypes: Our Lady Soul and the Miraculous Child. If they are refined in appearance, what about it? Surely we are not so naive as to equate squalor and ugliness with sincerity? The holy figures of Bronzino appear to me just as evocative of religious belief as the most hideous, decaying Christs of Grunewald or the haloed Flemish runts of Rembrandt; it is simply that they do it in a different way and the belief they provoke is of a different quality. Beauty is just as devout as ugliness.

In this fine Bronzino which is now in the Detroit collection we see one aspect of womanhood superbly depicted. In Christian faith it is called the Divine Mother; in other beliefs it may be the Great Mother; whatever the form of belief, this aspect of femininity—the sustaining, protective, uplifting and ennobling element in the human spirit is deep in the heart of mankind. It seems to me that in this picture Bronzino looks forward four hundred and ten years to the declaration by the Pope of the bodily Assumption of Mary to Heaven, to sit with the otherwise male Trinity in the highest seat of splendour and power. This is woman

as God. Bronzino's Mary looks down with delight upon her Divine
Child, who is playing with—with what? With a globe of the world of
which he is Saviour and King. But the observer may very well see in
this picture of the Christian goddess her predecessors Isis and Semele,
for this is a truly religious, and not simply a sectarian, picture of womanhood in its aspects of love, wisdom, and mercy.

Now I invite you to consider another Bronzino which I mentioned
earlier. It is in the National Gallery in London and it is usually called
An Allegory of Love. Let me recall it to you. The central figure is a nude
woman, wearing a coronet of jewels; in one hand she holds an apple,
in the other an arrow. This is clearly Venus, and she is playing with
her son Cupid, shown as a boy of perhaps fourteen. And how is she
playing? He is caressing her left breast, the nipple between his fingers
as if exciting it. They are kissing, and since the picture was cleaned,
we can see that she is putting her tongue into his mouth. Interesting
play for mother and son, is it not? A naked child, laughing at them,
is pelting them with rose-leaves, and at the feet of this child are masks
of cheating and dissimulation, mixed with the thorns from the roses.
Behind the principal figures are one of a woman, in agony, apparently
Jealousy, if we understand her expression rightly; the other is a monster, for a rich gown conceals a body with lion's feet and a stinging
tail, and we notice these things after we have seen her exquisite, dissembling woman's face and the honeycomb which she is offering to
the principal players in the scene. We do not have to be great icono-
graphers to recognize this as Fraude, the Cheat. The whole scene is
displayed against a blue cloak, which is either being drawn aside or
thrown over the love affair, by a bearded figure and a woman, whose
face may—we must not be too eager to read meanings into expres-
sions—reveal either dismay or astonishment. Who are these two?
Plainly they are Time and his daughter Truth.

May I pause for a moment to tell you about the last time I saw this
picture? I found a group of school children, with their teacher, sitting
on the floor in front of it. The children were filling in some sort of
questionnaire. I asked the teacher what was going on and she said,
shortly, that the children were learning Art Appreciation. I looked over

the shoulder of one little girl—about ten, I suppose—to see what the questions were and was astonished that one of them was "Is this picture rude?" What on earth could it mean? The little girl had ticked the box which showed that, in her opinion, the picture was "rude." "Why do you think it is rude?" I asked. "Because that Lidy is niked," said the child, indicating Venus. I looked at some of the other papers filled in by the other children and found that they were all agreed that the naked human body, however beautiful, was "rude." Such is Art Appreciation in our day.

What do we make of this remarkable, arresting composition? It is another aspect of womanhood. This is not the divine love of the Madonna in the Detroit picture; it is erotic in the highest degree, and the mother is tempting her son to something not usually regarded as maternal. And yet—is it something we do not care to acknowledge? These days the papers are full of horror stories about the fathers who debauch their young daughters. But what is sauce for the gander is sauce for the goose, and I foresee that it will not be long before we are reading of mothers who debauch their sons, and any social worker or experienced magistrate has stories to tell about that kind of involvement. Are Time and Truth revealing or concealing this form of sexual passion? We shall see. Meanwhile, we all know plenty of mother's boys, and many households where the presence of the father seems almost to serve as a cloak of respectability cast over a lively affair—not overtly sexual, but certainly powerfully emotional, between a mother and her son. I suggest to you that Bronzino was not only a Mannerist, but in a comprehensive sense a moralist, as well. He knew the facts of life, including some that modern morality still does not choose to admit. The Fraud and Jealousy that play their part in many love affairs seem to have been strongly present in his consciousness. There is a fine Bronzino in the Museum of Fine Arts in Budapest in which once again we see Venus and her enamoured son; and once again a figure called Jealousy, but who might also be called Terror, or Horror, is prominent in the composition. The innocent, tempting figures of rose-crowned children are here as well. Are these not two aspects of the same love? This is what the literary man sees in these pictures—love in its divine and its all-too-fleshy aspects. The art critic sees the splendid technical accomplishment in composition and colour, but he makes no mention of what the pictures are saying to us. Speaking for myself, I am not greatly concerned that Bronzino was a Mannerist—which at the moment seems to be a bad kind of painter to be—but I am fascinated by him as a Moralist, which does not mean somebody who codifies and dictates what the behaviour of mankind should be, but someone who sees what the behaviour of mankind really is, and shows it to us.

Mannerism has been defined as a degenerate form of High Renaissance Classicism, which flourished between 1530 and 1590. But the most recent Mannerist picture to come to my notice was painted in 1977 by an American artist, Audrey Flack, and it leapt off the wall at me in the art gallery of the university in Tucson, Arizona. We can sometimes identify the models of Renaissance artists; do we not see the superb Simonetta Vespucci in several of the finest canvases of Botticelli, whose Madonna and whose Venus she was? And in Audrey Flack's picture we know at once whose life, and beauty, and unhappy fate, is displayed before us, because the picture is called *Marilyn* and two unmistakable faces of Marilyn appear in it, in a composition which includes some unmistakable moral symbols—cut and decaying fruit, grapes (always a fruit associated with the highest luxury), a rose in full bloom, a photograph of Marilyn as a child, luxurious drapery, and two reminders of the cruel passing of time—a watch and a burning candle. Over the whole picture broods an air of cheap, fleeting, sweet and pathetic beauty. I am told that this is one of three pictures in a series, which includes one of the Wheel of Fortune and another of World War II, and in all three the symbol of the burning candle appears.

Don't tell me that Mannerism is dead. It is not a technical style of painting; it is a way of feeling and thinking about life, the way of the moralist who sees and records and reminds, but who does not insistently judge. Bronzino uses the symbols of faith and mythology to say what he has to say. Audrey Flack is addressing another audience and she uses symbols of today but the fruit, the roses, the candle and the timepiece would have been familiar to Bronzino. But if she had chosen to show us Marilyn's fate in, for instance, a picture of Susanna and the Elders, or perhaps Danae in the Tower of Brass—Danae, you recall, was destroyed by an overwhelming love which visited her in the form of a shower of gold—how many of her viewers would have understood what she was saying? Because, I repeat, painters are always saying something, and in our time, when religion and knowledge of the Bible have sunk into a heavy eclipse—once, in a class of graduate students I met with a young man who did not know who Noah was!— and mythology where it exists at all has become an incomprehensible tangle, the language which painters once used with such eloquence is almost forgotten.

Do I regret it? Yes, I do, because faith and mythology summed up in themselves vast wisdom which we neglect at our peril. Yet, among what we assume to be educated and sophisticated people today this classicism of the Bible and mythology is a matter of ignorance and sometimes of downright hostility. I make no apology for quoting the very familiar words of Santayana, who might have been described as a Mannerist philosopher. He said: "Progress, far from consisting in change, depends on retentiveness... Those who cannot remember the past are condemned to fulfil it." The Bible, which has now sunk to the level of a book of admonition and law in the hands of people who profess to take it literally, remains perhaps the greatest compendium of history, philosophy, and fruitful reflection available to us, and as lately as our parents' time it was possible for public speakers to make allusions to it, in the confidence that virtually all of their hearers, highly educated or not, would understand them. And mythology, which was familiar to generations whose education included a good deal of Latin and probably some Greek, was a constant reminder of the ambition, downfall, and suffering to which mankind is liable. And where the Bible insisted that God is not mocked, mythology made it equally clear that the gods are not mocked. They were ever-present reminders that pride, and the stupidity that is inseparable from pride, goes before a fall; reminders that God, and the gods, are within us and must be cherished and listened to; reminders that we are not a glorious completion of the history of mankind, but beads on a string, which extends from the cloudy beginnings of life to whatever may be its conclusion. I must leave this theme or I shall begin to sound like a prophet, whereas I constantly remind myself that as a writer of fiction I am a moralist, an observer, and a recorder.

As an observer I have, of course, been aware of the remarkable increase in tension in the art world during the past few years. Suddenly, art news is big news and people who are not in the least interested in the picture itself are in some way thrilled to learn that Van Gogh's picture of some irises has sold for $59.9 million, and the fact that the artist himself lived and died in poverty gives a savour of commonplace romance to the affair. People love to think of artists as innocent sufferers and poor while with the stroke of a brush they are creating riches. When it is revealed that in 1987 Sotheby's turnover amounted to $699 million the most abject philistines are forced to admit that there must be something in this art stuff after all. When I agreed to come here to talk to you tonight I began to take more than my usual interest in the art news in the London *Times,* and read about the Chardin that fetched $192,000 and the Modigliani that fetched £2 million. A newly found and perhaps not entirely authentic Mantegna has an expected price of £600,000 put on it by Sotheby's, which is modest when one considers that in 1987 an unquestionably genuine Mantegna sold for £8.1 million. A Tiepolo has turned up for which £2.5 million have been offered, and for another Tiepolo £10 million have been realized. A Chardin goes at $192,000 and a head of a child by Greuze brings £125,000.

The reputations of painters have changed radically. In 1939 I could have bought a large canvas by Fuseli in London for five pounds, and I didn't buy it, though I coveted it, because I did not have a spare five pounds or a big wall. Today a good Fuseli will, as they say, set you back a few hundred thousand. Pictures which have what is called "association interest" by Winston Churchill or Noël Coward fetch handsome prices, though they are undistinguished as paintings. Two painters of association interest whose high prices give me special pleasure are Richard Dadd and Thomas Griffiths Wainwright. Dadd's dates are 1817 to 1886, and from his twenty-fourth year until his death he lived first in Bedlam—yes, the old hospital of St. Mary of Bethlehem for lunatics—and the greater part of his last forty years in Broadmoor prison for the criminally insane. On August 28, 1843, he went for a walk with his father, and cut his father's throat with a razor. He was otherwise an amiable man; fond of his father, but moody. In prison he had plenty of time to paint, and his wonderfully fantastic pictures have been, until recently, available at substantial but not amazing prices. But in 1983 his masterpiece, a picture of Oberon and Titania and attendant fairies, was sold at Sotheby's for just under £300,000. I would love to own a Dadd—not because he was a murderer but because his pictures appeal to me—but I came too late upon the scene.

As for Wainwright, he did his best work in Australia, where he had been transported in 1837 for forgery. He was not an amiable man, but he was a handsome one, and as well as forging he was suspected and tried for poisoning his mother-in-law, his uncle, and his sister-in-law. He was an art critic by profession, and he made one uncommonly perceptive statement in that capacity. He said: "I hold that no work of art can be tried otherwise than by laws deduced from itself: whether or not it be consistent with itself is the question." But he carried criticism too far for his own good; when he was accused of murdering his sister-in-law the murder could not be proven, but he so far forgot himself as to offer, as part of his defence, that she had very thick ankles. It was assumed by the court that there was only one place for a man so dead to all decency, and it was Australia. So off to Van Dieman's Land he was packed, and because of his talent he was allowed a good deal of leeway there, and painted a number of portraits of Australian citizens of means, who were not of the criminal class. Today, in Australia, to have a portrait of an ancestor painted by Wainwright confers a wholly understandable distinction. But if he had not been a gentleman-crook one wonders if it would be so.

May I pause for a moment in the logical progress of what I am saying for a few words in praise of Henry Fuseli, a painter who has only recently begun to attract the attention which I think was always his due. When we speak of Surrealism we are apt to think of it as a movement of this century, coming into being between the two World Wars. Some perceptive critics have indeed seen hints of it in the past, in the work of Hieronymus Bosch, and Arcimboldi, and indeed Goya, who used grotesquerie of subject and treatment to make statements that could not be made in any other way. But Fuseli is a greater figure in this group than is generally admitted. It was Thomas Griffiths Wainwright, the poisoner—who was, as I told you, an art critic—who explained his own great admiration for Fuseli when he said, "The little Swiss does not consider that an artist should paint only what he sees." Sees, that is to say, with the physical eye. Fuseli was one of those who painted what appeared to the mind's eye, and there is about his pictures a fascination of the sort we find in the wonderful stories of E.T.A. Hoffmann.

While we are pausing thus, I should like to confess my own strong interest in portraits and my admiration for portrait-painters, who are not a class of artists as highly considered in our day as I think they should be. But their art, when they are artists of high attainment, is perceptive and critical in a degree that other painters—even when they are masterly in their achievement—may not possess. I think of the words of a literary man, Thomas Carlyle, who said: "Often I have found a portrait superior in real instruction to half a dozen biographies . . . I have found that the portrait was a small lighted candle by which the biographies could for the first time be read, and some human interpretation made of them." That is a writer's opinion, and I have spent many happy hours in the National Portrait Gallery in London, in full agreement with Thomas Carlyle.

Now, to resume our thread of thought. We were talking of painters who are notable through their association rather than their demonstrable talent—politicians, playwrights, and poisoners. As well as these oddities, we have all seen the return to popularity of painters who dropped out of fashion, like the marvellously observant Tissot, and the ebullient, strongly flavoured Bouguereau. Pre-Raphaelites, once laughed at, have made a strong comeback, and for a good Burne-Jones you must dip deep into your pocket. Victorian narrative pictures, of the kind exemplified by *The Old Shepherd's Faithful Mourner* in the Victoria and Albert

Museum, where the body of the dead shepherd is seen receiving the tearful tribute of his dog, now sell at substantial prices. Animal pictures of
all kinds are eagerly collected, even dismayingly sentimental canvases of
kittens or puppies playing with balls of wool, or their master's slippers.
Indeed, there is hardly anything that cannot be sold today, if it exhibits
some workmanlike command of paint.

The enthusiasm is unbounded, and many countries that were, until
recently, indifferent to what their artists had done make a great clamour about what they call their Heritage. Scotland has begun to pay
huge prices, not for Raeburns, but for quite undistinguished work,
which can be shown to have some historical association. Indeed, the
word Heritage has achieved new and unaccountable meanings. I visited a museum in Canada a while ago, in which I was assured that the
splendours of my Heritage would be made visible. It proved to be
filled with Red Indian artifacts, and although I can claim some Red
Indian blood—about a teaspoonful, it would be, I suppose, after 150
years—I did not find my bosom swelling with anthropological pride.

But the word Heritage has become magical. Phillips, the auctioneer, says: "We have seen amazing prices paid for golfing and cricket
memorabilia. Tennis and football have started to take off in a big way,
and now it's the turn of boxing." Phillips is expecting £150 for a bust
of Tom Sayers, the last of the bare-knuckle boxers, and they are offering an inestimable treasure—a baseball signed by Babe Ruth. Art connoisseurs, of course, are scornful of this stuff, and refer to it as
"sporting tat." But what do you make of £5,000 which was recently
paid for a lock of Lord Nelson's hair? Or several hundred pounds for
an authentic cigar-butt, flung away long ago by the great Franz Liszt?
I recall that in the early fifties a Liszt cigar-butt, complete with a bell-
jar to display it, fetched only $25. Never before has Oscar Wilde's
remark that the only person who admires all schools of art with equal
fervour is an auctioneer, been so true.

One of the many magazines devoted to art and the world of the
saleroom has published for the last four years a list of America's Top
100 Collectors. That means that there must now be 400 top collectors and one wonders how far the list can be extended. The magazine

says: "Our research has been as extensive as ever—we've talked to dealers, auction-house experts, curators, art-world journalists and, in all
but a handful of cases, the collectors themselves." It is significant that
on this list of persons consulted, dealers and auctioneers come first.
That disturbs me, because, however admirable and honourable these
people may be, they are still essentially tradesmen, and in their words
about what the top hundred have bought they write and speak in
what, as a writer, I consider a very unchaste prose. They exult, they
bombinate, they scream in print, and however tactful they try to be
it is always the prices that fascinate them. And what do these giants
among collectors collect? Pictures, of course, and usually by living
artists. But they are not above Fabergé eggs, presidential manuscripts
(I hope they really mean manuscripts and not merely typescripts), toy
soldiers—100,000 of these in one collection!—and vintage photographs. I was amazed to discover that somebody collects work from
the Roycrofters, that group of handicraftsmen assembled by Elbert
Hubbard at East Aurora near Buffalo, where they tried to work in the
spirit of William Morris and fell desperately short of their aim. Have
you ever heard of Elbert Hubbard? One should not speak ill of the
dead, but before he died in the sinking of the *Lusitania* in 1915 he
spread pernicious views about art and filled the living-rooms of aspiring American homes with much shocking junk, which a few people
are now collecting. American Indian art, we learn, is "going through
the roof." *Art nouveau* is very popular, as well as art-deco and Tiffany
lamps, which we used to think of as expensive trade goods. One top
collector has the middle portion of a drip-painting which Jackson
Pollock once chopped into three when he was drunk; if you have
either of the other portions, he is certainly your man. Of course many
of the hundred collect unquestioned fine art, and what they think
about being lumped with these other hysterical enthusiasts the magazine does not record. The compiler of this list assures us that the old
adage "Buy what you love" is as true today as ever. We can only comment that love is a many-splendoured thing.

Why do they do it? Why are there more collectors of art and artifacts today than ever before in history? I have a theory—a literary man's

theory—and it has to do with Time. By acquiring objects from the past and the immediate present these collectors are trying to stop the clock, and to seize, so far as they can, a portion of the past and make it their own until, with their names attached to it, the collection goes into a museum and they are assured of a kind of immortality. Religion, as I have already said, has lost its grip on a very large part—perhaps a majority—of people in the modern world. The body of knowledge of the Scriptures and of the classics and mythology has ceased to be a common *lingua franca* of educated people; that splendid link with our cultural past has vanished except among scholars, who can rarely afford to be collectors. You must not suppose that I am grieving uncontrollably, because this loss to the educated and wealthy portion of mankind is simply an historical fact, and I do not suppose anything can be done about it. But in art hundreds of millions of people seek a sense of assurance about the past, and a link with the past. Those who can afford to do so make collections of their own, and the rest of us frequent museums and collections to refresh ourselves at the deep well of the past, even when we understand only in the most general terms what the artists of the past were saying and, as I have suggested, saying through a language once common to educated people. For the language of faith and classical literature, and mythology, the art critics have substituted, with some success, a language of their own, and the people who follow them look no longer at the *Madonna and Child with St. John the Baptist* or *An Allegory of Love* as portrayals of the Great and Divine Mother, or the Mother as Seducer and Devourer, but as handsome assemblies of planes and composition, and arrangements in tones of colour. Personally I suspect that they understand the pictures in the old way to a greater extent than they are willing to admit, because none of us wants to seem naive. But they look and look and look in extraordinary numbers. I read in the *New York Times* a few months ago— I am sorry that I have lost the clipping and cannot give you the exact date—that more people visit art museums in the course of a year than attend all the sports events held in the United States during the same year. That is an awesome statement, but it appears in the *Times* and if we begin to doubt the *Times* surely the heavens will fall.

What are all these people looking for? Some come for curiosity, but vastly more for beauty, for an enrichment and fulfilment that they cannot find anywhere else. It is for this reason, I think, that the galleries which confine themselves to modern art, though they are crowded, are not so popular as those galleries that show pictures of the past, arranged in some order, usually chronological. There is no difficulty in understanding why this is so. Modern art is demanding in a way the art of the past is not, or seems not to be to the unreflecting observer. Modern art does not speak the language of faith or the classical world; what it has to say is expressed by the painter as it arises from his unconscious, creative centre, and this may take the widest possible variety of forms. As with much modern poetry the forms and the symbols the modern painter employs are his alone, and they may not be readily understood by other people unless they bring a sophistication and a knowledge of an uncommon kind to the task. The language of modern painting is thus far a secret language, and it must be learned anew for each painter.

For this reason a special and subtle temptation assails the modern painter, if he does not happen to be quite first-rate, either as a painter or a person. It is the temptation to fake the secret language, and to paint mysteriously where there is no real mystery. Perhaps "fake" is too harsh a term. I doubt if many modern painters set out deliberately to hoodwink themselves, believing that what arises most readily from within is not therefore the real stuff. I know that this happens in literature, and the remainder tables of the bookshops are heavy with novels and books of verse written by people who demand that the public find a key to their secret language or climate of feeling. But with them the desire to write is greater than any genuine necessity, any overwhelming impulse, to write, and what emerges is showy but really feeble stuff.

A painter in a past age—in the seventeenth century, let us say— could not embark on a painting with a muddled and incoherent idea of what he was going to express. He could not depend on variable inspiration to carry him through. The language painters used was prescribed, and anybody who lost himself in it was judged incompetent.

There was also a level of technical skill that was expected, and those who could not rise to it were simply village daubers, who painted clumsy pictures of burgomasters, or ill-contrived Virgins and saints. Now you must not suppose that I am so stupid as to suggest that modern painters of the first rank have abandoned technique; they have adapted the traditional painter's technique to their manner without having much command of their matter.

I think that is why many gallery visitors are leery of ultra-modern pictures. They cannot judge them by any standards they know, and they are very much afraid of being taken in by a confident second-or third-rater.

That is why painters of the humblest order—the people who exhibit their pictures in the street—usually paint in the best imitation they can achieve of some bygone style. The people who buy a picture for twenty-five or a hundred dollars want something about which they can be confident. They are investing just as much of their capital, pro-portionately, as the Hundred Top Collectors.

Don't laugh at them. Many of us also want something about which we can feel confident before we admire it. A great name and an indis-putable history of informed ownership assure us that what we are looking at is the real thing, before we permit ourselves to—to do what? Here is where I approach a realm more congenial to the literary man than to the gallery-goer.

I think that what so many of us want is a picture in which we can invest something of ourselves, which I can only call soul. I know soul is a dirty word to many people; it is one of the four-letter words that even the people who write dirty words in spray paint on walls hesi-tate to use. But how else can I define that quality of trust and hum-ble acceptance with which we approach the great unknown things of life? There are not many among us who have been so irredeemably coarsened and battered by the vicissitudes of life that there is not, deep within us, something that cries out for belief and unquestioning trust. What we bring with us to a great gallery like this one is not, as a usual thing, the simple piety of the confessedly religious man or woman, nor is it the complex tapestry of understanding that makes scenes from mythology or classical learning evocative and enriching to us. But the yearning which was satisfied and enabled by that common language of the past—the language of belief and acceptance—is still there, and these pictures from the past give us an assurance of the continuity and value of life. People in past ages, we say, lived and felt to some degree in the mode of these wonderful pictures, and when we look at the pictures we can do so too. We reach out a hand to the past, and we feel a responding touch.

I must repeat that I do not undervalue the sheer beauty of the great pictures of past ages. But beauty is not an element that can be divorced from the thing that it illumines. The professors of aesthetics can haggle as much as they please about what beauty is, and there can be no doubt that we have to be taught to see it. But once we have learned our lesson, beauty seizes us and blesses us, and enslaves us.

There. You may think I have been speaking in a high fashion of ineffable things and matters for which there is no indisputable proof. But I have another string to my bow. It is a psychological string, and some of you may think it a rather dirty string, but I am unrepentant. In the human psyche the ineffable, the elegant, and the praiseworthy are inextricably mingled with the grubby, the commonplace, and the reputedly inadmissible. That is what keeps us sane. I want to talk now about money.

People are apt to talk stupidly about money, as though it were something shameful, or simply a means to an end. Not at all. Money is one of the aspects in which the soul manifests itself in mankind. It is adventure, it is aspiration, and an important means through which we invite the Goddess of Fortune to enter our lives. If I were the president of a bank I would have a fine statue of the Goddess of Fortune standing in the middle of every branch and I would have Cicero's great dictum "Man's life is ruled by Fortune, not by wisdom" embossed on all the bank's stationery. I suppose I am explaining to you why I am not the president of a bank. I doubt if many bank presidents would agree with me that money enables our souls to manifest themselves. When I say *soul* I hope you understand that I am not speaking of an intoxicating gas, rather like ether but pleasanter, which is the peculiar property of saints and girls who are still virgins. What I mean by soul is that mysterious element which nobody has ever been able to define that separates a living creature from a corpse. Soul is a lot of things; it is energy, of course, and it is also the secrecy and obsession that live in all of us, unless we are too near the corpse. And soul must have expression. It does not exist by itself. It is something that we invest in those things that can enlarge our lives, and one of the greatest of these is money.

Because this line of thought may be strange to you, and perhaps disagreeable, allow me to support what I am saying with a quotation from a Jungian analyst, Dr. Adolf Güggenbuhl-Craig. He writes: "Wherever soul appears there is secrecy, a secrecy that is expressed through many symbols. Initiation rituals designed to connect us to soul are shrouded in secrecy. The soul is often depicted as a hidden treasure in the woods, guarded by dragons in caves, etc. Second, fascination. Being concerned with one's soul is the greatest aim in life; losing it the greatest calamity. Third, strength and energy. The loss of soul results in weakness, while being in touch with the soul produces boundless energy." But, as I said before, soul has to have a habitation. In psychological terms, we have to project it on something. In the past many people projected their souls, understandably, on religion. In the present time, you have only to read the daily papers to see that great numbers of people have projected their souls on sex, and for some of them it appears as if the orgasm were a unit of currency, the new, unshakeable gold standard. But for many, the soul is projected on money, and I want to repeat that this does not mean that the soul is degraded by money, but rather that money is exalted by soul.

What do we do with our money? Even if we prudently tuck away a good deal of it, we spend most of it, and what we spend it on shows the nature of our souls. It shows what we are doing with an external, exchangeable symbol of the soul. All those collectors we were talking about earlier, the serious ones and the merely solemn ones, are projecting their souls into their collections, they are seeking to possess some portion of what was best in the past, and one might almost say that by so doing they are trying to slow down the flight of Time, or they may wish to stop Time altogether.

We are particularly concerned with Time nowadays because we are approaching the end of a millennium, and for some reason which I cannot begin to explain, mankind is fascinated by these millennial completions. When the last one was approaching, and the year 1000 A.D. was almost at hand, all sorts of extraordinary predictions were made, all sorts of monsters and portents were reported to have appeared, great wars were declared to be inevitable, and above all it was assumed that Christ would come again to earth, to judge the quick and the dead at a great Last Judgement. It was widely agreed that the Last Judgement would take place at Jerusalem, and years before the actual date, thousands of pilgrims from all over Europe set out toward Jerusalem on foot or, if they could afford it, on horses. They wanted to be there in plenty of time, presumably so that they could get good seats for the great occasion. It was altogether a most unhappy and ill-judged pilgrimage. Some of the travellers were killed by robbers; some were captured and sold into slavery among the heathen; some just never made it, and were lost somewhere on the way. Many, of course, did complete the journey, and hung around like discontented tourists, waiting for something to happen, and indulging in elaborate calculations designed to show that Christ was not really late, but that the pilgrims were early.

Now we approach another millennium, and I am sure that we shall hear of extraordinary things, and morbid or apocalyptic expectations. Indeed there has already been a lot of talk about the progression from the Platonic Month of Pisces to the Platonic Month of Aquarius, which will bring great changes in the character of human life. I take no sides in these matters. I merely point them out as evidence of the tendency of mankind to think along such lines, and understandably to dread the great changes that are thought to be imminent, because we always assume that change will be for the worse, and we fear it. What is more natural, then, than to seek out those things that do not change, that have abiding value and give an assurance of a great past, and to get them into our own collections if we can, or to visit them where they are already collected, if we cannot.

The modern enthusiasm for painting, I suggest, is in part linked to the human yearning for certainty at a time when uncertainty seems imminent; for links with a great past when the future seems menacing; for tradition when society is in flux; and, in short, for a means of slowing, if we cannot stop, the world clock. And the vast amounts of money which in one way or another are invested in this yearning, are, in fact, investments of soul, of life energy, of what is deepest and most prized. And one of the things we demand is the assurance of value, of tradition, of association with the great men of an earlier day.

What happens then, when it is discovered, as it so often is, that some great painting is not the work of the Master to whom it has been attributed—that it is by a lesser man, or a pupil? Even worse what happens when—horror of horrors!—it is shown to be a fake, painted within the last fifty years by some clever fellow, and palmed off on the credulous as the genuine article?

Faking goes on all the time and it operates on many levels. When a tourist goes to Paris and buys a Corot for $100 we do not waste pity on him. But when a serious collector, or a museum, buys a picture for hundreds of thousands, or millions, and it is shown to be a fake, what then?

The faker is regarded as a criminal of the worst kind. He has made the experts look foolish, which is unendurable, because experts of all kinds are our modern priests and we want to think them infallible. He has exacted from the public praise and high esteem for his painting which is not justified by the passage of time, and by association with a great Master whom we unquestioningly revere; he has dared to tinker with the World Clock. And high among his enormities is that he has made fun of money, and as money is a bearer of the projection of the soul he has blasphemed against the gods, which is to say against something very precious in every one of us.

Consider the case of that unhappy man, Henricus Van Mcegeren, who was discovered in 1947 to have been forging Old Masters. He had been accused of selling art treasures to the Germans during the years when his country was occupied by the Nazis, and he sought to clear himself by revealing that the pictures were fakes, painted by himself. But before the war, in 1937, he had pretended to discover a large painting of *The Supper at Ammaus,* which he declared was by Vermeer. Great numbers of experts examined it and declared without reserve that it was indeed by Vermeer. But after his exposure in 1947 other experts, and some who were the same, sneered at the idea that the picture could have been by Vermeer. They even asserted that the model for the face of Christ was one of the most highly revered countenances of our own day—that of Greta Garbo. Poor Van Meegeren was in very bad trouble; he was tried and sentenced to imprisonment, but he died before he could serve his term. The public obloquy which attended his unmasking was extraordinary, but he maintained great dignity at his trial. And he asked a question which nobody attempted to answer; later, a play was written about him in which his question took this form: "Yesterday, this picture was worth millions of guilders, and experts and art lovers would come from all over the world and pay money to see it. Today, it is worth nothing, and nobody would cross the street to see it free. But the picture has not changed. What has?"

Since then a variety of art critics have been attempting to answer that question, and some of them reach heights of indignation that give us the measure of their spirits. The only honest one of the lot, so far as I know, is Denis Dutton, who says simply, "The magic has gone out of it." Magic. That's the word. Length of time, association with a great name—these are magical elements, unbecoming the austerity of an art critic.

In the course of Van Meegeren's trial it came out that he had been hurt because his own paintings had not gained him substantial recognition. If you look at them, they are modern in subject and technique and they have little to say for themselves. But when Van Meegeren began to paint in the Old Language of art, and counterfeited the saintly innocence of Vermeer, he was acclaimed as great. The more sophisticated we are the more reluctant we are to admit that we are open to the magic of past time, and the greatness of Masters long dead. It seems simple-minded, somehow. It is when the faker exposes us, and especially the art experts, as simple-minded that the roof falls in.

Consider the case of Tom Keating, whom I mentioned earlier, and who died on February 12, 1984. He was an Englishman of humble origins, who had been a sign painter, then became a picture restorer, and found that he could paint like almost anybody you care to name. And he did. He painted a lot of pictures simply as Tom Keating, but they were not very interesting; competent but not remarkable. Then Tom Keating, who was a man of refreshingly irreverent mind, began, as he said, to flood the market with fakes, to show up the art experts and, as he said, "as a protest against merchants who make capital out of those I am proud to call my brother artists, both living and dead."

He was a true son of Mercurius. He said that his fakes could be detected by anybody with half an eye, and furthermore he inserted clues into his fakes—things that could not historically have been there, or things that should have leapt to the instructed eye, as when he used eighteenth-century paper for his Rembrandt drawings. These Rembrandt drawings, by the way, he did with quills and a special ink he made himself out of apple juice and Nescafé. If you are ever offered a Rembrandt drawing that somehow reminds you of breakfast it is probably a Tom Keating. He went farther. Before doing a fake he would write his name, or the word Fake, or perhaps a ruder word of about the same length, on the canvas with white lead paint; this meant that if the picture were X-rayed it would be shown at once as a fake. He lived to be sixty-six, and painted, as I said earlier, rather more than two thousand fakes. In 1977 he was arrested on charges of conspiracy and criminal deception, but it took many months to reach the courts, and in 1979 the charges were dropped because Keating was in very bad health. But the indignation against him is undying, and in some art circles to laugh about what Tom Keating did is a grave offence. Yet can we help laughing? We must be dull of soul if we are not amused by these convulsions in the ultra-solemn world of art.

A few years ago, in London, I visited an exhibition of fakes at the Tate Gallery. It was very refreshing, dispelling a lot of the smoke of incense from art. Without exception the pictures had great charm and quality as art. But they were fakes. Ought I to have been ashamed?

Are we too solemn about art? I think perhaps we are when Dr. Gilberto

Algranti can set up a gallery in London from which you can rent any one of 250 Old Masters, to brighten up your house for a cocktail party, or your daughter's wedding. A Canaletto will run you about £17,000 for a week. Dr. Algranti says: "This is not an activity for social climbers, but rather those concerned with beauty in the home." Yes, doctor. We hear you.

I am speaking to you not as a critic, or someone primarily concerned with painting, but as a writer, and understandably my perspective on the whole business of faking is different. First of all, of course, it makes such a very good story. Second, and more important, is the alarm it causes in the world of dealership, of extraordinary prices, of competitive connoisseurship. But most interesting, I think, are the reflections it arouses on the nature of Time, and Time's ability to create magic, and to cast a palpable but inexplicable wonder over pictures that were once simply the last to leave the atelier of some notable artist-craftsman, working for a patron with definite ideas of what he wanted. This is the magic which allows us to link ourselves with the past, and in one way or another to project, or invest something of our souls into the past. It is not impossible to describe, but it is rather difficult to explain.

The Daughter of Time, as you know, is Truth, and when we ask Truth for an explanation, she smiles and is silent. Sometimes, when confronted by a Van Meegeren, or a Tom Keating, she winks.

5

CAN A DOCTOR
BE A HUMANIST?

∽ℰℰ∾

Robertson Davies' last novel, *The Cunning Man*, published in 1994, is about the life of Jonathan Hullah, a physician. From Hullah's boyhood encounter with Mrs. Smoke, an Ojibwa medicine woman in Northern Ontario, the theme of healing runs through the book, and great respect is shown for unconventional methods. This is not unexpected since Davies himself had benefitted so greatly from learning the Alexander Technique to alleviate physical ailments.

His 1984 lecture makes it clear that Davies was devoting much provocative thought to the topic of healing long before the 1994 book. One of the most famous medical schools in North America, Johns Hopkins Medical Institution in Baltimore was a fitting location for the David Coit Gilman Lecture on November 18, 1984, arranged by his friend Dr. George Udvarhelyi. Besides the lecture, there were other enjoyable aspects of his visit to the old Maryland seaport city, as these excerpts from his diary show: *George takes me to the 14 West Hamilton Street Club, described as "an intellectual Men's Club" housed in a charming old early 19th century house and small in membership. Meet John Houseman who is to moderate the Symposium, and he is very much like his film self, a charming, distinguished, beautifully spoken man of wide culture and we get on very well. We both speak briefly at lunch. . . . After dinner Prof. Richard Macksey takes us to his house for drinks and to see his library, which is a wonder; reputedly 36,000 books, everywhere in a splendid*

old house, but especially in a library he adapted from a garage, two
stories tall, books floor to ceiling, heaped on tables, deep on the floor—
quite wonderful. Shows me some of his association books, chiefly
Ruskin, but he has much in this line including some Johnson. Asks me
to inscribe books for the College which I do with a will.

I am at a loss as to how I should describe what I am about to say to you. A lecture I fear it is not, for that would suggest that I was about to tell you something new about something I understand better than you do. A lecture should be on a subject that has discernible boundaries, and it should say something that only the boldest dares to contradict. A lecture should be informative and perhaps edifying, and if it should ever be published it ought to be richly bejewelled with footnotes. Above all, a lecture should be solemn. I have given lectures in my time, but I assure you this is not going to be one of them. If I had to describe my remarks this evening frankly—as if I were in police court and on oath, so to speak—I should have to call it a ramble over several subjects, portions of which may seem to you to be impudent, and portions of which will be ignorant, and portions of which may contrive to be both at once.

You see I know nothing about medicine, though I have, in the highest degree, the hypochondriacal curiosity about it that is characteristic of authors. Indeed I know nothing about any science whatever. I presume you asked me to talk to you now because you thought it might be amusing to hear what a literary man thinks about your profession. A literary man is supposed to know about people, and the profession of medicine is still loosely associated with people, though it seems to be moving rapidly toward a condition where it is principally involved with science. That is what I want to talk about: I want to beg you not to break off entirely your association with people, simply as people, because we need you, and you—even if only as raw material—need us.

When I was asked to speak tonight, I assented with glee, because I knew that it was an honour to give the Gilman Lecture, and I have a simple delight in honours which may be unbecoming but is also very human. I agreed to do it many months ago, and then, as tonight drew nearer, your co-ordinator, quite naturally, asked me for a title. Because I was very busy writing a novel, I was flustered and hastily replied with a title—"Can a Doctor Be a Humanist?" It is a bad title because it invites an immediate affirmative response. Of course a doctor ought to be a humanist. What I should really have called my speech is "How Can a Doctor Possibly Be a Humanist in a Society that Increasingly Tempts Him to Be a Scientist"—but as you see that is clumsy and much too long. Nevertheless, that is what I am going to talk about.

When I was a boy, if I went to a doctor he examined me gravely, asked questions that were searching without being positively embarrassing, and when we had both had enough of that he retired to a dirty little kitchen behind his consulting room, where he mixed up a few things he had lying around, and emerged with a bottle from which he instructed me to drink three times a day. It usually contained something that tasted of rusty nails and boiled rhubarb, and I received it reverently, because I regarded the doctor as a magician, and I knew that his nasty mixture had magical properties. But for many years of my adult life my various doctors have given me medicine—it tends to be in pill form nowadays—which plainly comes from a pharmaceutical company, and I leave his office thinking of him as a middleman between me and a large pill works. He has lost his magic. I want to make a few suggestions as to how he might regain at least some of his magic, and my recommendation is that the doctor should be, plainly and unmistakably, a humanist.

Do not suppose that I am hostile toward the modern marvels that come in the form of pills. Certainly not hostile but I have—I promised to be honest with you—a hint of scepticism. Of course I take the pills; I am frightened not to do so. But the reverence has gone.

Over the years, I have seen many medical certainties come, heralded by trumpetings and hosannas, which have in a few years died upon the ear, as the great discoveries faded almost into oblivion. Not all of these panaceas were strictly medical, but medical men seemed to believe in them. The first I recall, when I was a small boy, was

Auto-Suggestion, the discovery of one Emile Coué, and it was delightfully simple. All that was involved was that the sufferer from practically anything should fall asleep every night murmuring to himself a magical formula—what Oriental religion calls a *mantra*—and it was <u>Every day in every way I am growing better and better.</u> And people did grow better and better—for a while. Coué himself gained fame, but very little money: he made his discovery available for nothing. His cure—he was not a medical man but a French pharmacist—had its place in the long, foggy history of auto-suggestion, but the forces of evil were too much for it, and lots of people went down into their graves gasping out the wonderful *mantra,* and in a few years Monsieur Coué passed into oblivion, joining the advocates of colonic lavage and the people who thought that everything could be cured by eating bran.

His disappearance was not noticed, perhaps because he was not really medical in his advice; he was a primitive psychologist. And as he vanished, another truly medical wonder appeared upon the scene. It was called Focal Infection, and it was thought to be the cause of many of our mortal ills. As I heard about it, Focal Infection came principally from diseased teeth, and in my part of the world we were greatly impressed—indeed we were awed and humbled—by a famous dental surgeon who devoted all of his Sundays—for nothing, just for the sheer philanthropy of the thing—to pulling the teeth of the inmates of our largest mental hospital. Many of them, it was asserted, recovered their wits as a result of his ministrations, and rushed out of the asylum, praising God and His agent upon this earth, the great dentist. But something happened—I don't know what it was—and Focal Infection faded from view.

I shall not bore you with all the changes in medical enthusiasm I have seen. In the city in which I lived, as a young man, a doctor achieved fame that lasted for almost a year, treating cancer—apparently with success—with something-or-other he wrung out of rabbits. Penicillin came, and great claims were made for it, and indeed it is still extensively prescribed, and it was at one time believed to be a specific for syphilis and tuberculosis. Tuberculosis, a scourge in my own family, was banished, but a medical friend tells me it has not utterly gone, and from time to time one hears dark whisperings of syphilis.

Of course there were cures which have come and have remained, some of them for the most dreaded diseases of childhood, and everybody is immeasurably grateful. But—I do not wish to sound cantankerous, but the truth must out—as one disease goes, another seems to arise to take its place, and many of my contemporaries are struggling with ailments that were unheard of, or simply not identified, when we were young. Upon the whole, medicine has not succeeded in its nineteenth- and twentieth-century crusade to make mankind immortal, though life expectancy has been much increased, and some of the worst afflictions have been confined and mitigated. And for this we are deeply grateful to you, and the researchers and pharmaceutical geniuses who stand at your elbow.

It is not to the triumphs of the heroes of medicine that I wish to address myself tonight, but rather to the day-to-day, jogtrot practice not simply of family physicians but diagnosticians, specialists, and surgeons, for I have often heard members of your profession complain of the diurnal routine which, over a long professional life, may become rather a bore. You grow tired of the endless parade of the ailing, all of whom regard themselves as uniquely afflicted, but whom you know to be suffering from one or other of perhaps two dozen common, though not necessarily trivial, ailments. You may grow sick of a very bad disease yourself; that is to say, you may become sick of the human race, and its endless whining and beseeching. Behind your professional half-smile there may lurk an impulse to play some mercurial trick on a patient—in fact, to give him something really serious to complain about. The forbearance you show in the face of this temptation is beyond all praise.

What do you look like to your patients? You hope that you look like a trustworthy professional man, and so you do, in most cases, though not all. But you look like something else, to the wretch who sits in the chair on the other side of your desk. You look like a god. Oh, yes you do. Don't contradict me. Medicine may be your game, but the detection and identification of gods in modern life is mine, and I assure you that you look like a god. Your patient may not think so—not consciously. But about your head shines a divinity, and it is extremely likely that somewhere in your consulting room the identifying symbol of the god appears.

There are doctors who have no modesty about assuming the godlike *persona*. I have made a desultory study of the pictures that doctors hang in their offices, and to the reflective eye, they are revealing. They are usually of a kind that reflects warmly on the medical profession or perhaps on the doctor himself—a few watercolour sketches from his own hand, or that of his talented wife, for instance. The office picture I like least shows an old-time country doctor, driving his buggy and his tired old horse along a country road through the night. He is engaged in a race; in the sky above him flies a stork, and in a sling in its bill it carries a baby. Will the dear old doctor arrive in time? We are supposed to smile, while wiping away a tear. I do not like to speak evil of any man, but I believe this disgusting assault on the senses was the work of Norman Rockwell. Another standard decoration of a doctor's office in my youth was a monochrome reproduction of Sir Luke Fildes's famous picture *The Doctor* in which a doctor, professional and also godlike, sits in an attitude of reflection at the bedside of a sick child whose humble parents hover anxiously in the background, waiting for the great man to utter. But the one I like best had no title and needed none; its message was clear. On a bed lay the form of a beautiful young woman, stark naked and revealing—at least to the layman's eye—no sign of illness. But over the bed hovers the menacing figure of Death, horrible and skeletonic; Death is seeking to deflower the toothsome beauty. Will he? No, most decidedly he will not, for standing at the bedside, defying him with all the power of his fully clothed youthful manhood, is the doctor, who is going to save the girl. I imagine that picture sustained the doctor, who was a surgeon, through many a weary month of tonsillectomies and removals of glued-up gall-bladders. He was wondering when he would be summoned to that passion-fraught bedside.

But it is not of these boastful, obvious valentines addressed to himself that the doctor hangs on the wall of his waiting-room that I speak when I talk of the symbol of the god. I mean the caduceus, which has for centuries—indeed for at least five thousand years—been the special mark of your profession and the symbol of the power you have inherited from the past, and from the world of myth which is still a potent, if rarely recognized, force in our daily lives. Let us examine this symbol and see what it has to say to us. You know it well, have seen it countless times, but what have you thought about it, as having a bearing on your everyday life?

Of course it is the staff of Mercury. It is frequently described in literature. What does Spenser say?

> He took *Caduceus* his snakie wand
> With which the damned ghosts he governeth . . .

But who was Mercury? And what were the damned ghosts? In Greece he was called Hermes, but he did not have his origin in Greece. Hermes was a Greek adaptation of the Egyptian god Thoth, and when we speak of Thoth we are already five thousand years in the past. You have seen images of Thoth in museums; he is the god with a man's body, and the head of a bird, an ibis. He was worshipped as the inventor of the arts and the sciences, of music, of astronomy, of speech and of the written word. Thoth was translated by the Greeks as Logos, the Word. The god, in fact, of the intellect in its farthest reaches.

So the staff, representing the power of the god, has an ancient ancestry, but as Thoth bore it, it had no twining snakes. Those were Greek additions, and the legend is that one day the god Hermes—the Greek Thoth—came upon two warring serpents, who writhed and fought upon the ground at his feet. To restore peace the god thrust his staff between them, and they curled around it, forever in contention, but held in a mutuality of power by the reconciling staff. And there they are still, held in check by the power of Hermes from achieving a final victory in their struggle for supremacy.

What are the serpents? Are they damned ghosts? No: they are vividly alive and relevant. They are Knowledge and Wisdom, and in your profession the caduceus is a perpetual reminder that the god

Hermes—who is Hermes Trismégistus, Hermes the Thrice Great—requires you to hold them in balance and to keep one from devouring the other.

But, you may say, are Knowledge and Wisdom opponents? Not necessarily, but they may easily become so, for they are opposites and unless they are reconciled and each made a supporter of the other, they can make the staff of Hermes lopsided, and wanting in its true power. To lapse for a moment into the language of Analytical Psychology, Knowledge is an extraverted element in the doctor's psyche; it comes from without; it is what he acquires during his long and demanding education in order that he may direct it outward upon his patients. It is what you bring to bear upon the disease that confronts you in your patients. But Wisdom is an introverted element in the doctor's psyche; it has its origin within, and it is what makes him look not at the disease, but at the bearer of the disease. It is what creates the link that unites the healer with his patient, and the exercise of which makes him a true physician, a true healer, a true child of Hermes. It is Wisdom that tells the physician how to make the patient a partner in his own cure.

Instead of calling them Knowledge and Wisdom, let us call them Science and Humanism.

When the Greeks were ill, they often went to the temple of Hermes to pray, and their first prayer was "To which god must I sacrifice in order to be healed?" There were many gods then, and there are many gods now, though we usually pretend that there is only one, or else none at all. But the prayer is still one of great power, and I suggest that it is now the prayer of the physician: "To which god must I sacrifice in order to heal?" To which of the warring serpents should I turn with the problem that now faces me?

It is easy, and tempting, to choose the god of Science. Now I would not for a moment have you suppose that I am one of those idiots who scorns Science, merely because it is always twisting and turning, and sometimes shedding its skin, like the serpent that is its symbol. It is a powerful god indeed, but it is what the students of ancient gods called a shape-shifter, and sometimes a trickster. Science, during the past hundred and fifty years, has gained formidable new authority, and it is to Science that we owe the increased longevity of the race, and the control of many of the terrible ills that afflict mankind. Science may cure disease, but can it confer health? Like all powerful gods, Science seeks to be the One True God, and as it writhes about the staff of Hermes it seeks to diminish and perhaps drive out the other god, the god of Humanism.

I am telling you nothing you do not know already. I remember with pleasure a conversation I had a while ago with a young man who was studying medicine, who told me that one of the finest of his teachers said to his class: "When you find yourself at the bedside, don't immediately *do* something: just *stand* there!" In other words, hold Science in check, and wait to see what Wisdom does.

I am reminded of what I have been told about one of the most astonishing diagnosticians of this century, the late Dr. Georg Groddeck. When a difficult case was brought to him—which was often when other doctors had had a crack at the case and given up—he put the patient in bed in his clinic, and for two or three days did not see him; the patient was calmed by warm baths, cleaned out by gentle but searching enemas, fed small quantities of bland foods. Then, at last, Dr. Groddeck appeared, sat by the bedside and told the nurse to strip the covers from the patient. Then he placed his ear on the patient's abdomen, and there he listened for sometimes three hours, without speaking a word. He listened to joints. He sniffed the patient's breath and sometimes, dismayingly to the sensitive, he sniffed their privy parts. Groddeck, as many of you know, was not a pretty man, and it must have been rather like a nosy inspection by a hedgehog, or perhaps one of those gnomes one meets in fairy tales. But at last, when all the sniffing and listening and prodding with the fingers and thumbs was over, he began to talk to the patient and to ask questions that had been suggested by all the animal-like preliminaries. After a while, the great doctor began to make suggestions. He had found a diagnosis, frequently an unexpected and astonishing one. I hope I do not provoke nausea in any of my hearers by using the word "psychosomatic" but sometimes—certainly not always—his diagnosis was on

psychosomatic lines. Like all really great doctors, he acquired a reputation as a magician, but he laughed heartily when that was said to
him. He might well have said, as the great Ambroise Paré said three
centuries before him, "I dressed his wounds, and God healed him."

You see, of course, what Groddeck was doing. He was allowing the
patient to speak, in bodily sounds and smells, before the patient was
invited to open his mouth. And what had happened was that what
was deepest in the patient—not merely his disease—had been invited
to speak to what was deepest in the doctor.

Do you say, We cannot be expected to train yearly graduating
classes of Groddecks? Of course not. So many of your students come
to you, already such convinced worshippers of the Science snake, that
they do not want to hear about anything else. You have to be mindful of what we might call the Doctor Psychology, the cast of mind that
impels young men and women to want to join your profession. As an
outsider, I am sometimes impressed by the similarity of mental qualities that make doctors so very much like farmers. I am sure you all
know a few farmers, and many of them are admirable people, but
surely you have observed how fiercely impatient they are to questioning or restraint. They are loners. When they are standing in their
fields they will not allow anyone to offer an opinion on their work.
They are deeply suspicious of co-operative efforts and they are sometimes convinced that the whole of mankind is in league against them.
Is that cast of psychology familiar to you, in any degree? It may be
admired as a manifestation of the Hero Psychology, the determination to conquer, to rule, and to brook no interference. It is heroic,
certainly, but it is also pig-headed. Farmers of genius, like doctors of
genius, are uncommon. When we meet a great farmer we find that he
possesses no command of nature; he lets nature speak to him. It is so
with doctors.

You see where I am tending: I now want to talk about the other
snake, the Humanist snake, the snake which symbolizes not the
knowledge of Science, but Wisdom, that breadth of the spirit which
makes the difference between the first-rate healer and the capable
technician.

Those of you who are of a strongly scientific cast of mind are doubtless already impatient with me, because the personal slant that I am giving to my remarks is so painfully unscientific. It is a widely held belief among scientists that whatever derives from a single, personal experience is of slight value compared with what may be deduced from a statistical analysis of a large number of cases. Well, it is your own fault; you must not ask novelists to talk to you if you want statistical analyses, for their personal response to life is the strongest element in their character, and some of them display that ability to see through a brick wall that is so disturbing to the scientific mind. Again to employ the terminology of Analytical Psychology, the scientist is a man in whom thought and sensation predominate, whereas an author is usually a man of feeling and intuition. So you will not be surprised if I continue with a personal anecdote—a single experience—on the basis of which I mean to generalize.

When I was a young man, a student at Oxford, I became ill in a way characteristic of me and my family; I developed a ferocious cold and cough. Ordinary treatments achieved nothing, and I was sent by my tutor to his own doctor. "You'll find him first-rate," he said, "a very wise fellow." And so he was. His name was Dr. Raymond Greene, and with my Canadian experience of doctors he was not at all what I expected. He saw me in what must have been his consulting room, but it looked much more like a library, for it was lined with books and because I can read the title of a book at forty yards, I knew at once that they were not books about medicine. He had some excellent pictures, not of the Norman Rockwell or Luke Fildes variety. And his manner was most agreeable, but in terms of my experience utterly unprofessional.

He heard my complaint, and took a quick look at me and said in an offhand manner: "Oh yes, I'll give you an inhalant and something to control the cough. Your family tends toward respiratory illnesses, I suppose?" I said that was so. Then he said, "Now why do you suppose you are unwell?"

I launched into the usual North American students' rigmarole about the chill of the Oxford winter, the coldness of Oxford rooms, the prevalence of draughts—all of that. "But why are you ill?" he persisted. "Germs, I suppose." I had never been asked before to diagnose my own case. "Certainly germs," said Dr. Greene, "but you know perfectly well there are germs everywhere. Why have they been able to get their hooks into you? Why are you ill in the way you tell me all your family become ill, when they have need of an illness? That is to say when they need to look seriously at their life and where they are. Is it a girl? What about your work?"

It was my work, which—for reasons that need not detain us—was in a dreadful mess, for reasons that were not all my fault. We talked about that, and out of our conversation emerged some plans which, in quite a short time, put my work back on the rails. But then he said: "You know, you shouldn't put so much emphasis on your work. Only second-rate people do that. And then, of course, their work eats them up. Whereas they, of course, ought to eat up their work. My work would eat me up, but I keep it in its place by climbing mountains. And, do you know, climbing mountains makes me a better doctor."

I found out a few things about Dr. Greene, later on, all of which I read again in his obituary in the London *Times*, which appeared in December 1982. He was indeed a very distinguished mountain climber, a greatly admired physician, and—this is not perhaps as irrelevant as it may seem—the brother of the novelist Graham Greene. And the *Times* made it clear, to me at least, that he was a first-rate doctor because he never allowed doctoring to eat him up. He was a humanist first, and a physician second.

I recovered from my symptoms—the cold and the cough—and ever since I have been trying to follow the doctor's more enduring prescription, which was that I should not allow my work to eat me up. It has sometimes been a struggle, but my wife, who like all really good wives is an admirable physician, constantly reminds me of the danger. And I have often thought with gratitude of Dr. Raymond Greene, and blessed the day when I set foot in his consulting-room. Since then I have fallen into the hands of many doctors—few of whom have been humanists though some of them were remorseless scientists—and I have felt the full fury of the Snake of Knowledge, the Scientific Snake, when it rages and coils unchecked by the Snake of Humanism.

Dr. Greene, of course, was in a great tradition—a tradition I recommend you to explore, if you have not already done so. It would be long and tedious to discuss even a handful of the great humanist physicians, but I should like to speak briefly of three, the first of whom was the man with perhaps the most resounding name in all the annals of medicine—Philippus Aureolus Theophrastus Bombast von Hohenheim, commonly called Paracelsus, who lived from 1493 to 1541, and was thus, as you see, at his great revolutionary work just as knowledge of the New World became general. In his day he was a great revolutionary against authority, and his revolt was on behalf of science: were he living today I have no doubt that he would be lecturing, with all his terrible eloquence and daring, against the tyranny of unchecked science in an age when another new world, that of space, is in process of exploration.

He was essentially a humanist, you see. That does not mean that he was an atheist. Mankind as God's noblest creation, and inseparable from his Creator, was the theme of all his teaching. He said: "There is no field on earth in which heavenly medicine grows or lies hidden, other than the resurrected flesh or 'new body' of man; only in the 'new body' have all its words force and efficacy here on earth. This heavenly medicine works according to the will of the man of the 'new birth'; in him lie all the active virtues. For it does not operate in the mortal body, but only in the eternal body." This was not a priest speaking, or a man bound by the old medicine of Avicenna and Galen, but a man who was a pioneer in the dissection of the body. His life was a constant, turbulent search for wisdom—the wisdom of the Humanist Serpent—and it was he who said "The striving for wisdom is the second paradise of the world." I dare not recommend that you read all of his work, for it is extensive, but I urge you to take a look at some of it—there is an excellent anthology published in volume 28 of the Bollingen Series—because though at first it may seem puzzling, it is full of the sweet milk of humanist wisdom.

My next great humanist physician, who was almost an exact contemporary of Paracelsus, is François Rabelais, whose great novel about Gargantua and Pantagruel is probably familiar to you. Although he was a priest, and for a time a monk, he was primarily a doctor and another mighty rebel against the domination of the accepted wisdom of his time—which was university scholasticism. If he were living now, I am certain that he would be lambasting the self-delighted scientists with all the vigour of his wit and the irrepressible hilarity and irreverence that kept him perpetually in trouble. The commonplace opinion about Rabelais in our time is that he wrote a dirty book. Of course it is dirty: a true humanist is always mindful of the inescapable ties that hold mankind close to the grossest facts of life; his feet are in the dunghill, but his eyes are fixed upon the heavens. This is what makes the life of man absurd, and I am surprised that the modern Absurdists have never claimed Rabelais as the greatest of their ancestors. But absurdity was not all Rabelais saw in Life—and in that he differs from the modern Absurdists; he saw life as glorious, and hilarious. It may be said of him as it has been of a later humorist, "His foe was folly, and his weapon, wit."

He must have been a wonderful creature. Sometimes I think that if I were lying on my deathbed, and opened my eyes to see Dr. Rabelais standing beside me, I should either leap to my feet, or perhaps expire laughing with delight at the splendour of the world, and the folly of mankind. As I am sure you know, Rabelais himself is said to have died murmuring, "I go in search of the Great Perhaps." That is certainly splendid, but there is another tradition which I hold in equal esteem, which is that as Rabelais lay dying, the last rites of his Church were being administered to him, and the moment had come when the priest anointed his feet with the holy oil. It is said that then he was heard to murmur, "I must be going on a long journey; they are greasing my boots."

My third and last of these great humanist physicians from the past is one whose name is, I am sure, held in honour at Johns Hopkins. That is Sir Thomas Browne, the great physician of Norwich, who lived from 1605 until 1682, and whose first book, *Religio Medici,* is one of the treasures of English literature. The temptation of all who talk of Browne is to quote from him, and I must be strong with myself. Nevertheless, some quotation cannot be avoided. It was Browne who made that great humanist statement: "We carry within us the wonders we seek without us: There is all Africa and her prodigies in us." And some of his words might be taken as warnings against the stern certainties of Science, as when he says: "To believe only possibilities, is not faith, but mere Philosophy." May we not think he is protesting against that mighty force in the medical science of our day, the passion for the new, the latest, when he says: "If there be any among those common objects of hatred I do condemn and laugh at, it is that great enemy of reason, virtue and religion, the multitude: that monstrous piece of monstrosity, which, taken asunder, seem men, and the reasonable creatures of God, but, confused together, make but one great beast, and a monstrosity more prodigious than Hydra." Whenever I read that, I remember the mighty clamour about Focal Infection, of which I spoke earlier. Paracelsus, Rabelais, and Browne were all men deeply committed to religion, but in each of them was a wise scepticism, which kept them from fanatical enthusiasms. Christian theology is not much in vogue nowadays, but I think we would be wise to recall that two of the Virtues Christianity adopted from the Greeks and the Jews were Temperance and Prudence. In other words, do not let anything, even your work, eat you up and silence your common sense.

To talk of Sir Thomas Browne at Johns Hopkins is of course to recall a name held in high honour here, that of Sir William Osler. It is a source of pride to me that he was a Canadian, who received his earliest medical education at the Universities of Toronto, and McGill in Montreal. It has been said that his work here almost a century ago revolutionized medical education in Johns Hopkins, and indeed on the North American continent. He was truly a great physician, and he was also a splendid Humanist, and Browne's *Religio Medici* was a fixed star in a literary taste—a book-collector's taste—that included much that was finest in the literatures of several languages. He constantly adjured

medical students to read *Religio Medici*. I wonder how many did so?
But even if only a few did so a blow had been struck for the humanism that lay at the root of Osler's art as a physician.

I have told you that the great god of medicine was Thoth, and that
in time he was transformed by the Greeks into the Thrice-Mighty
Hermes. But he underwent a further transformation, and a psychologically very interesting one, because among the Romans he was
called Mercurius, and in the course of that change he took on new
attributes. He kept all his splendour as the god of intellect, but the
psychological expansion and perception of the Romans saw in him
also the shadow side of intellect, which is sometimes trickery and char-
latanism, and always of wit, of ambiguity and of the merriment which
accompanies quickness of wit. When you are working under the influence of Mercurius you cannot always subdue the element of fantasy,
of duality of meaning, that accompanies genuine, deeply felt knowledge, and without which that deeply felt knowledge cannot be transformed into wisdom. Mercurius was the god of the alchemists, whose
supposed desire was to change base metals into precious metals. But
we know now that the best of the alchemists were at work to change
many things that were in themselves inert and dull into the splendour
of wisdom. Knowledge may enable you to memorize the whole of
Gray's *Anatomy* or Osler's *Principles and Practice of Medicine* but only
wisdom can teach you what to do with what you have learned.

Osler, great man that he was, could not escape the mischievous
aspects of Mercurius, and in your library here you preserve a full
record of the medical opinions of Osler's Mercurial self, whom he
called Dr. Egerton Yorrick Davis, many of which were published as
papers in the most respectable and learned medical journals. I am sure
some of these are well known to you. For instance, his hair-raising
and hilarious account of the childbirth customs and sexual shenani-
gans of the Caughnawaga Indians, which he managed to impose on
some of his colleagues who were children of Hermes, but had not yet
graduated to be children of Mercurius. I am sure you all know his writings on that distressing, inconvenient ailment, strabismus of the penis.
These were signed by Dr. Egerton Yorrick Davis, but the hand was

the hand of William Osler. He simply could not be solemn, twenty-four hours a day, year in and year out, about medical science. These writings were in the true spirit of Rabelais, and distressing though they may be to the wholly solemn members of his profession, they convince many of us that Sir William would have been the ideal doctor for us, because he took neither himself nor his vast knowledge with total, unremitting solemnity. And that, ladies and gentlemen, is one of the marks of the true humanist, who pays appropriate heed to the left-hand snake that coils about the staff of the caduceus. To confuse mere solemnity with real seriousness is to forget that the trickster-god lies always in wait to pull the rug from under your feet.

That word caduceus, by the way, means also the staff of the herald, and it is the privilege, and also the duty of the true physician to be the herald who brings great news, transporting enlightenment, to his patients. Does he not also bring news of Death? Why do you think that news may not be, to the philosophic mind, transporting and enlightening? Grave news but is it always bad news?

Will you allow me, before I finish, to surrender myself to the influence of Mercurius—who is also the god of writers, as I am sure you know—and suggest to you a truly Mercurial, humanistic approach to your work as physicians. It is an approach which might, given a chance, revolutionize medical practice. Even if it did not do that it would give you a great deal of not wholly innocent fun.

What is the great evil, the pervasive malaise, that overshadows the whole of mankind at present and is frighteningly on the increase, everywhere and among all kinds and conditions of men and women? Is it cancer? No, it is not. Is it the ravages wrought in society by smoking tobacco, which is now under such discussion and attack by the most zealous of your kind—the group which, so many years ago, leapt on the bandwagon of Focal Infection? It sometimes seems to me, as I look back over my life, that smoking has achieved the status of the Ultimate Curse which was, in my boyhood, conferred upon masturbation. That indulgence, the youth of all civilized countries were assured, would sap the intellect, bring about rot of the spine and loss of the reason, and within measurable time destroy the vigour of the race. Perhaps it did so, for I see the evidence everywhere about me. But to my astonishment I find that masturbation is no longer reprehended, but tolerated, and even advocated by some of the most advanced medical and psychological minds. Novels have been written about it, and grave matrons speak of it without a blush. But now tobacco has usurped its place and yet I say to you that tobacco, dangerous addiction though it be, is not the worst affliction of our age.

What is it, then? I shall tell you. It is, quite simply, *stupidity,* which seeps, like a corrosive poison through every level of society, and lays its blighting hand on every aspect of social, professional, political, and cultural life. To whom may we confide the task of attacking this pervasive blight better than upon yourselves, to whom we look for so much that is concerned in the betterment of mankind?

It is not always easy to diagnose. The simplest form of stupidity— the mumbling, nose-picking, stolid incomprehension—can be detected by anyone. But the stupidity which disguises itself as thought, and which talks so glibly and eloquently, indeed never stops talking, in every walk of life is not so easy to identify, because it marches under a formidable name, which few dare attack. It is called Popular Opinion, and sometimes the Received Wisdom of the Race. It looks as though it came from some form of mental activity or spiritual grace, but it does not, and its true name is Intellectual Stasis.

Unquestionably you have observed this dread evil among your patients. But have you ever mentioned it? Have you ever prescribed for it? In the nineteenth century it was not easy for a physician to tell his patient that he had syphilis; social delicacy inhibited him. So it is today with the even more dreadful social disease of stupidity. Something must be done, and yours is the profession that has the authority to do it.

You cannot expect governments to do anything about it. After all, their dependence on stupidity is notorious. Stupidity is the great vested interest, with holdings everywhere, and the full support of the media. And so it will be a long time before popular television programs are prefaced by a flash which says, "The Surgeon General warns that viewing what follows is injurious to your mental health." No, a wiser, more responsible agency than government must do what needs to be done, and that agency is the medical profession.

What can you—what, as humanist physicians, must you do—to fight stupidity? First, you must assure your own complete inoculation against this plague by massive daily applications of art, music, and literature. Then you must do the most difficult thing of all: you must be wholly honest with your patients.

"Madam," you will say to the woman who sits in your patient's chair, "We have dealt on the whole successfully, with your allergies, yet you tell me that you still feel dull, logy, unable to eat more than three large meals a day and drink more than three Martinis at a time. I am not in the least surprised. Your intellect, which is no worse than the average despite lifelong abuse, is under a cloud. Read Rabelais, and if that proves too strenuous, read the works of Mark Twain. For a weekend health workout, go to a festival of Marx Brothers films. Learn to laugh, especially at yourself."

That is not too hard. But what about the elderly man who complains to you that although he is in his mid-seventies his sex-life is still volcanic in its vigour, and he has just divorced his wife to give his full attention to a charming little creature of seventeen. Nevertheless, the fear of Death is upon him, even as he frolics in the harlot's embrace. He wakes up in the night sweating, with a chill about his heart. Now, here is a case that demands graver measures than that of the lady who merely feels that her life is dull.

"Sir," you will say: "You have been taken in by the popular magazines that assure you that sex in old age will bring you happiness, and perhaps immortality. Now, I am going to give you this card, which you must carry about with you, and read at least three times a day. Listen—

"'I could be content that we might procreate like trees, without conjunction, or that there were any way to perpetuate the World without this trivial and vulgar way of coition: it is the foolishest act a wise man commits in all his life; nor is there anything that will more deject his cool'd imagination, when he shall consider what an odd and unworthy piece of folly he hath committed.'

"That is by a very great physician, Sir Thomas Browne of Norwich. My prescription is that you should be content to leave to youth those delights that belong to youth. As for the Spectre of Death, when it frightens you, read this other card:

"'DEATH, be not proud, though some have calléd thee
Mighty and dreadful, for thou art not so:
For those whom thou think'st thou dost overthrow
Die not, poor Death; nor yet canst thou kill me.
From Rest and Sleep, which but thy pictures be,
Much pleasure, then from thee much more must flow;
And soonest our best men with thee do go—
Rest of their bones, and soul's delivery!
Thou'rt slave to fate, chance, kings and desperate men,
And dost with poison, war and sickness dwell;
And poppy or charms can make us sleep as well
And better than thy stroke. Why swell'st thou then?
One short sleep past, we wake eternally,
And Death shall be no more:

　　　　　　　　　　Death, thou shalt die.'"

If he obstinately continues to tremble, tell him that the man who wrote that died of typhoid fever, an illness that your profession has rendered almost unknown.

But what about the lady who presents herself to you complaining that although she jogs six miles every day, and has reduced her fat by forty pounds or so, she still *feels* fat, and her friends do not seem to notice any change in her appearance? "Madam," you must say, "It is true that you jog in the flesh, but are you jogging in the spirit? Your adiposity is metaphysical. You no longer are fat in the body, but you are still fat-headed. I recommend some strenuous mental jogging; I advise you to read a chapter daily of Gibbon's *Decline and Fall of the*

Roman Empire, and then read it again, and continue until your friends tell you that you look lithe and sinewy, that a new light shines from your eyes, and that your conversation and your comprehension of political and social life has improved immeasurably. Go at once, and busy yourself with your cure."

There you are, ladies and gentlemen. I have told you what to do: now go and do it, and bring about the great Humanist revolution in the practice of medicine. In your diagnoses, give full attention to the Left-Hand Snake.

I make no charge for this invaluable advice. I am myself above taking fees, because I am a Humanist, but I know that you must live, and when you have brought about enough Humanist cures not you, but your grateful patients, will insist that your fees be doubled. So—onward on behalf of the Left-Hand Snake. Forward, Children of Mercury, in the great assault upon stupidity.

With this stern injunction I bid you adieu.

6

REVIEWING GRAHAM GREENE

෴

The previous chapter included a description of Davies' helpful encounter at Oxford with Dr. Raymond Greene, "a humanist first, and a physician second." It notes that it is "not as irrelevant as it may seem" that he was the brother of Graham Greene.

Here in what is ostensibly a review of *The Captain and the Enemy* for *Compass, A Jesuit Journal,* Davies surveys Greene's work in general as "a novelist of extraordinary achievement."

From his diaries we know that this was written on December 27, 1988. The date is not insignificant, especially for those who believe that writers lead a life of luxurious ease, writing only when the Muse smiles on them. In fact, on a day when most households are dozing amidst piles of wrapping-paper and ingesting left-over turkey, Davies was hard at work exercising the writing muscle that kept him fit and allowed him to go on composing fine work till the end of his life.

How Catholic is Graham Greene? It is some time since we heard much about a school of Catholic novelists, but before 1939 there were several writers, of whom Greene and Evelyn Waugh were the most widely known, who were so described, and the Roman Catholic community, particularly in Britain, took justifiable pride in them. They seemed to carry on the work of Chesterton and Belloc, and in

D.B. Wyndham Lewis ("Beachcomber") they possessed one of the most brilliant humorists of the day. They were loyally supported and given a special sort of visibility by what may perhaps be called the Jesuit-Dominican element in the English-speaking world of intellectual Catholicism. How they were regarded by the Catholic community as a whole I do not know.

To the non-Catholic world they seemed often to be skating on very thin ice, and Greene himself came close to heresy. When *The Power and the Glory* appeared in 1940 and became a best-seller, it was known (probably by a "diplomatic leak") that the Holy Office had its doubts, and, although it did not condemn the book, it let it be known that it was "paradoxical," which is to say contrary or discordant to received opinion and belief. To the Protestant mind this objection seemed to flirt with Protestantism in its suggestion that a bad man cannot be a true priest; but Greene's whisky-priest was shown to have served God truly and to the point of martyrdom, when at last he was confronted with a desperate choice.

These points of Catholic theology are not for me to discuss, but I was sharply reminded on one occasion of the offence Greene gave among orthodox Catholics in Europe. My wife and I were travelling in Portugal in the spring of 1961, and wearying of the nineteenth-century tosh that was to be seen at the Teatro Nacional we asked if there were not some more adventurous theatre in Lisbon? In hushed tones our travel agency directed us to the Teatro da Trinidade, where experimental and "way-out" theatre was offered, and we took tickets for *A Casa dos Vivos*. After the curtain had been up for a few minutes we realized (having only the most trivial acquaintance with the Portuguese language) that the shocker we were seeing was nothing else than Greene's *The Living Room*, and that the play was interpreted in the most extreme of Catholic taste. Thereafter we were on firmer ground, for we knew the play well as a staple of English-speaking theatre at the time. The culminating moment came when the broken old priest—represented in this production by a *jeune premier* with silvered hair but otherwise in robust health—asked the heroine how many times she had had sexual relations with her lover; she whispered her reply, and what followed in the theatre astonished us, for ladies in mantillas rose and were escorted from their seats in a condition of shock, by gentlemen who were affronted at this public indecency. There was a large number of sailors in the gallery, presumably in free seats given to them by some well-meaning group, and the sailors began a near riot, hissing, cat-calling, crying Shame and Harlot in voices accustomed to shouting down the storms of the Atlantic. When the uproar died down at last, fully half the audience had fled, and the play continued what was to us its dramatically interesting, but by no means outrageous, course. The Catholicism of Lisbon was decidedly not that of the world we knew, where Catholics took *The Living Room* pretty calmly, and we understood that the pride taken in Greene's work in Farm Street did not extend to Latin Europe.

Greene is a man who creates storms, from time to time, by the intransigence of his opinions. In 1937 he destroyed the English magazine *Night and Day,* which he served as film reviewer, by a notice he wrote about the film *Wee Willie Winkie,* of which Shirley Temple was the star; Greene suggested that the exploitation of Miss Temple's infant charms was somewhat less innocent than a casual observer might think. Twentieth Century-Fox, the makers of the film, sued for libel and, although the case was settled out of court, the size of the settlement ruined the paper. Not for the first or last time Greene had allowed good taste to overbear good sense.

Perhaps it is because of the un-English sharpness of his opinions that Greene is so often criticised in terms that suggest a Continental, rather than an English sensibility, as when that shrewd critic, J. B. Priestley, declares that he is "somewhere between the worlds of Mauriac and Malraux." Yet he has himself often asserted his intellectual debt to a decidedly English and by no means Catholic poet, none other than Robert Browning. He quotes with approval the words from *Bishop Blougram's Apology:*

Our interest's on the dangerous edge of things.
The honest thief, the tender murderer,
The superstitious atheist, demirep

That loves and saves her soul in new French books—
We watch while these in equilibrium keep
The giddy line midway: one step aside
They're classed and done with. . . .

Nobody can say that Bishop Blougram is not a Catholic, but he most decidedly is not a Lisbon Catholic. Greene's lifelong preoccupation with what he calls "the appalling strangeness of the mercy of God" is not for the timid of any persuasion. One must feel some pity for the makers and maintainers of Catholic orthodoxy who have to grapple with Catholic writers like Greene, and, in our nearer time, Anthony Burgess, who want to have a crack at theology but are under little obligation to make their opinions palatable to the guardians of the faith.

Not all of Greene's works are troublesome to this degree. His latest short novel, *The Captain and the Enemy,* is not a book which will bother his most Catholic admirers. It will give the accustomed pleasure to his readers, for it is written in his admirable, spare style and the story it tells is a good one. I do not want to commit the sin of so many reviewers, who tell the tale so completely that it becomes almost needless to read the book—for people who read books only for their stories. Let it be enough to say that the principal character, Victor Baxter, finds when he is twelve years old that his father—the Enemy of the title—has lost him in a game of backgammon to an adventurer and con-man known as the Captain. The Captain gives Victor into the keeping of his mistress, named Liza, who brings him up, the Captain visiting them irregularly, and providing them with money irregularly. But the boy is loved, however oddly and gloomily, and he develops a warm admiration for the Captain and a fear that the Enemy may somehow intrude once again into his life. When Victor is a man, Liza dies and Victor goes to Panama to take the news to the Captain, who proves to be engaged in shady doings, running marijuana from Colombia, and muddled in that world of moral obliquity which has come to be known as Greeneland.

At last the Captain is faced with a moral decision, and his essential moral worth asserts itself. If you want to know how this happens, you must read the book yourself, for as I have said, I am not the sort of reviewer who considers it his job to read books for you. The denouement is a gripping and convincing one, and Greene's powers show no sign of diminution in his eighty-fourth year. And why should they? Writers mature slowly—if there is anything in them to mature—and retain their powers as do painters, composers, and sculptors, when men and women who are not artists are relinquishing their hold on life.

The word "artist" which I have used to define Greene, is not applied to writers as readily as to musicians or sculptors or painters, because the medium in which they work—our language—is used by everyone without any particular thought or regard for economy or form. Language is the common drudge of every sort of experience and it does not enter the heads of most people to use it with any conscious skill or effectiveness. Indeed, too sophisticated a use of language may arouse suspicion of insincerity, as our politicians well know, when they seek to impress themselves on the electorate. Only the occasional Churchill can strike the thrilling string and get away with it. But the serious writer is an artist and language is his medium, and the way he employs it is of the greatest interest. Greene has said that "creative art seems to remain a function of the religious mind," and it is this quality of awareness of another world, against which the actions of this world must be measured, that explains his warm admiration of Trollope, of one of his earliest influences, Stanley Weyman (not now widely read but a redoubtable craftsman in the world of adventure which Greene has made his own), and of course Robert Browning. Greene's world is certainly not that of Trollope; he is a tougher and more economical workman than Weyman; of Browning he grasps the intellectual and spiritual content, though the poetry seems to elude him there as it does elsewhere. There is nothing of the poet in Greene.

We are strongly impressed by this characteristic when we read his fragmentary but trenchant criticisms of Shakespeare. The playwright was, he concludes, too much a friend of the Establishment—almost the running-dog of Tudor capitalism, with his eye on fruitful investments in land, a great house in Stratford, and a coat-of-arms. So

Shakespeare, in modern jargon, was not a "committed" writer. It does not occur to Greene that a great poet may see through commitment, as he sees through much else that engages another sort of literary artist. Says Greene:

> Isn't it the story-teller's task to act as the devil's advocate, to elicit sympathy and a measure of understanding for those who lie outside the boundaries of State approval? The writer is driven by his own vocation to be a protestant in a Catholic society, a catholic in a Protestant one, to see the virtues of the capitalist in the Communist society, of the communist in a Capitalist state. Thomas Paine wrote, "We must guard even our enemies against injustice."

This is admirable, of course and Greene has made it his credo as a master story-teller. But it is going too far to say it is the story-teller's "task." The literary artist is under no obligation to beat the drum for causes, however good. The task of the great poet is certainly otherwise, to see every man simply as a man and not as in some measure an embodiment of a political or religious belief. But it is absurd to fault Greene because he does not think and feel like any other writer, Shakespeare included. His credo has made him a novelist of extraordinary achievement, and his artistry has made him something more admirable—dare I say it—than an irreproachable Catholic.

7

THE NOVELIST AND MAGIC

The University of Toronto, where Davies taught for twenty years, is the setting for several of his novels, most notably *The Rebel Angels* and *The Lyre of Orpheus*. Beginning with a reference to Michael Bliss, a solidly non-fictitious History Professor, and to a parallel lecture by the home-grown novelist Margaret Atwood, this particular lecture was very much a University of Toronto event, given as part of the Wiegand Lecture series there. Yet from that local base Davies takes the listener (and now the reader) on an astonishingly far-ranging tour. Few now remember a 1953 film (set on "a campus not unlike our own") entitled *Monster on the Campus*. Yet that film is engagingly described, along with *Faust, Hamlet, The Old Curiosity Shop, War and Peace,* Huxley and Joyce, not to mention the beliefs of Freud and Jung, as Davies' imagination takes wing, clearly inspired by the theme of magic.

Equally fascinating is his revelation of his own encounter with magic. Few of his readers will be aware of the vision that gave the central image, and indeed the title, to his novel *The Manticore*.

His diary records his pleasure at the success of the speech on November 8, 1989 when he was introduced by the former President of the University, Claude Bissell. It also reveals—amazingly—his shy belief that, at the age of seventy-six, he has finally mastered the art of public speaking: *To the auditorium of the Medical Building, which is crammed to the doors and people sitting*

on the stage. Give my Wiegand Lecture to great applause; Brenda
says I have never been better, and Claude Bissell, who introduced me,
said he had never heard me better. Worked like a Percheron, and got
very hot, but the material was good and every point told. At last I feel
that I have passed my test as a public speaker.

When I was invited to give this lecture Professor Bliss told me
that you were to hear Miss Margaret Atwood talk about the
novelist and science, and that you would like me to talk about the
novelist and magic. Miss Atwood's task, though not an easy one, was
clear; many novelists have written about science, including Miss
Atwood herself. As well she may do, for she has a family background
in science, as did Aldous Huxley, who introduced scientific material
into almost every novel he wrote. I remember from my school days
the interest that was caused by Sinclair Lewis's novel *Arrowsmith* (1925)
which described in detail the temptations and travails of a young scientist; a great many medical students saw themselves in Martin
Arrowsmith, for scientists, in their tenderer moments, are by no means
immune from the soft solicitations of fiction. But I know virtually
nothing of science, and have only once introduced a scientist into the
cast of characters in a novel of mine. That was Professor Ozias Froats,
who appears in *The Rebel Angels;* his special interest was in human fae-
ces, which he hoped to prove was a much more important diagnostic
element than had been previously considered. I know that my portrait of Ozy Froats caused some laughter among scientists, and some
indignation, as well. Yet I had a good source for my idea—no less than
a statement of Sir William Osler, about his use of this despised substance in the diagnosis of tuberculosis, and his intuition that it might
yield much greater information to a determined researcher. And to my
delight, just after that book had appeared, a friend of mine who is a
medical man told me that some work on this very subject had recently
attracted attention. But I know why my scientific readers laughed: my
description of Professor Froats's experiments was not scientific, but
novelistic; it was written to be comprehensible to readers who might

have no scientific knowledge whatever, but who must be persuaded by me that Professor Froats was a great man, with a great idea. It was written also to illustrate one of the themes of the novel, which was that value and beauty are often found in places that people ignorantly despise. I needed an unrecognized great man in my story, and I had to make him great in my own way.

That was certainly the method of the novelist. But had it anything to do with magic? I suppose that is what I am to talk about now.

As I presume that a great many of you are scientists, you will expect me to define my terms. What is science? I put the question last summer to an old friend of mine who is a distinguished gastro-enterologist. I expected that it might take him some time to answer, but nothing of the sort. He replied at once. "Science is the systematic study of nature," said he. Admirable. What, then, is magic? A possible definition is that magic is an attempt to control nature. When the witch of olden days put her evil spell on the beautiful princess, she attempted to control nature and destiny, and in the story she succeeded. When Macbeth sought out the Weird Sisters to discover what the future held for him, there was much mumbo-jumbo with "fillet of a fenny snake . . . eye of newt and toe of frog" which was perfectly justified, psychologically, because it helped to focus the occult powers of the witches and to deepen the credulity of Macbeth. Here again was the theme of value concealed in what seemed to be disgusting. The Witches were trying to control nature, and in the drama they did so very effectively. An Indian Rain Dance is an attempt to control nature, and I am told that it sometimes brings rain. Prayer of any sort is an attempt to control nature, and he would be a bold man indeed who declared that prayer was at all times ineffectual. But I must beware, if I can, of getting into the misty ground where magic and religion mingle, for that belongs to another lecture, and I have no intention of giving it.

Does the novelist seek to control nature? Sometimes he does, for the novelist feels himself free to use anything that is needed by his story. Why he makes this grandiose claim is something that I shall talk about later. For the moment, let us look at a few instances in which a novelist has asserted something as a fact which is demonstrably untrue from a scientific point of view. But the novelist has made his point, which is not precisely scientific, unless you are prepared to regard psychology as a science. I shall address that subject later, as well.

Let us make a start with a novel which may not be familiar to everyone here, but which was enormously popular for at least fifty years after it appeared in 1894. It is *Trilby*, by Georges du Maurier. It sold innumerable copies, it became an extremely successful play, and it has been made into at least two movies. It is the story of a beautiful artist's model in Paris, named Trilby O'Farrell, who has a splendid voice but nobody can bear to hear her sing because she has no ear. Trilby's singing is a joke until she falls under the influence of an evil German-Polish musician named Svengali who demonstrates that when he has hypnotised Trilby she can be made to sing not merely in tune, but with the most exquisite musical taste—which is, of course, Svengali's. Between them they make an immense musical sensation, and have all musical Europe at their feet, until at a concert Svengali dies of a heart attack while conducting the orchestra, and at once Trilby begins to sing in her old, off-key, stupid manner, and is hooted from the stage.

This is the ever-popular story of the charismatic genius who achieves his fulfilment through another person, and of the woman who is incomplete without the man who evokes her finest qualities. The public eats it up, and very properly so because although it is not science it is magic, and people—I venture to say even some scientists—have a great appetite for magic.

Georges du Maurier wrote another very popular story called *Peter Ibbetson* (1891) in which a pair of lovers, who are separated by an unhappy fate, are able to meet and express their love in their dreams. The public was enchanted by it, and it became the theme of an opera.

Why were these books so popular? Because they gave convincing expression not to what was demonstrably true, but to *what the public wished were true.* People love to attribute demonic powers to hypnotists, who know how limited, though medically useful, their powers are. It could even be said that *Peter Ibbetson* was prophetic, for it is a commonplace of our day that people who have been widely separated may converse and, I suppose, make love, by means of the telephone. Nobody calls that magic nowadays, because once a magical wish, or a miracle, has been made available to everyone, it is no longer magical.

Another story in this category, still popular and known to every literate person, is R.L. Stevenson's *Dr. Jekyll and Mr. Hyde,* which appeared in 1896, before Sigmund Freud had demonstrated by psychoanalysis the extraordinary duality of man's nature. You remember it. The admired medical man, Dr. Henry Jekyll, discovers a potion which turns him into a creature wholly evil, who acts out, as we now believe, the submerged and inadmissible side of the perfect doctor's nature. It is a Freudian tale, and it is also a Calvinist tale, for, as I hope to mention later, there is nothing in depth psychology which was not known to theologians and literary artists for centuries before Dr. Freud gave it a scientific ground.

The popularity of Stevenson's tale is not hard to explain. Most of us are aware of, and frightened by, the figure of Mr. Hyde in ourselves. We keep Mr. Hyde safely in the cellar-dungeon, but from time to time we hear his murmuring, and now and then he escapes. Every day in the pages of the newspapers, we read of the exploits of somebody's Mr. Hyde. As readers of Stevenson's great story, we like to play somewhat dangerously with the terrible insight it contains.

We are all aware of the modern literary genre of Science Fiction, though we may not read it. It had its beginnings long ago, but it came into extraordinarily sharp focus with some novels at the beginning of this century written by H.G. Wells. When we read them now, we are astonished at their amazing prophetic quality. *The War of the Worlds* (1898) is about an invasion from Outer Space, which is a favourite bugaboo of millions of newspaper readers today. *The Time Machine* (1895) tells of travel through time, which is still unachieved, but who is to say when it will become a fact? *The Food of the Gods* (1904) tells of a biological catastrophe, and every day we are warned of just such horrors that will come if we do not immediately mend our ways and check our wholesale pollution. *The War in the Air* (1908) is very much a horror of our time.

Let us permit ourselves a brief digression, which is, however, not wholly without relevance to our subject of the novel and magic. I do not know much about Science Fiction, but I am told by those who do that some of its products are admirably written and rooted in science which does not outrage the spirit of genuine scientists. But there is a vast amount of Science Fiction on a lower level, which dribbles off into Science Fiction films and has an active life in SciFi Comics and Horror Comics, and these things number their audience in millions. What they exploit is not science, but the fears and the dreams which are only partly admissible of people whom I must call illiterate, although I know that in doing so I offend those people who are devoted to the principle that all people are created equal, and that what I call literacy is just a kind of academic snobbery. But these people of whom I speak are the very people who, in an earlier day, found food for their dreams in a crass form of religion. They were the people who invented and embraced tales of miracles worked by holy images, of visions vouchsafed to simple folk who were assured by a saint or even some more elevated religious figure that they would be cured of their ills, or that some extraordinary disaster would happen if there were not a widespread repentance among the faithful. Let me assure you at once that I am not deriding miracles or cures produced by faith, but I am expressing my incredulity about the frequency and the mechanical nature of their operation.

Only last year I visited a church in the Southern United States, which contained the mummified body of the bishop who had built the church. The body was covered with pieces of paper on which the people who made up the church's congregation had written their prayers for restored health. According to your ailment, you pinned your supplication to the relevant part of the body—for migraine, the head, for rheumatism, the hip, for weak heart, the breast, and so forth. I was assured that countless cures were achieved in this way, if the messages to the saint were accompanied by an appropriate gift of money.

Did I leave that church with my nose in the air, despising the simple folk and their wonder-working image? No, I most certainly did not. Those people had faith, and they knew what to do with their faith. The people I pitied, without despising them, were their innumerable fellow-citizens who have no focus for their faith, but in whom the roots of faith are still alive, and who seek hungrily and foolishly for something to do with the power they feel, but do not—even in the vaguest and most superstitious sense—understand.

These are the people who, in New York, visit a sort of supernatural supermart, not far from Wall Street, where there is a collection of astrologers, numerologists, occultists, and other wonder-workers who will, for fifteen dollars for fifteen minutes, give you a "reading" and advice about your love-life and your career and your most intimate problems. Who visits them—because the place is crowded every noon-hour? I have it on the authority of *The New Yorker* magazine that a great part of their clientele is drawn from young workers in Wall Street, who say that it is as good as a visit to your analyst, and very much cheaper.

I speak of New York, but of course this sort of thing is found everywhere. Not long ago on Bay Street a small boy, whom I judged to be of Hispanic origin, pressed upon me a handbill advertising the services of a lady who would tell me my most intimate secrets and rearrange my life on very favourable terms. And the Personal columns of our newspapers contain advertisements promising everything the world of irresponsible magic can afford.

What is it these faithless, deprived people want? You do not have to read hard volumes of philosophers to find out. Read the comic strips; go to the cheaper sort of movies, and you will find out at once. They want marvels. They want magic, and they have put behind them the faith of their fathers which offered them marvels and magic, as much as they could absorb, linked to a firm ethical teaching.

I am a keen movie-goer. Sometimes I go for art, sometimes for well-planned narrative or adventure, and sometimes to find out what my fellow-creatures desire, in their heart of hearts.

In this latter category I have long remembered a film, made in 1953, called *Monster on the Campus*. The scene was a campus not unlike our own, and one of its admired figures was a brilliant young biologist. There may be some of his kind in this audience. His future was glorious, not only in his profession, but in the realm of love, for he loved and was loved in return by the President's daughter. Their love was pure. That is to say, it went no further than the mauling and face-chewing which Hollywood considers pure but interesting. Need I say she was a blonde? Indeed, her blondness may have been more authentically scientific than any other element in the film. It was the good fortune of the young biologist to receive from the East Indies a specimen of extraordinary scientific interest; it was a coelacanth, which we were told was a fish long thought to be extinct, and therefore a relic of primeval times. When the crate containing this monster was unloaded at the laboratory, some nasty-looking juice leaked out of it, and a passing dog lapped it up. Later that day the dog became uncontrollable—a ravening monster—and had to be shot. Nobody except the audience put two and two together, but we in the audience shrewdly caught the inference. We were not astonished, therefore, when the young professor, opening the crate, accidentally caught his arm in the coelacanth's jaws, and received a tiny bite; like a good scientist he put a Band-Aid on it and thought no more of the matter. But oh!—brace yourselves for this—when next the moon was at the full the campus was invaded by a primitive creature, not to be described as human, who terrified everybody. The police could not catch him, for he had a great turn for tree-climbing and jumping on the roofs of buildings. This monster, it appeared, had an unappeasable appetite for blondes, and it was not long before the President's daughter found herself in his loathsome embrace. The police had no alternative but to shoot him. As he lay on the ground, seemingly dead, he underwent a transformation. Slowly the cave-man gave place to the handsome young biologist. The President's daughter, looking as bereft as it is given to a Hollywood blonde to look, hung over him, as an elderly scientist explained that the evil juices of the coelacanth must have infected him and, at the full of the moon, returned him to an era unimaginably older than our own, when the appetite for blondes was less perfectly under control.

The audience in whose company I encountered this piece seemed well pleased with it. They had had a dose of science, and they had also been given a strong shot of magic.

I may say that this appetite for blondes among primitives is powerfully evinced in the popular film *King Kong*. Are we to assume from this indirect evidence that it is not really gentlemen who prefer blondes?

Even so absurd a work of science fiction as the film I have just described to you includes a few scientific trappings and exploits the modern notion that the world of wonders is now to be approached by priests in white coats, rather than magicians in conical hats and robes embroidered with signs of the zodiac. But in all of these tales, good and bad, the marvels are likely to happen to a single person or to a small group of persons. That is what seems to me to be unscientific about them. Surely a scientific fact must be authenticated by scores, by hundreds, of experiments which all yield, if not precisely the same result, results which are near to being identical? But when the Blessed Virgin appears to a group of children at Lourdes, we cannot demand that she reappear to people of all sorts until the scientific world is satisfied. The unscientific man or woman wants some marvel which applies to him alone; he does not concern himself with what his neighbours feel about it. And it is here, I think, that the magic of the novel, or the play, or the poem, satisfies a deep longing in the human breast. It is wholly personal.

When the Ancient Mariner suffers his long misery after the slaughter of the albatross, we do not demand that at least eighty per cent of the personnel of the British Navy suffer a similar anguish of the soul before we believe in it. When, in the second part of *Faust*—I mean Goethe's *Faust* and not the popular opera—Dr. Faust encounters a whole world of archetypal figures who carry him into realms of experience to which only a supremely great poet holds the key, we do not require that every doctoral student in science undergo the same revelations. When Hamlet encounters his father's ghost we do not call for a Gallup poll to discern how many men have seen the ghost of their respective fathers. These marvellous revelations, which come deep from the soul of man, are embodied in literature as the experiences of single people, and we are ready to share their enlightenment without demanding what would be called scientific truth to back them up. We, as single readers or playgoers, share these experiences willingly, and regard them as valid in so far as they strike some responsive chord in ourselves. Why are we willing to do this?

Now we are getting into deep water, and not everybody is willing or able to swim in it without a lifebelt. In the early days of the Christian church, one of the church fathers asserted that the soul of man was naturally Christian. I cannot agree with him, but I am convinced that the soul of man is naturally religious. And very properly you will require me to say what I mean by that.

Let us begin with the word religion. What does it mean? There are two popular derivations. One is from the Latin verb *religare*, which means to tie, to fasten, to assume a yoke. People who accept that derivation think of religion as adherence to a creed, a system of belief which dictates conduct and man's approach to the unseen world. But there is another derivation, which cannot be dismissed, from the verb *relegere*, which means to consider, to ponder, to examine, and this is the derivation I myself prefer, because it implies a freedom to examine and reflect upon every sort of experience in a personal way. It implies that fullness of life which is both illuminating and consuming, as it is implied in that saying of Christ's which is not in the Gospels but which is quoted by one of the earliest of the church fathers—Origen—and which is: *"Qui iuxta me est iuxta ignem est qui longe est a me, longe est a regno"*—and if my Latin is not of the sort you are used to, that means "Whoever is near to me is near to the fire, whoever is far from me is far from the kingdom." That fire is surely the consuming splendour of life which, from time to time, we may experience if we strive to do so. It is not something which we could endure all the time. It is the *striving* which demands our best energies and our uttermost intuitive powers. That striving is familiar both to scientists and to writers, if they accept their work with full seriousness. We remember Einstein's comment that the physicist is the truly religious man of our time. But what the scientist is able to reveal to us of that splendid fire is concerned with the world of nature and of fact. The writer strives to communicate as much of the fire as he can apprehend in terms which speak personally to individuals in his audience. One voice speaks to one hearer. When the writer succeeds, the means he uses to communicate what he has apprehended may seem to many readers to partake of magic.

This is not, of course, the magic of which I spoke earlier, by which ambitious people sought to control life, but it is the magic which is necessary to the writer if he hopes, even in the slightest degree, to describe and reveal life.

We are the inheritors of what may be called the Freudian Revolution. It began in 1900 when Sigmund Freud published his revolutionary book, *The Interpretation of Dreams.* For several years the book was neglected; the intervention of the First World War kept it from reaching the English-speaking world until the twenties, though it was translated in 1913. Acceptance of what Freud had to say was understandably slow. The interpretation of dreams had for centuries been the province of people who had no scientific standing, although they were eagerly sought out and patronized as they have been at all times in history. People of a religious turn of mind—the wearers of the yoke of which I spoke a few minutes ago—were quite ready to accept Joseph's interpretations of the dreams of Pharaoh, but they were certain that their own dreams were the result of indigestion or garbled memories or simply of the irrationality which they assumed was the whole world of sleep. At least, that was what they pretended. Many of them were credulous about dreams, as people have always been. But what Freud said, and what has now become accepted by great numbers of people, even when they do not really comprehend it, is that the human mind is vastly greater than the portion of it that asserts itself in consciousness, and that we all live a life of immense psychological complexity which influences us in ways that can only be approached with caution and a wary pragmatism. Dreams are messages from that otherwise inaccessible part of the psyche. Since 1900 Freud and his followers have heard and interpreted millions of dreams, and still there is no simple key to the dream world. Every dream is the creation of an individual psyche, and no general agreement about symbolism can be reached, for everybody's symbolism is personal.

Although Freud's approach to the human psyche—and I remind

you that the word means "soul"—was as scientific as such pioneering work can be, there were plenty of people who insisted that he was reverting to magic and occultism, and one of the great battles of his life was to establish his findings on a scientific basis. So much so, indeed, that he refused to pay attention to things which asserted themselves in his clinical experience which he thought would drag him toward the occult, of which he had a horror. It remained for his rebellious colleague and pupil, C.G. Jung, to take a brave step into the world of what was called the occult, which simply means hidden from view, and therefore mysterious.

Jung was a man who was, if I may say so, much less hag-ridden than Freud. He did not have to brave the anti-Semitism of the Viennese scientific world, and because he claimed descent from Goethe he was inclined to examine the world of art and literature in a spirit which Freud thought unscientific. Jung didn't care. He plunged into the science of the past, not because he believed it, but because he wanted to see why people in the past—people no less serious and intelligent than himself and Freud—had agreed to believe in it. Alchemy? What made so many highly intelligent people devote their lives to a study which was on the face of it irrational? He took the plunge and it may be said that he redeemed alchemy from the discard into which it had been thrown, revealing its psychological rather than its physical importance. Astrology? Well, was it not an ancestor of astronomy, devised by people without telescopes and with a cultural background that led them to describe what they could apprehend about the stars in terms which do not agree with modern science? But Jung devoted quite a lot of experimentation to astrology, and came up with the finding that, while it was about fifty per cent nonsense, it was also about fifty per cent worthy of consideration. (This was not, I hasten to assure you, the sort of astrology that you find nowadays in newspaper columns and fashion magazines which never, never, never predict an evil fate for anyone.) He gave a great deal of study to religious beliefs—to Gnosticism in particular—which the Church had long ago condemned as damnable, and he discovered that the Gnostics were no more damnable than any other group who sought to live according to a strict creed, and that they had possessed some psychological insights which were only damnable to a Church that would not tolerate psychological speculation except on its own terms.

These, however, were by-works in the immense amount of speculation and psychological exploration that Jung was able to cram into a busy life as a practising psychiatrist, a life that extended to eighty-six years. For the purpose of our discussion today—a purpose which I assure you I have not forgotten, however far I seem to be ranging from it—I think that his most important assertion as a psychologist was that Evil is a reality, and not just a departure from Good, which is the norm.

Like so many apparent novelties in human thought, this is really a re-assertion of something that used to be assumed as part of everybody's belief. But strict Church doctrine for many centuries had insisted that Evil was simply a *privatio boni,* a temporary falling away or lapse from Good. The writers and chroniclers of the Bible believed no such thing. "Be not deceived; God is not mocked: for whatsoever a man soweth, that shall he also reap." "The imagination of man's heart is evil from his youth." "God will not do wickedly, neither will the Almighty pervert judgement." "The wages of sin is death." But sin has fallen out of fashion and many people who have never heard of the doctrine of the *privatio boni*—sins as a simple and temporary lapse of Good—are none the less loud in asserting it. The murderer, the rapist, the mass-killer, the torturer, the terrorist, are not evil people; they are sick, and we must try to cure them, and if that means keeping them at the public expense for several decades, so be it. There is no such thing as Evil, and if something that looks uncommonly like it asserts itself, it is part of the burden of our humanistic philosophy to rebuke it as mildly as we know how.

Don't be alarmed. I am not calling for a revival of capital punishment or the lash. I am saying that Jung, from his very large clinical experience and his observation of the world about him, believed in an element of Evil which was separate and autonomous, and which was at work in human life, and—to return to our original theme—this is a belief which many writers of the highest attainment have believed also, and the struggle between Good and Evil has been the substance of much of their most powerful work.

The century which is coming to an end has experienced Evil as have few previous ages in human history. Three of the most extensive and murderous tyrannies known to mankind—those of Stalin and Hitler and Pol Pot—have flourished in our time. War has lost any chivalric glamour it may have possessed and has become a horror involving whole populations, and extermination on a scale unparalleled. Creeds which we thought belonged to the Middle Ages have shown themselves to be alive and more fearfully powerful than ever before. But do we talk of Evil as a force in the world? No, we prattle about economics and historical inevitability and all sorts of things which avoid the root of the problem. God and the Devil as contenders in the human drama have been banished from the stage, and that is profoundly irreligious. Irreligious in the sense of the word that I presented to you; it is failure to consider, to ponder, and to examine the world of man as it is. Certainly our politicians never do anything of the kind.

Our artists, however, make the attempt whenever they are people of sufficient stature to undertake such work. It is frequently complained that their work—their paintings, their music, their books—are chaotic either in form or content. This is an entirely just criticism; their work may be chaotic—though it is not always so—because it reflects the chaos of the world about them. They feel that they should do this, and in that feeling lurks a temptation to which many artists—writers in particular—fall victim.

The temptation is to become the artist *engagé,* the writer who addresses himself to the problems of his time, describing them, and thereby trying to persuade the world to come to terms with them. It sounds splendid, doesn't it? The writer as the possessor of a specially acute perception, of a particularly rich compassion, of a heart aflame with disgust and revulsion at the wickedness of mankind—is that not his duty, his highest calling? And certainly it is true that many fine books have been written under this impulse. But the temptation is to think that these huge themes are the only important themes, the truest themes, for literary art. The temptation for the technically capable but intellectually second-rate writer is to say to himself: "Where is there trouble? Where is there misery? Where is the action? Where can I find a cause to support my next book? How can I show myself a person of overflowing compassion? Where can I drop a rain of tears?" This is the temptation of the Devil himself, and for one Solzhenitsyn there are a dozen fakers who are indignant and compassionate because indignation and compassion pay very well, and such books are considered to be "serious" by people who enjoy vicarious compassion. You do not find much magic in these books of the *engagé* writers, and although they may enjoy an immediate success they do not last very long, for new miseries arise to require the compassion that was expended on the old ones. Being sorry for mankind has nothing much to do with attempting to understand mankind.

I mentioned Solzhenitsyn a moment ago. He is not as much in the public eye as once he was. There are many people who regard him as an outstanding example of the writer *engagé,* because he deals with huge themes. Yes, but how does he deal with them? Always in terms of individuals upon whose lives the great themes have overwhelming influence. His books are stories about people, not primarily about history or politics. Tolstoy's extraordinary novel *War and Peace* does the same thing; the fates of individuals give the book its fascinating power. It is only at the end, when Tolstoy cannot control his passion for theorizing and philosophizing and nagging that the book goes off the rails, and we bog down in an explanation of what Napoleon might have done if he had been Leo Tolstoy. But when he is at the top of his form as an artist, and keeps the philosopher in check, he talks about people. And that is what the best novels do, and it is in relation to people that they exercise their magical power by re-shaping observable fact to suit their own ends.

They must do so if they hope to make the effect on their readers which the readers desire. Let me offer an extreme example. How long is it since you read Dickens's novel *The Old Curiosity Shop?* If you have read it at all you surely remember the death of Little Nell, which is described at length and with a great deal of pathos and—it must be said—quite a lot of sentimental unction. Critics have made cruel fun of it. But if you read it with an open mind, you understand and feel what Dickens means by it. The pathos of a life cut short in youth, the fragility of life itself, the sadness which we feel when virtue and goodness of heart in a single life are lost to the world, arise palpably from the page and we are moved, unless we are suffering from an excess of rationality. We may not be drowned in tears as we read it, for that is not the fashion of our time, but we understand why Dickens wept as he wrote it. This is the writer's art on a high level.

I ask you to contrast the death of Little Nell with the death of another child in a novel much closer to our own time. It is Aldous Huxley's *Point Counter Point,* in which he describes with a good deal of clinical detail the death of a little boy who has meningitis. Huxley was a man who had a strong scientific bias, and he spares us nothing of the child's agony, and we are glad when it is over. But are we touched in our innermost feeling? I don't think so, because the child's death is a gratuitous horror. It seems to be lugged in to make our flesh creep. Little Nell dies of something that is not identified; meningitis is a dreadful reality. What we remember from Huxley's book is likely to be the fear which that death inspires in the child's grandfather, who realizes that his own death must be approaching, and he dreads it with all the power of a pitifully egotistical nature. He seems almost to think that the child's death postpones his own. Huxley, in some of his critical work, makes cruel fun of the death of Little Nell, and we may perhaps think that he wrote of the child's death in his own novel in order to show us how a clear-eyed, unsentimental, unweeping, remorselessly modern spirit faces such an event. But the effect of Little Nell's death is unforgettable, however we may regard it, and for the life of me I cannot even remember the name of Huxley's unhappy little boy.

What is the difference? Is it simply modernity contrasted with nineteenth-century sentimentality? Not at all. If we read *The Old Curiosity Shop* with real critical feeling we know that the death of Little Nell is a contrasting passage with the death of the wholly evil, terrifying monster Mr. Quilp. Not long before Nell's death we read of the shocking end of Quilp, whose evil deeds are coming to a culmination where escape is his only recourse, and in seeking to get away from his pursuers he takes a false step, tumbles into the filthy waters of the river, and drowns horribly. It is not in the single death of the child, but in the two deaths in which Good and Evil meet with their reward, that the power of the end of the novel resides. It is in such passages that the genius of Dickens is manifested, leaving Aldous Huxley as a brilliant novelist of vastly lesser powers.

Dickens has dealt with the great theme of Good and Evil, in both of which he had unbounded faith because—if we believe some of his most recent and most perceptive critics—he knew both those elements in his own nature. Huxley nowhere in his work shows much concern with Good, and he seems to regard Evil as a thing of chance, an unmotivated horror in a world without direction.

James Joyce once said that the measure of a book was the quality of the mind from which it sprang. That seems to be a truism, but like many truisms it is often overlooked. The great literary artist concerns himself, in a thousand contrasting ways, with problems of Good and Evil, both of which are realities in his own vision of the world and of mankind. Oh, but you may say, look at Jane Austen: where do you find such elements in her work, which is seriously, and often extravagantly, admired? Well, look at Jane Austen again, and see what you find. She did not write of Good and Evil as did her contemporary and admirer, Sir Walter Scott, but she knew what the score was, if I may be permitted a wholly uncritical term. Speaking of Jane Austen, Scott himself said: "The Big Bow-Wow strain I can do myself like any now going; but the exquisite touch, which renders ordinary commonplace things and characters interesting, from the truth of description and sentiment, is denied me." Scott spoke with the generosity that was characteristic of him but his point is a valid one. Not everything a novelist may wish to say needs to be said in the Big Bow-Wow strain, and the comic genius of Jane Austen is incontestable. But God preserve us from a literature written wholly by Jane Austen and her kind. The Big Bow-Wow strain is a necessity of literary art, and fine-honed social comedy will not reach the full span of human concern.

Fine-honed social comedy, in the Jane Austen sense, is not, however, the only kind of comedy, or the greatest kind. There is a tendency among readers generally, and even among many academic critics, to consider Tragedy a literary mode very much superior to Comedy. I don't agree. Comedy does not mean simply making people laugh. It is not the art of the stand-up comedian, the wise-cracker. It is a way of looking at life which explores some of the noblest aspects of the human spirit. The greatest comic writer in our language was Shakespeare. Oh, I do not mean those often painful scenes in which clowns crack jokes that have lost their point. I mean the totality of those wonderful comedies that made us feel, when we have seen them well presented on the stage, that life is great, and that the human spirit is unconquerable. Shakespeare's most splendid scenes of comedy are often those in which nobody makes a joke. I have long cherished a remark by G.K. Chesterton, when he said that *A Midsummer Night's Dream* was one of our greatest explorations of the mysticism of happiness. It is a happiness that is remote from obvious fun, although *The Dream* has some fine examples of that sort of comedy. But it is not the wild humour of the Athenian workmen who decide to act a tragedy, but that wonderful moment when the bewitched weaver, Bottom, awakes from his enchantment and tries to recover the marvels that he has experienced that presents us with Shakespearean comedy at its peak, emanating from what Chesterton once again calls "the god-like and inexhaustible carelessness of a happy man." We do not laugh, or laugh very hard, at that scene, but when it is well acted we are enveloped in tenderness, and wonderment, and rich fulfilment—in the truth of Comedy, in fact.

Both Comedy and Tragedy can be faked. There are people who think they have experienced Tragedy when they have simply been made to feel miserable. And there are people who think that they have encountered Comedy when they have been made to laugh, without much regard for what they are laughing at, or where their laughter comes from. But in our impressible world, I think it is easier to fake Tragedy than Comedy, and what some critics call "the tragic sense of life" may often mean no more than a sense of the disappointment of one's personal life. Tragedy and Comedy, in their finest flights, are elevating, enlarging, and produce a quality of serenity and courage.

Are Tragedy and Comedy everlasting? Are they part of the spirit of man, archetypal in their grasp on our concept of life, on the very matrix of existence? I wonder if this is so. Tragedy and Comedy, as we know them, extend only from the fifth century B.C., and that is not a long time in the story of man's mind. How long is it since anyone wrote an unmistakable tragedy? I should put it at 1896, when Ibsen wrote *John Gabriel Borkman*. And what do you find in that? Is it the fall of a great king or a hero? No, it is the long dissolution of a financial genius which I suppose is the modern equivalent. Perhaps some of you are eager to tell me that *Death of a Salesman* is a tragedy, but I cannot agree; as Sidney says, "Tragedy concerneth a high fellow," and Willy Loman is not a high fellow; he is a duplicitous Bagman. But it is of interest that in presenting the fall of Borkman and also of Willy, both authors have to resort to the kind of magic which—I assure you I have not forgotten it—this speech was intended to discuss. But allow me one further excursion into a bypath which is not really a bypath.

Why is Comedy tending more and more to become mixed with pathos? Why is Tragedy no longer stark in its approach to the fall of a great man? It is surely part of the Freudian Revolution, and I need not remind you that Freud was a great admirer of the genius of Henrik Ibsen. But it is not to Freud, but to Jung, that we must turn for an answer to the question I have asked, for Jung reminded us of the curious Neo-Platonic theory that the history of mankind proceeds in Aeons, each measuring about two thousand years, and which are equivalent to the Houses of the Zodiac. We are now in the last few years of the Aeon of Pisces—the Aeon of the Warring Brothers—and as we have been somewhat tiresomely reminded by popular music, we are drawing near to the Aeon of Aquarius the Water Carrier, which is regarded as the sign of *the union or reconciliation of opposites*. According to some calculations we shall enter that Aeon decisively in the year 1997, but there are other astronomers—not astrologers, I may say— who put the date somewhere around the year 2154. But these changes do not come about suddenly, and there will be no unmistakable bump when the Age of Aquarius finally arrives.

What will it bring? We already have some hints of a reconciliation of the Warring Brothers in the move toward the blending of Tragedy and Comedy that I have mentioned. We no longer see life quoted so much in terms of black and white, of Evil as opposed to Good, of God as wholly divorced from the Devil. The sentimentality of which I spoke earlier is a shallow evidence of this evening-up; the sentimentality that insists on seeing the good in every man, however apparently evil his actions are, is balanced by the determination of the media—who dictate so many of our accepted ideas—to belittle and diminish people whom we might once have imagined to be great. Thus we have biographies of statesmen and philosophers which are eager to show their worst side, revealing every petty vanity and sexual peccadillo, and biographies of criminals, like Gênet to speak of one, which declare them to have been unrecognized saints. There will be a lot of sentimental nonsense to be waded through before we reach the truth of the Age of Aquarius, but already there are evidences of a mature acceptance of what the future may bring.

Many of these are to be found in literature. In poetry, certainly, and in drama, but I think most insistently in the novel, which is the foremost literary genre of our time.

It would be tedious to go into this question at length, and anyhow it would call for a series of talks, and not one, to make any detailed exploration of the theme. Let me confine myself, therefore, to the work of James Joyce, an extraordinary and not in every way a pleasing genius, who is known to us chiefly through two extraordinary novels: *Ulysses,* published in 1922 and very slowly accepted as a masterpiece above the prejudices of censors and people whose only eyes were in the back of their heads; the other great novel was *Finnegans Wake,* which appeared in 1939.

If you have read them, or one of them, nothing that I can say will enlarge your understanding of them. But many people have not read either, for they are difficult books, written by an egotist who could not imagine how better mankind might spend its time than in poring over his works. Therefore allow me to give a hint or two at what they contain.

Ulysses, as the title suggests, is about a man who undertakes a great voyage, and in this case the traveller is a Jewish advertising salesman called Leopold Bloom, and his journey is through the city of Dublin, from morn to midnight. The likeness between Bloom as Ulysses, Stephen Dedalus, the young schoolmaster, as Ulysses' son Telemachus who seeks and finds his father, and Molly Bloom as Penelope, the wife of the hero, is clear and detailed, but it is done with such subtlety that we must nudge ourselves to see the Heroic tale in the bourgeois doings of these Dubliners. But the hero-tale is there.

Finnegans Wake is a much more difficult book, and in some places it seems to be impenetrable. *Ulysses* makes extensive use of the "stream of consciousness" technique, and of parody, and in places it takes off into high realms of fantasy, without ever losing its grip on the reality of Dublin life. But *Finnegans Wake* begins in the middle of a dream, and continues in that dream for 628 pages of the most demanding, exasperating, dense, incomprehensible exploration of the consciousness of the dreamer that you can imagine, expressed in language that mingles portmanteau words, words in several foreign languages, arcane words from past literature, quotations, passages of lyric beauty, and outrageous puns. Reading it is like nothing so much as wrestling with the Giant Briareus with his hundred arms and his fifty heads, all of them shouting and laughing.

Yes, laughing. Even the most penetrating of critics sometimes miss the point that these two extraordinary novels are huge comedies, in which the depths of experience and the fantasy life of man are explored with the torch of the Comic Spirit. The history of mankind, and the human and mythical elements in what goes to make up that history, are all shown in the dream life of an unremarkable Dublin pub-keeper, and at least we can discern that Joyce is saying that every man and woman contains the truth of every man and woman who has ever lived, and that truth is cloaked in the muddy vesture of everyday life.

This, I put it to you, is the magic of the novel. I suppose we must embark on the question of where it comes from.

I do this, I assure you, with reluctance, because I do not really want to talk about the way I write my own novels, nor do I wish to seem to liken my own novels to the very great works of which I have already made mention. But what alternative have I? I have already said that the novel is wholly personal in its appeal; one reader, with one book, encounters the mind of one author. Not all the science in the world can explain or chart the different ways in which the book reaches its reader, and I, as one author, cannot speak with any knowledge or authority about the way other authors work. Of course there are similarities in the broad method, but every writer works in his own way and cannot effectively embrace any other. So I have no alternative but to talk about myself as a writer of novels.

When I first began to write novels I was often criticised for elements in the plots which seemed to the critics to be inadmissible in any serious work of fiction. This was the first mistake of the critics; being Canadians, they could not conceive that any right-minded fellow-Canadian would write novels that were not meant to be taken in the spirit of serious realism. They knew about Humour, of course; they recognized it; and they gave it cautious acceptance, but it was a genre by itself, a thing for which one was awarded the Leacock Medal; humour ought not to spill over into serious work—for there was still hope that somebody was going to write The Great Canadian Novel, and the critics were damned sure it wouldn't be funny. But in my early novels they were presented with works that were formal, funny, and appeared to lack that higgledy-piggledy quality which the critics thought was characteristic of serious life. They objected to my use of coincidence, because they never noticed any coincidences in their own lives, although I—being religious in the careful, observant psychologically alert sense of that word—found plenty of coincidences in mine. They objected to my style, which they thought needlessly formal. What they did not see, or did not choose to admit, was that I was writing comedies, and comedies freed from that necessity to simulate the humdrum quality of ordinary life which was at that time thought to be the mark of a good novel.

What most annoyed them, however, was my way of introducing things into my novels which hinted at what they called the supernatural—at a life existing at the same time as ours, and influencing ours in a variety of great and small ways, and sometimes intervening in our lives decisively. But I did not mean these things to be supernatural because that is a stupid term. No, my novels were simply psychological, and for a variety of reasons I was strongly aware of these psychological elements, was heedful of them, and could not keep them out of any story I thought worth telling. I was not interested in realism in the ordinary acceptance of the word; my realism was psychological realism and the way in which it manifested itself in my stories could not be accommodated to a narrower conception of reality. "Mr. Davies, as usual, makes his obeisance to the Dark Powers," wrote one critic. And indeed I did so, because to me those powers were inseparable from my vision of life, comic though it was. And to me they were not dark, but numinous. I was not a photographer, catching in black and white what the lens of the camera could see; I was a painter in oils, including what I, as an author, could see.

Why? It is here that I have to tell you one or two things which I have not spoken of in public, because I thought they would be misunderstood. But I have now come to a time of life when I really don't care very much whether people understand me, because I have spent my life trying with my best efforts to understand myself. I am one of those creatures—by no means uncommon—who were called by Bernard Shaw, in his discussion of the character of Joan of Arc, Galtonic Visualizers. It is not a very good term but it strives for scientific accuracy and therefore I offer it to this scientific audience. Things of importance come to me not in philosophical reflections, but in flashes, in sudden perceptions of the unseen, indeed I suppose I must say in visions. It is not, I assure you, because I have a screw loose, but because my arrangement of screws is wholly personal. As a child I had these perceptions, and I did not talk about them even to my mother, because they seemed odd, and private. I once, as quite a young boy, saw something in the sky which was so astonishing that I treasured it without knowing in the least what it was. I could take you now to the very place in the street where, on my way home from school, I saw it. It was not for another thirty years that I learned from my study of Jung that it was a vision of the Unus Mundus, the One

World, the Totality and interdependence of all things. Don't ask me why a schoolboy should see such a thing. I saw it, and that's all there is about it, and later on it crept into my novels and plays.

Once, as a child, I was frightened very powerfully by a witch, a figure of evil—of evil transcending anything I had ever knowingly encountered in my life. It was in the attic of our family house, where I was playing, when suddenly I knew that the witch was there, in a cupboard; I could see her through the cupboard door. For a very long time—it might have been half an hour, but probably it was less—I was frozen, not daring to move a muscle, while the evil creature stared at me with a chilling smile. She knew me, and her knowledge was not benign. When at last I escaped I dared not speak of it, and thought I should never get over it.

I did so, however. I was nearer sixty than fifty when I met that witch again, in a dream. She fixed me with her glare and her smile, and as I dreamed I thought I should once again be frozen by that spell. Not so. I roused myself, and walked toward her, holding out my hands. "Can't we be friends?" I said. And believe it or do not believe it as you will, the witch became a benevolent figure, took my hand, and was terrifying no longer. I did not need an analyst to tell me what that meant. It meant a measure of self-conquest.

All my life I have met from time to time strange figures, sometimes witches, sometimes ghosts, and I have learned not to fear them. They are the way in which I encounter truth, or whatever of truth it is given to me to understand. And it is this painfully gleaned truth that I seek to impart in my novels, and I have a great many letters from readers that make it plain that many people have responded to my truths, for which I make no extraordinary claim, but for whose validity, limited as it may be, I have no doubt at all.

One of the assertions of C.G. Jung, whose work has served to explain to me many things which would otherwise have remained dark, is that people may encounter in dreams or visions things of which they have no previous knowledge. One of his favourite examples was of an illiterate Negro prisoner in an American jail, who had a vision that was explicable only in terms of a very old and somewhat obscure Egyptian legend. The man could not possibly have read about it, or heard about it, and he was not a man of uncommon intellectual powers. What he saw, said Jung, was something that exists in the Collective Unconscious of mankind. It exists, and apparently from time to time some part of it makes its way to the surface of the mind of some living person.

I have had an experience of that kind. Some years ago I was at work on a novel, the central character of which was a man of complex but ill-comprehended character, and his personal problems had driven him to drink. I don't like the word alcoholic. It has a Nice Nelly sound that troubles me. My character was, to put it grossly, a boozer. As I wrote about him, I knew quite a bit about him, but it wasn't in focus; I did not know quite what I intended for him. Novelists have these problems.

One day, after lunch, as I was sitting in the open air, in that condition of abated consciousness which often follows lunch—no, I wasn't asleep, and I do not suggest that lunch is a key to the visionary world—I saw two figures approaching me. One was a beautiful young woman, dressed in classical garb, with flowing hair and an air of confidence about her which was immediately arresting. On a golden chain she was leading an animal; it had the body and head of a lion, the clawed feet of a dragon, a tail which was barbed as the tails of scorpions are barbed in ancient art, and it had the anguished face of a man. What on earth was it? As the vision faded I scraped about in my mind for a name for that curious creature, and after consulting a dictionary of mythology I had it. The creature was a manticore, a thing composed of a man helplessly trapped in the attributes of beings that were less than human. When I came to myself I knew that I had the clue to my book and my character. I called the book *The Manticore* against the advice of my publisher— publishers are not often visionaries—and rather a large number of people have liked it, if I may judge by its continuing popularity and the letters from readers it has inspired.

There you are. You asked me to talk about the novelist and magic, and I have done so, and as you see, the magic isn't magic at all, when once you know how it comes about. It resides in a realm that has always existed, and from which such works as *A Midsummer Night's Dream* and *The Ancient Mariner* have arisen, as well as many such humbler literary creations as my own. I am not, as you see, a writer *engagé* in the usual sense of the term, but I am a writer deeply immersed in the only world of which he can hope to have any indisputable knowledge—the world of himself. Unless the writer is prepared to write unsparingly and sometimes painfully of himself, he hasn't much to say that has the ring of truth. He may cloak what he has to say in a formal style, as I do, and in a comic mode, as I do, but the source from which his writing comes is neither formal nor comic in essence, but is turbulent, pressing, and vital, and it is a world where Tragedy and Comedy have mingled.

I have described the writer to you in terms that mark him as the religious man—religious in the sense in which I defined the word earlier. Not as the expounder of a creed, or the zealous supporter of a cause, but as one who approaches life with care, and indeed with reverence; who examines everything he can as carefully as he can; he is not afraid of a paradox or an outright contradiction in what he finds, and in some cases is one who points the way to the thoughts and preoccupations of the future.

In our century extraordinary efforts have been made toward the exploration of the universe about us, and the culmination of that work has been the landing of man on the Moon. In spite of all the fuss, that didn't amount to much. There were people who said that it was merely to show technological superiority to Russian science, and that may be so in part. There were those who said that it achieved nothing much except to leave an utterly irrelevant flag and some rubbish on a hitherto unviolated planet, but that is not the whole truth. What that venture did do was to mark the beginning of an exploration that will in time take man deep into a world now unknown, which may contain secrets of which we cannot even dream. Space travel is one of the most enlarging adventures to come in the Age of Aquarius.

You notice that I said "*one* of the enlarging adventures." There is another fully as important and perhaps more important without which space travel will mean little. For what is the point of sending men and women into space whose personal lives are lived on the surface of the mind, whose perceptions are clouded by ignorance of themselves, whose understanding of what mankind is does nothing to fit them for great adventures. Bravery is not enough. Technology is not enough. Psychologically unevolved men and women may be both brave and fine technologists. The other great adventure of the future is the exploration of the coming to terms with the innermost self, the well-springs of humanity, the linking of the daemonic and the civilized, the joining of hands between Apollo, the Giver of Light, and Dionysius, the Lord of the Dark Forces, the recognition that God and the Devil between them unite to make a third power which must be encountered and so far as possible comprehended.

Has that anything to do with the novel, which you pick up, put down at will, use to beguile an idle hour and perhaps think of as a modest contribution to the ever-changing culture of the time?

Well, yes, it has, if you will permit me to be shameless in asserting the essence of the art of which I am a humble but careful practitioner. For the novelist, indirectly perhaps but persuasively, he hopes, is pointing you in the direction of the new discovery, the new conquest, the great new adventure. That is, if you want to call it by an ambiguous name, his magic, his enchanter quality.

And if you do not believe a word I have said, I have at least done what you asked. I have talked about the novelist and magic.

8

MY EARLY LITERARY LIFE

On January 27, 1988 the distinguished Canadian magazine *Saturday Night* celebrated its 100th anniversary with a gala dinner in Toronto. As the equivalent of American publications such as *Harper's* or *The Atlantic*, the now-monthly magazine continues to play an important role in Canadian intellectual life.

At the time of the celebration the magazine's editor was John Fraser, who in 1995 followed in Robertson Davies' footsteps to become the fourth Master of Massey College in the University of Toronto. It was appropriate that he should invite Robertson Davies, a former literary editor of the magazine and possibly its oldest ex-employee, to deliver the toast to the magazine that was at the centre of the evening's festivities. Few of those present suspected that Davies' memories of the magazine would extend back to the time before he could read, or that his memories of working there from 1940 to 1942 would be so clear. Or, indeed, that he still bore ink-stained scars from that time; the insensitivity of the evil Mr. Croucher in his words "still rankles here in me buzzem!"

On July 16, 1988 Davies noted: *Write to John Fraser, whose August issue of* Saturday Night *displays my speech toasting the old paper very handsomely, though there are some drawings of what a bad artist imagines me to have looked like in my twenties, and the wedding picture of Brenda and me which we both dislike.*

When I was first asked to propose this toast, I was horrified to discover that my association with *Saturday Night* goes back for seventy years. It began in my childhood, because *Saturday Night* used to come to our home. My father was a journalist, my mother was a writer—a newspaper writer—so the whole family was in the trade. And when I was a very little boy I remember that on Sundays my parents sat reading a very large newspaper printed on glossy, coated stock which, I understood, was called *Saturday Night*. That was during the years of the First World War and I learned to write from *Saturday Night*. But I did not learn to read from it, because what I used to do when my parents had finished with the paper was to get a pencil and copy the big headlines and work out the letters in that way. I never understood what they meant and nobody ever told me, but that was what I did.

I recall that my father used to read the first section of the paper, which was full newspaper size; that part was about international affairs and primarily, of course, about the Great War. I was very much aware, from what he read, and what he said, and what he read aloud to my mother and to my brothers, that this conflict was between two extraordinary antagonists: one, a Mr. Lloyd George, who was of overwhelming nobility and splendour because he was Welsh, like my family; and the other was a monster, an incarnation of evil, who was the German emperor, Kaiser Wilhelm II. I used to see, in the *Saturday Night* pages, caricatures of Lloyd George, hair flying splendidly with the excess of his zeal and patriotism as he exhorted other people to fight. And also, the picture of the cringing, evil German emperor, wearing a helmet with a spike on the top of it, with extraordinary upturned moustaches and a sneer that would chill the blood of a crocodile. There were occasionally caricatures of his son, Prince Louis Ferdinand, who was always referred to as "Chinless Freddie."

My mother, meanwhile, as my father was reading this inflammatory stuff, was reading the section of the paper that was given over to fashion and society. Because in those days, *Saturday Night* devoted a great many pages to society and everybody was interested in it. I should like to think that the editor would reinstitute that enthusiasm and that in Canada we would get some real society and not just a coven of committees devoted to the assistance of the dystrophic and the paraplegic and the AIDS-ridden and *les misérables* who seem to have taken the forefront in our world at the moment.

Later on, I began to read *Saturday Night* myself, and I was particularly interested in the middle section, which was devoted to literature and the arts. And what I especially liked were the theatrical pictures that were printed of actors who were going to appear in Toronto in the week following the date of publication. They were splendid; indeed, splendid in a sense which the younger among you cannot conceive at this moment. It was an era when the theatrical profession was either beautiful or distinguished. The ladies were elegant, beautiful, stylishly dressed, marvellously coiffed, splendid creatures, inspiring even to a very young boy (mind you, young boys are very easily inspired). And the men had an air of hauteur and distinction, a height of white collar and a splendour of cravat, that has utterly disappeared from the theatrical profession, which has become now, I fear, a congeries of scabby detrimentals who never seem to wash their hair, and I don't want to look at their pictures any more. But, in those days, the pictures of the theatre people were transporting, and I looked at them with the keenest interest. And also, I read the theatrical reports by Hector Charlesworth, which were witty and charming and interesting and never cruel, though sometimes pointed. And I read the work of a man, who is not much remembered nowadays, called Peter Donovan. The thing about Peter Donovan was that he was funny; and in those days it was permissible for publications like *Saturday Night* to be funny. Peter Donovan (whose famous pseudonym was P. O'D) was very funny indeed. I wish the spirit of those days would return, when somebody in *Saturday Night* could be knowingly and intentionally and pointedly funny.

Well, now we hasten on in our story to the year the war began, 1939, when things were very, very bad in the theatrical profession, of which I was a member. I remember vividly waking up one morning in

London, in England, and discovering that the government had closed all the theatres indefinitely and that over 5,000 actors in London alone were out of work, and I was one of them. There was no job for me there, so I came back to Canada, where I thought I might conceivably get employment, and it was not easy to find. *The Globe and Mail* was going through a mid-life crisis which has existed with it for fifty, sixty, and seventy years, and in wartime could not bring itself to appoint anybody to such a frivolous position as that of a theatre critic. So, although I banged upon their doors, I got no job there.

While this was going on, I was summoned by my country to be considered for military service. Well, now, I didn't respond with a whoop and a holler, because I had heard about people getting killed in the First World War and I had no particular interest in following their example in the Second. However, I went along and got examined. I assure you I went into the examining pavilion a young Hercules and I came out an ignominious wretch. I was utterly rejected. I had been aware that, sometimes, my apprehension of things at a distance was dim, but I had not expected to be condemned as blear-eyed. I knew that, occasionally, I didn't catch everything that was said at great distances, but I didn't know that I was really rather tediously deaf. And I had had occasions of exaltation which I put down to the mercurial nature of my temperament, but I didn't realize I had vertigo. I was turned down on these points because the Canadian army had all the blind, deaf, and dizzy people it needed already.

I assure you, I crawled out of the doctor's office almost on my hands and knees. I still had not got a job and I needed one very badly. Then, suddenly, something extraordinary happened. These coincidences—Jungian coincidences—occur from time to time in my life. The news appeared in the papers that the literary editor of *Saturday Night* had died in a boating accident on a lake near Ottawa. He was a man named Hal Sutton. Well, I thought, now there's a job I might conceivably aspire to. But, you see, I had been so well brought up that I thought the death of a literary editor such a grievous affliction that for two or three weeks, certainly, the magazine would close down entirely, and it would be shameful to intrude upon their grief. But I met a friend of mine in the street, and I told him what my intentions were and what my feelings were, and he said, "Don't you believe it: you get in and apply right away. And don't send your letter through the mail, take it down and put it through the letter box at Consoldated Press." I thought he knew what he was talking about, so that's what I did, and the very next day I received a phone call from the editor, Mr. B.K. Sandwell, asking me to come and talk to him about this application that I had made.

I went. I was terrified of Mr. Sandwell, but Mr. Sandwell was charming, pleasant, and put me greatly at my ease. We talked for a very short time. I'd expected to be grilled, but I wasn't grilled. And then Mr. Sandwell said, "Well, that seems very satisfactory. Let's go and talk to the publisher." So, we went to talk to the publisher, and I've never talked to such a publisher in my life, before or since. We went into a magnificent office which was panelled in some splendid, I expect exotic, wood. And there sat, not a grim-visaged male, but a charming lady. She was Miss Sutton, and she was the publisher of *Saturday Night*, and she was, indeed, the aunt of the man who had so recently died. I expected her to be suffused with grief, but she was not.

So I talked to Miss Sutton and I very quickly discovered that Miss Sutton was not interested so much in my literary qualifications as in my personal life. "Are you married, Mr. Davies?" she said.

"Yes, Miss Sutton. I am."

"Have you any children?"

And I, blushing deeply, said, "Well, no, Miss Sutton, but it is now early November and my wife and I hope that before the end of the year . . . um . . ."

Miss Sutton became all smiles and we got on admirably, and the interview, again, was uncommonly short. Miss Sutton said, "Now, there is only one thing still to consider: what salary would you expect?"

Well, I was prepared for that one, because I had consulted my father by telephone and my father said, "I know for a fact that B.K. Sandwell gets five thousand dollars a year for being editor of *Saturday Night*. Now, you must not consider that you are worth as much as

B.K. Sandwell, so you must put your salary somewhere slightly below half what he gets, but not too far below."

So, I was ready for Miss Sutton and I said, "Well—ah—I think that perhaps forty-two dollars and fifty cents weekly would be about right."

And Miss Sutton looked grave, as publishers always do, and said, "Well, I think, possibly, we could agree on that."

And so we did.

I said, "When do I begin?"

And Mr. Sandwell said, "You begin at once. You come in the day after tomorrow. Tomorrow is press day; come in the day following."

So I did. And I met the staff and the staff were delightful people. There was Mr. Sandwell himself, of course, who was the editor. And there was Pat Richards, who was the financial editor and a very big wheel in the affair because he gave advice about how you invested your money. In those days, you could still write to *Saturday Night* and ask, "What do I do with my money?" and Mr. Richards would send you a personal reply telling you what to do with it. Mr. Richards, I always thought, was a man of extraordinary self-denial, because he never worked upon his advice to get rich himself: he just let other people get rich on what he suggested. Mr. Richards had an assistant called Wessely Hicks, who did the layout of the paper. He was very kind to me and showed me the ropes. And there was Miss Bernice Coffey, who did fashion and society, and what were then called, reprehensibly of course, "women's affairs."

That was the whole staff except for the secretary, Miss Watson, who like all good secretaries cloaked her steely core in boundless charm. One of her main jobs was to protect Mr. Sandwell from the bores, time-wasters, and certifiable lunatics by whom he—like all editors— was beset all day. I began to realize why they needed somebody in an awful hurry. If you reduce a staff of six by one, you're in considerable trouble.

But there were all sorts of people who appeared who worked on the paper occasionally. One was Karsh, the photographer, at that time very much at the beginning of his career, who was doing a lot of photography for *Saturday Night*. There was the photographer who worked regularly for the advertising department, whose name was Jaycocks, a delightful Englishman. Jaycocks taught me a lot of things about photography, which I've never forgotten. One time I said to him, "Jay, all the food that you photograph for the food advertisements looks so absolutely delicious. Why is that? You know that most of it is awful."

And he said, "Well, it's simple, you see. They get everything ready and then I get a can of varnish and pour it over the whole thing, and it brings out that wonderful, delicious gleam which everybody admires in the pictures."

Now, *Saturday Night* at that time was not an independent journal. It was a publication put out by a firm called Consolidated Press; it had a very large group of papers, which are what are called "trade papers." They were *The Canadian Founder and Die-Sinker* and *The Canadian Leather-Pounder and Fuller* and *The Canadian Nail-Drawer and Wire-Pusher,* and all those things, and they were money-makers, every last one of them. *Saturday Night* was the black sheep of the family, because, although it was the most illustrious paper of the group, it lost money pretty consistently. And for that reason we were perpetually under pressure from the group who ran Consolidated Press. You see, Miss Sutton had established a sort of Byzantine Empire and she was the empress at the top of the heap. Below her were a group of palace eunuchs, so to say, who did all the work, and these were, some of them, very curious people indeed.

I remember the first day that I was at work on *Saturday Night*, I filled out a lot of papers about what pension I would get when I was seventy, and all those things you do when you go to work in your early days on a paper. Very shortly afterwards an extremely small, but globular, man appeared in my office, a man full of self-esteem, obviously, and he said, "Here are your forms."

I said, "Yes?"

He said, "Well now, look at them. I can read every word you've written."

I said, "Yes?"

He said, "Well now, I'm going to tell you something, because I'm a man who's achieved a good deal of success in the world of business, and you are a young man just entering the world of business. And I want to tell you that nobody who succeeds in the world of business ever writes legibly." And he then proceeded to scribble something on a paper, and he said, "That's my signature."

And I looked at it and I thought, "Yes, that's his signature. I don't know what his name is, but that's his signature." And then he marched away, having conferred upon me this inestimable boon. I've never forgotten it, and I have gone right on writing as clearly as I can.

There was another man who quickly appeared in the door of my office, hissing strangely, and I later on discovered that this was evidence of an inveterate malignance against literary editors. He was the assistant business manager and he bore the Dickensian name of Croucher. Mr. Croucher was the thorn in my flesh and the bane of my life, because Mr. Croucher would appear on publication day with an advertisement which simply had to be squeezed into the literary pages. He would insist that this be done and it had to be done, because I was junior to Mr. Croucher and could not say him nay. And I remember my lowest hour was one day, when we were just about to go to press, and Mr. Croucher came in and said, "I've got to have three inches, a column wide, for an ad on your page, your first page." He got it, of course. It was an ad for "Pussy-foot Closet Tanks." In order to wedge it in I had to cut three inches of deathless prose by myself. I resented that. I resent it still. It still rankles here in me buzzem!

I made other acquaintances very quickly in those first days at the paper. One was the compositor who took care of the literary pages. He appeared, suddenly, a gigantic man, and made strange noises, and pointed and jabbed and made signs, but I knew exactly where we stood. He was a type of printer that you don't see any more, because printing has ceased to be that kind of trade. But in those days a great many people who were deaf mutes became printers, and this man was a deaf mute. He was a wonderful fellow, a first-class printer and a great friend. He was understanding and amusing and we got on admirably. He would point, sign, make motions, and I would write in my ridiculously legible handwriting and, in that way, we got along splendidly.

I also got on not very good terms, but on very intimate terms, with the proof-reader, who was an Englishman, and a demon grammarian. He was much distressed by me, but I didn't worry too much, because he was much distressed by everybody. He was distressed by Mr. Sandwell; he was distressed by the whole paper. None of us seemed to know any grammar as he understood grammar. He was particularly dismayed by what he called my objectionable abuse of the colon. He explained this further: it was a kind of syntactical AIDS he was talking about, a deficiency syndrome. He wrangled with me about this all the time that I was at *Saturday Night*, which was well over two years. We never reached an agreement.

But I eventually found out how things went, and I remember the very first review that I wrote as book editor was of a collection of Ogden Nash's poetry and the headline which I wrote for it was "Golden Trashery of Ogden Nashery." And a lot of people thought that was very un-*Saturday Night*. But Mr. Sandwell thought it was just fine.

A lot of people had odd ideas about what the literary pages in *Saturday Night* should be like. In my very first week, a dignified and beautifully dressed gentleman suddenly appeared in my office without a by-your-leave, and proceeded to select books from the shelves and set them aside, obviously about to put them into his briefcase and carry them away. I made enquiries. What did he think he was doing, I asked.

"I am going to review these books," he said.

Well, I thought, this is Waterloo. And I said, "You know, really, when I want you to review a book, I will see that it is sent to you in plenty of time for you to get on with it." Meanwhile, I snatched the books and put them back on the shelves. This was terrible, because he went away looking daggers. And I discovered, because Miss Watson was looking white and shaken, that this was no less a grandee than Professor Pelham Edgar, of the University of Toronto, and it was as though, in modern terms, I had shot Northrop Frye. Nobody that I was, I had given Pelham Edgar the bum's rush! He never darkened the door of *Saturday Night* again during my time there. But I felt that I had not entirely missed the mark, because I noticed, when I went out to look around and see what the carnage was like, that Mr. Sandwell, whose door was always open, was shaking with laughter. And so I decided that everything was all right.

One of the pleasures of my work was a weekly chat with Hector Charlesworth. He had been editor, had then become one of the earliest broadcast administrators in the country, and had returned to journalism, as music critic of *The Globe and Mail* and as a reviewer and occasional critic for us. He was a splendid figure, of Edwardian elegance; he loved to tell how in his younger days he had often been mistaken for the Prince of Wales (later Edward VII). Indeed, he had sometimes shown himself on a platform on the prince's train, when the prince himself was on another platform, causing some confusion among the loyal souls gathered at country railway stations. Two princes! It was like an *Uncle Tom's Cabin* company with two Topsies. He was always handsomely dressed, and every week he had his beard trimmed by a female barber whom he spoke of as "Madame Queen"—the name of a character in the "Amos 'n' Andy" radio programme.

He was a fountain of anecdotes about the theatre of the late nineteenth century, and as this was an enthusiasm of mine I became his disciple. As a critic, I think he was strong as a judge of acting, rather than of plays, and his recollection of differences in the performance of *Hamlet* by a variety of leading players was detailed and perceptive.

He was wonderfully courteous to women, and a great, and respectful, celebrator of the beauty of actresses. I remember that once, when we had become strong friends, he said, "I want to show you a picture of my wife," and he drew from his pocketbook a Victorian photograph of the kind that used to be called *"carte de visite"*; it was of a wonderfully pretty girl of not more than twenty, wearing one of those tight bodices down the front of which marched a procession of charming little buttons. This was Kate Ryan, who, at the time we were talking, was a bedridden invalid whose chief entertainment was the pursuit of innumerable lawsuits—something she had inherited from her father,

Peter Ryan, a brilliant Liberal politician who was, it appeared, irrepressibly litigious.

Hector belonged to a bygone age, and a very good age it must have been. His kindness to me was all the more warming because there was no reason why he should have paid any heed to me whatever. Indeed, when I look back at my days on *Saturday Night* it is of the kindness of Hector Charlesworth and B.K. Sandwell—gentlest and firmest of editors—that I think first and last.

And so, on and on it went, and I enjoyed my time at *Saturday Night* immensely. One of the things that I did was to try to popularize Canadian wine. We were getting out a Christmas edition. B.K. said, "What can you think of that would be novel?"

I said, "Well, somebody saying something good about Canadian wine."

He said, "You go ahead and try that."

So, my wife and I tried a number of recipes, and I printed an article under a pseudonym, a feminine pseudonym—it was the custom in the paper at that time—saying that if you heated it, and put enough spice in it, and added a few glasses of brandy to it, it made an admirable punch. And this was an absolutely fiery success. I became the white-haired boy of the Canadian wine industry and I can still feel the caress of Noah Torno when he talked to me about that article later on.

In the course of time I left *Saturday Night* to take up other employment which was necessary for one reason or another—reluctantly, because I loved the place.

It is, par excellence, Canada's intellectual paper. It has been so for a hundred years. It has, at its very best and sometimes when it wasn't at its very best, been a mountain breeze among the smogs and miasmas and hypocritical fug of Canadian life. We must treasure it for that reason and, as we look back to its past with admiration and affection, we must look forward to its future with expectation, with very great hope.

And so I ask you to drink a toast not to *Saturday Night*. Let us call it "our paper."

9

LITERATURE AND TECHNOLOGY

"If democracy is not to prove a gigantic mistake, the many must have only the best, and that does not always mean the fastest or the easiest."

"I cannot understand how it is possible to neglect what a man is and the way he lives when one considers what his artistic work adds up to."

Insights like this abound when Davies tackles the subject of literature and technology. Beginning with a look at how new technology, such as the word processor, changes the way an author writes, in this speech he brings his thoughts to bear on wider topics, from *Vanity Fair* to the mystery of artistic creation and its relation to the unconscious.

The speech was given at the Ontario Science Centre in Toronto as part of the Tuzo Wilson Lecture Series. Wilson, a distinguished geologist best known for his work on tectonic plates, was not only a former Director General of the Science Centre but an old friend. Indeed, when Davies, the founding Master, was engaged in the task of establishing Massey College, he was delighted to have Tuzo Wilson become one of the original Fellows in 1963.

On November 11, 1989, a significant period before the lecture date of November 26, Davies wrote in his diary a tribute to his wife: *Finish the Wilson Lecture and think it not bad. Read it to Brenda who likes it and makes some good criticisms, as usual. She is by far and away my best critic . . .*

I am going to talk to you, in part at least, about Literature and Technology, though how that will work out I cannot be sure, for, although I know something about literature, I am very much a novice in the whole world of technology. I am not even sure what it means. Of course I know what the dictionary says it is; it is the application of science to practical or industrial things. And I cannot pretend that it lies outside the sphere of my experience, because I live in a house that has a telephone and electrical power, and is heated by a sophisticated system activated by oil, and I drink cleansed water and am quite often in buildings where the air is circulated and its temperature controlled by technical devices. Technology touches me at every aspect of my physical life. But that is not the same thing as saying that I *understand* technology. Whenever something goes wrong with any of the things I just mentioned, I have to get somebody—referred to usually as "the man"—to put it right, and what he does and how he does it are mysteries to me.

I am happy to find that there is now a word for me as I relate to these things. I am a technomoron. I am a man of words and I glory in that splendid title. Technomoron; it has resonance.

When it comes to Literature and Technology I confess that I am more than usually puzzled, as I cannot really convince myself that the two things have any connection. Perhaps they have connections that I have not yet discovered. Let us see.

As a writer, I receive a great many letters, some of which are from schoolchildren. They are curious about what it means to be an author, and a question they always ask is: "Do you have a word processor?" Sometimes children come to see me, face to face, and when they ask this question I reply, "Why would I want a word processor?" They say: "It's the way everybody writes now," and they tell me about their own experiences with word processors, which they value greatly because the machine can spell, and it is easy to make corrections on its offprints, and it is quick and you can have as many copies as you like of what you have written.

If I am not in a particularly benign mood I reply that I am rather a good speller myself and my secretary is infallible, and that the machine cannot spell a lot of words I wish to use; the machine has a restricted and commonplace vocabulary. In my sort of work speed is not the most important thing, and writing done too quickly always has to be done again. As for having as many copies as you like, I never want more than one copy. My secretary urges me to use carbon paper to make at least one extra copy, and I have been warned by all sorts of people that if I ever lost my single copy I should be in great trouble. To which I can only reply, simpleton that I am, that I have never lost my single copy and I hate carbon paper, which is dirty.

I am not being completely honest with these children, because I use an electric typewriter, which is certainly a technological marvel, but I want to find out why they are so enthusiastic about word processors, which they think are wondrous and indispensable. I tell them the old story about Mr. Sam Goldwyn, who picked up a volume of the *Complete Works of Shakespeare* and said, in admiration, "And to think he wrote it all with a feather." I explain to the children that writing is not a technological process, and to rely on technology to do what you cannot do with a feather, or perhaps a lead pencil, is to fall into grievous error.

I assure you I am not a dinosaur. I do not wish to return to candlelight and the horse-drawn vehicle. I have investigated the question of word processors. I asked the man from whom I get typewriters, and who also sells word processors, what he thought about the matter. He is an honest man, and what he said was this: "The word processor is a marvel for everything connected with business, because it can do tabulations brilliantly, it allows for unlimited correction by the easiest possible means, and it produces as many duplicates of a document as you want. But you are not interested in speed; it would take you six months to master a word processor completely, although I can teach a secretary to do all she needs to do in two weeks. You live in the country and, knowing you, I am sure you would need a service man at least every two weeks, and that would be fifty dollars a call, exclusive of his cost of transportation. You are better off without one."

I listened to these words of wisdom and was grateful to my friend for his frankness. So I asked another question: "Does not the word processor tempt its user to over-write, to say too much, because it is so easy?" "Oh yes," he replied; "they certainly encourage blather and many business documents are needlessly extended because they are so easy to make. Business people are very innocent and they are impressed by bulk."

That, again, was frank and I knew it to be true, for every week I throw away yards of stuff written on word processors that people have sent me. This is always marked, "For your information." But it is usually information I don't want and haven't asked for—speeches by politicians, reports about things I don't want to know, masses of figures in which I have trouble locating my bank balance, which is all I require. Word processors tempt people toward profusion, and my work is writing the best prose I can manage, in which profusion is almost the worst of sins. I want to say what I have to say in the clearest, briefest manner I can achieve, and you may take it from me that the work is slow.

I get letters that are obviously written on word processors, and they are always too long. I have read novels and essays written on word processors and they are always at least one-third too long. Anything that tempts me to write at self-indulgent length is the work of the Devil, and whatever word processors may be to the world of business, they are not for me. I must be slow. I must be deliberate, and I must not work with anything that gets between me and what I really want to say, the best way I can say it.

Of course, as an author, I rely heavily on technology, but the technology must be applied by somebody else, when I have done the best I can, in my own slow way.

For twenty years I worked as a journalist, and I left the world of journalism just before a gigantic application of a new technology in printing revolutionized the newspaper and magazine world.

You know what I mean. When I was a journalist the job of putting a newspaper together and printing it was a highly sophisticated application of techniques which were, in essence, the work of the blacksmith. Printers worked with metal. What I wrote went to men who converted it into lengths of metal on a machine called a Linotype, which was in its day a miracle of technology. When my father was a young man, learning the printing trade, everything that appeared in a newspaper had to be set up by hand, with movable type, one piece of metal for every letter, space, and mark of punctuation. It was a true craft. It was a slow process, even when the printers were quick and expert, and it employed a great many skilled compositors, as they were called. Modern technocrats called that "work-intensive." The Linotype could do rapidly in an hour what five hand-compositors could do, and it put a lot of men out of work, of course. And when the Linotype had done its job, all those trays of type had to be assembled on stone tables into newspaper pages, and then another process known as stereotyping came into play, which made moulds of those pages, again in hot metal, which were transferred to a large printing-press, which in its turn printed the newspaper at great speed. We thought that technology had gone as far as it could. Those printers were highly skilled workmen, proud of their job, which demanded a four-year apprenticeship to master. Then came a technological revolution.

Nowadays newspapers are produced by what is really an elaborate system related to photography, and all the setting is done on miraculous machines which are often worked by women, as they do not demand the physical strength which used to be part of the qualification of a printer. Printing of this new sort produces not only newspapers but books and everything else that appears nowadays in printed form. This is one aspect of the new computer-based technology.

Much has been gained. Printing is now clean work, and in the old days of metals and oily, thick printer's ink it was dirty work, however skilful the men might be. It is very quick work, for several processes have been made redundant. But in the old days—not so very old, but now gone forever—a printer took pride in the aesthetic appearance of his work and he knew certain things that machines cannot be made to do. He knew, for instance, how to make all the lines on his page present an even appearance when printed; it was an art called "justifying." The machines cannot justify, and so the pages they present are often enough to turn an old-fashioned printer grey, for they are full of ugly gutters and cramped or loose lines. The machines do not speak English, or any other language, so they have no idea where a hyphen ought to appear in a word that comes at the end of a line. Consequently you are likely to find even the word "and" printed as "a" at the end of one line, followed by a hyphen, with the "nd" on the next line, which is ugly and illiterate, and un-aesthetic. Maddeningly and confusingly, the word "the" may well appear as "t"—hyphen—"he." Tee-hee—and that, of course, is laughable. Old-fashioned printing had still something of the art which was a necessity to printers from Gutenberg down to twenty years ago, and that has gone. And because it is so quick, the modern work is often careless, and even in an expensive modern book you will find errors of spelling which are there simply because the old, tedious art of the proof-reader has been superseded by the slapdash bad manners of the machine, which has no mind.

There are things, of course, which the machines know, or think they know. They think they know how to punctuate, because a system of punctuation has been built into them. But they don't seem to know what a colon is, and as I use colons rather often, I conduct a running battle with machines and the people who own them, who assure me that the colon belongs to the past. This is nonsense. The colon is invaluable, and the machines will have to learn, just as they will have to learn about justification and the proper placing of hyphens.

They will also have to learn that when I quote from some old author who spelled differently from the machine, the wishes of the long-dead author must be respected, and the machine will have to mind its manners.

This is my complaint: These machines have no manners and no conscience, for these are human traits, and machines are not human yet, though only God knows what they may become with the passing of time.

I have another complaint against these machines, and some people think it a frivolous one. It is simply that they offer what they print in such hideous type. I was brought up in a printing family where typography was taken seriously as a minor art, which it is. The letters of the Roman alphabet which we use are all related, in some fashion, to the letters inscribed on Trajan's Column in Rome; the great typefaces designed and originated by the great type founders of the past, and which bear the names of Bodoni, Bembo, Caslon, and many others, are exquisitely proportioned to combine legibility and beauty so that the printed page is a thing to rejoice the eye, and a worthy interpreter of careful thought to the receptive mind, and sometimes of genius to the astonished and re-created mind. The hideous, deformed letters produced by the word processor or the computer are barbarous, and for no conceivable reason except that their designers wished them to be barbarous. All too often the word technology is synonymous with ugly. Self-conscious ugliness is bad morals and bad manners, and I want nothing to do with it. I forbear to speak of the disgusting paper which goes with these machines. They appear to be capable of working only on paper which is an offence against a great craft.

Am I making myself clear? I am no enemy of technology; I just want better technology, and if it is not available, I am happy to go on doing things the old way, even if it is the hard way.

I am sure that you have already grasped my point. Writing, either as an art or simply as a means of conveying necessary or desirable information, does not begin with technology. It is the job of technology to make such writing available to those who desire it, and at present it does that job with questionable literacy. Literacy is not just good manners: it is a guarantee of some measure of thought.

If this sounds obvious, I must assure you that it is not so to the schoolchildren who are now made familiar with computers at school, and often with word processors at home. Children delight in complexity, for good reasons; they have the whole complex world before them to discover and master. It is not quickly apparent to them that good writing has its origin not in complexity but in simplicity, and that speed and rapid reproduction have nothing whatever to do with it. Good writing belongs to a world and a concept of life and art which were already old when printing—which was the technological revolution of five hundred years ago—came into being, and the former laborious method of reproducing books by careful hand-copying was outmoded. Printing was a powerful force in the spread of democracy, and we all know that democracy means the rule of the many. But I will not be moved from my conviction that if democracy is not to prove a gigantic mistake, the many must have only the best, and that does not always mean the fastest or the easiest.

I must repeat: I am not an enemy of advanced technology, but technology touches what I do—which is to write books—only when the book has been given its form by the writer. And how is that done?

Nowadays the word "creativity" has become immensely popular. Everybody, beginning with the youngest child, is assured that something called creativity lies within his grasp, and that for his soul's good he must be as creative as he can manage. There is a good deal to be said for that idea, but when it is linked with democratic education, it can be mischievous. It is perfectly true that many people can draw and paint and make up tunes and write—after a fashion. Sometimes, in children, quite interesting things result from this conviction. But it is an indisputable fact that as people grow older this creative ability wanes and usually disappears altogether. Believe me, I speak from long experience as an editor and also as a teacher. It is in the realm of writing that I have the most experience and the most claim to be a judge. I have been on panels which have considered writing by amateurs, who feel themselves possessed of some gift, more often than I now like to remember, and it has been my experience that the older the contestants are in these affairs, the less truly creative they become. They want to write, but unhappily they want to write like somebody else, whose work they admire; they do not offer anything which is indisputably their own.

This is not wholly bad. Many writers have begun by imitating established masters, but very soon they discover that they cannot say what they themselves have to say disguised as somebody else. They must find their own voice and their own way of looking at the world, and follow that even if it means failure. But there are very many aspiring writers who never proceed so far as making that discovery. They are discouraged because their imitations do not quickly win them the recognition they want. And therein lies an important truth. They want *recognition,* and if writing will not bring it, they stop writing. What they want and—I apologize for the obviousness of what I am about to say, but many truths are obvious—what they want is to be *recognized as writers,* far more than they truly want to write. If they are real writers nothing—not failure or obscurity or misunderstanding—will stop them, and often it is a long struggle before they win any sort of acceptance. Sometimes, indeed, acceptance never comes. It has been my melancholy duty to read manuscripts by people who were undoubtedly writers in this sense of total commitment, but who lacked enough gift or talent to win them any attention from the world.

These words—talent and gift—are bitter words, for the thing they describe is not common, and no amount of effort and certainly no word processor or other appurtenance of writing will bring it into being.

Let me tell you a sad story. I knew a man who wanted agonizingly to be a writer. There had been one writer who was a member of his family whose ability the world had acclaimed. This man—he was a Canadian, and indeed a Torontonian (and, of course, nobody is more unquestionably a Canadian than a Torontonian)—had the good fortune, or the ill fortune perhaps, to be quite rich. So he secured for himself a fine house, and in it he fitted up a study which contained everything he thought a writer could need or wish. It was a panelled room with a fireplace in it, and it was hung with excellent pictures. There were cases of reference books and dictionaries and thesauruses and of course the works of many esteemed modern writers. It had a desk which was in itself an invitation to brilliant writing, because it was a costly antique, polished to the highest lustre. But he also had all the technological equipment that the innocent heart could ask—a magnificent electric typewriter, and a dictaphone, and a Xerox machine and God only knows what else, so that his inspiration could be caught on the fly, so to speak. Having assembled all this splendid equipment, he sat down to write. And he sat. And sat. And nothing came. Not long afterward he died. The doctors gave some scientific name to what killed him, but I have a powerful intuition that it was disappointment. You see, he wanted to be a writer, but that could not make him one. This is both a farcical and a sad story.

Let me tell you another, which is wholly farcical. I do not tell it simply to amuse you but because it contains several dreadful truths. I knew a man, knew him very well, who was a journalist, and a pretty good one. He could write acceptably about anything you gave him as a subject. This man had the mixed fortune to marry a woman who was extremely ambitious. I did not know her well, but she thought she knew me, and she was not impressed by what she knew. I wrote books. It could not, therefore, be beyond the power of an intelligent man with an ambitious wife to do the same. She said so, to several people. "If Rob Davies can write a book, Johnny can write a book," she declared; "I know he has a book in him." She was determined to get that book out of him, and she knew just how to do it. Every night she fed him, as well as her abilities as a cook made possible, and then she sent him to a room where there was a typewriter, and there he was to write his book, and when he was released at about ten o'clock, and rewarded with a bottle of beer, he was to show her what he had written. But after a few weeks the poor wretch could bear no more; he knew he was not writing a book, he was just spoiling paper, and he rebelled. He was too intelligent to deceive himself, though I think he might have deceived his wife. (There is more than one way of deceiving a wife.)

There is no use whatever trying to write a book unless you know that you must write that book or go mad, or perhaps die.

Let me explain at once that when I say *book,* I mean a work of fiction or poetry which has some claim to be regarded as a work of creation. I do not mean a travel book or a history book, or a biography, because although these books may be works of art if they are good enough, written with taste and elegance, they have their subject matter provided by travel, or world affairs, or somebody's completed life. Art may be manifested in the way they are written, but the original inspiration comes from somewhere outside the writer.

The kind of writing I am talking about was described in a short verse by Henrik Ibsen, that mighty, unforgiving genius who knew every sort of trouble and struggle that can come a writer's way. He wrote:

> To live—is a battle with troll-folk
> In the realms of heart and head:
> To write—is a man's self-judgement,
> As Doom shall judge the dead.

I have had those grim words always in my mind since I became a writer, and the older I grow the more I am awed by their terrible truth. Let us consider them for a few minutes.

The battle with troll-folk—what is it? It is impossible to make it really clear to people who have never experienced it, and they are many. The trolls are part of the dark forces of nature, and of mankind as a part of nature; they are the inadmissible parts of ourselves that we rarely face—if we ever face them—and of which we are ashamed, and by which we may be horrified. They are the parts of ourselves which suggest that we do mean things, dishonest things, grudging and vulgar things, even criminal things. They are the thoughts that suggest to us how convenient it would be if someone who complicates our life were out of the way—dead, perhaps. They are the thoughts that make us write a revengeful and destructive review of a book by a rival or someone we detest, making it seem that we have held the scales with the uttermost scrupulosity. They are the thoughts which make us deny promotion to a junior, simply because we do not like his table-manners. And they are the thoughts of a rejected junior, who thinks he has been denied promotion because of his table-manners, when everybody else knows that it is because he is not up to the job. They are the thoughts that make the judge find against the driver of the Rolls-Royce, when there has been a collision with a Ford, whatever the rights and wrongs of the case may be. It is the troll-folk who make mankind little and mean, and who also break up marriages, provoke murders, or cook the books of a charity to promote a political cause. It is the troll-folk who make us pretend that the worse is the better cause, and prove it with clever argument, for the trolls are greatly gifted in argument.

The troll-folk are everywhere and hard at work. In old mythology they are misshapen dwarfs who work deep in the mines, and many of those mines are in our own hearts and heads. As I said, there are plenty of people who say they never see the troll-folk. Watch out for those, because they are innocent, and after a certain age innocence is a dangerous quality.

The troll-folk, I may say, are brilliant technologists, because they had their beginnings as ingenious mine-workers.

So there are the troll-folk, against whom we all have our deeply personal struggle. Now, what about writing, which Ibsen says is a man's self-judgement, as Doom shall judge the dead?

I am often asked if any of my books are autobiographical. To most of these enquirers I answer that they are not autobiographical at all, because they do not report the facts of any part of my life. That is not a wholly honest answer, because the true answer is not something which children or literal-minded people can understand. There are people to whom the complex truth is less comprehensible than the simple lie. To ask an author who hopes to be a serious writer if his work is autobiographical is like asking a spider where he buys his thread. The spider gets his thread right out of his own guts, and that is where the author gets his writing, and in that profound sense everything he writes is autobiographical. He could not write it if he had not seen it and felt it deeply. Sometimes letter-writers tell me that the women in my books are wholly unreal, because they have never met any women like them. There is a rude answer to that sort of criticism, but the proper answer is: "Have you met women like Lady Macbeth, or Juliet, or Rosalind? When did you last meet a woman like Beatrice Esmond or Shaw's Saint Joan? Have you ever met a woman precisely like Becky Sharpe, or Lucy Ashton, of the Lammermoor Hills?" All of these women, who have become exemplars of many kinds of femininity, are the creations of men, and they seem to millions of readers to be as convincing as Jane Eyre or Mrs. Dalloway, who are the creations of women. Nor are women writers behind their masculine colleagues in their perceptions of masculine nature. Are there better portraits of a certain type of impotent, self-honouring scholar than Mary Ann Evans's portrait of Mr. Casaubon, or of bull-headed masculinity than Tom Tulliver, from the same splendid hand, known to fame as George Eliot? The work of the best writers is bisexual: the man finds the women in himself, and the woman finds her men in the same creative womb.

I know that most of you are familiar with the story of the woman who said to Gustave Flaubert, "How could you possibly explore a certain kind of female nature as you have done in your character of Madame Bovary?" To which Flaubert replied, with total sincerity: "Madame Bovary, c'est moi." The real writer deals not with masculine or feminine, but with human nature, as he has observed it in life and as he finds it in himself.

He does not make these discoveries easily or without pain. This is the self-judgement of which Ibsen speaks in the terrifying four lines that I have quoted to you.

Does he do it with a word processor? I do not say that he could not do so, for that would be very stupid. I say only that in the examples I have quoted, he has done it by a slower method, which gives unlimited time for reflection, and does not tempt to easy, exuberant work.

When I was asked to speak to you today, several questions were put to me, as themes which I might explore. One was: "Does a word processor change the way we think and create?" I believe I have answered that one already. It depends on what you suppose thinking and creation is. If you think it is work that can be hurried up and made easy, the answer is Yes. But if you understand that thinking and creation are extremely difficult work, the answer is certainly No. If you will pardon an impudent generalization, I think that if Shakespeare had owned a word processor he might have written not thirty-six plays in his twenty-odd years of work, but seventy-two or perhaps—if he

had really put on speed—he would have written one hundred and
eight. What they would have been like I leave it to some computer-
technologist to tell us.

I am not being wholly frivolous. Some of you may be acquainted
with the name or even some of the works of Lope de Vega, the Spanish
contemporary of Shakespeare who wrote something like 1,500 plays.
He is said by his admirers to present a picture of unparalleled mental
activity, but it is quite a while since one of his plays appeared on the
world stage. What he might have done if he had owned a word processor I shudder to think.

I am not, you must understand, presenting a case for the writer
whose output is small. That would be foolish, for most writers of great
stature have written a good deal. But mere bulk is not the measure of
a literary artist's capability. He does the best he can, and like a cow
we judge him by his butterfat content and not by the number of pails
he fills.

Again, I was asked to comment on "the synthesis of art and technology." I have done that; the art comes first, and then technology
puts it in a form by means of which it reaches the public. It cannot
be called a synthesis; the two processes are wholly different.

I am sure I need not labour the fact that with all technological
devices they cannot do better than the human creature who puts them
to work is able to understand and direct. I have been talking to you
about a quotation from Henrik Ibsen, the great Norwegian dramatist.
I quote him often, for he was a very wise man. Not long ago I quoted
him in an address which was transferred from tape to word processor
by a girl who had never heard of him, and I was astonished when my
address came back to me to find that I had quoted somebody—a
Scotsman, perhaps—named Henry Gibson. No technology is proof
against human error and human ignorance.

To return to the questions I was asked to consider in this speech,
one which is basic to the whole matter is, "Does a word processor
change the way we think and create?" I can't see how it can possibly
do so, unless we are so delighted with the machine itself that we allow
it to dominate us. Anything the machine can do happens after the

thinking and creating have taken place. Some consideration of what thinking and creating really are makes this abundantly clear.

It is possible to define thinking in elaborate terms, but perhaps you will allow me to define it as exercising the mind otherwise than by passive reception of somebody else's ideas. That covers a lot of ground. In the restaurant you say, "I think I'll have the salmon," when everybody else has chosen the roast beef. You have *thought;* you have made a personal choice; you have not tagged along after your friends. If you are a great philosopher, attempting to come to terms with the question of being, you may say, "I think, therefore I am," and immediately you have opened up a vast field of argument and speculation. It is this power of speculative thought which raises man to his pre-eminent place in nature. No other creature is so aware of itself in so many ways as we are. No other creature has knowledge of the remote past, or any power to influence the future. The higher animals possess some measure of choice, some ability to learn, some consciousness of themselves as separate from their fellows, but of our sort of thinking they are quite unaware. This power of thinking depends to a high degree on our possession of language—language of great flexibility and variety, which enables us to formulate our perceptions of the world with a consciousness of past and future, and of possibility.

What has a word processor to do with that? It can record, it can tabulate, it can assemble material of all kinds, but somebody must have thought of everything it does before it can do it. The word processor may speed things up, but as I have already said, speed is not always important to serious thought, and the necessity for speed—which the machine may impose upon a careless or innocent user—may reduce the value of what is thought. The machine is valuable only after the real work has been done.

As for creation, I do not think that a machine has any effectiveness whatever. For what is creation?

May we call it imaginative thought? That word "imaginative" opens up a world where no machine can intrude. What is imagination?

I do not want to get into a discussion of extreme complexity on this subject, though I cannot avoid the subject itself. I am not a philosopher, but I do work of a sort which is called creative, and I must confine myself to talking about what I know. And in order to do that I must talk of something which you may dispute, which is related not to philosophy but to psychology.

In this extraordinary century in which we live, we are all affected in some degree by what I may call the Freudian Revolution, which had its beginning exactly in the year 1900 when Sigmund Freud published his revolutionary book called *The Interpretation of Dreams.* Everything in that book rests on Freud's theory of the mind, which was not original with himself, because it had always been familiar to artists of all kinds, writers included. But Freud put it on a scientific basis, and proved it scientifically by his work with hundreds of patients; it has been extended and refined by the subsequent work of thousands of psychologists and psychoanalysts, some of whom disagreed with Freud about matters of detail, but all of whom begin their work with his discoveries and formulations. The effect of the Freudian Revolution has been to enlarge to an immeasurable degree our ideas about how the mind works and what the mind is. One of the things we now know, unless we have neglected the subject altogether, is that the mind works on several levels and that the process we call thinking is only one of these and perhaps not the most important.

It was Bertrand Russell, a philosopher who surely knew what he was talking about, who said that "intellect, except at white heat, is apt to be trivial." And how many of us dare say that we have ever thought at white heat? And what does thinking at white heat mean? Freud asserted that it was not the often superficial ratiocinative process, but something else which reached into another realm of the mind, which Freud and his followers call the unconscious mind.

What is the unconscious mind? It is that part of the mind which lies below the area of wholly conscious thought, in which there lies a mass of memory, recollection, emotion, and—this is what many people wish to reject—a great many things we did not know we knew but which may well up from the unconscious mind when it is working creatively. This sort of knowledge is most apt to assert itself suddenly, in a flash, and frequently surprises the person to whom it happens.

Creative people have always known this. Artists, poets, romancers, and also scientists know that they have always worked in this way. I included scientists because some of their most extraordinary revelations and perceptions of the nature of things have come to them in this way. Einstein of course worked out his revolutionary theory of relativity by long and exhausting thought; but the intuition that lay at its root came in a flash, and when it had come he did the hard work which proved that the flash was an overwhelming and scientifically defensible theory, and not just an illusion. We all know the story about Newton recognizing the theory of gravity when he saw an apple fall from a tree. The work by which he refined and asserted that astonishing insight is explained in his writing, and is plain for anybody to see, and it followed the fall of the apple. Both Newton and Einstein, of course, were ripe subjects for inspiration; they were certainly not scientific ignoramuses.

I once asked an eminent scientist—I will not name him but will content myself by saying that he was the last Canadian to be awarded a Nobel prize for his work—whether he got his best ideas in sudden intuitions, or by elaborate trains of speculative thought. He replied without hesitation that the intuition came first, and then the hard work was finding the intellectual means by which the intuition could be asserted as a truth, or at least a matter for careful discussion.

It is so also with writers, if they are writers of any considerable attainment. Frequently schoolchildren ask me, "Where do you get your ideas from?" The answer, which usually puzzles them is, "I don't get my ideas; they get me." That is the simple truth. Writers of many kinds have said the same thing, in different ways, for centuries.

I write novels, and a good novel is a work of art. How good my novels are it is not for me to say, but I try to make them as good as I can. A very good critic has said, "A truly great novel is a tale to the simple, a parable to the wise, and a direct revelation of reality to a man who has made it a part of his being." That sort of novel does not make its influence felt because it arises from a simple job of invention; it is rooted in something much deeper, something which comes at least in part from the unconscious mind, and which says something more significant about the story it tells.

What kind of thing? Nobody will be content with a single example, but we have not time for an extended discussion of this matter. Let us look at something that teaches you without appearing to do so. There are countless examples, but the one I bring to your attention is a novel which I expect many of you have read, even if you have not looked at it recently. It is Thackeray's *Vanity Fair*.

What is it? Everything is contained in the title. It is a story about some not very remarkable people, who live lives that are amusing to read about, but which in themselves are trivial and sometimes despicable. It is in part about a young adventuress called Becky Sharp who resents the humble station into which she is born and is determined to climb and claw her way into another kind of life where the world will have to take account of her. It seems to be about the surfaces of life and the pettiness and triviality of society. But every now and then in that book there is a sound like the tolling of a great bell, which reminds us that all this nonsense is played out against the march of history, against the fall of Napoleon, the making and breaking of nations and empires. And when we hear the bell we think: is this sort of life really worthy of rational beings? Is this sort of struggle what life is really about? How can people devote their energies to such petty achievements and foolish ends? And we realize what a very moral novel *Vanity Fair* is.

From what does it spring? From the life of its author, who had cause to know, if ever a man did, what the costs and exactions of a society life can be. As a young man Thackeray had a fortune, and it seemed that his future was a glowing one. But he foolishly blew away his fortune, and had to face the task of supporting himself as best he could. He fell deeply in love and he brought two daughters into the world whom he loved very much. But his wife became mad and he had to bring up his daughters without her, at a time when girls sorely needed a wise mama to launch them in society and show them how to take their proper place in the carefully ordered world. Thackeray had to be both Victorian papa and a mama as well. In middle life he fell in love with a woman who encouraged him until his love became a nuisance to her, and then she made her husband reject Thackeray with great cruelty and self-righteousness. And all through his life he was plagued by a particularly exhausting form of ill health.

Do you find any of this described in *Vanity Fair?* No, you do not. But the distillation of that experience, and the promptings of the unconscious mind of a true artist, brought about the great novel which still rings true, although the sort of society it describes has almost vanished from the earth.

I have done something in the last few minutes which is supposed to be bad criticism. I have linked the life experience of a writer with his work. But I cannot understand how it is possible to neglect what a man is and the way he lives when one considers what his artistic work adds up to.

The time is near when I must draw to a close, so I would do well to go over some of the things I have said, and try to pull them together. I was to talk about literature and technology, was I not? And what I have been saying suggests that what is important in literature is not to be approached by technological means, which belong to quite a different kind of life and work. Now, you may object that so many of the writers I have mentioned lived long ago, and are thus irrelevant to our subject. I don't agree. All the writers of whom we have any intimate knowledge have worked in the same way, through a most careful and respectful solicitation of their own unconscious processes, and by building upon what they bring to the surface.

I suppose that at some point I am expected to make some comment about my own work, though I am reluctant to do so. My novels have been both praised and disliked because of elements of what people call the supernatural in them, which strain the credulity of readers who insist that a novel must be an uncompromising picture of life—by which they mean what they themselves can see of life. But

I myself do not see life in tones of grey, nor do I believe that all human affairs are limited by what is called "realism," meaning a photographer's vision of what is obvious to the most limited inspection. I reject the term "supernatural." If I perceive something, surely it is natural? If there is anything unusual about it, it is the clarity of my vision. All my life I have been too much aware of the part that what we call chance, but which might also be called destiny, plays in everybody's affairs, and I have also been aware of the existence of ghosts where most people refuse to see them. I assure you that I do not mean spooks in white sheets; no, I mean the persistence after death of the influences of people who cannot be forgotten or discounted as influences in the lives of their children. Hamlet's father's ghost is no outmoded dramatic device in a play which is now nearly four hundred years old. It is a part of Hamlet's soul. There are many of you here who have not freed yourselves from the ghosts of your fathers, and perhaps more particularly of your mothers, and because they haunt you, they also haunt your children, your lovers, and sometimes even your friends. That is part of what heredity means, and it deserves careful attention. I try in my novels to come to terms with aspects of life which many people do not observe, or choose not to observe, but which I feel are determining elements in what we do with our lives. Need I emphasize that the promptings that move me to this sort of writing come from the unconscious, as well as from the most careful observation I can command of my daily life and the lives of the people about me? Life is not a movie-show, projected flatly on a flat screen. It is a drama, in three or more dimensions, with some of the most important things happening off-stage. I have described life as a World of Wonders, and my metaphor for that was a travelling show of freaks and cheats, and also of extraordinary people, capable of goodness and even on occasion of nobility. My novels are rooted in my own vision of life, and what gives them vitality comes as much from the unconscious mind as from unresting observation of the visible world.

Of course there is another element in the writer's work which I have not mentioned, because it is not immediately applicable to our theme.

But I must speak of it now, because to neglect it entirely would be to give a lopsided picture of what literature is.

It is a form of art, and all artists must work in some medium or other, whether it is paint, or stone, or pure sound—as with musicians—or with words, as writers do. The way a writer uses words is one of the things that defines him. He may be an extremely careful, conscious artist, like James Joyce in our own century, who takes many years to complete a book of great complexity and variety of meaning. Or he may be a writer like Dickens, who works at lightning speed, and seems careless of the technicalities of language, but who achieves extraordinary effects apparently by the profusion and diffusion of his means. This technical variety, I suggest, is not so much a matter of conscious choice as of the unconscious process, from which the writing springs. This is why it is quite impossible to write in the style of another person. There is always a tinny sound about such writing, because it has its origin in the wrong place.

Nor is it by words alone that the writer produces his effects. It is by the form he gives his book. There are writers whose work we can analyze almost as we analyze music, showing how brilliantly he produces his effects by the use of recurrent thematic matter, or by the assembling of paragraphs and chapters which seem to move at different speeds, and of which the careful reader must be heedful if he is to feel the full effect of what is written. A modern example is afforded by Sylvia Townsend-Warner, whose exquisite novels and short stories are still seriously undervalued. The writer may disguise great seriousness of purpose beneath an appearance of frivolity, which deceives imperceptive readers into thinking that he is no more than a funnyman. And here Evelyn Waugh gives us a brilliant example. Or the writer may seem to deal in simplicities, like Ernest Hemingway, but the simplicities are anything but simple in the effects they produce.

I could go on at length, but I shall not do so because I am sure you have taken my point. Once he has dredged the depths of his unconscious, the writer must clothe what he has to say in the garments most suited to it, and that is the second most important aspect of his art.

Inspiration first: the promptings that cannot be faked, or compelled to arise from the depth where they have their being. The style second: and that may be a very elaborate and consciously sophisticated creation, or it may be a simplicity which, as I have said, is by no means simple.

Now, do you think either of these things can be assisted—not to say evoked—by technology of any kind? If you do, I have spoken here in vain.

10

A CANADIAN AUTHOR

"Even now when I visit New York, I have a haunting fear that I may be detected as an unrepentant Tory, and tarred and feathered." When he was awarded the Medal of Honor for Literature by the National Arts Club in New York on February 24, 1987, Davies was conscious that he was the first Canadian to receive this signal honour. It was as a representative of his country that he chose to speak, and his reference to his own unrepentant Loyalist forebears and to tarring and feathering will resonate with all readers who are familiar with the New York scenes in *Murther & Walking Spirits*, in many ways the most personal of his novels.

Among the friends and dignitaries mentioned in the diary entry that follows, "Nick Meyer" is Nicholas Meyer, author of *The Seven Per Cent Solution* and a Hollywood film-maker; Jean Sutton Straus was then the province of Ontario's representative in New York; and Robert MacNeil, an ex-patriate Canadian, was a respected New York television newsman who has gone on to become a distinguished author.

His diary records the following impressions: *Dress and are ready when called for by Leslie and Joanna Garfield, who drive us to the National Arts Club, on Gramercy Park, a New York area unknown to us and reminiscent of London. The Club House is an old mansion, hideous in the 19th century manner, but also dignified and impressive and admirably suited to the sort of Club this is. Large, handsome*

rooms. A large crowd; they have had to have an annex to the din-
ingroom; this is a great compliment. . . . After dinner, speeches: Robert
Johnstone, our Consul General who spoke admirably, briefly, and in
terms that made me blush: said I was doing what Joyce had done—
"Forging in the smithy of my soul the uncreated conscience of my
race"—very flattering—but I think it's true, and brilliant of Johnstone
to discern it . . . Nick Meyer speaks with surprising eloquence and
grace. Jean Straus speaks charmingly and elegantly. Robert MacNeil
says what he thinks I have done for Canada. All this reduces me almost
to speechlessness, but speak I must. And I do, and it is received with
blush-making kindness.

O n such occasions as this, the speaker has obligations he cannot neglect without gross discourtesy. He must express his pleasure and gratitude for the award he has received at your hands, and I do that, with unfeigned enthusiasm. He must say how complimented he is by your presence, and once again I do so heartily. He must thank those who have spoken so generously of his work—and again I do so; their generosity is warming and encouraging, for I am at the beginning of yet another book and I need encouragement as much as if it were my first. He may suggest that he is unworthy of the award and of your friendly encouragement, but he would be unwise to do so with too much conviction for he may inadvertently carry his point, and you may feel that there had been some mistake. I accept this award without false modesty or demurral, because I think that it reaches beyond me toward a group of writers in my own country whom you have seen fit to recognize through me, and I respect and honour your intention.

Canada has come into the larger world of literature rather suddenly. We have always had writers, and some of them were good, though few gained a hearing beyond our own border. But in something like a quarter of a century Canadian writing has begun to take a place in the very large world of literature written in English (on this occasion I do not pretend to speak of what our writers have done in

French). Nor has our writing been confined to the English-speaking world; we have travelled widely to many lands, in many languages. Last month *The Times* of London said of our writers, "they have crammed a century of change into a generation." During a period when so many Canadians have been chattering in fashionable despair about a "crisis of identity" for our country, Canada's writers have been examining that identity and presenting it to the rest of the world. As Aldous Huxley has said, poets and novelists do more to form the idea of a national character than any other group in society. A national literature is a mirror in which the nation sees its face. Canadian writers have been busily silvering and polishing the mirror for home use, and at the same time painting a portrait which other lands have inspected with interest and friendly approval.

Geography is a great creator and conditioner of literature, and if there is one thing we Canadians have in undiminishing abundance, it is geography. Ours is the second-largest country in the world, the largest being, of course, our near neighbour, Russia. In our huge land mass we have a population not quite half the size of Poland. Our other near neighbour, yourselves, has a smaller land with ten times our population, but even so you are by no means crowded. Some Canadians, and some of them in high places, cannot stop comparing us with you, and demanding to know why we do not do some of the things you do, the way you do them. The answers these people give, when they choose to give an answer, are usually concerned with economics. But there are elements which go into the making of a people that are vastly more important than economics. The land itself is one of them, and the greater part of our country is more ancient than, for instance, the island of Manhattan, where we are at this moment. I cannot believe that this extraordinary antiquity—not antiquity of man, for it extends far beyond the era of man—does not affect our people, and do much to determine our character. With the land goes the climate, and ours is a climate that makes men watchful, reserved, and somewhat disposed toward melancholy. We have the chilly distinction of possessing the coldest national capital in the world, compared with which Moscow seems positively Californian. The land and the climate are all-pervasive, and we know that the blackest or most turbaned new-comer to our country will have descendants who will, within three generations, be Canadians in spirit.

Our history is not like yours, for you were born of revolution, and our roots are deep in a dogged loyalty. The people who first settled our country were not like your Pilgrims, or the handful of powerful aristocrats who settled in Virginia and thereabout. The stories of most of our earliest settlers were sad ones, and not the least unhappy was the tale of those supporters of the British cause who, at the time of your Revolution, were compelled to go north and begin life afresh. Many of my own forebears were of that group, and even now, when I visit New York, I have a haunting fear that I may be detected as an unrepentant Tory, and tarred and feathered. There is an element of loss and betrayal in our history which even yet tends to make us an introverted people, with the particular kind of inner strength that introversion implies. No, we are not like you, though if you come to our country on a visit you may not be strongly aware of having left the United States. But stay with us for a year, and the difference will be amply apparent. We do not wear our hearts on our sleeves.

Out of such people comes the literature I represent at this moment and which you have chosen to honour. Once again I thank you. But although I feel that I stand here for many others I must necessarily speak in my own character, and I should like to say some-thing about what it means to be a Canadian author, from my own experience.

I imagine that it is something like what it must have been to be an American author a century or a century and a half ago, when your country's literature was still young. Louisa Alcott wrote amusingly about the curiosity she provoked as "the woman that wrote the books." Of course, as a woman, she was a double oddity, for it was a time when people spoke patronizingly of "lady novelists." People rapped at her door when she was trying to work; they peered in at her windows; sometimes they managed to get into her house and stole pens from her desk; she was asked for advice on a variety of unlikely subjects; it was assumed that she lived a life of adventure and very possibly of dubious morality. It was assumed also that she had time to devote to any cause that anybody wanted to promote, and that she would be delighted and honoured to drop her work and hurry off to make a speech. It was also assumed that she was an ever-flowing source of her own books, which, as she obviously got them for nothing, she would be happy to give away.

Times have not changed greatly, but in our day the post office and the telephone have added new terrors to the writer's life. "Do you get many letters?" people ask me. Yes, I do get many letters. Not as many as if I were a film star, but sometimes more than I can cope with, because I have a conviction that every letter should be answered. If some one is kind enough to write to you saying that they like your work, common courtesy demands that they should be thanked. But it is not these courtesy letters that are vexatious. The troublesome ones are those that hold out offers of a position as a writer-in-residence at a university, somewhere—often very far away. Such a position would, the writers explain with disarming enthusiasm, give me a chance to be among young people and encourage young talent—possibly even to discover a genius. It is not easy to reply in evasive terms. The people who write such letters know very little about authors. What author wants to leave his workroom, where he is surrounded by happily familiar mess and disorder, to live in a university residence and eat residence food? He knows that he will get no work done while he is surrounded by young people, who may be delightful in their uninhibited youth, but scare off the Muse by their noise. As for encouraging young talent, most of the writers I know are doing their uttermost to preserve and encourage middle-aged or even elderly talent, and if they met an undoubted young genius they would probably poison him, as Salieri is supposed to have poisoned Mozart. Indeed, the dark side of the literary character, the shadow of the man of letters, seems to be unknown to the people who seek writers-in-residence. They think authors are jolly good fellows, and I cannot bear to tell them the truth.

Then there are the people who are looking for somebody to make a speech, and they think an author would be just the right person to fill a "slot"—they always talk about "slots"—in their program. Very often these speeches are to be made far away—as far as California or Texas—and the writers generously offer to pay the fare of the author, as well as a generous fee. Their goodwill and their generosity are overwhelming. But one must not underestimate their craftiness. They write now, in February, to ask for a speech to be delivered next February. Therefore the writer has to be ingenious in his refusal. It is no use saying that he is writing a book: surely he cannot make such a task stretch over a whole year? It is futile to say that on the date mentioned he must attend his grandmother's funeral; they will set detectives to work to discover that his grandmother is in robust health and shows no signs of decline. It would never do to write and say that the author does not really like making speeches, that he is of a shy and reticent character, and that the thought of facing an audience arouses all the skin diseases, catarrhs, and mysterious aches that he includes in his hypochondriac's repertoire. A man who is prepared to expose himself on paper must surely have no objection to facing an audience? Come on, man, rouse yourself and fly to Texas, where an eager audience awaits you!

What these kind people do not understand is the profound physical inertia of authors—and by authors I mean producers of fiction, and not explorers, or people who have written a book explaining how to attain sainthood by some special diet. Authors hate to move. Authors are Stoughton bottles.

Are there any among you who do not know what a Stoughton bottle is? Many long years ago, on this continent, there flourished an elixir, a cure-all, which had been devised by a man—I think he was a pharmacist of some sort, or possibly just a tent-show witch-doctor—called Stoughton, and he presented his nostrum in a bottle of a squat, broadly based appearance which seemed not to sit upon the druggist's shelf, but positively to have taken root there. And thus the Stoughton bottle became a byword for sullen inertia. My grandmother used the term frequently, and more than once she applied it to me. "Don't just sit there like a Stoughton bottle," she would say, unaware that she was addressing an embryonic author.

Ladies and gentlemen, behold a Stoughton bottle! I assure any of you who may feel some uneasiness about what I have said when I speak of speech-making in these terms that I do not include the sort of speech-making in which I am engaged at this moment. To speak to a sympathetic audience of literary people is quite a different thing from flying—O, most dreadful of all forms of travel!—to speak to an audience of strangers in Texas. In such circumstances as these I am quite a different creature—a Stoughton bottle transfigured. A Stoughton bottle with wings, you might say. Authors, or perhaps, I should say this author, will certainly make speeches, but not to fill slots.

The telephone is something quite different. Now and then I meet people who say, "Why don't you have an unlisted number?" There are two reasons. The first is a modesty which I know you will understand. Lord Byron once remarked that he did not mind having his portrait painted, but he felt that sitting to a sculptor for a bust was like making a pretension toward immortality. I feel the same way about an unlisted telephone number. To refuse to speak to people who want to speak to me demands a thickness of crust that I simply do not possess.

There is another reason—I said there were two—and it is this. The telephone certainly permits people to gain entry to your house whom you would not dream of admitting through the door. But it may also be a herald of unexpected good fortune. When my telephone rings, it is always possible that it is somebody bringing me good news, of a magnificent inheritance, or an offer to dine with the great or even the merely wealthy, on equal terms. Sheer curiosity, without which an author cannot exist, demands that I be available by the phone.

Calls announcing good fortune do come over the wire now and then, but less often than calls from high-school students who want help with essays; often they say encouragingly that they are studying a book of mine in class, and are at a loss to understand it. About a year ago I had a typical call, at nine o'clock at night, in which a young man whose voice was changing, said, "Say, are you the fellow that writes the books?" When I admitted that I had certainly written some books, he continued: "I've got to write this essay, and I have to hand it in tomorrow morning, and I wonder if you could give me some help with these-here Jungian archeotypes?" To hang up the receiver at that moment would have been the act of a stony-hearted monster; here, obviously, was a soul in torment, and so I proceeded to get myself into a proper mess. I explained that Dr. Jung's theory of archetypes was complex and not easily explained in a few words. Then, with goat-like and fatal stupidity I went on to say that an archetype was a pattern of experience common to all of mankind, and that the pattern was greater in its power than any individual experience of it. I said, thinking he would know about such things, that falling in love was an archetypal experience. "Like how?" said the boy at the other end of the line. I plunged even deeper. I soon became aware that what I was saying was, in Shelley's fine phrase, "pinnacled dim in the intense inane." I found myself trying to imagine, from the sound of his voice, what my enquirer looked like. With the awful folly of an author, I tried to shape my answer about falling in love to what I supposed he might have experienced. I attempted to enter into his feelings. "You have surely fallen in love?" I said. "Naw, I can't say I have," was his reply. Here was a Romeo who had not even met his Rosaline. How long I floundered on I do not know, but it seemed an eternity. His answers took on a tone of incredulity, changing to hostility. He seemed to think that I was evading his question, that I was toying with him in a whimsical and unfeeling fashion. "Am I supposed to tell that to my teacher?" he demanded. A vision of his teacher swam into my consciousness, and I lost my self-control and told him in unsuitable terms what he could tell his teacher, who had encouraged him to get me on the phone and make my life intolerable. "I guess what you're trying to say is—" he began, and I gave a scream of pain. "I'm not trying to say it: I've said it as best I can," I roared. He hung up in disgust and, I am sure, disbelief.

As a novelist I have been described by many critics as a moralist. I find no fault with that. One of our finest Canadian writers, Margaret Laurence, who died a few weeks ago, said that every serious novelist is at heart a moralist. My notion of a moralist—the belief on which I base my writing—is someone who observes the vicissitudes of life and tries to discern in them some patterns, some lasting truths that govern what happens to us as we meet whatever fate has in store for us. A moralist is not one who teaches a system of morality. He is someone who points out as interestingly as he can that if you play with fire you will get burned; that the dog returns again to his vomit and the sow that was washed to her wallowing in the mire; that two and two do not merely make four, but just as often they make twenty-two; that God, or the First Cause, or the Life Force or whatever you want to call it, is not mocked, and that the mocker will unfailingly get his lumps, and it is vanity to think that he may not get them in some other world than this, or in some aspect of this world of which he has no understanding. That is what I am saying, and saying it as entertainingly as I can manage.

Because, you see, I am strongly of the opinion that a novelist's job is to be entertaining, not in a trivial or shallow way, but in such a way that his readers will want to finish his book, and perhaps think about it. I know it is old-fashioned, but I do not myself like novels that set puzzles for readers, or snub readers, or determinedly abuse and bamboozle readers. Some years ago when Vladimir Nabokov was asked what quality he thought was of the greatest importance in writing, he replied that it was something he described by the Russian word *shamanstvo,* which he interpreted as meaning "the enchanter quality." I agree with my whole heart. As a boy I was captured, and have been held forever, by Sir Philip Sidney's description of a real, unmistakable writer: "he cometh to you with words, set in delightful proportions. . . . and with a tale, forsooth, he cometh unto you with a tale, which holdeth children from play, and old men from the chimney-corner." My dearest hope is that when all else has been said, that might be said of me.

Thank you for this award. I assure you that I shall cherish it.

II

LITERATURE AND

MORAL PURPOSE

∿୧୨୬

Davies was back in New York again three years later, this time to
give The Erasmus Lecture at the Institute of Religion and Public
Life on April 15, 1990. The theme—"how far literature may be
expected to discuss moral problems and what contribution it can
make to their solution, without being untrue to itself"—is one
that has engaged authors and critics, not to mention theologians
and dictators, down through the centuries.

Davies tackles the theme with great imagination. He also leav-
ens the high seriousness of the subject by dealing with "literature
which is moral before it is artistic," and in the process devastates
Little Men, Beautiful Joe ("Joe was a sort of Canine Christian, and
what was more, a Total Abstainer"), *Little Lord Fauntleroy,* and their
like. He also gives personal testimony about the creation of novels such as *Fifth Business:* "I assure you that as I wrote those books
I had no sense of moral purpose whatever. I have never thought
of myself as a moralist."

As a performer, however, Davies was a conscientious and
thorough professional. He prepared this particular speech two
months in advance, in time to incorporate, at his wife's suggestion,
the paragraph that mentions Hemingway and Faulkner and other
twentieth-century moralists. We notice that already, in February,
he knows just how long the well-polished piece will take to read
in performance in April: *Read the Erasmus to Brenda; she likes it*

but says that all the literary references are to 19th century books and should say something about living or recently dead authors. Very sound criticism and I insert a paragraph doing so, but explain that my chief references will be to an earlier day, and to acknowledged classics. Speech runs 50 minutes, without laughs or breaks; will be an hour in performance.

It is tedious when a speaker begins by protesting modestly that he is inadequate to the task before him, that he is the last person who should have been asked to discuss the theme of his address, and so on and so forth. We are apt to dismiss such wincing disclaimers as belonging to what Goldsmith called "The decorums of Stupidity." But the fact is that speakers often do feel inadequate to their task, and I am one of them at this moment. "Why, then, did you accept our invitation to speak?" you ask. I did it because I was intrigued by the theme you proposed, and wanted to think about it. I may even have been so vain as to suppose that I might say something illuminating about it. But as I thought, and wrote, and wrote and thought, I was driven to admit that I had bitten off a very large chaw, and that I could only chew a part of it. I understand that there is to be a discussion arising at least in part out of what I am about to say; perhaps you will be able to take the subject farther than I can.

The subject is "Literature and Moral Purpose." It is not a particularly engaging title, but your Director and I were unable to come up with anything better that was equally descriptive. What I am going to talk about is how far literature may be expected to discuss moral problems and what contribution it can make to their solution, without being untrue to itself.

I suppose I had better make some attempt to define or to give some general notion of what is meant by moral purpose. Is it not to give some guidance toward whatever is good as opposed to what is evil? At once we meet a difficulty, for in some parts of the world things are considered to be good, or at least within the bounds of reasonable conduct, which are condemned elsewhere. Consider pederasty and sodomy, for instance, which were tolerated in the pagan world, but which until about the middle of this century were thought to be immoral in the Christian and Judaic world. But now the Christian and Judaic world, or a considerable part of it, has done a moral U-turn and what was condemned is tolerated, if not countenanced, even among members of the clergy, who are expected to be moral exemplars.

Presumably this is because among the seven Virtues, the Natural Virtues are regarded as less needful to the good life than the Supernatural Virtues. If one has Faith, Hope, and Charity one may presumably manage with a smattering of Justice, Fortitude, Prudence, and Temperance. But these are very deep and stormy waters, and only subtle theologians can swim in them. As a literary man—specifically a novelist and a playwright—I must keep within the bounds of what I may be expected to know. And what I know is this: virtually all novelists, playwrights, and poets of serious artistic purpose become inevitably involved in problems of morality, but such writers are on dangerous and artistically ruinous ground when they allow their work to be dominated by moral purpose.

I cannot think of an exception to this statement; perhaps you can, and you will have your chance to object to what I have said. And I must make it clear that when I speak of literature I mean poetry, fiction, and drama. Philosophy and avowedly moral disquisitions I cannot discuss, because it is about imaginative literature that I suppose you wish to think today. But when I speak of great works of imaginative literature which have an avowed moral purpose I think at once of *Paradise Lost,* in which Milton the artist so overreached Milton the theologian that Satan emerges as by far the most interesting character in the poem, and we are all drawn to admire him; in *Paradise Regained,* where Satan is reduced from the proud rebel to a much lesser tempter and schemer, the genius of Milton seems to be less happy. Or consider *The Pilgrim's Progress,* which is remorselessly and unanswerably moral, so far as it goes, but which lives by the beauty of its style and its succession of vivid portraits and pictures. When we were children, did we ever want to be Christian, as we read that book? Would we not have yearned more toward one of the lesser roles, even that of Giant Despair? Reprobate children that we were, we thought that Christian was rather a pill, and that the others were full of exciting life.

Literature which is moral before it is artistic is rarely on the level of Milton or Bunyan. When I was a boy I was a voracious reader. I would read anything even if it were only the directions on a bottle of medicine. My home had plenty of moral literature on its shelves, and I was urged to read it, for my betterment. There was lots of other literature, as well, but I was—not forbidden, but discouraged—from reading it as it was said to be "beyond me" which I quickly discovered meant that it dealt with life pretty much as life was, and not as the determinedly moral writers wanted me to think. My parents had both been brought up in uncompromisingly Christian homes, and so we had many books which they had won as Sunday School prizes— which meant that they had good memories, rather than aggressively contrite hearts.

How awful those prize books were! I shall not bore you with too much detail about them, but I must mention one which was called *Striving To Help.* It was about a noble boy whose father was a business failure, through no fault of his own, but because evil men worked against him. The boy possessed a boy's printing-press, equipped with rubber type, and he single-handedly lifted his family out of despair by going into the printing business; he sought orders from temperance societies to print their notices, and thus he killed two moral birds with one stone, although evil boys often altered the bills he printed to give them a pro-alcohol bias. But he won through in the end, because right always triumphs. He was very decent to his father, and never rubbed it in that his father was a failure. To his mother, of course, he was an object of almost hysterical adoration. There was an Oedipal element in this story, which, at the time, I did not appreciate.

I have since wondered if some of those writers of moral tales for youth knew just what they were doing. Even Louisa May Alcott— unquestionably a writer of substantial gifts—included puzzling things in her books. Think of *Little Men,* which I read with avidity. One of the little men is a boy called Ned, and he is a boy of wavering moral character; but at Plumstead School he comes under the influence of Professor Bhaer, a German pedagogue, who had an unusual method of discipline. When Ned is naughty, the Professor does not punish him—oh, no—the Professor makes Ned strike *him* on the hands with the cane, as hard as he can, until Ned is reduced to tears, because he dearly loves and admires the Professor. Even as a boy I thought there was something decidedly kinky about the Professor. But did Louisa May Alcott know it? She was not wholly without kinks herself. But let us return to the noble boy in *Striving To Help*.

That boy made me feel very cheap indeed, for I too had a boy's printing-press, and it produced the messiest, worst-spelled and most despicable work that anybody had ever seen. The most abject temperance society would have scorned to employ me. Fortunately my father was not a failure, or my family would have sunk under the weight of my ineptitude.

Noble boys in fiction were the bane of my life. My family subscribed, on my behalf, to a journal called *The Youth's Companion*, which originated in Boston, and every month it arrived, heavy with tales of noble boys who imposed their moral superiority on everybody around them by much the same sort of admirable industry. In my dark heart I hated those boys. They were unfailingly noble in their behaviour toward girls, and I confess that there were times when my feelings about girls fell below their standard, because I knew quite a few girls, and they were divided between the voluptuously desirable, and beastly little sneaks and tattle-tales.

Only one thing saved me, I now believe. The boys in the Sunday School books were all English, and the boys in *The Youth's Companion* were all Americans—usually Bostonians. I was a Canadian, and I grew up believing that Canadians were different—a lower order of being, incapable of morality in its highest reaches. One of the satisfactions of being a Canadian is that one is not expected to be a good example.

I gagged on tales of moral animals, like *Beautiful Joe*. You may not have encountered this powerfully moral dog, who met with much of the world's evil in the form of wicked and cruel masters. But Joe was a sort of Canine Christian, and what was more, a Total Abstainer; Joe's lips never touched alcohol. But I knew a few dogs in real life, most of whom were idiots, and whose moral behaviour was well below Joe's standard, for Joe lived a life of unwavering chastity, and the dogs I knew did not.

I could not stomach *Little Lord Fauntleroy,* who presented me with the political puzzle especially hard for a Canadian. What was that boy, and what did he do? He was an American, but by chance he inherited a title and went to England and became a Lord, and thereafter was remorselessly democratic toward anyone who kept it firmly in mind that he *was* a Lord, and behaved accordingly. The Little Lord existed to hammer home two things that were presented as mighty truths: we must be democratic and we must recognize the moral superiority that goes with poverty. It was easy, I thought, to be a democrat if everybody toadied to you, and I wished that the Little Lord could spend a few days at the school I went to, where to be known as a tireless reader (for I could not conceal it) was to be an outcast. Many of my persecutors enjoyed the blessing of poverty but it did not seem to improve their characters. They were savage, jealous, and without bowels of compassion.

My sanity was saved by the books I read on the sly. Dickens, where evil people were plentiful and often rich, successful, and attractive. Thackeray, where snobbery seemed to be the mainspring of much of the action. Thomas Hardy, where life was complicated by opposed moralities and the uncontrollable workings of Destiny, and where God was decidedly not a loving Father. I did not know it at the time, but of course these were the works of literary artists who observed life with keen eyes, and wrote about what they saw, as their widely varying temperaments enabled them to see. When I myself became a writer, it was these whom I chose to follow, as best I could, and not the aggressive moralists.

When I went to Oxford I fell in with a young man in my college who had already been ordained as a Presbyterian minister. He found out that I had ambitions as a playwright and he conceived of a great scheme: we would collaborate on a series of plays based on the great moral tales of the Bible—The Sacrifice of Isaac, Moses and the Golden Calf, Naboth's Vineyard, and the like. I would write the plays, and he would supply the theology, the moral fervour, and zeal and keep me from going astray. I pointed out to him that in the eighteenth century Mrs. Hannah More had produced, in 1782, four *Sacred Dramas*, and they were *Moses in the Bulrushes, David and Goliath, Belshazzar,* and *Daniel*. Even the authoress could not really like them. She wrote: "It would not be easy, I believe, to introduce Sacred Dramas on the English Stage. The scrupulous would think it profane, while the profane would think it dull." My friend the young dominie was not daunted: we would succeed where Mrs. More had failed. But I was not convinced. In my childhood I had seen sacred dramas—*Queen Esther,* and *The Prodigal Son*—and even in such a stage-struck child as I they produced a profound ennui. I had a lot of trouble getting rid of that ambitious young parson, I may tell you.

It was because I had changed my personal definition of the word "moralist." For me it meant not someone who imposes a moral system upon his art, but someone who sees as much of life as he can, and who draws what conclusions he may. What courses of action lead to what results? Are there absolute standards of good and evil? To what degree is what appears to be acceptable to society rooted in the truth of a particular man or woman? To what degree may the acceptance of a popular or socially approved code of conduct define or perhaps distort a character? Where do the springs of behaviour lie; to what degree may they be controlled; how far is a human creature accountable to his group, or his country, or his professed belief (or unbelief) for what he does? How far is it permissible to talk of what a human creature "makes" of his life, and to what degree does an element of which he may be unaware in himself "make" his life for him? How far may we accept the dictum that life is a dream, and that we are creatures in that dream, which is being dreamed by something of which we have no knowledge? These, it seems to me, are the concerns of the true moralist. He is an observer and a recorder; he may not permit himself to be a judge, except by indirection.

In what I am about to say it may seem to you that I dwell heavily on writers of the nineteenth century and earlier, to the neglect of writers of the century in which we live. Of course there are many writers of comparatively recent times who might be discussed; one thinks at once of Hemingway and Faulkner in the United States, and of Graham Greene, James Joyce, and that resounding moralist Evelyn Waugh in Great Britain; Marcel Proust's great novel is virtually a long disquisition on vanity, and much might be said of Thomas Mann, of Günter Grass. In the drama, one of the most deeply searching moralists of our time is Arthur Miller, and in Britain Alan Ayckbourn, under the cloak of sardonic comedy, presents us with some complex moral problems. But of these and of more recent writers I shall say nothing, because the nearer a writer is to us, the more varied debate and opinion become. Therefore I have stayed with writers of an earlier day, about whose work the dust of dispute has in some degree subsided.

It may appear to you that I have weighted the scales unfairly against books of avowed moral purpose by talking of Sunday School prizes, and publications for children. Certainly there have been widely accepted works of fiction and drama that are not so simple. I think of the famous play *George Barnwell, or the London Merchant* which was written in 1731 and enjoyed something like 150 years of popularity on the stage. It was often performed on holidays as a moral warning to apprentices who, like Barnwell, might fall into the company of evil women and—what was worse—rob their masters. One thinks of *Uncle Tom's Cabin,* powerful both as a play and a novel. There were books like *Danesbury House,* which Mrs. Henry Wood wrote in 1860, and which won a prize of one hundred pounds from the Scottish Temperance League because of its description of the evils of drink; this was the first of Mrs. Henry Wood's remarkable flow of novels, all of which were extremely popular—and all of which were of a determinedly moral tendency. But their morality has not been able to save them, for a simple reason: morality changes from age to age and her morality was dictated by her society. The deeper truths about human nature, which form the foundations of great drama and fiction, are of more enduring stuff.

Compare, for instance, Mrs. Henry Wood's most famous novel, *East Lynne*, with Tolstoy's *Anna Karenina*. The theme is the same: a married woman falls hopelessly in love with a man who wearies of her; she destroys the peace of her husband, and is estranged from her beloved child; in the end, having ruined her life, she dies. But in *East Lynne* her infatuation is dealt with very heavily on the basis of what Mrs. Grundy might think. Who can forget the line from the play, spoken by the heroine's father: "O Isobel! you, an Earl's daughter! How utterly have you forgotten yourself!" Tolstoy treats Anna's defection as it reflects on the career of her husband, who is brilliantly portrayed as a wronged, if unsympathetic, man. But chiefly Tolstoy tells us of the moral destruction of Anna herself, of her abandonment to a passion which she finds overwhelming but which seems from the outside to be merely foolish. We see Anna's ruin and her final realization of what she is and what she has done, and her suicide. Anna Karenina is pitiable, and she is almost noble in her passion, but we cannot escape the realization that she is also something of a fool. Not so the heroine of *East Lynne;* she sins, and she is rapturously forgiven; much of her conduct must be described as sneaky, but nobody seems to care; she dies at last in a glow of virtue, mourned by her husband, whom she has treated badly, as if she had been an angel all her life. Anna dies because it is her fate. Lady Isobel dies, one suspects, to make all the other characters feel cheap.

Why has Anna Karenina lived, whereas Lady Isobel is forgotten by all except a few hobbyists like myself? Because in *East Lynne* the cards are all stacked to the benefit of the principal character, the repentant sinner, the woman whose sins are forgiven her chiefly because she is the heroine of a popular novel. But Anna Karenina is a human being, not a doll devised to perform in a doll's drama. Anna's faults are plain for all to see, and the morality of the novel dips far below the surface of what was considered moral in the Russian society of the 1870s. We read it now, in a very different moral climate, for its fine understanding of what may happen when passion overcomes prudence, which is a timeless theme, and the way in which Fate may intervene in an apparently ordinary life.

Of course not all fine fiction is written at the Tolstoy level. There are many literary artists who do their best to represent man in society, and man at odds with society, whose literary gift does not take them into the front rank of writers. A gift is not to be commanded. We know how grievously Tolstoy himself sank in the latter part of his career when he often wrote to prove a point and drive home a lesson, rather than to record what he saw and what he understood intuitively from what he saw. The genius of fiction seems to be always at war with orthodoxies, always resistant to established creeds because the literary artist is drawn toward those things which are exceptions to orthodoxy and which seem opposed to creeds. And this is not because literary artists are necessarily rebellious (though some have been so) but because they are wary and unrestingly observant. They are well aware of the sunlight, but they are driven also to examine the shadow that it inevitably creates.

If I seem to be talking as if writers have an orthodoxy of their own— an orthodoxy of unorthodoxy, so to speak—a determination to go against the grain of society, let me disclaim any such intention at once. Writers are not unrestingly intellectual in their approach to life; indeed, some acquaintance with the history of literature shows how far authors, in the main, fall below the determined intellectuals in their power of analysing and theorizing. I once got myself into some trouble by saying that authors are not, as a rule, highly intelligent. People attacked me and contradicted me because they were certain that anyone who can create plots and characters must be a person of powerful intelligence. But I defend myself by saying that I do not take intellectuality, as it commonly appears in society, with entire seriousness. The power to argue strongly, and what I may call the puzzle-solving and examination-passing cast of mind, is often the possession of people of arid and limited perception and uneducated heart. In art, and in science as well, it is the power to see what other people do not see, to jump to conclusions *and to be right,* to see through a brick wall, in short to be creative, that counts. Intuition is an abused word, but if we define it as the power to apprehend things without the intervention of a reasoning or logical process, we are talking about something which is not intelligence in the accepted sense of the word. Anybody who has tried it knows what a poor tool logic is when it is applied to questions of human conduct. A very great logician defined intuition as "the perception of shadows" and it is the perception of shadows that is at the root of the greatest poetry, and fiction, and drama.

Because they are not unrestingly intellectual, writers may not be strongly aware of the intuitive impulse that drives. Consider a novel which has survived for almost four centuries, and is still regarded as one of the great masterpieces of world fiction. I speak of *Don Quixote*, by Cervantes.

Its story is of the adventures of a gentleman whose wits have been turned by reading old books of romance and chivalry; he equips himself absurdly with miserable armour and an old and wretched horse, and he rides forth in search of adventures. Their story is not told with tidy literary art; it is a rambling and often coarse tale of the foolishness of a mad old man who is mocked, beaten, and humiliated until, on his deathbed, he understands the folly of his delusion.

The book is often read superficially. More often it is not read at all, by people who are nevertheless aware of it, because the story is familiar from stage, film, and operatic versions, and has given our language the word "quixotic," meaning actuated by impracticable ideals of honour. But if we read the book carefully and sympathetically we find the secret of its extraordinary power. It is the first example in popular literature of the profoundly religious theme of victory plucked from defeat, which has strong Christian implications. The Don, who is courteous and chivalrous toward those who ill-use him, and who is ready to help the distressed and attack tyranny or cruelty at whatever cost to himself, is manifestly a greater man than the dull-witted peasants and cruel nobles who torment and despise him. We love him because his folly is Christlike, and his victory is not of this world.

Is this what Cervantes meant? I cannot say, for I am not a Cervantist, but this is certainly what he wrote, and we know that such a book could not have been written except by a man of great spirit. This is the puzzle which has led some impetuous critics to assume that a writer is sometimes an *idiot savant* who writes better than he knows, and who, of course, needs critics to explain him to the world, and probably also to himself.

The theme of victory plucked from defeat, and the folly which is greater than conventional wisdom, is at the root of many novels. One of the best and most enduring is Charles Dickens's first success, *The Pickwick Papers*. When we first meet Mr. Pickwick he is an almost buffoonlike character, but when he is unjustly imprisoned his character deepens and he becomes aware of the misery and injustice which are part of the society in which he lives. By the end of the book Mr. Pickwick is a man of real worth. It is interesting and very important that Mr. Pickwick is dependent on his valet, Sam Weller, a streetwise youth who is to him what Sancho Panza is to Don Quixote; that is, an element of common sense and practical wisdom that is lacking in his master. When we think about it we see that the great virtues are exemplified in these four people: Don Quixote and Mr. Pickwick possess faith, hope, charity, justice, and fortitude, but they need their servants to supply prudence and temperance. A character who possessed all the seven great virtues would never do as the hero of a novel; he would be perfect, and in consequence unsympathetic, for we are impatient and suspicious of human perfection. But when a hero who has most of the virtues is partnered by a helper and server who has what he lacks, great and magical fiction may result.

Did Dickens know what he was doing? Here I am on safer ground than I am with Cervantes, for Dickens has been one of my lifelong studies, and I think he knew exactly what he was doing, in this and in all the novels that followed *Pickwick Papers*. Dickens's life showed him to be a man who was far from intellectual, and sadly astray in much of his personal conduct, but when he was at his desk he was in total command, and he knew very well that, after a shaky start, he was working with a great theme.

What, throughout his career, was Dickens doing? There are critics who insist that he was a great social reformer, a scourge of the society and laws of his time. So indeed he was, though a careful study of his work suggests that he was often *behind* reform rather than before it. His famous attack on the iniquitous Yorkshire schools that existed as places to conceal and forget illegitimate children, came after those schools had already been attacked and were in the process of being investigated. Certainly he attacked the Civil Service and the Court of Chancery savagely in *Bleak House,* but whether any changes resulted as a result is open to question. The world has a strong tendency to separate what it reads in novels from what it experiences in real life, and, although a reformer like Dickens may rouse public indignation, it is carrying things a little too far to attribute reforms to his interventions. Abraham Lincoln may indeed have said that Harriet Beecher Stowe's *Uncle Tom's Cabin* started the American Civil War, but one suspects that in his heart he knew better. So, was Charles Dickens moved by moral fervour when he wrote?

Yes, he was in part, but he was moved more strongly and effectively by something else, and that was the instinct of an author—a very great author—that worked within him. There were plenty of reforming writers in his time, and in some of them indignation burned more fiercely than it did in Dickens. There was one, Henry Cockton, whom you may well be excused for not knowing, who wrote a very popular book called *Valentine Vox* (1840) which was a furious attack on the private asylums for the insane which, during the nineteenth century, served very often as prisons for inconvenient relatives. There is some reason to believe that *Valentine Vox* had its effect in provoking investigation, but who reads it now? Why? Because Cockton was no Dickens and except for eccentrics like myself his book is unreadable. So, what was it Dickens had, which places him so high in the ranks of writers in English, that Henry Cockton lacked? It was the instinct, the nature of the author. Can it be defined? Let us try.

It was Plato who first said that we gain our knowledge of the world about us by means of four functions, which we may call Thinking, Feeling, Sensation, and Intuition. Thinking is reasoning, untinged by emotion; Feeling is the forming of what are now called "value judgements" on the basis of emotion; Sensation is the quality which gives us the physical reality of things—of height, depth, softness, hardness, distance, temperature, and all such palpable things; and last is Intuition, which is the perception of possibilities. We all have these four functions in some measure, but one is likely to be dormant and thus determines our approach to life. Please do not ask me to defend this opinion. If you don't like it, argue with Plato. I bring it up because it is useful to the present discussion. The author is likely to be particularly strong in Intuition.

It is Intuition that enables the writer to see beyond the facts of a situation, to embroider and extend their scope, and to discover possibilities which do not appear to the Thinker, for instance, or the Sensation man. I used to tell my students that every Monday morning the story of *Othello* was reported in the morning papers, but it took a Shakespeare to see its possibilities. I reminded them also that Henrik Ibsen said that he read virtually nothing but the Bible and the newspapers, because it was there that he found all he needed for his dramas. Human experience is not illimitable; the same things tend to repeat themselves in all our lives; it is the individuality of our response that gives them their personal quality. Dickens encountered the same poverty, squalor, meanness, magnanimity, and heroically endured pain in the London of his childhood that was met with by his boy companion, Bob Fagin, but it was his intuitive quality which enabled him to people the scene with Mr. and Mrs. Micawber, with Bill Sykes and Nancy, with Dick Swiveller and the Marchioness, with Uriah Heep and the grandiloquent Crummleses. I think it is superficial to say that he invented his characters; rather it should be said that he discerned them in the welter of life and experience that pressed upon him; he saw the gold in the ore, and he made the gold palpable to his readers, then and now.

The vitality of Dickens's work, I suggest, lay not in his indignation over long-dead abuses; there was plenty of indignation in Victorian England. It was in his extraordinary perception and illumination of the life that lay about him, inanimate as well as animate. He was not nearly so aroused about the incompetence and dishonesty of the hospital nurses of his time as he was fascinated by the incompetence and dishonesty of Sairey Gamp and her partner Betsey Prig; he did not care so much about the grinding slowness of the Court of Chancery as he cared about Miss Flyte, whom it had driven mad, and the

Jarndyce family, whom it impoverished. When he looked at the Lord Chancellor seated in his court, wigged and gowned and attended by all the splendour of precedent and ritual, he was not a lawyer who had reached the top of his profession, but Old Krook who sat in his nearby junk-shop surrounded, like the Lord Chancellor, by the dusty evidence of ruined households and broken lives.

It tells us nothing to say that Dickens was an artist. Why was he an artist, and what did his artistry incline him toward, as a writer? Not, I think, to causes far better pursued in Parliament and the newspapers, but to people and things and the raw stuff of life in which he saw wonders hidden from other eyes. If you want to find out what Dickens's opinions on social subjects were, apart from his novels, read what he wrote for the popular papers he edited; you will be astonished at how commonplace and un-Dickensian many of those articles are. The editor was driven by moral purpose: the great author was driven by intuition.

Do not mistake me. I do not say that Dickens lacked moral purpose; he had as much as the next man and more than many. But it was not moral purpose that made him a great writer.

There have been writers, and good ones, who have rejected any suggestion of moral purpose in their work. Vladimir Nabokov wrote, in a letter to a friend, "Writers have no social responsibility," and certainly he admits of none in his own novels. But in the three published volumes of his lectures on Western Literature he has to recognize the powerful social responsibility of Tolstoy and Dostoyevsky, to name no others. Unless one writes extremely astringent novels, as Nabokov himself did, it is difficult to avoid some influence of social responsibility because it appears to be something deeply rooted in human nature. Ever since *Aesop's Fables* mankind has had a strong appetite for stories from which a moral is drawn directly, or in which some moral attitude is implied.

If you truly want to discover what people expect from what they read, forget about great writers and masterpieces for a while, and look at the bulk of popular novels—the kind of novels that sell in the hundreds of thousands in drugstores and airports, and which are never reviewed in the literary papers. G.K. Chesterton, a perceptive and unjustly neglected critic, wrote in 1905, "Men's basic assumptions and everlasting energies are to be found in penny dreadfuls and halfpenny novelettes." To rise above that level, but to deal still with a genre of literature that is hugely popular, consider the detective novels that sell in such astronomical numbers, and are eagerly passed from hand to hand by enthusiasts. I do not suppose that many of their readers ever give a thought to moral purpose, but their attitude could be summed up as "Vengeance is mine; I will repay, saith the Lord." Scores of detective novels are rooted in the words of Exodus: "And if any mischief follow, then thou shalt give life for life, eye for eye, tooth for tooth, hand for hand, foot for foot." And in these stories, so various in their form and so widely separated in the kind of society they depict, who is the instrument of the Lord's vengeance, who brings the thief or the murderer to his just reward? It is the Great Detective, of course. Perhaps, like Sherlock Holmes, he is the Thinking Man, the cold reasoner. Or he may be the Man of Feeling, as in Chesterton's Father Brown. He may be the aristocratic Lord Peter Wimsey, or the immobile intellectual Nero Wolfe. In the work of Miss P.D. James, the acknowledged queen of the modern detective story, he may be Adam Dalgleish of New Scotland Yard, who is a poet when he is not on the trail of a murderer, and plainly a Man of Intuition. But whatever Platonic type he may belong to, anybody who has given even superficial attention to medieval religious drama recognizes in the Great Detective the figure called Divine Correction. He is the restorer of balance, and dispenser of justice, working on behalf of a higher authority.

What higher authority? The mass of readers might balk at calling that authority God, but they might agree to calling it Poetic Justice, the desire deep in the human heart to see evil punished, however delightedly as readers they may have bathed in that evil for two-thirds of the book.

Even in the much-abused television series, and the movies where the villains wreak hideous punishment on the Good Guys, the Good Guys must triumph in the end, or there would be outraged protest from armies of viewers.

You may say that in this the public is having its cake and eating it too. I make no denial. That has always been the public's way, whenever it can be managed. It is neatly summed up in the story about the little boy who burst into his mother's drawing-room, crying: "Ma— I caught a toad, and I bashed him and jumped on him and ran over him with the lawn mower till—(suddenly seeing the parson, who had come to tea)—till God called him home." The moral attitudes of the majority of people are not intellectually reasoned but they are deeply rooted. Evil must be punished, one way or another. But while the Evil is going on we do not want to miss a gunshot, or a blow, or a drop of gore. As an English satirist wrote, a century ago:

It's human natur, p'raps—if so,
Oh, isn't human natur low!

Perhaps, in a more generous mood, we may say that human nature is not so much low, as unreflecting. It is people like ourselves who have determined to reflect on this theme of literature and moral purpose, and I have put forward my opinion that literature at its higher levels must beware of allowing moral purpose to assume a dominant place in its creation. Moral purpose, if it asserts itself as it has done in much of the finest literature we possess, will come unbidden from the place where literature of the serious kind has its origin, and it will be part of the fabric of the whole work, and not something that can be abstracted and discussed as an element in itself.

Consider a novel acknowledged to be great, from the French Literature of the nineteenth century. I speak of Gustave Flaubert's *Madame Bovary* (1857). In it we follow the brief life of Emma Bovary, who is fated to live in provincial dullness, with a dull if worthy husband; she is not a woman of strong character or intellect; she has been sentimentally educated, and what intelligence she has is poorly employed; she seeks a broader life through ill-fated romances with men of no greater intellectual or moral stature than herself, and in the end she dies wretchedly, a disappointed woman. It sounds a dismal theme, but as Flaubert treats it, it is transfixing in its depth of understanding and its illumination of a kind of life that is led by millions of people. Is Emma treated by the author with compassion? No, she is treated with justice. Has the author no pity for Emma? It does not appear, but it is plain to the understanding reader that the author has great pity for mankind. It is not the pity that slops and gushes, nor would it be just to Flaubert to say that it attempts to be godlike. It is the pity of the observer, the recorder of things as they are, rather than as they should be.

It is significant that on a famous occasion when a lady said to him: "How could you write so profoundly about Emma Bovary? Where did you find your extraordinary understanding of woman's nature?" Flaubert replied: "Madame Bovary, c'est moi."

He spoke the simple truth. A writer finds his themes and his characters in the depth of his own being, and his understanding of them is an understanding of himself. This is not to say that Don Quixote is Miguel de Cervantes or that Mr. Pickwick is Charles Dickens in any simple sense. It is to say that Cervantes and Dickens are capable of the Don and Mr. Pickwick; they embrace the character, not because it is an obvious part of their own nature, but because it is a possibility which they are capable of seizing and bringing to a fictional life. They have intuitions of the Don and of Pickwick, as Flaubert had his intuition of Madame Bovary.

Incidentally, it is nonsense to say, as some extreme feminists say now, that a man is incapable of writing perceptively about a woman; nobody, so far as I know, has ever said that a woman is incapable of writing perceptively about a man. George Eliot, one of the truly great writers of the Victorian age, could draw men with a breath-taking verisimilitude and perception. It needs no genius from the genetic laboratories to tell us that in every man there lies a substantial, physical element which is feminine, and that in every woman there is a substantial genetic element of masculinity. Authors, it appears, have unusual access to this contra-sexual side of themselves, which is not only mental, but physical. Heavy books are written now to explain this androgynous element in human character, but great numbers of people of all sorts have always been aware of it, and artists of any significance have always been among their number. Perhaps we may say of the author what Walt Whitman said of himself: he is large, he contains multitudes.

You will expect me to develop this theme of intuition, and I shall do so, but it will be necessary for me to speak of personal experience, if I am to make what I say real to you. What I am about to say is not prompted by vanity, but by the fact that only by telling you what I know from my own experience to be true, can I hope to carry conviction.

When people speak of intuition they seem as a usual thing to mean some sudden leap in the dark, some instantaneous flash of enlightenment. Certainly that is intuition of one sort. But there is another kind of intuition, which is the slumbrous, slow-moving kind, and it is not so widely recognized.

Some years ago I wrote a book called *Fifth Business,* which attracted a flattering amount of attention. For six or seven years before I wrote it I was very busy about some work that demanded the best of my attention, it seemed, and all of my energy. I had been entrusted with the task of setting in motion a new college in my university, exclusively for graduate students. But however hard one works at a task, one is never totally absorbed in it. Personal matters, family matters, involvements of all kinds must be given their necessary attention. And in addition to these things, one is never free of one's fantasy life, or the life that asserts itself in dreams. During all the years that I was busy in the way I have described, I was visited from time to time by a scene which appeared in my fantasy life— when tired, or when dropping off to sleep, or when travelling in an airplane when a better-organized man would have had his lap full of papers and letters.

I have called it a scene, and that is what it was; the action in it was slight, but the picture was vivid. The picture was of a village street; it is six o'clock at night and as it is two or three days after Christmas it is dark; snow is everywhere. Two boys are in the street; one is hurrying home to his supper, and the other calls abuse after him and throws a snowball at him; I know that inside that snowball there is a stone and that it can hurt, and that it is meant to hurt; just as the snowball is about to find its mark, the first boy dodges suddenly in front of two people, a man and a woman, who are walking in the street, and the snowball hits the woman on the head; she falls to the ground.

There it is. An incident which takes about thirty seconds to act out. Does it mean anything? It recurred so often that I decided that it was stupid to ignore it any longer, so I called up the scene and invited my imagination to do what it could with that material. In a very short time I knew who all the people in the fantasy were, and what the outcome of the incident was. The book demanded to be written. And as I wrote, over a period of several months, the remainder of the story and its outcome appeared as they were needed. And not only did the story of *Fifth Business* appear, but other aspects of the same story which made up two subsequent novels, resulting in a trilogy.

I assure you that as I wrote those books I had no sense of moral purpose whatever. I have never thought of myself as a moralist. What I was writing about might be summed up in two themes: first, that the result of a single action may spread like the circles that expand when a stone is thrown into a pond, until they touch places and people unguessed at by the person who threw the stone; in my story it took sixty years for the flight of that stone-laden snowball to expend itself; second, I wanted to explore the matter of childhood culpability for evil-doing—may a child be guilty of true evil? And what may be the outcome of deeply felt childhood guilt?

These, I protest, are a novelist's themes and it was as a novelist that I treated them. I was surprised when some critics decided that I was a moralist. Of course there were moral aspects of my story, but to me they were of far less importance than character and incident. Character and incident were the results of intuition, not of careful intellectual work, and when critics wrote about the book as if I had decided on a moral theme first and then cloaked it in fiction, I was at once amused and indignant.

This, I am sure, is the way that real books—I mean books which are not simply manufactured for the market from themes popular in the market—get themselves written. They have already formed themselves deep in the unconscious of the writer, from which they can be coaxed, or dragged, when they will not emerge gently and readily. Before a word was put on paper, the book existed as a possibility.

This accounts, I think, for the unsatisfactory nature of some very great books, when they are looked at from the viewpoint of the literary critic. Critics appear to have in their minds some sort of Platonic Ideal of what a novel should be, and any novel that does not conform to that ideal they declare to be "flawed." I once asked a member of this Druid circle if she could name any novel to me which was not flawed. After melancholy reflection she declared that she could not. Even Henry James, the high priest of the finely crafted novel, showed flaws, at points where outraged artistic instinct refused to be bullied in the name of academic excellence. We all know these great, flawed books. *War and Peace* is a horror to the literary critic, but it is a work of unquestioned greatness. So is *Moby Dick,* which seems at times as if it would exhaust the patience of the most besotted reader. Dostoyevsky and Balzac never know when enough is enough. But would we wish to be without any of the great, flawed masterpieces? No, we would not.

Nor would we say that we valued them first of all for the emphatic moral purpose that unquestionably appears in them. Again and again as we read the great works of fiction—and I apologize for the fact that I have almost wholly neglected poetry and drama, but our time is not without limit—again and again as we read the great works of fiction we hear voices afar crying, "God is not mocked: For whatsoever a man soweth, that shall he also reap"; "The dog is turned to his own vomit again; and the sow that was washed to her wallowing in the mire." But can we find any evidence that these things were written up over the desk of the great author? Why then, do they assert themselves in his work?

I have said that I am not a moralist. Nor am I a philosopher or a theologian. So when I suggest, or tentatively hint, that perhaps morality is part of the structure of man, that it has some archetypal root, I am not speaking as anything but a novelist. You are the experts on the subject, and it is for you to say your say.

I am all ears. But I do not imagine for a moment that anything you say will change the way I write, for you are theologians and moralists and I am that quite different creature, an artist. Neither the greatest nor the least of my kind, but still—an artist.

Having said that, let me hasten to add that I do not use the word "artist" in any grandiose sense, nor do I claim particular status because I apply it to myself. The word, traced to its origin, means simply "a maker," and not necessarily a superior being, though, as Aldous Huxley said more than sixty years ago, we live in a time when anybody who chooses to call himself an artist seems to imagine that the world owes him a living. Literature is unquestionably an art, but we must be cautious in whatever claims we make for it.

Everyone is aware of the sad plight of Salman Rushdie who has offended the world of Islam. I shall not say anything about the rights and wrongs of that matter, because I do not know enough about it to do so usefully. But I was sorry when, in a recent public address, Mr. Rushdie appealed to what he called "the sacredness of art" to justify what he had written in *The Satanic Verses*. An age that has often urged us to regard the Bible simply as literature is no time to throw a cloak of sanctity over a novel. Art has no over-riding "sacredness" that lifts it above the other works of man. Some books, because of their splendour of conception and execution, are unquestionably art on the highest level, and are so valued. But their glory does not spill over onto the run-of-the-mill works of the journeymen of literature, and writers are on shaky ground when they think otherwise.

So, to sum up, I have given an opinion that literature may indeed have a moral purpose when the moral judgement rises naturally from the work of art and is answered by a strong inner conviction in the reader. Morality which is applied cosmetically to catch a particular taste is found in many books, but not in the best books. I have confined my remarks pretty well to fiction, and of fiction I may say that it is by its nature a secular form of art, taking the whole of life as its province, and impatient of bonds of any sort, including those of popular morality. But if, as I suspect, some moral purposes exist deep in the psyche of man, they are certain to rise to the surface in literature of the highest order.

I 2

THE MCFIGGIN FRAGMENT

It is ironic that this spoof of literary scholarship should itself surface long after its original publication in 1970, when it was specially printed for members of the Leacock Symposium on
October 30 of that year.

The Canadian humorist Stephen Leacock (1869–1944) was a
figure of special interest to Davies. Since much of his own early
writing—either in the *persona* of Samuel Marchbanks or his own
"Salterton" novels—was humorous, he found himself automati-
cally paired with Leacock. In fact McClelland & Stewart, the
Canadian publishers, asked him to write a brief critical biography
of Leacock, and in 1969 he actually interrupted the writing of *Fifth
Business* to produce it. A year later he delivered *Feast of Stephen*,
an anthology of his favourite Leacock works that is still in print.

Leacock and Davies had much in common in their backgrounds. Both were raised in Ontario and attended Toronto's
Upper Canada College ("Colborne College" in the Davies novels). There Leacock continued as a teacher, before eventually
becoming an Economics Professor at McGill and a popular best-
selling humorist almost from the publication of his first books,
Literary Lapses in 1910 and *Nonsense Novels* in 1911.

In his Afterword to *Literary Lapses* Davies called Leacock "a
great writer—one of the greatest we have ever possessed," but
he came to modify that opinion, regretting, in Judith Skelton

Grant's words, that "Leacock had simply not matured as a writer." But he admired Leacock's success as a performer. "People who went to Leacock's lectures laughed until they hurt themselves; they laughed until mildly disgraceful personal misfortunes befell them."

The three Leacock pieces referred to here are among his most famous. In Davies' words, "'Boarding House Geometry,' written by a man who had lived in seventeen different Toronto boarding-houses during his student days, could not be improved by the addition or subtraction of a single word." (Among the most famous Postulates and Propositions are these: "The clothes of a boarding-house bed, though produced ever so far both ways, will not meet;" and "Any two meals at a boarding house are together less than two square meals.")

In "Hoodoo McFiggin's Christmas," which lends its name to this piece, Leacock deals with the fate of young Hoodoo, "the son and heir of the McFiggins, at whose house I board," and whose Christmas presents are irredeemably useful and sensible.

The "McFiggin Fragment" is a high-spirited satire on earnest literary scholarship. Canadian readers will especially enjoy the solemn listing of "the T. Eaton Co." (the ubiquitous department store) as a source of the paper, while the all-important provenance of the document is established with the words: "It is sufficient to say that it has one, and it is a beauty."

A final thought: from 1942 to 1963 Davies and his wife and three daughters lived in the Ontario town of Peterborough, a place not unlike the "little town" (Orillia in real life) satirized by Leacock in his *Sunshine Sketches* and elsewhere. At one point Davies and another accomplished prankster, his Peterborough *Examiner* colléague Ralph Hancox, devised a carefully aged historical fragment that showed one of the town's revered founders in an unflattering light. Presented with this convincing but dismaying evidence, the worthies of the local historical society chose to suppress it, to the delight of the hoax's perpetrators.

The major desideratum in modern Leacock studies is a consideration in depth in his sources. Virtually until the present day the
unscholarly belief has been held that he produced his works from his
own unaided fancy; the absurdity of any such idea is immediately
apparent to editors trained in modern research techniques. Certainly
there were sources, and influences; if his value to scholarship is to be
established, as distinguished from mere popularity, they must be found.
Obviously the most desirable thing would be evidence that he wrote
all his work under the influence of someone else. A line-by-line comparison of Leacock's writings with those of Thorstein Veblen would
unquestionably yield much of value. Failing this (no grant can so far
be obtained for the many years of intensive work such a task would
entail) examination of Leacock's personal papers is the next best thing,
and we are pleased to be able to offer members of the Symposium this
fragment of a diary kept by Leacock during a very brief period in the
autumn of 1888, when he was beginning his second year as a student
at the University of Toronto. Its relevance as source material for later
works so varied as *Diner de Fameel at the Boarding-House de McFiggin*,
Boarding-House Geometry, and *Hoodoo McFiggin's Christmas* calls in
imperative tones for full scholarly treatment.

The Document measures 28 mm by 21 mm and is a single ruled
sheet torn from a Student's Jumbo Notebook originating with the T.
Eaton Co. (a firm of stationers active in Toronto at the relevant date).

Provenance: as two major Canadian universities are competing for
purchase of the document, details of its provenance must be withheld
for the present. It is sufficient to say that it has one, and it is a beauty.

Thurs. Sept 27: need a boarding-house & George says 12
Harbord St. pretty good. Run by a Mrs. MacFarlane. Fat. Tight
corset. Wants $1.50 per week for third-floor back room and full
board. Offer 95c. She says not a cent under $1.50. Got to $1.05.
An hour later we close at $1.45, but she throws in my laundry.
Meal times: breakfast 6:30 to 6:45, dinner 12:15 sharp, supper 6

sharp. Drag my trunk up. She follows, cautioning abt. linoleum. Can't help as Internal Organs do not permit. Room has bed and chair and window at floor level and iron rod for clothes behind curtain with funny stains on it.

Fri. Sept. 28: miss breakfast by two mins but make dinner. Cold corned beef. Eat a lot to balance off the bkfst. Supper, corn beef warmed, with limp cabbage, and tapioca pud. Meet family. Mr. MacFarlane works on street-railway. Has rupture. Says St. Rlwy a cruel boss. Son Homer a dude. Celluloid collar and dirty-shirt necktie which he calls Ascot; salesman. In anvils. Other board-ers one Potts, a printer at Ryerson Press. Literary. Quotes a lot. A Miss Bertha Buller, yellow hair and loud blouse. I ask her what she does. Homer laughs coarsely and Mrs. McF. says None o' that here now and flushes up from the corset. Miss B. says I am forelady in the Reconditioned Human Hair Works.

Sat. Sept. 29: meet Homer on stairs. Wears a clean celluloid col-lar that looks familiar. I say, Hey there, but he laughs and says Don't say Hay before my horse. Wish I could think of witty replies like that. But it looked like my collar.

Sun. Sept. 30: Mrs. McFarlane says no breakfast on Sundays. Irreligious to expect it. Sit in my room and brood. Sunday din-ner is corned beef and cabbage at room temperature. Homer and Mr. McFarlane wrangle abt. money and Mr. McFarlane shouts Boozer and Homer shouts Who are you calling a boozer you old no-hoper and Mr. McFarlane shouts You know well enough who I'm calling a boozer, and Mrs. McFarlane shouts Honour thy father and thy mother if you expect free board and room in this house & Miss Buller shouts Aw why don't youse all go into the alley if youse want to fight and Potts murmurs O Sabbath rest by Galilee, O still small voice of calm, and sneaks out. I fol-low him. Do you think Homer pinched my collar, I ask. He says, They knew he stole, they knew he knowed, they didn't tell or make a fuss but winked at Homer down the road and he winked back the same at us, Kipling. My advice is lock up your collars.

Mon. Oct. 1: after bkfst. I give Mrs. McFarlane notice I will be leaving on Thurs. She squawks and sort of faints against the stove and says you better give me a month's notice. I say no, I have read Landlord and Tenant and my collars are not common property. She says I am sharper than a serpent's tooth. I hope so. After Vandersmissen's class look for a new boarding-house.

13

READING

An invitation from Yale, perhaps the greatest of America's universities, drew Davies south to New Haven to deliver the prestigious Tanner Lectures in February 1990.

These two lectures, with their deceptively simple titles, reveal evidence of much hard work, which is confirmed by his diary. Some of this lecture's contents are surprising, with Tom Wolfe's then-current *Bonfire of the Vanities* finding itself in heady company. Both lectures later appeared in book form under the title *Reading and Writing*, published by the University of Utah Press, publishers of the Tanner Lectures each year.

February 20th. I lecture at 4:30: packed house and people sitting on the floor. But I cough horribly and find it a strain. But the applause is long and warm and everybody seems pleased. I am drenched in sweat and must change shirt.

There was a day when, if I were asked to give a lecture, I would search for some recondite subject on which I would be able to amaze my hearers and add to my reputation as a man of wide and various knowledge. But as time passes I find that either my hearers are growing wiser or I am growing stupider, and the likelihood that I can astonish them becomes more and more remote. So when I was asked to give the Tanner Lectures I decided that my best plan was to talk about things that everybody knows and attempt to stir up some discussion which would give the really clever ones a chance to show their strength. That is why my lectures bear the simple titles "Reading" and "Writing."

Every one of you, I am sure, reads and writes, and some of you do so professionally. That means, in our time, simply that you are paid to do it, and not that you are necessarily greatly gifted at those pursuits. Professionalism as applied to reading and writing is a subject on which I shall have some rather severe things to say, because I think the word *professional* is misleading and exerts a bad influence. I shall tell you why later. At the moment we must talk a little more of the actual words *reading* and *writing* and perhaps agree about what they mean.

Most people on this continent can read and write in some degree, though the number of those who cannot is disgracefully large. An astonishing number of those who can read and write think that they do so rather well. I spent twenty years as a journalist, and I met all kinds of men and women who prided themselves on what they called their "communication skills"; they would tell you, with an unconvincing show of modesty, that they thought they could write "a pretty good letter." It was my duty as an editor to deal with their pretty good letters, and I never ceased to be astonished at how badly people expressed themselves who did well in the world as lawyers, doctors, engineers, and the like. When they were angry they seemed unable to focus their anger; they roared like lions, and like lions they roared on no identifiable note. When they wished to express grief they fell into cliché and trivialized their sincere feeling by the awful prose in which they expressed it. When they were soliciting money for charity, they pranced and cavorted in coy prose, or else they tried to make the reader's flesh creep with tales of horrors that may have been true but did not sound true. I used to wonder what made them write as they did, and whenever I was able to find out I discovered that it was because of the dreadful prose they read and the way they read it. They admired cheap stuff, they imitated cheap stuff, and they appeared to have no understanding of how they cheapened their own minds and their powers of expression by doing so.

Do not suppose, however, that I intend to urge a diet of classics on anybody. I have seen such diets at work. I have known people who have actually read all, or almost all, the guaranteed Hundred Best Books. God save us from reading nothing but the best. But God deliver us from contenting ourselves with a steady diet of mediocrity, for it is mediocrity, rather than downright trash, that influences the majority of readers.

Very often nowadays we hear and read the pitiful wails of those who are convinced that reading is in deep decline. They blame television and the movies for this state of affairs. I wonder very often how they square their conviction that nobody reads with the evidence of bookshops everywhere and the proliferation of paperback books which, if not cheap, are at least cheaper than the hardback originals. Most people must be reading or so many books would not be published every year, and it is possible today to be very well read without ever buying a book in hard covers. The literary community, too, seems to be growing at an astounding pace. Wonderful young new writers are hailed every week by eager reviewers. You can hardly throw a stone in the street without hitting somebody who has written a book. People are ready to lay down money in quite substantial sums to listen to authors read, even though most writers are wretched readers. Has there ever been a time when the writer was such a cult-figure as he is today? Every time a writer brings out a book his publishers pay to ship him all over the continent so that people may gaze at him, and marvel at him, and ask for his autograph. Every time a young writer produces something, older writers like myself are entreated to write some words expressive of their awe and delight at the effulgence of his genius. The papers carry news of the large sums that authors are paid as advance fees, sometimes even before they have put pen to paper.

Ah, but there I go, exposing myself as a creature from a bygone age. These new writers do not *put pen to paper*—they put forefinger to word processor, the new device which is supposed to take so much of the pain out of authorship. I do not myself use a word processor, because I am what is now the fashion to call a technomoron. I have no skill with machines. I fear them, and because I cannot help attributing human qualities to them, I suspect that they hate me and will kill me if they can. However, I am here not to expose my ineptitude but to talk about reading. What I have been suggesting is that there is more reading today than ever before in the history of the world, and that most of it is of no importance whatever.

We all have to read far too much. Every day the mails bring us handfuls of material, of which some part must be read, or skimmed. If we are in business, or in the academic world, we have to read essays and documents relating to our work. It is unheard of now for a government body to bring out a report that does not run to a thousand pages; nobody can read it all, but many people must read some of it. We have to read countless letters, often simply in order that we may throw them away. We are deluged with stuff that must be read, and to meet the needs of busy people, procedures of speed-reading have been developed which enable anybody who has mastered the trick to grab the contents out of a mass of print without reading it seriously. Very often all the speed-reader gets out of his speed-reading is the intent of the material read: he does not assess its value, nor does he base his opinion of what is said on the way the case is argued. Indeed, he cannot be said to have *read,* except in the most superficial sense.

It is unfortunate that this craze for rapid reading has infected the universities, where, if anywhere, careful and considered reading and rereading ought to be the rule. Departments of English provide their students with Reading Lists which explain what writers and what works will be dealt with in particular courses. It is understood between the students and the faculty that nobody is expected to read all the books on the list; students are asked only to "acquaint" themselves with what is on the list, so they finish their year's work with a once-over-lightly acquaintance with a staggering array of masterpieces. I do not complain of this procedure: I do not even think it of doubtful honesty. I have seen it at work over many years, and it is a fact that students emerge at the end of the year somewhat less illiterate than they were when they went in. Can one reasonably ask for anything better? But has it anything to do with reading?

Of course it can be argued that reading too much is just as pernicious as reading too little. I can recall from my undergraduate days a girl who used to moan, when she was slightly drunk: "I've read everything on the Senior English course lists, and where has it got me?" What she meant was that her reading had not provided her with beauty, or charm, or sexual irresistibility. That girl had gobbled eight plays of Shakespeare, a play by Ben Jonson, all of *Pamela,* the whole eight volumes of *Clarissa,* eight novels by Dickens, one by Thackeray, one by Trollope, a large wodge of Henry James, a substantial vegetarian mass of Bernard Shaw and God knows what else, and at the end of it all her mind was as flat as Holland. All she had gained were thick glasses and a bad breath, doubtless the result of literary constipation. I once asked her if she had read Browning's *The Ring and the Book,* which was an enthusiasm of my own. She had not. She said it was "not required reading" and that was that. But T.S. Eliot was required reading, and she had read him to the bone, without any discernible effect. She did not even get a First Class in her finals. She was the most over-read girl I have ever known, but she still said "Between you and I." God deliver me from all such.

To speak only for myself, I read a great deal of varied material, including several newspapers. Perhaps because I come of a journalist family, I have never scorned newspapers as many people do. I have long been mindful of the words of Henrik Ibsen, who, when he was asked what he read, replied that he read only the Bible and the daily papers, and there he found everything he needed. And indeed, if you read the newspaper perceptively, you will find the great themes of the Bible, of Homer, of Shakespeare, repeated again and again. When I was a teacher I used to tell my students that if they thought the plot of *Othello* farfetched, they had only to read the Toronto *Globe and Mail* any Monday morning to find that the plot had been recreated and re-enacted in some suburb over the weekend. It is from newspapers that I collect such information as I have about the supposed present crisis in education. By no means all that is said looks backward to some imaginary time when the world was filled with keen and perceptive readers. I have a clipping from a letter to the *Times* of London, in which the writer declares:

> Your correspondent of October 15, 1990, bemoans the influence
> of television, and says it is the task of teachers to teach children
> to become readers. Surely the task of teachers is to make children more effective and critical users of information from all
> sources, of which television is one of the most important. I am
> a book lover; I have acquired many hundreds and written a few.
> But the day of the printed book which has been our staple
> source of information for 500 years, is now passing. Education
> must look forward, not back.

It sounds eminently reasonable, does it not? It has that calm, no-nonsense ring which impresses speed-readers. But I think the writer is wrong on several counts. I cannot believe that the day of the printed book is passing. A book is such a convenient object; you can carry it anywhere. You can go backward in it, and reconsider something that it said yesterday or last week. You cannot do that with television. The book can present abstract ideas, which television cannot; unless you can take a picture of something, it has no news value for television. Finally, I do not agree that education must look forward at all times; real education looks backward, and gives you a sense of the past against which to measure the present and forecast the future. Television is a good educational tool, but it has its marked limitations. The convenience of the book, as I have described it, will ensure a long life for it, unless we bring up a race that has forgotten how to read.

There are people who declare that we are doing precisely that. A revealing test was made, several months ago, by an international body which estimated the literacy—in which was included mathematical literacy—of twenty-four of the most advanced countries on earth. Unhappily, your nation (the United States) came twenty-fourth on the list. Do not think I am exulting; my country ranked twenty-third. The young people of this continent were found wanting in every important skill—and you will remember that mathematical skills were included. They read badly—which is to say that they could not intelligently relate the content of a paragraph of prose—and they could not express themselves in writing in simple, unambiguous, grammatical sentences. In your country this has caused an understandable uproar, and subsequent investigation has revealed that nearly a million children in the United States graduate from high school every year unable to read at the level expected of eleven-year-olds. Enlightened employers are spending heavily on remedial classes for secondary-school graduates. Think of that—the bosses now have to educate the workers because the schools have failed to do so. The New York Telephone Company recently rejected several thousand applicants for a handful of low-level clerical jobs because none could summarize a simple paragraph. When your Scholastic Aptitude Test authorities attempted recently to impress the school authorities with the importance of reading and writing, and attempted to introduce one—only one—compulsory essay as a test of analytical and communicative ability, radical educators, politicians, and other lobby groups protested that such a test discriminated against black and Hispanic Americans and recent immigrants. To put it bluntly, the inabilities of the disadvantaged minorities were to establish the standard for the nation.

So what is to be done? Is all lost? Not at all, but the salvation lies not with the government bodies but with individuals—with hundreds and thousands of men and women who decide that this diseased concept of democracy shall not prevail. Whenever I talk in this way—and I have been doing so for more than thirty years—somebody is sure to protest that I am proposing the establishment and recruitment of an intellectual élite. My reply is enthusiastic agreement: that is precisely what I am doing. What is an élite? Is it not a body which values the best above that which is less good? Your country has never hesitated to let it be known that it leads the world in certain respects. You do not insist that your national standard of living should be that of your humblest citizens. You do not inhibit scientific research lest some less fortunate country should feel left out and protest that your scientists are élitist. Your moral standards as expressed by your politicians are the wonder of less ethically grandiose folk; I have always thought your invincible morality was a heritage from the Pilgrim Fathers, who were so unremittingly moral that the Old World couldn't stand them for another minute and kicked them out. You do not conceal the fact that you are the wonder of the world. But in matters of intellect you are strangely unwilling to assert yourselves. Although many of the world's leading intellectuals are citizens of the United States, you do not, as a nation, take pride in the pleasures of the intellect, enjoyed for their own sake, as adjuncts of the truly good, well-rounded life.

I wish you would give it a try. But let me say at once that I am not calling for some great national movement, with a president and several vice-presidents, and innumerable committees, and of course a vast drive for funds, and fortnightly meetings, and prizes for those who recruit the most members, and special prices for the old and the crippled—excuse me, I mean the disadvantaged. Anything of that sort would be wholly against the kind of gentle but insistent change in the national life that I most earnestly wish to see. What I call for is a multitude of revolutionary cells, each composed of one intelligent human being and one book of substantial worth, getting down to the immensely serious business of personal exploration through personal pleasure. Your nation was born of revolution. Don't I know it! My Canadian forebears were Loyalists, who lost in that war and had to make a run for it to a new country. Why not another and equally decisive American Revolution—a revolution of the intellect? Why are we on this continent so afraid of using our brains?

Am I preaching to the converted? I wish I thought so, but you will excuse me if I have my reservations. I have known far too many university graduates, in this country and in my own, who, as soon as they have received the diploma which declares them to be of Certified Intelligence, put their brains in cold storage and never use them again until they are hauled away to the mortuary. What, you will say, do you speak thus of our doctors, our lawyers, our—God bless us all—our graduates in business administration? Yes, I do. Surely we all know scores of professional men and women who, apart from their professional concerns, seem not to have enough brains to butter a biscuit. They probably had intelligence once. But when their university had given them its blessing, they thought that enough had been done for one lifetime.

Anybody who cares about the matter knows that the intellect requires constant attention and renewal. The notion that someone who has graduated from a university has thereby been victualled for a long voyage through life as an intelligent human creature, is totally contradicted by common observation. And when I speak of intellect, you must not suppose that I mean merely that really rather humble ratiocinative ability—that power to reason about the ordinary concerns of life and to reach conclusions from given facts. I do not even mean that same ratiocinative faculty carried to a higher level, where it attacks complex, but still wholly finite problems. I use "intellect" to include all that vast realm of thinking and feeling that goes beyond the merely puzzle-solving work of the mind and establishes, so to speak, the very fabric and atmosphere in which life is lived and from which it is perceived. And when I talk of education I have no desire to belittle the powers of reason, but only to assert the power of *feeling*, the power of *sympathy* in the true meaning of that word, which enlarges our understanding of every aspect of our lives. We are quick to say that it is man's power of abstract thought that separates him from the animal world, but how rarely do we say that it is man's power to *feel* through a broader spectrum of emotion and sympathy that also makes him human—and, because human, capable of conduct that ranges from the godlike to the villainous.

There are many ways of educating our feelings, but I recommend reading as that which is most ready to hand. We can all do it. But *do* we do it?

I beg you to pardon me if I seem to stress the obvious in what I am saying. I do so because it is so obvious that it is often overlooked or undervalued. I do not suppose there are many present here who would dispute my statement that literature is an art, and that as an art it is able to enlarge and refine our understanding of life. But do we treat it as an art? Consider the care we take when we listen to music. Do we attempt to do so in a room full of people who are talking, and who interrupt us frequently for opinions? Do we increase the speed of the hi-fi in order that we may get through a symphony in time to rush away and do something else? Do we stop a recording partway through a movement because we have to fulfil some demand of ordinary life, then start the machine up the next day at the same place, to finish what the composer was saying? Do we skip here and there on the record or tape, looking for tunes that appeal to us, or rejecting passages of exposition that we find dull? No, of course we do none of these absurd things and would condemn anybody who did do them as a barbarian who had no feeling for music. Why? Because we regard music as an art, and our civilization demands that serious and sometimes almost religious attention be paid to it.

Literature, however, is something quite other. It is the drudge, the unconsidered odd-job man of the arts. Who among us can say that when he reads he does not rush, and skip, does not stop in improbable places, does not indeed commit the literary sin against the Holy Ghost, which is to gobble a book in order to be able to say that he has read it, without having given the book a fair chance to declare to him why it should have been read?

I have already agreed that much of the reading we have to do is unworthy of anything beyond superficial attention, but when we take up a book that is a work of art, or is so intended by the author, should we not treat it better? The worst offenders in this realm are book reviewers. I know, because I have been a reviewer myself, and I have been ashamed of the superficiality with which I read books in order that I might be able, within a certain fixed time, to deliver some sort of opinion about them. One's opinion about a book should surely rise slowly from the impression that the whole book has made, perhaps a considerable time after it has been read. Of course that cannot be the way a reviewer works, but certainly we should bear this fact in mind when we read reviews, which are written often in great haste, to establish the reputation of the reviewer, rather than to give a careful assessment of what an author has worked very hard to make as good as he can.

Now I am going to talk about the way in which I think a book *should* be read, and if what I say seems unbearably simple-minded I ask you to hear me to the end. First of all I think it is desirable to put aside some time for reading—perhaps an evening, or an hour, or half an hour, or even fifteen minutes, but a time in which to read and do nothing else and pay no attention to anything but the book.

We can read any way we please. When I was a boy, and was known to be fond of reading, many patronizing adults assured me that there was nothing I liked better than to "curl up with a book." I despised them. I have never curled. My physique is not formed for it. It is a matter of legend that Abraham Lincoln read lying on his stomach in front of the fire; you should try that in order to understand the extra-ordinary indifference to physical comfort that Lincoln possessed. I have read about children who "creep away into the attic" to read, and Victorian children's stories are full of children who cannot read any-where except in a deeply embrasured window seat. You have to find your own best place for reading, and for most of us in the Western world it is sitting on a chair with a decent light—though for Lincoln-ians, of course, firelight is the thing. I have forgotten those people of whom it is said that they "always have their noses in a book." This makes reading difficult, but as I have said, you must suit yourself.

You then read your book, somewhat more slowly than modern edu-cationists recommend. Remember, you are trying to find out what the book has to say. You are not straining to reach the end, in order that you may read something else. If you don't like the book, you do not have to read it. Put it aside and read something you do like, because there is no reason at all why you should read what bores you during your serious reading time. You have to read enough boring stuff in the ordinary way of life, without extending the borders of ennui. But if you do like the book, if it engages you seriously, do not rush at it. Read it at the pace at which you can pronounce and hear every word in your own head. Read eloquently.

I know this is heresy. People who teach reading are dead against what they call "verbalizing." If you verbalize, you lose time. What time are they talking about? Time is one of the great hobgoblins of our day. There is really no time except the single, fleeting moment that slips by us like water, and to talk about losing time, or saving time, is often a very dubious argument. When you are reading you cannot save time, but you can diminish your pleasure by trying to do so. What are you going to do with this time when you have saved it? Have you anything to do more important than reading? You are reading for pleasure, you see, and pleasure is very important. Incidentally your reading may bring you information, or enlightenment, but unless it brings pleasure first you should think carefully about why you are doing it.

Everybody used to verbalize as they read. Indeed during the Middle Ages people read aloud, and everybody knows the story about the scholar who had to discontinue his studies because he had a sore throat. Because they verbalized—I hate that word, but I can't find another—they truly took in—drank in, one might almost say—what they read and it was impressed on their minds forever.

Verbalizing is also one of the best critical procedures. If you meet with a passage in a book that seems to you to be, in some way, dubious or false, try reading it aloud, and your doubts will be settled. The trick of argument or the falsity of emphasis will declare itself to your ear, when it seemed to be deceiving your eye. Lots of young people come to me to ask my advice about writing. I haven't much to give them, and if they think anyone but themselves can teach them to write, they are sadly mistaken. I am fond of a story about Beethoven, who was approached by a young man who asked how to become a composer. "I cannot tell you," said Beethoven; "I really don't know." "But you have become a composer yourself," protested the young man. "Yes, but I never had to ask," was the answer. I tell the young people who come to me to try reading their work aloud, to see how it sounds. "Oh, but I'm not writing for performance," they say. "Oh, yes, you are," I reply, and often they are mystified. But in truth writing *is* for performance. The great works of imagination—the masterworks of poetry, drama, and fiction—are simply indications for performance which you hold in your hand, and like musical scores they call for skilled performance *by you,* the artist and the reader.

Literature is an art, and reading is also an art, and unless you recognize and develop your qualities as an interpretative artist you are not getting the best from your reading. You do not play a Bach concerto for the solo cello on a musical saw, and you should not read a play of Shakespeare in the voice of an auctioneer selling tobacco.

The business of verbalizing, of reading so that you hear what is read with the inner ear, is an invaluable critical method when you are reading poetry. Much of what passes as poetry is perishable stuff. Not long ago I was making a comparison between the *Oxford Book of English Poetry* as it appeared in 1900, edited by the late Sir Arthur Quiller-Couch, and the latest edition, edited by Dame Helen Gardner. It was an astonishing revelation of change in taste—in the taste of scholars of great reputation who as critics command respect. But I permitted myself—critical worm that I am in comparison with these godlike figures—to wonder if Sir Arthur and Dame Helen had taken the trouble to read aloud all that they offered to the world, with justifiable confidence in their authority, as a survey of the best verse of five centuries. Had Sir Arthur ever really tested "A garden is a lovesome thing, God wot," on his tongue?* If he had done so, could he have missed that what he took for honey was saccharin? Perhaps so; there are elements in literary taste that seem not to be things of reason but of something relating to time, which determines taste. When Dame Helen includes

> Lay your sleeping head, my love
> Human on my faithless arm†

most of her readers will applaud, but what will readers say in another seventy years? Modern disillusion is unlikely to last forever, and nothing rings so hollow as the angst of yesteryear.

Reading to hear, rather than merely to comprehend, explains much

---

* Thomas Edward Brown, "My Garden."
† Wystan Hugh Auden, "Lullaby."

about the poetry of earlier days. Old ballads, which seem somewhat simple-minded, with their bleak stories and their repeated refrains, when they pass over the eye, leap into vivid life when they are heard, because they belong to a tradition of poetry which has not renounced the delights of rhyme, rhythm, and the quality of incantation which our distant forebears valued in poetry. Poetry which has decided to do without music, to divorce itself from song, has thrown away much of its reason for being, and a recognition of the element of music in poetry narrows the gap between, for instance, Keats and Byron, which might appear to a reader who had never *heard* them to be almost unbridgeable. Until quite recently there was an academic fashion for looking down on Tennyson, who was said to be mellifluous but simple-minded. But *listen* to Tennyson, and his music will tell you something that the closest sort of mute analysis cannot do, and his stature as a poet is restored and perhaps increased thereby.

I have been talking about poetry, and I do urge you to renew your acquaintance with it, if by chance you have not been reading much poetry lately. Perhaps this is the point at which I should advise you, if you are reading for pleasure, to read several books at once, and to keep on your table a book of poetry, as well as a novel, some essays, and perhaps a play or two. The notion that you have to read solemnly through one book before you can allow yourself to take up another is simple Puritanism, probably left over from childhood. If you choose to be an epicurean reader, which is what I am recommending, there will be times when nothing but poetry will satisfy your appetite, and you must have poetry readily at hand. Perhaps you like to keep up with what the young poets are doing, and that is admirable, but I urge you also to read some poetry that has been tested by time, and which does things that the moderns do not seek to do, or perhaps—I say this almost apologetically—cannot do. One of the things I miss in modern poetry is joy, exuberance, sheer delight in life. That is a quality that preserves a poet marvellously.

Ty hye, ty hye! O sweet delight!
He tickles this age that can

> Call Tullia's ape a marmosite
> And Leda's goose a swan.

Who writes charming invitations to pleasure in a kind of splendid gig-
gling frolic like that nowadays? Not the people who write lyrics—if
they may so be called—for rock music; their joy seems to have its
roots in disarray of the mind. But the little squib that I have just
quoted springs from joy that is unalloyed, and it was written in a time
when the plague and war and the ill will of nations were just as prevalent on the earth as they are today, and the average expectation of life
was about thirty-two years.

I myself have a taste for Browning. There are times when nothing
but Browning will do. He is not particularly musical, and that is odd,
because he is one of the few poets who was a technically trained and
skilled musician. His language is knotty and there are times when his
reader feels like

> The old man of Ashokan
> Who loved to chew wood, mostly oaken;
> Very often he'd quip
> With a smile on his lip,
> Ah sho' can gnash oak in Ashokan.[*]

Browning's tough colloquialism used to be held against him, and as
an undergraduate I encountered professors who would quote:

> Irks care the crop-full bird?
> Frets doubt the maw-crammed beast?[†]

—and then go off into paroxysms of dusty academic mirth at what
they thought was Browning's wilful clumsiness. But once you have

---

[*] Morris Bishop.
[†] Robert Browning, "Rabbi ben Ezra."

accustomed yourself to his voice, Browning has golden things to say, and I have been a lifelong champion of *The Ring and the Book,* which is neglected by many readers because it is long and intimidating. But it is also a very great poem, and you do not have to read it all at once. But to sense its worth you should read in it, and reread, at various times in your life. Frequently it recalls to me the Loathly Damsel of medieval legend, who was repellent at first encounter but who, when embraced, changed into a girl of inexhaustible charm, wisdom, and beauty.

What I have just said about rereading is a point I should like to stress. The great sin, as I have said, is to assume that something that has been read once has been read forever. As a very simple example I mention Thackeray's *Vanity Fair.* People are expected to read it during their university years. But you are mistaken if you think you read Thackeray's book then; you read a lesser book of your own. It should be read again when you are thirty-six, which is the age of Thackeray when he wrote it. It should be read for a third time when you are fifty-six, sixty-six, seventy-six, in order to see how Thackeray's irony stands up to your own experience of life. Perhaps you will not read every page in these later years, but you really should take another look at a great book, in order to find out how great it is, or how great it has remained, to you. You see, Thackeray was an artist, and artists deserve this kind of careful consideration. We must not gobble their work, like chocolates, or olives, or anchovies, and think we know it forever. *Nobody ever reads the same book twice.*

Of course everybody knows that, but how many people act upon it? One of the great achievements of literature in our century is Proust's *À la recherche du temps perdu;* in the edition I have it runs to twelve convenient volumes. In my experience people tend to read it when young, and never to look at it again. But it is not a young person's book. Of course young people should read it, but they should go on reading it or reading in it during the life that follows. When I read it as a young man, the homosexual exploits of the Baron de Charlus seemed extraordinary dispatches from an unknown world; nowadays, when one can meet a mini-Charlus every day of the week, the extraordinary quality has gone. But what has not gone—what is indeed freshly understood—is Proust's serious and compassionate treatment of this theme in a book of many themes. Charlus is one of those great characters whom we know better than we know most of our contemporaries, and his creator's attitude toward him and his tenderness toward the Baron's dreadful disintegration enlarge our own sensibility, and give us a different attitude toward excitable protests on behalf of "gays"—as for some reason they are called, in our own very different, un-Proustian society. The Baron would have shrunk from being typified as "gay."

So it is also with another towering creation of this century, James Joyce's *Ulysses*. One cannot, of course, measure what Molly Bloom's magnificent soliloquy at the end of that book has done to enlarge and reshape our ideas about women, but one knows that its influence has been vast. When Sigmund Freud asked his supposedly unanswerable question—"What do women really want?"—he had not read what Molly wanted or he would have phrased it differently. It is not that she *says* what she wants, but she makes us *feel* what she wants, and it is something far beyond the range of any sociological or psychoanalytical answer. Molly wants to live on a mythological level, and that certainly does not mean that she wants to posture as a goddess or indulge in any pseudoclassical antics; it means that she wants a largeness of perception, a wider dimension of life, a psychological freedom that the modern world does not give her. She wants a rich simplicity. And that is the whole thrust of the book. Unaware of the fact, Leopold Bloom and Stephen Dedalus are living out a great classical theme in their dingy Dublin lives, and the greatness of what they are doing eludes them. Eludes them not because they are stupid—they are nothing of the sort—but because it is part of our fate never to see our destiny as a whole or discern the archetypal forces that shape our lives. Molly does not see these things either, but she has an intuitive sense of them, and thus she is able to long for them when the men, corseted in reason and logic, cannot draw so near to this aspect of truth.

Ulysses is a wonder, and we can recur to it time and again with the certainty of finding new pleasures and new insights. It is also one of the funniest books in our language. The fun lies not in obvious jokes;

it is in the grain of the prose, and it rises from the extraordinary mind of the author. When we read, we must always be aware of the mind that lies behind the book. Not that we may be wholly persuaded by it, or that we should have no minds of our own, but that we may share it and be shown new meanings by it. Also that we should assess it. When I was a professor I seemed to meet a great many students who were wholly possessed and beglamoured by Oscar Wilde, and some of them were, for a few weeks, mini-Wildes, dealing extensively in *réchauffé* wit of the 1890s. Sometimes I suggested that they examine, not the refulgent surface, the shot-silk elegance of his prose, but whatever they were able to discern behind it of the mind that had created such beautiful things. It is a Fabergé mind, and although we should not like to be without Fabergé, we should not wish to make him our standard of artistic achievement. There are people who insist that Wilde ranks with Congreve as a great writer of comedy. Consider both minds: Congreve was wise—worldly wise as well—in a degree that Wilde never achieved, kindly, good, generous, fatuous man that he was.

Joyce is an Irishman of a different stripe, and Wilde's admirers might describe him as a dirty-fingernails writer. If Joyce's fingernails are dirty, it is because he has no objection to grubbing in the dirt, if the dirt has anything to tell him. And he has taught us one of the lessons of our century, which is that the dirt has very important things to tell us, because it is from the dirt that we all spring, and no disease is so fatal to an adequate understanding of life as over-refinement, which is inevitably false refinement. For refinement of feeling is surely a quality we bring to everything we touch, and not something which cuts us off from a great part of human experience. Modern hygiene has banished much of the physical dirt of an earlier day, but the lessons that are hidden in the dirt must not be forgotten.

Of Joyce's other remarkable book, *Finnegans Wake,* I shall not speak, because I have not yet come to any conclusions about it. I know few people who have read it, and of those, I meet fewer still who appear to me to have come anywhere near to understanding it. I grope in it, holding a candle that is plainly marked "Manufactured by C.G. Jung and Co., Zurich." It is not a candle that Joyce would have approved—he hated Jung because Jung told him something he didn't want to hear—but the Jungian candle is the only one I have.

I hope you do not think that I am being trivial, or treating you with less than proper respect, because I am talking so much about novels. When I was an undergraduate there were still academics who thought novel-reading an inferior sort of literary enjoyment. But a good novel has its roots in life as surely as a good poem and usually more truly than the work of most essayists. It was when I was young that I read the opinion of a critic—popular at that time and now almost forgotten—John Middleton Murray, that "a truly great novel is a tale to the simple, a parable to the wise, and a direct revelation of reality to a man who has made it part of his being." I have never forgotten that, and I test the novels I read by its acid, seeking for gold, for gold plate, and for dissembling brass.

The simplest function of the novel is the tale, but only someone who has never tried it thinks that the discovery and relation of a tale is simple work. The wish to be told a story never dies in the human heart, and great storytellers enjoy a long life that more subtle writers sometimes envy. Consider the stories of Sherlock Holmes. Unless you are beglamoured by them, they are queer reading. The mysteries that confront the great detective are tailor-made for his style of detection; they are puzzles suited to a particular puzzle-solver. Confront Holmes with a simple back-street murder or theft, and he would probably have to confess his inferiority to the Scotland Yard bunglers he despised. But the tale-telling is so skilful, the contrast between Holmes and Watson so brilliant, the upper-middle-class level of crime which is all that Holmes will touch (you observe that he has no truck or trade with the likes of Jack the Ripper) is all so deftly handled by Arthur Conan Doyle that he has created a legend that seems to be increasing sixty years after the death of its creator. Will Virginia Woolf last so long? It seems to me that I see the mists closing in as her novels give place to scandalous revelations about her life.

Then comes the parable. What is a parable? A moral tale, is it not? Such novels are very popular because, whatever appears on the surface, our time loves a display of moralism; innumerable novels are rooted in

the words of St. Paul: "Be not deceived; God is not mocked: for whatsoever a man soweth, that shall he also reap." That is the message of
Tom Wolfe's hugely popular best-seller *Bonfire of the Vanities*. What is
its message? It seems to be couched in modern, rather grotty language:
keep your nose clean; don't risk everything for the big bucks; never trust
a dame. But behind this street wisdom is the wisdom of Paul, served
up with the pepper and tabasco that persuades so many innocent readers that they are getting something undreamed of in the past.

Now, what about the book which is a direct revelation of reality?
We all have our favourites, and they are the books that accord with
the reality life has brought to us. We cannot hope to grasp total, all-
embracing reality. For many people these are the great blockbusters—
novels like *War and Peace, Crime and Punishment, The Magic
Mountain, Middlemarch, Remembrance of Things Past.* I have known
people who found this sort of revelation in *Don Quixote,* which I can
understand but not accept as my own; I have known others who found
it in *Tristram Shandy,* which I confess puzzles me. One must find one's
own great novels, which seem to illuminate and explain portions of
one's own experience, just as one must find the poetry that speaks
most intimately to oneself. For one reader it is Shakespeare's *Sonnets,*
for another Wordsworth's *Prelude,* for another *The Ring and the Book.*
And so it would be possible to go on elaborating and extending lists,
because the choice is great and individual preference the final factor
in making a choice. And in addition to these milestones on the most
travelled roads, the real enthusiast for reading will find byways, like
the works of Rabelais, or Burton's *Anatomy of Melancholy,* or the mag-
pie accumulations of John Aubrey. It is absurd to speak of these books
as byways, but I do so because I do not meet many people who read
in them frequently, or indeed at all.

How dull he is being, you may think, as I draw near to my conclusion. How like a Professor. He is simply parroting Matthew Arnold,
with his tedious adjuration that "Culture is the acquainting ourselves
with the best that has been known and said in the world, and thus
with the history of the human spirit." But I assure you that I mean
no such thing, and I have always had my reservations about Matthew

Arnold, who was too cultured for his own good; he seems never to have listened to the voices which must, surely, have spoken to him in dreams or in moments when he was off his guard—voices that spoke of the human longing for what is ordinary, what is commonplace, vulgar, possibly obscene or smutty. Our grandparents used to say that we must eat a peck of dirt before we die, and they were right. And you must read a lot of rubbish before you die, as well, because an exclusive diet of masterpieces will give you spiritual dyspepsia. How can you know that a mountain peak is glorious if you have never scrambled through a dirty valley? How do you know that your gourmet meal is perfect of its kind if you have never eaten a roadside hot dog? If you want to know what a masterpiece *The Pilgrim's Progress* is, read *Bonfire of the Vanities,* and if you have any taste—which of course may not be the case—you will quickly find out. So I advise you, as well as reading great books that I have been talking about, read some current books and some periodicals. They will help you to take the measure of the age in which you live.

I hope you are not disappointed in the advice I have been giving. Certainly I have not flogged you on to feats of endurance and intellectual stress. Quite the contrary, I have urged you to relax, to read more slowly, to reread books that speak to you with special intimacy, to act out your fictions in your minds, as if you were a great theatrical director with infinite choice in casting, in decor, in all the adjuncts that produce a convincing atmosphere. I have urged you to allow your poetry to sing to you so that you may hear the authentic bardic voice wherever it is to be found. This is reading for pleasure, not to become immensely widely read, not to become an expert on anything, but to have read deeply and to have invited a few great masterpieces into your life. Again, I suggest that you should read deeply, rather than widely.

Many years ago—it was in 1960, in fact—a book of mine was published by the late Alfred Knopf, called *A Voice from the Attic;* it bore that curious title because one of our Canadian poets had described Canada as "one and none, pin and pine, snow and slow, America's attic," and I was speaking from that attic. When it was published in England it bore the less provocative but probably more descriptive title

The Personal Art—and that personal art was reading. Its first chapter was titled "A Call to the Clerisy," and it said rather the sort of thing I have been saying in this lecture. It proposed that an educated class should recognize itself in North America, and take into its own hands the literary influence which had been pretty much abandoned to the universities and the academic critics. By an educated class I certainly did not mean people of substantial means with university degrees; I meant anybody who knew how to use a public library and did so with zeal and devotion. I expressed no enmity toward the academic critics but I did say that I thought their professionalism and the need they had to establish personal reputations made them less-than-perfect guides for the public at large. I called for the rise of self-recognition of a group of readers whom I defined as "those who read for pleasure, but not for idleness; who read for pastime but not to kill time; who love books but do not live by books." And to that group, the members of which are to be found everywhere, I applied the almost forgotten word *clerisy.* It is not so aspiring as *intelligentsia,* which is a word that frightens many people. I once had a friend who was applying for a position in a large financial house—a rather senior position—and when he was being interviewed by the Big Boss, the Big Boss said, rather truculently: "Do you consider yourself a member of the intelligentsia?" "No," replied my friend, "a member of the intelligentsia is what I aspire some day to be." I need hardly tell you that he did not get the job. Rich people are usually afraid of an intelligentsia, because intelligentsias have so often been used as stalking-horses for revolutionaries. But *clerisy* is a mild term, one might almost say a Trollopian term. It could not frighten the most neurotic banker. And the clerisy do not want to take anything from anybody; they merely want to recover what was their own in those distant days before so much of our intellectual life was abandoned to the universities. They want to have a say in the world of books. They want the world of books, through them, to have its influence in the national life—social and political. To return, somewhat apologetically, to Matthew Arnold, they want the history of the human spirit to have its influence in the history of our own times.

14

WRITING

In his diary entry for the second Tanner Lecture Davies used the Virgilian Latin expression for surprising news when he reported on the curative powers of "nose drops and whisky": *Mirabile dictu, get through without so much as a cough and am greeted with long and enthusiastic applause. Brenda says a triumph. So now hard part of the work is over.*

In the first lecture I talked of reading and now the theme is writing, but of course you understand that the two are inseparable for the purposes of such a discussion as this. With respect to reading, I am only one voice among millions, but in matters of writing I may claim to be one among thousands, for, although it sometimes seems that everybody in the world wants to write, comparatively few really do so in any serious sense.

Like every author who has achieved even a modest measure of success, I get bagfuls of letters from aspiring writers who ask me questions that make it plain that they are unlikely to do anything very much in that art—for it is an art when it is practised creatively, and by that I mean in the writing of poetry or drama or fiction, and in a slightly lesser degree in the writing of philosophy, history, and essays. As you see, I exclude criticism, for although some critics do write admirably in the technical sense, I cannot persuade myself that their work is creative. If they wish to disagree with me—and as a usual thing they do—that is their privilege.

The people who want to be writers are often seekers after a formula, or even a magic spell, which they are hopeful will bring them to their heart's desire. For they are very serious—serious, that is to say, in their desire to be known as writers, though they are often reluctant, or unaware, in everything that is involved in the actual work of writing. They think that a writer is a romantic creature, widely admired and amply rewarded. So they write to me—and to thousands of other writers, I am certain—asking, "How did you become a writer?"

If I have time I give them an answer, because I take them seriously and think that if they are sufficiently determined to write to me it is common courtesy to reply. But my answer is unlikely to give them comfort, because I tell them that I never became a writer: I was born a writer. My family, even beyond the confines of my parents and brothers, were writers, by which I mean that they were journalists ranging from simple reporters to writers of political comment, essays, reviews, and editorial opinion. Consequently I grew up supposing that everybody wrote; wrote to order, to length, and to time, and received payment for it. I think I must have been at least twelve years old before I became aware that not everyone writes and that indeed many people find it a task of daunting complexity and difficulty. But I was bred to the trade, and at school, and later, I was a great enterer of contests where money prizes were offered for essays. "That's *my* money," I thought, without any particular vanity; I knew I could get it, I delivered the goods, and I got it.

Apart from this confidence, I had other advantages. My parents were strict grammarians, and my brothers and I learned the English language by ear, which is not wholly a good way to learn, because I still have trouble identifying grammatical structures by name, although I know them as matters of usage. Any publisher's reader can throw me into confusion by asking technical questions. Not only were my parents grammarians, they were demon pronouncers and enunciators, and often there was a dictionary on the family table, to be a guide in pronunciation and usage, and I well remember the scene of Homeric mirth and derision when my older brother pronounced "truculent" as if the first syllable were "truce."

I think this was a good way to bring up a boy to be a writer. Acrobats start their children on the high wire as soon as they can walk, and a writer ought to begin before he has graduated to solid food. But as you will see, not everybody has my good fortune, and I can hardly offer the people who write to me Mrs. Poyser's advice: "You must be born again and born different."*

I know several writers, and they did not begin as I did. They became writers because that was their destiny, I suppose.

If somebody is truly a writer, he will find it out and he will understand that if there is any romance attached to the vocation, it is balanced by a number of unromantic circumstances, for the biographies of writers make it clear what a tough and enduring breed they are. There have been writers who have burst upon the world, to its astonishment and delight, but most writers have to establish a reputation over a period of time. That is where the toughness comes in; early discouragement is the rule, and much work is done before important lessons are learned.

Speaking for myself, my great wish was to be a playwright because the theatre was, and still is, the chief pleasure of my life. But I wrote seventeen plays before I found that I was not to be a playwright, because my conception of comedy was not to the popular taste. I was thirty-eight before I turned to fiction and fared rather better, though I swear I was writing my novels from the same source, and in the same vein, as I had written my plays. So I became a novelist and an essayist.

Another question that my letter writers often ask is, "When do you write?" To which the only honest answer is that I write when I can. For the greater part of my life, the luxury of devoting the best hours of the day to my writing has been denied me. I have no one to blame but myself. I have always had a job. For twenty-one years I was a

---

* George Eliot, *Adam Bede.*

journalist, and for much of that time the editor of a daily newspaper. I was then invited to join the faculty of the University of Toronto as— this is ironical for a failed playwright—a specialist in English drama. I was also appointed as the head of a college for graduate students. Thus for forty years I had a full-time job, and I wrote usually at night, when the day's work was done.

I do not in the least regret it. To begin with, my job meant that I was able to pay my own way as a writer. I have never received a grant to enable me to write, and I value that freedom very highly. I could not square it with my conscience to take money to enable me to do something that I was not sure I could do—and I swear to you that I have never set to work on a book with complete confidence that I would be able to finish it in a way satisfactory to myself. I have been criticized for my attitude toward grants to writers. I am told that the modern grant-giving bodies are the descendants of the aristocratic patrons of the past. My only reply is that Dr. Samuel Johnson seems to me to have said the final word on those aristocratic patrons, and I do not believe that their modern descendants are really indifferent to what happens to the money they hand out. Nothing—including grants—is for nothing. We hear much high-minded prattle in these days about the writer's freedom, and I think he best asserts his free- dom when he refuses to take money from anybody to do what he himself has chosen as his life's work. Robert Graves has said that a poet who writes for money will be rejected by the White Goddess, from whom all true poetic inspiration comes. I think this is true of all seri- ous writing and I do not think Graves's reference to the White Goddess either fanciful or superstitious: she is the only real patron and if you are not content with her patronage she will not care. But in the final summing-up, rather than in the royalty statement and the pub- lisher's returns, it is her patronage that will mark you as an artist or merely a glossy hack.

For academic projects the rules are probably different, but for the creative writer I see no possibility of accepting handouts and main- taining total freedom. Let the writer get a job, and look after himself, and be under no obligation to call anybody "Massa."

There was another reason why I thought my best course was to earn my living as I pursued my work—by no means remunerative for many years—as a writer. It kept me in touch with the world of realities. If you read the lives of writers, you will find that very few of them have been reclusive. Flaubert was so, but not Stendhal or Balzac. Dickens's life was a whirlwind of charitable obligations. Tolstoy ran a large estate. Dostoyevsky met the world at the gaming table, and Proust met it in the salons of the aristocracy. Anthony Trollope was a senior civil servant. I will not burden you with a tedious list of examples, because I am sure you know the truth of what I am saying. The worst thing that can happen to a writer is to draw in upon himself and his work until he knows nobody except other writers; he is then reduced to the literary desperation of writing a book about a man who is writing a book, and when he does that we know he is finished. I was always glad of the association with a wide variety of people that my work, first as a journalist and then as an academic, made necessary. I particularly valued the association with people much younger than I that the university made inescapable. It is very bad for a writer to become imprisoned in his own generation.

I have another point to make about the value of doing something in the world other than being a writer. The daily task keeps you from writing too much. You are not obliged to keep bread in your mouth, and in the mouths of your wife and children, by snatching at every occasional article, by attending political jamborees as a "special observer," by patching other people's work together to make a television program, or accepting commissions to write things for big corporations that look like books but are in fact a low form of hackwork. Even if you are a successful novelist, it is not in your best interest to have to bring out a book every year in order to please your public and build up an income from paperback sales. I am sure we can all think of writers who write far too much; their talent has become diseased, hypertrophied because of continual gross and indecent solicitation of the imagination. If you reply that Balzac and Dickens did it, I invite to you look at the infinitely larger number of writers who have done so to their hurt.

How the work is actually done is in part an exploration of drudgery, of daily application, of heaping up the pile of finished pages as the beaver builds his dam. But if you are really a writer, you probably like that drudgery better than anything else you could possibly be doing. It is during those hours of drudgery that you are most in touch with what is of greatest value in yourself. You are creating something, and therefore you are to some extent an artist; you are doing it by means of the technique you have painstakingly acquired, and perhaps mastered, and therefore you are a craftsman, and there is a special delight in plying one's craft.

Again I recur to the questions I am asked by the people who write to me. Young people—schoolboys and girls who are put up to this kind of pestering by their teachers—often ask, with youthful bluntness, "Where do you get your ideas from?" My usual, perfectly honest reply is, "I don't get them; they get me." If you have to rummage around finding something to write about, perhaps your vocation is less insistent than you suppose. Often these young inquirers read a book of mine—read it once, in the desperate rush which is apparently inseparable from modern education—and then they tell me what it means. Or rather they inquire about what it means indirectly, by a form of words that fills me with the desire to kill them. They look me in the eye and declare, "What you're trying to say is . . ." and that is where I choke them off, roaring, "I'm not *trying* to say anything; I *am* saying it with all the art and skill that I have acquired in a lifetime of hard work." But what I really ought to say is, "The book does not call for your reductive, half-baked explanation; it exists, and to you it may be a tale or a parable, or a direct revelation of reality; you will gain nothing by pulling it to pieces. It is like a clock, and if you observe it understandingly it will tell you what time it is in my life and yours, but if you pull it apart you will have nothing but a handful of junk." I do not often go so far as to say this, because I know that these children are being taught a system of criticism which is only criticism of a low order, and which is really an escape from direct experience of a work of art. I do not wholly blame the teachers; they are confronted with classes of students whose understanding is of the uttermost variability, and to talk about art to such a chance assembly is to embark on stormy and dangerous seas. The teacher's job is to teach, and artistic sensibility is not to be taught, so it must be feigned. I must say in justice that from time to time I encounter students who really do know what a book is and approach it as a work of art, and receive from it whatever a work of art is able to give them at a time when they are still green in understanding.

About adult critics I shall not speak. They rank from sensitive and deeply intelligent writers whose opinions must be respected, even if they are not shared, on down the steep descent to the large group whom Yeats dismissed as "sciolists and opinionated bitches." Every time a writer publishes a book he must run the gauntlet of criticism, the worst of which comes from—again I quote Yeats—

A leveling, rancorous, rational sort of mind
That never looked out of the eye of a saint
Or out of a drunkard's eye.[*]

I am speaking to you very personally. Whenever I meet with harsh or scornful criticism—and I assure you that I do, with each new book, encounter some of this—I reflect that my first novel came out in 1951, and it was dismissed by a majority of critics as an amusing but inconsiderable piece of work; but it is still in print, and sells pretty well, and some very intelligent people write to me who have found it much to their liking; whereas the criticism is forgotten and many of the critics are dead and rotten. The best advice I know for the writer on the matter of criticism was given by Thornton Wilder; he said that a writer should certainly read criticism of his work and give it adequate but not prolonged consideration, or else he would find that the critic had wormed into his mind and was writing his next book. To which I

---

[*] William Butler Yeats, "The Seven Sages."

would add that it must always be remembered that the critic is seeking to enhance his own reputation, and may not be wholly scrupulous about the way he does it.

When reading reviews, it is necessary to consider the way in which they are written. If a critic can really write, it is probably worthy of your attention. But many critics are miserable craftsmen in the art they seek to guide.

Perhaps it is too much to expect the author to distinguish at all times between serious criticism and newspaper and magazine reviewing. The latter is likely to be hasty, and undertaken by someone under stress and perhaps burdened by a sense of his own peripheral relationship to literature. But there—is one to regard anything that is published as "literature"? How much of what appears every year must be dismissed as honest in intention, but trivial in attainment?

To return to the aspiring writers of whom I spoke a few minutes ago, and who eagerly seek guidance about how to become writers, where are they to look? Not far, for there are all kinds of books that profess to teach methods of writing, fiction and non-fiction, poetry and the steamiest sort of prose. I bought one such magazine when I was thinking about what I would say to you. From time to time I receive through the mail offers to teach me to write, by some infallible method, but I have never had time to accept them. But in preparation for today I thought I had better find out what these helpful people were offering. The cover of my magazine proclaimed "How to Write Passionate Love Scenes . . . and Still Respect Your Typewriter in the Morning." Much is suggested in that title. Is the reader to expect that he will not only learn to write passionate love scenes, but that he will himself experience them vicariously? To a certain sort of mind, the prospect is alluring. The imaginative preparation, or foreplay; the turning down of the sheets, so to speak; the actual writing, or deliciously prolonged orgasm; the sense of achievement, of having transformed erotic fantasy into art. And you can do it over and over again, without fatigue or disgust—

. . . thus, thus, keeping endless holiday
Let us together closely lie, and kiss,

There is no labour, nor no shame in this;
This hath pleased, doth please, and long will please; never
Can this decay, but is beginning ever.[*]

I was astonished when I read the article to find it quite sensible; its counsel was, "Don't overdo things." But the title, as it appeared on the cover—that was aimed straight at the eager, desirous heart.

The magazine was full of advice, which may be good. I don't know because little of it concerned me. I don't particularly want to know "how to write irresistible non-fiction" nor do I want advice about computers because I do not own one and could not manage it if I did. I don't worry about collecting from slow-paying magazines. I don't want to know how to improve my writers' group, because I shrink from the notion of writers' groups; I don't want to master the building block of poetry and don't believe such a thing exists; nor do I seek "a playful guide to being a Southern writer." I was grateful that at Christmas nobody gave me the foolishly suggestive "Take an Author to Bed" poster. I am interested that the magazine calls loudly for novels in which "safe sex is eroticised and characters are sensuously—and routinely—conscious of their own and their partners' health" because this shows that the magazine really has its heart in the right place and wishes to be associated with a "caring community." Literary aid against AIDS, in fact.

As a writer, I have my share of intuition, and as I looked through that magazine I had a strong sense of the sort of reader at whom it was aimed: a lonely person, whose youth was slipping away; a reader who will hopefully cut out the coupon that is appended to an advertisement that begins, "You Can Make Up to $9,800 in 24 Hours!" and which describes the literary life as "The Royal Road to Riches"; a reader unsophisticated enough to believe that writers live marvellous social lives, eat and drink very high on the hog, and have access

---

[*] Ben Jonson's translation of Petronius Arbiter's poem which begins "Foeda est in coitu et brevis voluptas."

to unlimited, apocalyptic sex. A wistful reader and, I fear, an untalented one.

It is very sad. People of that sort do not, so far as I know, imagine that they could learn to write music by mastering a few easy tips, or that they could paint pictures that anybody would want. What on earth makes them think that they can be writers? It would be interesting to talk about that.

I should be sorry if you received the impression from anything I have said that I regard writing as being wholly remote from the ordinary concerns of life, and unheeding of what is going on in the world. The world around the writer presses upon him as it does on everybody else, and alters his way of working, although I do not think it alters what he most seriously works with, and has worked with ever since the printed book became generally available.

Ever since 1945 we have heard a great deal about the writer who is said to be *engagé,* meaning involved in current affairs and politics and social movements. The idea is one which many people, including some good writers, have found attractive. It seems to get the writer out of his solitary cell and into the forum. He devotes his skills of persuasion to manifestly good causes—or causes which seem good at the time—and politicians and demagogues and leaders of all kinds like to see a few writers on their side; it suggests an intellectuality which may not otherwise be strongly apparent. Unquestionably some writers are deeply moved by political and social causes, and they write with power to support whatever they think is necessary to bring about a better world. Every revolution has had a few writers involved in it at the beginning; by the end they are frequently either disillusioned or dead. But it would be wrong to dispute their sincerity or their goodness of heart.

There are many more writers, however, who regard themselves as *engagé* because it gives them a direction they would not otherwise have. It is a truism to say that a writer writes best when he writes of something that presses deeply upon his consciousness, and demands to be heard. It is from the depths that real inspiration rises. But there are scores of writers, sufficiently successful to attract attention from a public which knows their names if not their works, and upon whom nothing really presses very strongly. They want a theme; they want something that gives direction to their work. They are looking for a cause, and a vast array of causes lies open to them, waiting for them to make a choice.

They write books about all sorts of things—the wretchedness of the drug addict, the hard lot of the black people, the Spanish population, the native people, the misery of the woman who needs an abortion, or hasn't had one, or has had one and wishes she hadn't, the problems of the woman who has to make her way in a man's world where, literally, every man's hand is against her; indeed the misfortune of womanhood is almost unlimited in its profusion of themes. They espouse causes of every sort, and they are especially indignant about groups which, for one reason or another, are victims of discrimination. They are very severe upon The Rich, who are so wanting in compassion for the misery which gives rise—or seems to these writers to give rise—to their wealth and privilege. The world of such writers as these is filled with mute, inglorious Miltons, to whom they are eager to lend a voice.

Do not suppose for an instant that I am jeering at any of these themes, all of which have their validity as the understructure of fiction. But I am—well, not jeering, but certainly questioning the quality of the writing which emerges when a writer seizes upon a theme because it is for some reason popular, rather than because he has any strong initial feeling about it. Very often such writers try to make up for this want of depth of inspiration with a mass of research, which they insert into their books with a shoehorn, and which impresses readers who are awed by bundles of facts. When I read about a novel that it has been "extensively researched" I take it as a warning signal.

Unquestionably there are writers who are truly *engagé* and whose writing is powerful and moving. Such a writer, for instance, is Nadine Gordimer, whose novels about affairs in South Africa are justly celebrated. But when you read them you know that they have been deeply felt, rather than merely "researched," and that they are descriptions of life as it is, and studies of individual character, rather than polemics directed against a political regime. To revert to a classical example, it is the deeply felt passages and pathetic characters in *Uncle Tom's Cabin* that convince us, not the abolitionist harangues.

As opposed to the writers whom I have been describing are those who do indeed write about what presses most powerfully and insistently upon them, and it is in the work of such writers that we most frequently encounter that quality of individuality that is called "style." Style is an elusive quality, and one of the amusing things about the world of criticism is to watch critics chasing it, like children trying to put salt on the tail of a robin. They invent categories of writing, and then try to confine writers within these critical jails, talking of "minimalism" and "post-modernism" and "magic realism" and a dozen others, as if these things had real existence and were not simply gases extracted by the critics from works of strong individuality. Of course there are writers—writers modestly gifted but full of industry and aspiration, like the ones who write about politics and social wrongs—who leap from their chairs crying, "By Gum, that's it! I've been a minimalist all these years and didn't know it!"—and henceforth are increasingly minimal (if you will pardon the contradiction in that phrase) until finally they achieve total nullity. A style, or a special quality of writing, is not something that can be pulled on like a shirt. You cannot, so to speak, decide to "join the minimalists." Unless a style rises irresistibly from within the writer, as evidence of his individuality, it is not a style. It is a mannerism, an affectation, and, although it may be amusing for a while, the time will come when the writer finds it is getting in the way of his real talent. I do not say that there are never writers who do indeed find a new or apparently new way of writing. Unquestionably there are, somewhere, a few genuine "minimalists" who may never have thought of themselves in that way until the critics baptized them; but their minimalism is their gift, and other writers imitate it at their peril. For any writer, unless he is a young beginner looking for his own style, to imitate another writer is to confess a fatal want of talent.

Writers who would never think of imitating anyone else must, however, give heed to the literary atmosphere in which they work. You cannot write fiction nowadays in the mode of a century or two centuries ago, unless you are doing so for well-understood reasons of pastiche. All my life it has been one of my pleasures to read novels of the early nineteenth century. Not, I assure you, only the novels of the masters, but the second-raters, and even sometimes the third-raters. They are not half so bad as you might suppose. They are full of entertainment and they offer wonderful glimpses of past life and past ideas. It takes a surprising amount of talent to be even second-rate, and Bulwer-Lytton and Harrison Ainsworth and Charles Lever were very able craftsmen and by no means intellectually trivial. But one of the things I envy them as I read is the leisure with which they could lay out their stories. They back into their narrative like a reluctant horse being coaxed between the shafts of a cart. If they are writing about a family (and when are they not doing so?) they tell you its background and ancestry in a degree of detail which is quite astonishing. Dickens has parodied this approach marvellously in the first chapter of *Martin Chuzzlewit*. If they are writing about a battle they do not spare you a detail of what the ground was like, and what the commanders made of it. Indeed Tolstoy comes as near to spoiling *War and Peace* as a genius can come to destroying a masterpiece, by telling us what he would have done if he had been Napoleon. We forgive these writers, because we know that they are writing for a public which had apparently immense time for reading novels. Of course they had nothing of the kind; they had precisely as much time as we have today, but they didn't have the movies and television to compete for their leisure. Even Sir Walter Scott—unquestionably a great genius—was prolix to such a degree that I confess to you, in my shameless seniority, that I have never been able to read most of his novels without a great deal of skipping. I don't have to read about his moors and his mountains— I've seen 'em, and all I need is to be told that something is happening on a moor and a mountain to conjure up in an instant what may take him three or four pages of heavy, and to me confusing, prose to describe. When I was a boy my parents and their friends used to go into ecstasies about Hardy's description of Egdon Heath in the first chapter of *The Return of the Native*. But in these days I, and hundreds of thousands of others, have visited Egdon Heath, or have seen some other heath of equal literary weight, and although I value Hardy's art, I would not dream of trying to do myself what he has done, nor would any living writer I can think of. Nor would I wish to manoeuvre a pair of lovers into the likelihood of a sexual union as gingerly as do the writers of the nineteenth century. Like so much else, sex has speeded up.

The movies and television have made it necessary for modern novelists to get on with the job as fast as they decently can. All those immensely skilful techniques of cutting and montage and general sharpening of the technique of narration in which film and television are so adroit have influenced modern writing. Henry James, giving advice to writers, cried, "Dramatize, dramatize, dramatize!" Give as much actuality as you can to the scene of your story, but do not linger over it and make it a primary element in what you are writing. The visual imagination of the modern reader is much greater than that of his great-grandparents. It is said, cynically but with a terrible ring of truth, that the modern film is made for viewers with the intellect of a twelve-year-old. Emotionally and intellectually this may well be true, but the visual imagination of a twelve-year-old today is acute. If something is happening in a city street, he does not need the street to be set before him, garbage can by garbage can. He has seen all the city streets he needs on the large screen or the small one.

So it is also with scenes of action. A great novelist, like Trollope, moves from scene to scene with a deliberation that readers would resent in a modern novel. And writers of lesser quality, like Wilkie Collins, who was thought to write so sensationally that his work was almost dangerous to young readers, seem almost to crawl, as their narrative proceeds. The modern novelist, who has to compete for his readers with the devotees of the little screen, cannot do anything of the sort. He must get on with the job, and he can depend on his readers to be as brisk as he is in developing the narrative.

The narrative—that's the great matter. Not so very long ago writers like E.M. Forster and Virginia Woolf could be dismissive and even contemptuous of mere narrative. But it must be said that their art was sufficient to conceal a serious want in their works, but not all writers can follow where they trod, nor would they wish to do so. Nowadays there must be narrative—a story—because the readers want it, and if the writer has an eye on a possible film or TV version of his books, it is an absolute necessity.

I am often asked by young people, whose idea of success as a writer is involved in the notoriety and the money that come with film and television versions of a novel: "When are they going to make a movie of one of your books?" I have to say that I do not know. Film directors have shown interest in my work, but they always confess to me that they cannot interest the money which goes into making a film in anything so peculiar as the kind of books I write. Where's the hero, for whose role some popular young star could be engaged? Even worse, where's the heroine? I have been told by more than one film director that my most popular novel is impossible for film, because the heroine is described as one of the ugliest women in the world, and where's your star who would put up with that? The stories, they say, are great, but the characters are simply not translatable into film, unless, of course, I permit extensive revision along film lines which are by no means broad in their scope.

Once or twice I have tried to talk to film people about my ugly heroine. I explain to them the extraordinary psychological fascination of the medieval legend of the Loathly Damsel, whose splendour of spirit is confined within a hideous body, and she becomes beautiful only when she is understood and loved. I advise you not to talk to resolutely Hollywood minds about the Loathly Damsel. Their eyes glaze, and their cigars go out, and behind the lenses of their horn-rimmed spectacles I see the dominating symbol of their inner life: it is a dollar sign. The minds of vendors of popular entertainment are set in cement. Their recipe for success is: The Mixture as Before. They sincerely believe that success can be repeated endlessly, and it is against their resistance that any sort of originality or freshness must assert itself.

When Henry James said, "Dramatize, dramatize, dramatize," what, in fact, did he mean? His own works made it clear that he did not call for what used to be called "a rattling good yarn." Simple narrative, though he thoroughly understood it, had no special hold on him. He was too great a master to neglect it, and when one is called upon to do so it is quite possible to say what his books are *about*. The story is clear enough. Something happens. This distinguishes him from many writers who have sought to follow in his steps, who have been so over-whelmed by the rich allusiveness and implication of his style that they cannot see the wood for the trees, and they write books and short stories which are not, under examination, about anything very much; they are stifled by over-refinement, and it is wholly false to imagine that James was over-refined, whatever the intricacies of his expression. Think of his plots, and it is surprising how tough they are; they might have served Ibsen. His decisive action, however, is psychological. So what did he mean by his urgent advice to dramatize?

I think he meant, simply, that the writer must *show* what is happening; he must not describe it coldly, as might a bystander. Things must happen to his characters. Because so much of the action in James is psychological, an obtuse reader or writer—and people of cultivation and extensive education are perfectly capable of being obtuse—might suppose that nothing is going on. But as P.G. Wodehouse—a master of narrative art in quite a different milieu—once said, action in a plot is not simply a matter of the one-eyed Chinaman coming up through the trapdoor and shooting the butler on every page. Thrillers depend on such obvious devices, but great novels are psychological as well as physical in action, and a first-rate novelist must have psychological insight, as well as a story and a style.

To continue for a little longer with narrative, I want to stress my own conviction that it is vital to serious writing. Some writers are impatient with it, and the great example is Shakespeare, who seems not to have cared much about physical plots; and his work abounds with examples where he has seen beyond a perfunctory and almost incredible plot—*Measure for Measure* gives us an example—to a psy-chological action that results in a great play. A very simple onlooker could find pleasure in the tale, and doubtless over the centuries many simple-minded onlookers have done so. Narrative preserves a piece of writing as graces of style alone cannot do. The great example is *The Arabian Nights' Entertainments,* in which the sorceress-mistress of the Great Shah continues her narratives so compellingly that she cannot be resisted. The tyrant must permit her to live if he is to hear how the tale ends. There must be something of Scheherazade in any serious writer of novels, and that is what I want to talk about now.

Much of what I wish to say is summed up in a remark of the late Vladimir Nabokov, when he was discussing the writing of André Malraux: "The longer I live the more I become convinced that the only thing that matters in literature is the (more or less irrational) *shamanstvo* of a book, i.e., that the good writer is first of all an enchanter. But one must not let things tumble out of one's sleeve as Malraux does." He was referring to the clichés, imprecisions, and pretentious passages in the work of Malraux, which in Nabokov's opinion almost ruined him as a writer to be taken seriously.

What is *shamanstvo?* Russian friends have translated it for me as "enchanter-quality." Not simply stage magicianship, where one may perhaps allow things to fall out of one's sleeve, like the inept Malraux, but the real quality of the enchanter, the weaver of spells who may, through his spells, reveal unexpected and marvellous things about life, and thus about ourselves.

How does he do it? Is *shamanstvo* something that can be learned, or acquired by hard work? Here I come to a difficulty, because in our democratic age it is thought to be indefensible to suggest that there is anything that is not achievable by anybody. We know it is not so, but we turn our official, our public face against it. We encourage children to think that they can do anything. We praise them as creative, when in fact their drawings and stories are original only in that the children have no technique and have not yet set any bounds to their aspirations; they will learn to do that soon enough. But the fact has to be faced by anybody who seeks to work in any of the arts that there is no substitute for talent. As a musical friend of mine says, "If you haven't got it, you've had it." Art is much older than democracy, and art is uncompromisingly élitist. Devotion to the magazines, like the one of which I have spoken, which promise big money and quick success, will not make you a writer of any substance, and neither will the most stifling immersion in Matthew Arnold's best that has been known and said in the world. Writers of any substance are a special breed of people, and apart from their gift, it is not a breed that is necessarily agreeable or interesting.

If you want to be a writer, and are not one, you may take comfort in the fact that you are not a vulgarian, like Dickens or Balzac, or a bounder like H.G. Wells, or an embezzler like O. Henry, or an unwashed bully like Samuel Johnson, or a jailbird like Cervantes or Bunyan, or a pitiful self-deceiver like Wilde, or a sour invalid like Pope, or a hypocritical drunk like Addison, or an unlucky gambler like Dostoyevsky, or a snorting, sneering snob like Nabokov. You are a delightfully normal, admirable, lovable human being—you are just not a writer. You may have a splendidly rational intellect; very few writers have ever been so endowed though they have sometimes an uncanny gift for seeing through a brick wall. You may be an accomplished amorist and have a catalogue of your conquests like Don Giovanni; few writers have ever been good at that game. You may be rich; writers are never rich, even when they have plenty of money; there is something in their make-up that prevents them from ever feeling really rich. You may be happy, and a happy writer is virtually unknown, even among humorists; indeed humorists are often very sad men. I urge you to rejoice in your luck. If you haven't got *shamanstvo* you haven't got it, and that's that.

But we need not give up on our search to find out what *shamanstvo* is.

> Tell me, where is shamanstvo bred
> Or in the heart, or in the head
> How begot, how nourished?
> Reply, reply.

Well, I think we have decided, for the moment at least, that we do not know how it is begot, but we may profitably look to see where it is nourished, and we will begin with language.

It is extraordinary how few people have any real feeling for language, or any sense that it is one of the greatest and most inexhaustible playthings with which our human state has presented us. It is an unhappy truth that education, or partial education, which is all that most of us can claim as our own, seems to be destructive of the sense of language. It is often among simple people that truly effective and poetic expression is heard. I once heard a Welsh countrywoman in a bus talking to a friend about a local politician: "Every word he says is like a scratch from a rusty nail," said she, and I was struck by the novelty and aptness of her words. At the college where I spent twenty years we had a cleaner, a tiny woman of no great strength but mighty spirit, and one day one of our young men, a notable melancholic, said to her, "Nelly, are you happy?" To which she responded with a radiant face, "Happy! I'm so happy sometimes I have to wake up in the night, just to laugh!" Education seems to rid us of this directness with language. But a writer must have it. His language may be spare or it may be profuse, he may lean toward the demotic and the colloquial, or he may like to juggle with torches and sharp swords, but he must have a way of using words that commands attention, not by its singularity necessarily, but by its aptness, or sometimes by its reduction of a complex idea to an astonishing and revealing simplicity.

Language preserves a work of literary art when the ideas it contains have become familiar, or perhaps even unendurable. We delight in the plays of the Restoration because of their strong, vigorous, and elegant deployment of language, although the society they depict and criticize is very strange and perhaps repellent to us. The plays of Bernard Shaw are perhaps more powerful today than they have ever been, for although the notions they put forward are now old hat, the way in which they are put forward is so delightful, so classically chaste in expression, so unexpectedly funny even after the twentieth hearing, that we cannot be without them. Language in such writing as in these plays is not the drudge of the intellect but the winged horse of poetry, even though the plays appear to be in prose. We must never underrate what Thomas Mann so slyly called "the finer and much less obvious rhythmical laws of prose."

During the past few years a number of writers seem to have sickened of the simplicity of language which used to be considered a mark of quality.

Prefer the familiar work to the far-fetched.
Prefer the concrete word to the abstract.
Prefer the single word to the circumlocution.
Prefer the short word to the long.
Prefer the Saxon word to the Romance.

What excellent advice it is, and how it was beaten into my generation of schoolboys. And, of course, with my inheritance, it was dinned into me at home, along with the totally false assurance that if I ate my crusts I would have curly hair. But one may tire of even the best advice, as one may tire of writing according to those precepts. Would we wish to be without the heraldic splendour and torchlight processions that are the sentences of Sir Thomas Browne? Would we wish to sacrifice the orotund, Latinate pronouncements of Samuel Johnson? Would we wish that Dickens had written in the style recommended by the brothers Fowler, who framed the rules I have quoted; what would then have happened to Seth Pecksniff, Wilkins Micawber, and Sairey Gamp, I ask you? The Fowler brothers, God be with them, were writing for the guidance of, most probably, civil servants, and among civil servants *shamanstvo* is an undesirable quality. But a writer who possesses *shamanstvo* will not consent to be bound by such precepts, any more than he will consent to wear shoes that are several sizes too small. He delights in language, and he frisks, rolls, and wallows in it when he feels that way.

You can think of modern writers who send their readers scampering to the dictionary. Anthony Burgess, Paul Theroux, John Fowles, Samuel Beckett, Kurt Vonnegut, Peter De Vries, and of course Nabokov, who loved to bemuse his readers with a word that he, not born to the language, used with elegance. The great example of course is James Joyce, but there have been few writers except Beckett who have followed in his steps without ungraceful stumbling. Some time ago I was sent a copy of *The Oxter English Dictionary,* which gave examples of unfamiliar words used by modern writers. I was one of them, and I confess that I was surprised that the word *glamour* in its true sense was thought strange: I had always thought it meant enchantment, in either its noun or adjectival form, but apparently many people think differently. The word *lickerish,* which I had always understood to mean lecherous, is apparently unfamiliar, though in my childhood it was used by children both in its true sense and of that black candy with which we used to threaten our teeth. You never can tell what words will seem strange to your readers, and probably the best course is to pay no attention, and let them find out, if they wish. If they don't wish, perhaps they should confine their reading to the works of Barbara Cartland, who has, at the age of eighty-nine, just sent her latest romantic novel to her publishers. It brings her score up to five hundred books, and not a thing in them to puzzle the pretty head or bring a blush to the cheek of the Young Person.

Language is part of *shamanstvo,* for you cannot weave a spell without words. But words alone are not enough. A story is not enough. To weave the spell the writer must have within him something perhaps comparable to the silk-spinning and web-casting gift of a spider; he must not only have something to say, some story to tell or some wisdom to impart, but he must have a characteristic way of doing it which entraps and holds still his prey, by which I mean his reader. He must have a way of saying his say which is not that of the civil servant painstakingly explaining the applications of a tax, but which comes to the reader with a special, unmistakable, individual grace. And where does that come from? My own ideas on that subject may not appeal to all of you, but I am convinced that this special quality is the product of the writer's access to those deeper levels of his mind that the depth psychologists call the Unconscious. It is not a particular possession of the writer, this Unconscious, but the ability to invite it, to solicit its assistance, to hear what it has to say and impart it in the language that is peculiarly his own, is decidedly his gift and what defines him as an artist. He may not be—very probably is not—fishing up messages from the Unconscious that astonish and strike dumb his readers. It is more likely that he is telling them things that they recognize as soon as they hear them—you see I am recurring to my earlier insistence that what is read should be heard and not merely apprehended by the eye alone—but which they have not been able to seize and hold and put into language for themselves. I know of no instance of this quality more concentrated or more powerful than the second part of Goethe's *Faust,* where a world of insight and wisdom and spiritual enlargement is given form, and when we read it—or better still if we have an opportunity to see it well realized on the stage—we do not find ourselves in a world unknown and strange, but rather we know that we are in a world that has always existed within us and which for the first time we begin to apprehend.

Of course *Faust* is not the sole example of this refreshing and life-enhancing revelation. We find it in great novels. Dostoyevsky said that you do not have to go outside the mind in order to find God and the Devil, and he spoke truly. We find portions or glimpses of this revelation in novels which have been written with *shamanstvo* in some degree. Such books tell us what we have in us to know, but have not fully seized by our unaided efforts.

Thus the book which may be a tale to the simple reader—and the tale comes first, as I have tried to make plain—or may be a parable to some who like to explain what lies behind the tale, may also be, at its best, a direct revelation of reality which, when it comes, leaves us enlarged and in possession of some new ground in the exploration of ourselves.

15

CHRISTMAS BOOKS

Davies was regularly approached for articles by newspapers and magazines from many parts of the English-speaking world. He was reluctant to accept these offers whenever such an assignment interfered with the central matter of finishing his latest book.

When the *New York Times* approached him for an article in the fall of 1991, however, the timing was perfect. *Murther & Walking Spirits* had just been launched, engaging him in the usual promotional activities, but he was between books. He was therefore pleased to write this article on the books of Christmas Past on October 6 and 7, which appeared on October 28, 1991. Christmas, presumably, was a little early that year.

There are many people—happy people, it usually appears—whose thoughts at Christmas always turn to books. The notion of a Christmas tree with no books under it is repugnant and unnatural to them. I had the good luck to be born in such a family and, although my brothers and I were happy with such insubstantial gifts as skates, toboggans, and the like, we would have been greatly disappointed if there had been no books. My father expected the latest Wodehouse, and some vast wad of political recollections—the *Life and Letters of Walter Hines Page* when I was very young and the awesome six volumes of Lloyd George's war memoirs, much later, were the sort of thing that he, and he alone in our family, could read—and my mother wanted and received novels of idyllic rural life by Mary Webb or Sheila Kaye-Smith.

For me, a standby for years was the annual collected volume of the English boys' magazine *Chums,* through which I chewed greedily, consuming the historical serial (the boy who did wonders in the army of Wellington or the navy of Nelson); the contemporary serial (the boy whose mother sacrificed to send him to a good school—these were all boarding schools—and who emerged victorious from some scandal in which he had been accused of theft or secret drinking, and carried the school to victory in the great cricket match); the comic serial, about disruptive groups of boy conjurors, boy ventriloquists, and boy contortionists who reduced their schools to chaos and their masters to nervous prostration by their side-splitting japes and wheezes. None of these wondrous boys were in the least like the boys I knew in Canada, but that merely gave them the appeal of the exotic. In between the pages of these I read the articles about careers (civil servant, church organist, veterinary) and about how to make a serviceable violin out of a cigar box and some picture wire.

I particularly relished a column of comic backchat between two wags named Roland Butter and Hammond Deggs. Here is a sample of their wares: RB "Why did the djinn sham pain and whine?" HD "I dunno." RB "Because the stout porter bit 'er." HD "Oh, crumbs!" It was not until much later in life when I came under the spell of Demon Rum that I savoured the full richness of that one.

Before Christmas there was always a period of expectancy during which my parents urged me to read Dickens's *Christmas Carol.* Every year I tried and every year Christmas Day and new books arrived to find that I had got no further than the appearance of Marley's ghost. I was a slow reader, moving my lips and hearing every word, but I knew the story. It was inescapable. At school no Christmas passed without several children being dragooned into a re-enactment of the Cratchits' Christmas Dinner, for the entertainment of parents. Early in life I developed a distaste for the Cratchits which time has not sweetened. I do not think I was an embittered child, but the Cratchits' aggressive worthiness, their bravely borne poverty, their exultation over that wretched goose, disgusted me. I particularly disliked Tiny Tim (a part always played by a girl because girls had superior powers of looking moribund and worthy at the same time) and when he chirped, "God bless us, every one," my mental response was akin to Sam Goldwyn's famous phrase, "Include me out."

No doubt this was not a proper state of mind for a child, but there were ways in which I was a tediously improper child.

Later in life I became devoted to the *Carol,* though never wholly reconciled to the Cratchits. The book is a magical creation, defying every rule of taste and intellectual decency, but casting a spell that cannot be resisted. Of course it is a book which permits us to eat our cake and have it too; pestered and belaboured as we all are nowadays by organized charity (that Briareus whose hundred hands are all extended on behalf of causes and diseases of which we have never heard) we rejoice when Scrooge sends the charity-collectors away with a flea in their ear. We are not stony-hearted, we are not deaf to the cry of the needy, but when, apparently from nowhere, the Society for the Relief of the Ruptured Calithumpians sends us an expensive piece of three-colour printing demanding a handout right now, and no two ways about it, we have a fellow-feeling with Scrooge, and may even murmur, "Bah! Humbug!"

On the other hand, when we have sent out the last envelope containing a cheque, how we feel our souls to be cleansed, as was that of Scrooge on Christmas morning, when he woke to find that the Three Spirits who had visited him were creatures of a redemptive dream. We love Scrooge in both his phases.

It is a measure of Dickens's genius that he could write a book of such unabashed sentimentality and yet make it irresistible—so much so, indeed, that it is scarcely exaggeration to say that it brings a blessing with it. But there are times when genius is uncomfortable company; it nudges and overwhelms. So we may turn to other Christmas books for an enjoyment that is quieter. I am astonished to meet many people who do not know Thackeray's wonderful *The Rose and The Ring.* He wrote it at Christmas, in 1854 in Rome, to amuse a little

American girl, the daughter of friends, who was recovering from malaria. He called it, "A fireside Pantomime for Great and Small Children," and indeed it is like an English Christmas pantomime, with its good and evil fairies, its lost princess, its extraordinary transformations and its enchanting lightness of heart, but it is a story of much deeper and wiser qualities than those. The original manuscript, illustrated by Thackeray in his most charming pen-and-watercolour style, is in the Morgan Library, and it is a little book of transporting beauty. A reproduction was made in 1947 and if you are very lucky and know a really good book-dealer, you may be able to get one.

Or, if you want a realistic description of what Victorian Christmases were like, look at chapters twenty-one to twenty-three of Anthony Trollope's *Orley Farm,* where you will find three different groups celebrating the great day, and not a gift or a carol among them.

Christmas is the best time to read ghost stories. Really good examples of this sort of writing are rare; unless an author possesses the right sort of genius he tends to tell us how frightened we are, instead of frightening us against our will. But there are masters, and Henry James must be high on any list. Was his mastery of this other-worldliness something rooted in his father's Swedenborgianism? There is a collection of his ghost stories compiled by Leon Edel which is truly alarming. It does not make us scream; it makes us look uneasily over a shoulder, which is a much subtler effect. The great and only Henry has a powerful rival in Montague Rhodes James, who composed his ghost stories in the best traditional mode, because he wrote them to be read aloud to small groups of friends. My father-in-law had the great luck to hear one or two of these at Cambridge, as an undergraduate, and he said the effect far exceeded that of any ghost-film he had ever seen. A ghost story cannot survive a crowd or too much light. M.R. James does not make us scream either (who does, indeed?) but in "Oh Whistle and I'll Come to You, My Lad," he has written a story that never fails to give me the shudders, which is the highest tribute a ghost story can exact.

I have tried my hand at ghost stories myself; they present an irresistible challenge. But my ghosts were meant to amuse, rather than to frighten, for I have never understood why a ghost must be a miserable creature. But is a funny ghost a true ghost? Why not?

To write a Christmas story without believing in Christmas—without, that is to say, giving some credence to its religious origin and its transcendent spirit—is, I think, an impossibility. And yet—and yet—what splendid gifts the Imp of the Perverse has brought to the foot of the Christmas tree. Who would wish to be without Robert Benchley's "Christmas Afternoon," in which he tells us of the Gummidge family enduring its "dragging, devitalizing *ennui*" which gives rise to the yawns, snarls, and thinly veiled insults that are too often heard at the family Christmas party. And S.J. Perelman's Christmas playlet, *Waiting for Santy,* which stands Clifford Odets on his head and gives him a hearty shake; would we be without it? And H.L. Mencken's "Christmas Story" in which a great-hearted infidel, a brewery salesman, gives a vast, inclusive Christmas party for the bums of Baltimore, the point of which is that they do not have to be grateful, or filled with Christmas spirit, or repentant for their sins. But the bums are slaves of tradition and ritual, and when the mountains of turkey, the dirty burlesque show, and the bushels of cigars have been exhausted they are driven, like lemmings at the brink of the abyss, to do the accustomed thing, to confess, to sing hymns. The way of the high-minded infidel is hard.

No, we would not wish to be without these anti-Christmas delights.

My own favourite book for the season is no longer the *Carol;* my children have children of their own, and anyway I know the book by heart. Every year I return to Max Beerbohm's *A Christmas Garland,* surely the most brilliant, most hilarious book of parodies in our language. As with *The Rose and The Ring,* I am continually meeting people who do not know it.

It is assumed by many parodists that their imitations of notable writers must have an acid aftertaste, must sting and deride their originals. The great parodists, however—and Beerbohm is surely first among their small number—write from affection and admiration which are not, however, wholly overwhelming. They can see the clay in the foot of the idol, but they know that it does not go much above the ankle. Beerbohm writes parodies of Henry James, Kipling, Wells, Chesterton, Hardy, Galsworthy, Conrad, Shaw—there are seventeen in all—and every one is a marvellous evocation of its original, but seen slightly askew, as if in a mirror with a whorl in it. My favourite is "Fond Hearts Askew," which parodies a writer now virtually unknown but a mighty seller in his day, Maurice Hewlett, author of *The Forest Lovers* and foremost exponent of that begemmed and bedizened style of historical fiction that Beerbohm called "Tushery." You do not need to know Hewlett to find it enchanting and hilarious.

It is the *Garland* I turn to at Christmas, now. A long haul, my friends, from Roland Butter and Hammond Deggs.

16

WORLD OF WONDERS

ॐ

Davies was involved with the annual summer Shakespeare festival at Stratford, Ontario from the outset. He was a friend of the first director, Tyrone Guthrie, and an original member of the board from 1953 until 1971. In 1979 he and Brenda Davies were honoured by being made Permanent Members of the Festival.

Davies' influence at Stratford extended far beyond that of the usual board member. He wrote the three books that recorded the first years of the Festival, and even assisted in the adaptations of historical plays there. In his biographer Judith Skelton Grant's words: "At intervals Davies has also written half-a-dozen articles for the Festival's souvenir programs, given five papers at the Stratford seminars and three public lectures, and contributed to *The Stratford Scene 1958–1968*."

Perhaps none of these can have been as congenial as this lecture, which allows us to hear Robertson Davies, Man of the Theatre, discuss the play that has been made of the work by Robertson Davies, Novelist. This lecture was presented on June 14 and June 19, 1992, in the Avon Theatre during The Stratford Festival Celebrated Writers Series, when his own novel *World of Wonders* was adapted for the stage by Elliott Hayes, a young playwright tragically killed in a road accident not long after.

He wrote to a friend in August of that year: *The enclosed program offers an excuse for my delay in answering your last, splendid*

*letter. To say that I have been busy with the play is not quite true for
I have not taken a direct part in getting it on the stage. But its production involved me in a surprising amount of work, including two lectures that I gave about the problems involved in making a novel into
a play; they were very well attended, to my surprise, because I did not
think people would be greatly interested in such a subject, but they
were and the questions they asked afterward were searching and
probing in a surprising and complimentary way. The man who did the
stage version, Elliott Hayes, is an experienced playwright and did an
excellent job, in which I did not interfere at all. The audiences were
large and very pleased with the play, and on the whole it has been
a decided success.*

*The production was elaborate and expensive. Because it is about
a conjuror and illusionist it was necessary to show some of his illusions, and the audience loved them. Perhaps the most popular was
at the very end of the play, when Eisengrim, the conjuror, took the
notes that had been made by the man who wanted to make a television show of his life, and threw them out into the audience, where
they flew up into the roof of the theatre and disappeared! A very good
ending for a play about magic—the magic of the stage, and the magic
of life.*

I am going to talk to you about the novel called *World of Wonders*,
and about the play, *World of Wonders*, that you are going to see this
afternoon. I shall attempt to explain in what ways they are alike and
in what ways they differ, and why. I do not really know why you want
to hear about these things. Why don't you simply go to the play, and
enjoy it as a play? But that would be against our national character. We
Canadians are gluttons for instruction; we dote upon lectures. (I am
like that myself: I would much rather listen to somebody lecture
about— let us say—a cholera epidemic in Calcutta than go to Calcutta
and take part in it personally.) A lecture is a peaceful experience, lulling
to the senses and enlarging to the intellect without being too exciting.
But when it comes to giving a lecture myself, about something that is

very near to me, it is an entirely different matter; I am suddenly over-come with reluctance. I don't want to talk to you about what I do, how I do it, or why I do it. You have the completed product. Do you care how it comes into being? Surely my job is to offer you the completed product, not to take you on a tour of the workshop.

Why do I feel like that? Because writing a novel, if you do it seri-ously, is an act of creation. It is not simply a matter of invention; you do not just make up a story and write it out. You live with the book that you are writing for many months, during which you have to dig it out of yourself, often with discomfort and even pain. You do it with every ounce of sincerity and devotion you possess. And when it is done you say "That's that" and dismiss it from your mind. It is fin-ished, complete in so far as you can make it so, and you don't want to dig it up and examine it and go through all that act of creation again. Indeed, it can't be done.

There is more about the act of creation than what I have told you; when you have once finished your book, you have finished it for all time. You cannot go back and redo it or alter it, because you wrote it in the first instance as your instinct told you it should be. If you tin-ker with it afterward, the chances are very great that you will make a mess of it, because second thoughts in these matters are rarely best.

A famous instance concerns one of the greatest of playwrights, Henrik Ibsen. Many of you will be familiar with his play *A Doll's House.* It ends, you will recall, when the wife Nora tells her uncom-prehending husband why she must leave him to save her soul. It is one of the most powerful scenes in all drama. It is the considered work of a master. But it gave such great offence that when it was to be per-formed in Germany, and the demand for an altered ending was so insistent, Ibsen was forced to yield, and wrote a happy ending for the play. The German critics, you see, who had read the play said it was psychologically impossible that Nora should leave not only her hus-band but her three small children. (Critics are all great psychologists, and understand life much better than authors.) So Ibsen wrote a syrupy conclusion in which the pull of motherhood was too much for Nora, and she sank to the ground, crying, "Oh, this is a sin against myself, but I cannot leave them." You can imagine the joy and relief in the audience. Ibsen himself described this change as "a barbaric outrage," and so it was. It serves us today as an example of what tinkering with an already completed work of literature can do.

At various times in my life I have been asked to prepare plays or film-scripts based on my novels, and I have had enough experience to know that for me it is a hopeless task. What I have written once, in a particular form, I cannot change into something else.

This is not to say that it cannot be done. Somebody else may do it and do it very well. That is what has happened with *World of Wonders*. Elliott Hayes has prepared a dramatized version of the book and in my opinion he has done it admirably. The evidence of his success is that what has emerged in his stage version is a radical re-working of the material of the novel *in dramatic terms*. That is something quite different from preparing a stage version of the novel as it exists. Many of you, I dare say, have sat, as I have, through dreary plays which have been gouged out of the novels of Dickens. They stick too closely to the original, novelistic form. They are not Dickens and they are not plays. Of course, in later years some fine films have been made from Dickens, like the imaginative and deservedly successful *Nicholas Nickleby*. The serial effect of a novel—the narration of one incident after another for a reader who carries the whole of what he has read in his mind—is quite a different thing from dramatic action. The play, *World of Wonders,* gives you as much of the novel as the stage can absorb in about two hours. That is because the actors and the other stage artists concerned in the production of the play can give you instantaneously and through the eye and ear a vast amount of what the author has to express in prose, and in prose that does not bore you with too much tedious instruction. A playwright may rely heavily on his actors to push the action forward, and very often a nod or a glance from an accomplished actor will do what the author has to do in a careful paragraph of writing.

The author is, in his own way, a playwright or a film director, but he has to be the scene painter, the orchestra, and a whole cast of actors in order to make his effect. What he does is a solitary act of creation.

What the playwright and his colleagues do is a complex work of collaboration. The final effect of the novel or the play may be just the same, but the method of reaching the audience or the reader is wholly different.

Did I say that the author's work was a solitary act of creation? That is not quite true. He is a collaborator every time somebody reads his book. The reader must join with the author in bringing the book to life. In the theatre of his mind the reader must put the characters on stage, hear their voices, take pleasure in their individuality. Certainly that is what the author hopes. But is that the way we invariably read books? Do we not read at too fast a pace? Do we not sometimes skip parts that may be very necessary to the totality of the book, but which do not happen to please us at the moment? Do we really exert ourselves to bring the book to life? You cannot imagine how passionately the author hopes for good readers, who will exert themselves to find the energy and the colour in his book which he has worked so hard to put there. Real reading—the reading that brings the book fully to the understanding of the reader—is hard work of a special kind, and not everybody is equally gifted as a reader.

Thus, you see, the playwright or the adapter has advantages that the author may envy. But the author has his advantages, too. The actors in the play can convey all the action, and quite a lot of the psychological complexity of the novel upon which the play is based, but there are some things that elude them.

When you are watching a play you must catch it on the fly, and if it is a complex structure, and if the ideas it contains are touched on lightly, you may miss a part of what is being offered. One of the themes of *World of Wonders* as a play is that growing up, sharpening your wits, and indeed becoming yourself is a lifetime pursuit; you do not achieve all the maturity that can be yours on your twenty-first birthday. The play illustrates this, but it is put into words only once, when Liesl says: "You gain your mastery of your art at the cost of your innocence." The line may slip by without catching your attention and understanding. But it is important, and if you were reading the book you might wish to stop and think about it. Is it true? Has it been so in your own life? Is innocence too high a price to pay for mastery of something important? What is innocence and how do you distinguish it from stupidity? This is the advantage of the printed page; you may squeeze your orange of all its juice before you go on to the next thing. Not only do you read: you may reread, but you cannot ask actors to go back and repeat themselves, or give you a few minutes in which to think.

In *World of Wonders* there are basic truths that underlie the novel, which the novel can insist upon without arousing the hostility of the reader. Let me try one or two of them on you.

> Be not deceived; God is not mocked: for whatsoever a man soweth, that shall he also reap.

> As a dog returneth to his vomit, so a fool returneth to his folly.

> Vengeance is mine; I will repay, saith the Lord.

> A merry heart doeth good like a medicine: but a broken spirit drieth the bones.

> A fool's mouth is his destruction, and his lips are the snare of his soul.

In a novel it is possible to demonstrate these truths without preaching too strenuously at the reader; they are very much more difficult to show on the stage, for each one is the subject for a play in itself. A novel is a much more complex structure than a play can dare to be. A play has one or two themes, but a novel may have many.

In other words, a novel may deal extensively in ideas, but a play which is too much concerned with abstractions will be at serious risk of alienating its audience, which comes to the theatre to see something happen, not to hear about what might happen.

Let us talk for a while about the novel which underlies the play called by the same name. What is a novel, anyhow?

It has been said with, I think, great truth, that a good novel is a tale to the simple, a parable to the wise, and a direct revelation of reality to a man who has made it a part of his being. What is the tale of *World of Wonders?*

The book is the third volume of a trilogy, which is now called *The Deptford Trilogy*, because it is about the lives of three men all of whom were born in the little village of Deptford, in southern Ontario. These three achieve fame, in three wholly different ways: one becomes an important financier and entrepreneur, whose career is crowned by his appointment as Lieutenant-Governor of Ontario. One becomes a schoolmaster and teaches for forty-five years at a famous boys' school in Toronto, but his fame rests on his books about saints, and he gains a reputation as a hagiologist. The third endures a hard fate for many years, but at last achieves a curious fame as the world's foremost magician, conjuror, illusionist. The great financier is not wholly surprising as one who came from a very small place; the historian and hagiologist is more surprising because his enthusiasm is a strange one for a man raised in a Presbyterian family in a Canadian village; the third, the magician, is very surprising, for we do not expect anyone like that from a background wholly innocent about the world of theatre and sophisticated showmanship. The really surprising thing is that the lives and fates of all three men are linked by a single happening, which might be described as an accident—if you do not happen to agree with Dr. Freud that there are really no accidents, and that in this life what happens to us is determined by what we are. That is a hard doctrine, but it deserves attention.

What was this accident? It happened at 5:58 o'clock p.m. on the 27th of December, 1908. Two of the boys, Dunstan Ramsay and Boy Staunton, both ten years old, had been playing, and had quarrelled. Staunton threw a snowball at Ramsay, and Ramsay, sensing that it was coming, stepped out of its path, and the snowball hit a woman on the head. The shock to her was great, for concealed in the snowball was a stone; she collapsed, was taken home, and a few hours later gave premature birth to her son Paul, the third man in the trio.

I called it an accident. But what sort of accident was it? Certainly it was not an inexplicable or unmotivated happening. Ramsay dodged to avoid the snowball, but just how did he dodge? Did he dodge in front of the woman who was hit, and if he did so was he not guilty of her injury, and its consequence? How much did he understand of what he was doing? Certainly he understood the consequence, and suffered pangs of guilt for it all his life. Indeed, it may be said that the guilt of this incident was the most powerful force in shaping his life.

As for young Staunton, who threw the snowball, what do we make of him? A stone concealed in a snowball is a dirty trick, and as it happened, an evil deed. But to what extent is a child capable of evil, and to what degree is it exonerated from the consequences of its actions? This is a point on which I have opinions that are not the usual ones, for I think children are much more aware of what they do than we are inclined to think, and that they are capable of evil behaviour, and that the evil is intentional. Nowadays we are very sentimental about children, but I do not think we understand them as thoroughly as we imagine we do. Anybody who truly remembers what it was like to be a child remembers also the gigantic egotism and self-will of the child, which is controlled only by physical weakness and to some extent by fear. After the snowball found its mark, and the supposed accident became a village scandal, young Staunton denied all knowledge of it, and threatened young Ramsay with dire reprisal if he ever told what he knew. Staunton refused to face the truth, and denied his guilt, and it appeared that he had wiped it from the record of history.

And what about the third man, little Paul Dempster, who was hurried into the world untimely and thus, as he says later, robbed of eighty days of Paradise—the Paradise of the womb where all is love and protection? What happened to him would kill anyone who was not a born survivor. He suffers many external degradations and miseries, but his worst trial is that for many years he has to live the life of Nobody; he is the secret mechanism that works a sideshow trick—a card-playing automaton—and no one is supposed to know that he exists; he has been robbed totally, it appears, of humanity and personality. But he overcomes it and he borrows a personality from a man he idolizes, a great romantic actor, whose double it is his job to be in plays where a double is required. But he does not gain a personality of his own until his idol is dead, and then it is a personality so burnished, so splendid that it persuades huge audiences to regard him as a truly great man. It is only his closest friends who know his secret, which is that he is the deprived child who was robbed of eighty days in Paradise, and is determined to make the world pay for it.

That is what he does. How he does it I shall not tell you, because you are going to the play to find that out, and I would be a spoilsport if I let it out now. But in the end Paul Dempster, who has become Magnus Eisengrim, is a great man, and one of his two best friends is Dunstan Ramsay, who has been haunted all his life by two things: that he brought about Paul's premature birth by a failure of decency on his own part, and that Paul's mother, even in her madness, was a saint of heroic virtue. As for the third man, Boy Staunton, he dies mysteriously.

Ever since the first of these three books, *Fifth Business,* appeared I have been plagued by people who demand of me, "Who killed Boy Staunton?" Why they ask I cannot tell, because it is as plain as a pikestaff who killed him. The explanation that is given in one of Magnus Eisengrim's magic illusions says: "He was killed by the usual cabal: by himself, first of all; by the woman he knew; by the woman he did not know; by the man who granted his inmost wish; and by the inevitable fifth, who was keeper of his conscience and keeper of the stone." Nobody dies of a single cause, but of a complexity of events. The doctor who signs the necessary certificate may write "Cancer"—but what led to the cancer? A man may die, as Boy Staunton did, in part, by achieving a life's ambition, and finding out how much it is worth. And often there is, as the Brazen Head says in the illusion in the play, a fifth figure, whose involvement in the plot is necessary but not immediately observable.

Who killed Boy Staunton? "Vengeance is mine; I will repay, saith the Lord." But the Lord may use one, or several human agents to work out his design and manifest his judgement. And it may prove, if you wish to read the book on which this play is based, that the death of Boy Staunton was not the death of a criminal, and it may even be regarded as a mercy, considering the point which had been reached in his life.

It is not simple, you see. Life is not simple. Art is not simple. Perhaps only television is simple. I have been a writer now for over fifty years, and during that time critics have had a great deal to say about me, some of it good and some of it bad. But one of the things that has been said, and said often, is that as a writer I am a moralist, and I think that that is true and perceptive criticism.

What is a moralist? It is not, of course, somebody who preaches some system of morality which is supposed to make good people and a good world. A moralist is not an exponent of a creed. A moralist is somebody who observes life as carefully as he can, and draws conclusions from what he sees. He sees that fashionable enthusiasms about behaviour are short-lived, and that some things appear to be so self-evident that it is no exaggeration to call them truths. They are not new. Truth does not deal in novelty, but in age-long endurance. Because some of the truths the moralist observes have been given unforgettable expression in the Bible, there are people who think that the moralist is an enthusiast for Biblical morality. Not at all; there are portions of the Bible that make any sensitive person's flesh creep, they are so cruel and unforgiving. The moralist is not a cheapjack follower of the Old Testament—or of the New Testament, for that matter. He sees what he sees and he records it. And what does he see?

Whatsoever a man soweth, that shall he also reap.

As a dog returneth to his vomit, so a fool returneth to his folly.

A merry heart doeth good like a medicine: but a broken spirit drieth the bones.

A fool's mouth is his destruction, and his lips are the snare of his soul.

And a very great deal more, along the same lines. And if the moralist happens to be a writer, that is what he bases his writing on—the observation of the way life appears to work, by very old rules.

I wonder how many of you are familiar with Rudyard Kipling's poem, called "The Gods of the Copybook Headings"? I bring it up now to show that authors of recent time are just as powerfully aware of the way in which basic morality works as were the wind-and-sand-blown prophets of the Old Testament. Listen to this:

As it will be in the future, it was at the birth of Man—
There are only four things certain since Social progress began:—
That the Dog returns to his Vomit and the Sow returns to her
   Mire,
And the burnt fool's bandaged finger goes wabbling back to
   the Fire;

And that after this is accomplished, and the brave new world
   begins
When all men are paid for existing and no man must pay for
   his sins,
As surely as Water will wet us, as surely as Fire will burn,
The Gods of the Copybook Headings with terror and slaughter return!

That is tough talk, but morality *is* tough talk, which is why silly people try to brush it aside as old-fashioned and irrelevant to life as we—our wonderful, wonderful selves, toward whose perfection mankind has been striving ever since the Big Bang—as we understand, or misunderstand it.

I said some time ago that a novel of any weight is a tale to some readers, a parable to others. Is *World of Wonders* a parable? A parable is a story which points out a truth in terms of physical action. Does *World of Wonders* point out a truth? Oh yes, lots of truths. One might be summed up in the popular saying You Never Can Tell. You never can tell where something quite extraordinary and unexpected will come about. In a little Ontario village three men may be born so closely together that their lives run parallel courses, who may influence the world in quite different ways. Boy Staunton, after all, did do a remarkable job of distributing and assembling materials during the Second World War: Dunstan Ramsay made a lot of people aware of saints who were by no means disposed by nature or training to pay any attention to saints: Paul Dempster, when he became Magnus Eisengrim, brought wonder and marvel into the lives of countless people whose lives were very short of those elements. And all of these three men were linked by a single action that needed only a few seconds to take place—the throwing of a loaded snowball.

Part of the parable element in my story is that every action brings its reaction, and that you cannot always foresee what the reaction may be. If you throw a stone into a pool, the ripples will spread and spread until they reach the shores and continue as an impulse long after the ripples have ceased to be visible. After all, we are now assured that the Big Bang which occurred such an incalculably long time ago, set in action impulses that have resulted in such astonishing creatures as you and me and the complex world in which we live. The throwing of that snowball at 5:58 o'clock p.m. on the 27th of December, 1908, set up ripples which continued long after the death of Boy Staunton, sixty years later, when he was discovered in Toronto harbour, locked in his expensive car, with a stone clenched in his mouth. The ripples included Paul Dempster's wretchedness as a boy and his triumph as a man, and Dunstan Ramsay's long expiation of his guilt toward Paul's mother, and his preoccupation with saints.

Another element of parable in the novel is its demonstration of the truth—not a moralist's truth but a scientific truth—that nothing exists without its contrary. There is in all things a positive and a negative, and this is as true of human lives as it is of everything else. The three men who are the principal figures in the story are examples of this principle.

Consider the case of Boy Staunton. He seemed to the world around him an enviable and admirable fellow—handsome, rich, attractive to women, able to discharge big responsibilities with ease and perhaps a touch of genius. Yes—but always in his life there was a hint of that stone-in-the-snowball philosophy, the determination to impose his will upon others which leads so often to overdoing things which could be achieved more gently. Handsome, yes, but male beauty fails as quickly as its female counterpart. Rich, yes, but the failure of riches to buy anybody his heart's desire is proverbial, and Boy's heart's desire was to shine in the eyes of the world as gloriously as his ideal, Edward, Prince of Wales, and he ends up as the Lieutenant-Governor elect of Ontario, which is a very honourable position, unless you happen to see yourself as a Prince. Attractive to women, yes; but does the man who is attractive to women ever take the trouble to know women as human beings, and not as extensions of his own egotism? Every gift that was showered on Boy Staunton had its opposite, and in the end it was the opposites that were his undoing.

What about Dunstan Ramsay? An excellent schoolteacher, and those who saw him on the job saw no more than that, and thought him a useful but dull fellow. But in the world of true scholarship his opposite was found, and he gained fame in a very special scholarly world—a fame quite unknown to his colleagues in Colborne College, for what has hagiography to do with a school for boys? But Ramsay's was a crippled life; the Calvinist, Presbyterian morality in which he had been brought up, and which forced him to think that he was responsible for the madness of Mary Dempster and the premature birth of Paul, made him a suffering, haunted man, who thought too much about God, and did not give enough heed to the Devil until the Devil confronted him and laughed at him.

And Paul Dempster, *alias* Cass Fletcher, *alias* Faustus LeGrand, *alias* Mungo Fetch, *alias* Magnus Eisengrim—surely his life was all tilted toward the negative side? No, not quite, for he attained fame and made everybody around him subservient to him. He dominated large audiences of people who paid handsomely for him to deceive them with his illusions. But for his splendour he paid, because it was a life without love, though at the end he achieved something which, if not love as it is generally understood, was a wonderful substitute and much more exciting than love often is.

There are other elements of parable in the book, but I will not trouble you with them now. If you haven't read the book it would be presumptuous of me to suggest that you do so, but if you want to sort out all the elements of parable that are in it, you cannot expect to get them from the play, which by its very nature passes you by so quickly that you cannot take in everything. That is not a failure of the play, of course. It is part of the delight of plays that we leave them feeling that we have not quite encompassed all that was said and done. If you ever feel that you have got everything out of a play at a single sitting, you may be sure that the play was, in theatrical parlance, a turkey.

I have spoken of a novel as a tale—a simple story for those who do not want to look beyond that. And I have spoken of it as a parable, which is to say a story that illustrates certain truths. But there was a third dimension to the novel, was there not? The critic spoke of it as being perhaps a revelation of reality. Does *World of Wonders* reveal anything of that kind? I hope it does. An important part of the revelation lies in the character of Liesl. If you have read the book you remember who she was: Fräulein Dr. Liselotte Naegeli, a very rich Swiss woman who is the business partner of Magnus Eisengrim, and the financier who enables him to mount his Soirée of Illusions so handsomely that all other magic shows look tawdry in comparison. She is also a woman of unusual cultivation and taste, and it is she who gives the Soirée of Illusions its quality that appeals to people who would not ordinarily be attracted by a magic show; it is she who provides the distinction which Eisengrim, who never had any education or much experience of the world of culture, could not provide. She is described on the theatre program as "Autocrat," and some of you will remember that Diaghilev used the same title in his relation to the Ballets Russes, and the name she used for stage purposes is Liesl Vitzlipützli. The name has made a lot of people ask questions; it is the name of one of the devils who served that great magician, Doctor Faustus, and it was Liesl's joke that she took this servant's name when she was, in fact, the final boss, the top-dog, of the show of which Eisengrim was the star.

Liesl is a great deal more than that, however. She is hideous. She has been deformed by a disease which attacks a few unfortunate people when they are adolescent, and which makes their growth extraordinary, so that they may have huge hands, or feet, or a grotesquely deformed skull. You might expect a woman so deformed to live a life of seclusion, but Liesl has fallen under the spell of Eisengrim, who has himself made something extraordinary out of a wretchedly deprived beginning, and whose influence on Liesl is such that she adopts the manner of a supremely beautiful woman and—Gorgon though she is—she has many lovers—of both sexes. Eisengrim owes much to Liesl; she made him a gentleman and rather better than that word usually implies. But Liesl also owes much to him, because he sets her free from the physical prison in which misfortune has locked her.

You do not achieve victories like that and remain a nice, well-bred Swiss lady with an interest in the theatre. Gaining a victory over life brings wisdom of one sort or another, and it has brought Liesl a wisdom that has made her a mischief-maker when she meets someone as tightly bound up in his psychological make-up as Dunstan Ramsay. Ramsay has never been in love. He has thought he was in love, but his extreme wariness of women, which came about because of his experience with his possessive, dominating mother, has meant that his love was always cautious; he always had a way of escape if things became too demanding. In love affairs he always swam with water-wings. It is Liesl who decides that it is not too late for Ramsay, in middle age, to find out about the real thing, and she sets about to seduce him. Not, I assure you, by playing coy games; she simply invades his bedroom in her pyjamas and goes straight to the point. The effect is magical. Ramsay is never the same again.—By the way, I should perhaps utter a warning to any ladies among you who think of trying Liesl's methods that it is not quite as plain sailing as it looks, and you had better stick to the methods you know.—The result is, that when they are all considerably older, we meet Liesl and Eisengrim and Ramsay all living together in her luxurious Swiss retreat. They are as happy as larks, all in love with one another and with themselves, and face old age with joy.

People have asked me if Liesl is the Devil. It is extraordinary what questions people ask authors about things that are very plain in the book. What is the Devil? Who is the Devil? Like God, one of whose sons he is—and if you don't believe me check with your Bible—it is uncommonly hard to define, and you are hopelessly lost if you attempt to define him simply in human terms. But of course, like God, he has his human side, and sometimes he has been called the Spirit of Perversity, or Contrary Destiny. I am not a theologian and I make no attempt to define the Devil. But I know that there is one thing he undoubtedly is: he is a personal element in everybody's nature, and he may be defined as everything that a man or woman condemns, detests, and is certain that he or she is not. Consider the characters in the novel, and in the play. Ramsay has never thrown off his Presbyterian upbringing, great expert though he may be in the remarkable world of saints. Ramsay does not believe that he can be the slave of passion, a violent lover, a man swept utterly off his feet by sexual fury. He does not believe that he can be a liar, a deceiver, a concocter of false history—in fact a thorough-going academic crook. But it is Liesl who shows him that he can be all these things, and what is more, glory in what formerly filled him with detestation. She sets him free. Not free to go to the dogs and become a villain, but free to know that villainy has a place in his make-up, and that the dogs are never very far away. This is the knowledge that brings on his heart attack, when he realizes that by keeping the stone that Boy Staunton hid in the snowball when both boys were ten years old, he was acting, perhaps creditably, as a keeper of evidence, but he was acting in a very different spirit as well; he had vengeance and bitterness in his heart; he was an agent of an evil impulse—fully as evil as the impulse that led Staunton to conceal the stone in the snowball.

There is a character in the story who does not make it into the play. He is an old priest who says to Ramsay: "If you would know yourself, however slightly, you must meet and shake hands with your personal Devil; you will probably find that he is not at all a bad fellow." The old priest is wickedly delighted to find that Ramsay's personal Devil appears as a woman.

Liesl is, you see, the feminine element in the novel. That village simpleton that Ramsay loved and Staunton married, and that charming English girl whom Ramsay was almost inveigled into marrying, are not very deep studies of femininity. But I think Liesl is. She teaches two men vital things about themselves and thus she completes their nature, just as her nature is completed by them, and I think that is what women do, when they are at their best. But certainly it is as his personal Devil that Liesl first appears to Ramsay.

Because I have been talking about God and the Devil, as I so often do, many people assume that I must be very religious. I am always surprised when people tell me that they are not at all religious. It seems to me that to live without religion is to condemn oneself to a world which is the psychological equivalent of de-caf coffee, non-alcoholic wines, fatless butter-substitutes, paper made out of reconstituted garbage, language dominated by "political correctness," and all that rubbish which is supposed to make life safe and inoffensive and hardly distinguishable from death. Only of course we never talk about death and hope to read in the paper some morning that science has found a cure for it.

But what is religion? The dictionaries tell us that the origin of the word is obscure. It may come from a Latin word that means associating oneself with something in the past, and wearing it as a yoke, or it may come from another word that means to go over things again, to think matters through, to remember, to correct. It is in this second sense that I would describe myself as a religious man. To give the most serious consideration of which one is capable to the elements in life which confront one seems to me to be following a path which is not content with simplicities, and which cannot reject or set aside the innumerable things in life which suggest purposes and powers of which we have only the most fleeting perceptions. The intervention in life of what must be called Fate, the purpose which is achieved by happenings that appear to have no explicable reason (or which may even fly in the face of reason), the sense which is familiar to everyone that he or she is not guiding his life, but is being impelled by something unknown and perhaps not in any ordinary sense benevolent— these are the things that make it impossible for me to accept any of the arguments advanced by people who feel that religion has exhausted its part in the life of man and is exposed, as Sigmund Freud argued, as an illusion.

But has what I have been saying any connection with my earlier talk about God and the Devil? Those words are a convenient shorthand for vast elements in the fate of mankind, in the fate of the world and the universe, and in the fate of every human creature which we cannot hope to pin down with definitions or scientific formulae and which we have to accept as vast realities far outsoaring the portion of reality which is perceptible to us. We have to reject the egotistical human notion that we can, or should, discover and explain everything.

What do we mean by religion? Many people cannot separate the words from orthodoxy—some code of belief that has been laid down and to which the religious person tries to adhere as best he may. The most influential orthodoxy in our part of the world is Christianity, and Christianity asks its followers to strive for human perfection, thereby bringing nearer that Kingdom of God which will bring peace and perfection to our world. It is here that I must disagree, respect-fully but firmly. I think perfection an inhuman and impossible ideal, because it ignores elements in human experience and history which cannot be wished away. These are the things which we sweep together under the heading of Evil, or to use the shorthand terms I spoke of earlier, the Devil. You cannot banish the Devil by being so good, or merely goody-goody, that he shrinks away from your presence, ashamed of himself. You must meet him eye to eye and hear what he has to say. You may even learn from him, as do all the chief charac-ters in *World of Wonders,* for every one of them has met the Devil and come away slightly scorched but immensely wiser—even Roland Ingestree, the man who wants no truck with anything that he would call supernatural, which is a word silly people apply to anything they do not want to include in nature. Ingestree belongs to that very large class of people—often highly educated and influential people—who truly believe that Man is the centre and measure of all things, the highest development of life, and that when the individual conscious-ness is closed by death, that is the end of the matter. They are not inter-ested in Man as the instrument of some vastly greater Will than they can comprehend, and they do not see their refusal as a limitation of their understanding. As for the Devil, they laugh. And laughing at the Devil amuses the Devil a great deal more than it amuses the laugher, because he knows how easy such people are to bring wholly under his rule.

Many of you, no doubt, will have understood from what I have said that I am a student and follower of Dr. C.G. Jung. But Jung asked for no orthodoxy among his followers, and no missionary spirit. I am not trying to convert you to my beliefs, but only to explain a very little about what lies beneath the surface of my writing. The aim is not, "Be ye therefore perfect, even as your Father which is in heaven is perfect"; the aim is Know Thyself.

And what has this to do with my novel *World of Wonders,* and this play that has been derived from it? I assure you, it has everything to do with it. The book attempts to demonstrate in really quite a humble way that many things we regard as certainties are not certain at all, and that two and two only make four in arithmetic and cannot be counted on to do so in life. Neat certainties have a very limited truth. But there are some things which, in a very large and general way, do seem to work themselves out in the widest possible variety of ways, but with consequences which are almost—notice that I say almost—predictable.

When I spoke earlier about a definition of a novel, there were three elements, were there not? A tale: yes, we have talked about the story of *World of Wonders.* And a parable: yes, we have talked about the demonstration, through the story, of some old truth. What was the third? It was "a direct revelation of reality to the man who has made it a part of his being." Surely that is rather a tall order? A direct revelation of reality? Is not the novelist taking himself rather too seriously when he talks of revealing reality? Yes, indeed that may be, but unless a novelist regards himself simply as an entertainer, that is what he hopes for. Of course he does not expect to succeed with every reader, but he tries. And in what ways does he try?

Now we are getting into deep water, because we are going to talk about Style, and under that heading monstrous quantities of nonsense have been talked and will be talked in the future. I shall try not to talk nonsense.

There is a Style for every serious writer. It is the evidence, shown in his writing of what he himself is. He may be an immensely serious man, like Tolstoy or Thomas Mann, and they seize us, and hold us by the weight of their determination to see life steadily, and in terms of almost photographic realism. Or he may be someone like Graham Greene or Evelyn Waugh, who appear to superficial readers to be concocters of adventure stories or funny stories, but whose moral weight is evident in every line they write and whose seriousness of outlook is beyond question. Or the writer may be a Dickens or a Balzac whose books illuminate our world so brilliantly that we never see life again in the same terms. The styles exemplified by these writers and hundreds more whom we cannot mention are of the uttermost variety, but there are labels, if you like labels, that may be attached to certain groups among them.

I said that some critics had labelled me as a moralist, and although I do not quarrel with that description it makes me rather uncomfortable. If I had to choose a label, I suppose I should be driven to the world of art criticism to find one; I think that if I am anything, I am a Mannerist. In saying that I am putting my head into the lion's mouth, for to many critics Mannerist is a dirty word. It implies an artificiality, or frivolity, a lack of artistic weight, which repels critics who are themselves utterly solemn—notice that I say solemn and not serious, which is quite a different thing—in their outlook.

If your idea of a truly great picture is Van Gogh's *Irises,* which has commanded the highest price ever paid for a picture, you will not like the Mannerist pictures of such triflers as Michelangelo, Raphael, El Greco, and others of the kind. My own favourite Mannerist picture is in the National Gallery in London, and it is Bronzino's *An Allegory of Love.* When I look at Van Gogh's *Irises* I see some irises and I am ready to yield to those who see more. But when I look at *An Allegory of Love* I see not only a picture of transfixing beauty, but a mass of ideas, suggestions, warnings, and jokes, and I don't know how you could get all of that into a picture unless you were a Mannerist. One of the figures in the composition is called Fraude—Fraud, Deceit, Double-dealing, Deception. It is the figure of a girl of delicate beauty, who holds out her hand in which there is a honeycomb; it is only when you look more closely that you see that she has the feet and claws of a lion, and a dragon's tail with a dart on the end of it.

Have you ever, in your own love-life—and you must have one—met with this figure? Have you ever wondered how Van Gogh would have painted it? Of course he didn't want to. But Bronzino wanted to say his say about the nature of Love, and this aspect of it—deceiving, cheating Love—and he had to be a very great Mannerist to do it.

He says so many things—far more than I can possibly talk about now. He says to the central figure, who is Venus—"Take care; that youth you are kissing so voluptuously is your son." He shows us Jealousy raving. He shows us Old Time and his daughter Truth, drawing aside the curtain to reveal what the world would like to keep secret. And Bronzino could not have shown us all these things if he had not been a Mannerist, and free from the chains of photographic reality.

May one talk of Mannerism in the writing of fiction? I don't see any reason why not. Some very great writers have worked in that mode. One of the greatest was Rabelais, whose name is known to everybody, but who is not much read, though he has splendid things to say to the world today, and especially to the academic world. To come nearer to our own time, and to name a writer who is very widely read, I would certainly call James Joyce a Mannerist, for he casts aside the chains of realism in order to show us, in his best known novel, how the life of a Dublin advertisement salesman can follow the pattern of the travels of *Ulysses* in the course of a single day. The effect is funny, tragic, astonishing, and wholly magical.

I write as I do because I need the grotesques, the Classical and Biblical echoes and the high colour to say what I have to say, and what I call reality. Some kind people have added the word magic. What is magic? Is it not the production of effects for which there appear to be no causes? Behind all magic there is an explanation, but it is unwise to seek it too vigorously; there are lots of things in life which are more enjoyable when they are not completely understood. A good piece of magic is a work of art and should be respected as such; it is a flower, not an alarm clock, and if you pull it to pieces to find out what makes it work you have destroyed it, and your own pleasure.

That is where fiction and the art of the theatre meet; they are to be enjoyed first, and any discussion as to what they are and how they work must take second place to that initial pleasure. In our modern world we are very eager to explain everything, codify everything, and reduce everything that is complex to whatever may be comprehended by the greatest number, because anything that is mysterious is undemocratic, and "élitist." That is a pitiful attitude when it is allowed to infect the world of art.

World of Wonders is just that: the book and the play were made for your pleasure, and your pleasure will be greatest if you accept them simply as what they are.

17

CONVOCATION ADDRESS

By the end of his life Davies had received no fewer than twenty-six honorary degrees from universities in a number of countries. In many cases he was able to relax and enjoy the honour without any attendant active duties. In others he was required to deliver the Convocation Address.

On this occasion the young people in the audience at Dowling College on Long Island heard something far different than the usual platitudes about the future lying ahead of them. Davies talked to them about their Innermost Self, their Soul, and about the need to read some poetry throughout their lives.

His diary records his visit to Long Island, New York, at the unseasonable time of February 13, 1992: *Directly to Dowling which has as its core a former Vanderbilt mansion—summer dwelling—they built their own canal to the sea! A reception for us in the Hunt Room; Hunt was the architect, and this room is a pun on his name, for over the fireplace is a sculpture of Diana, very naked, and there used to be a frieze of her hunting exploits, but a fire destroyed it. . . . Long Island, which I had assumed was rural, is a huge complex of estates and substantial homes. Great distances from place to place. I am urged everywhere to sign books, and everyone looks at me expectantly, hoping I will say something wise or funny. Flattering, but demanding. Many fans here.*

M r. Chancellor, Mr. President, ladies and gentlemen: I am most grateful to you for the honour you have conferred upon me and I assure you that I shall remember with warm satisfaction that you have chosen to make me one of your community.

Let me assure you, however, that I am under no illusion about my position in these ceremonies. Although I have received my degree alone, and am permitted to speak, I am, in truth, the least important graduate here today. I have done nothing in particular to earn my degree; I have undergone no anxiety as to whether, when the moment came, I might be found wanting and sent empty away; I do not depend on my degree to help me toward a place in my profession. Compared with the young people here who are receiving degrees which they have earned, I am a fraud. This is *their* day, and any acclaim at this ceremony is for them and their achievement. As the least of today's graduating class, I salute you, and wish you well in the work you will shortly undertake; it is my earnest hope that this day marks a decisive moment in your fortunes and that you will always look back on it with pleasure.

When I was asked to speak to you today, I was told in the plainest terms that I should speak for ten minutes, and not an instant longer. I know the hope that springs in the bosoms of university authorities when they utter such warnings, and as one who has suffered under long convocation speeches, I have taken the words of your President seriously. I shall speak for ten minutes. Approximately.

What am I to say? Of course I must give you advice. And of course if I wanted to, I could say a great deal that is depressing about the troubled world into which you are now making your entry, and the problems and miseries that face you. But I don't want to do that, because I don't really think that times are any more difficult for young people starting out in life than they have ever been. They are different, in superficial ways, but not really more demanding. Your fate will be the usual one: a few will, in the eyes of the world, succeed spectacularly; the majority will get along pretty well; and a few will end up in jail.

When you reassemble in twenty-five years for a class reunion, look around to see what proportion are unavoidably absent. There is always a curious, not wholly admirable, satisfaction in doing that.

But—advice? I have lots of advice to give you and everybody else. Advice is a large part of my professional stock-in-trade. But today I must remember my ten minutes, so I shall give you one piece of advice and no more. But it is important, serious advice. I mean every word I say. And here it is.

As you make your way in the world, practising your profession, finding friends, finding companions in domesticity, bringing up children, trying to put by substance to guard you against the blows of fate, you will certainly be tempted to neglect the one person who is, beyond all others, your deepest concern and whose well-being is of overwhelming significance every day of your life. I mean your Innermost Self.

If this occasion took place a hundred and fifty years ago I would not talk about your Innermost Self. I would talk about your Soul, and you would understand me. But in our day the Soul is out of fashion—at least by that name—though people function exactly as they did in the time of our great-great-grandparents, when Souls were all the rage. But whatever you call it, it is the fundamental, animating element in your intellectual and emotional life, and you must be very careful of it. Who knows—it may last longer than you do.

We live in an age when the care of physical health has attained almost to the stature of a religion. People eat extraordinary and disagreeable foods and dose themselves with pills and supplements to ensure the uttermost perfection of healthy diet. They flog themselves to the most distressing exertions, hoping thereby to bully their bodies into some sort of exaggerated well-being. Creature comforts hallowed by centuries of acceptance as friends to man are now condemned as vile indulgences, harmful to the standers-by, harmful to the unborn, noxious and disgusting as well as ruinously expensive. It appears as though everybody under the age of fifty were convinced that by making their lives unbearable, they might extend their existence forever. Yes, it really seems as if they hoped that they might never die.

THE MERRY HEART

But what kind of lives are they thus preserving? Are they happy? Are they fun to be with? Are they wise? Do their contemporaries and their children hold them in high respect? Very often these questions must be answered with a resounding No! As Henry Thoreau said a century and a half ago, the mass of men lead lives of quiet desperation. If he were living today he would have to amend that statement to include women, who can be every bit as desperate as their brothers. As they jog and diet their way among us, the faces of such people are masks of despair. Do you want to join them?

If you don't, here is one way—just one way among many, but in my ten minutes I can't explore many ways—to avoid it. It sounds simple, but it isn't, if you take it seriously.

Get yourself a good anthology of poetry, and keep it by your bed. Read a little before you go to sleep. Read a little if you wake up before the alarm goes off. Read a little if you wake up in the night. When you are idle during the day—on public transport, or at a committee meeting—let your mind dwell on what you have read. One book will last you a long time. Indeed, it may last you a lifetime, but I hope you may acquire more books of poetry as time goes on. Read, not as people tend to read fiction or history, to get to the end of the book, to have the reading over with, to be able to say "I've read that." No; reread. Read until you find that you are reading the poem without actually looking at the words. Hear every word in your head. Do not skim; do not read quickly, any more than you would play a piece of music absurdly fast on your hi-fi, simply to get it over with. Read, listen to and savour the words, and the sense.

Oh yes, the sense. Because that is what poetry is. It is the distilled good sense or emotion of someone especially gifted in wisdom of some sort. Modern poetry has turned its face against rhyme and metre, which are two of the most vivid evidences of poetry. So be sure you read some of that poetry which was written before the modern austerity took command. Read it even if you don't agree with what it says. Read it even if you think it is saying something obvious. Read it because it feeds your Innermost Self, enlarges it, keeps it alert, refreshed and in good order, so that it never allows you to sink into despair or dullness, or some fashionable stupidity.

Poetry is part of the sustenance we take on board for the long voyage of life. Don't imagine it is easy, and don't give up when you find that it is hard. Tussle with the difficult things, and in the end they will reveal their meaning to you, and that meaning may help you over many a difficult place.

Meaning may come slowly. Long ago, when I was a small boy, we had books in school called "Readers" and they were anthologies of all sorts of prose and poetry, some of which we had to learn by heart. That was before the days of educational theorists who knew exactly what a child might be expected to understand at a particular age, and who thought it madness to give a child something to read which was not immediately comprehensible by the dullest wit in any class.

Thus it happened that, when I was eight years old, I had to memorize the following poem:

It is not growing like a tree
In bulk, doth make men better be;
Or standing long an oak, three hundred year,
To fall a log at last, dry, bald and sere:
A lily of a day
Is fairer far in May,
Although it fall and die that night;
It was the plant and flower of light.
In small proportions we just beauty see;
And in short measures, life may perfect be.

Not a poem that a modern educational theorist would give to children of eight, I think. Yet we mastered it, insofar that we knew what it meant that largeness, and bulk, and long endurance, though excellent in themselves, were not the only standards by which quality of life was to be measured; a small, perfect thing had its place too, and by no means an inferior place.

So there it was. It was not for another ten years that I discovered that the poem was part of a Pindaric ode written by a man named Ben Jonson, a friend of Shakespeare's, to comfort some people who had lost a dear friend in youth. And all my life I have known that poem and have come to love it. And I was so vain as to think I understood it.

I know better now. I am quite a bit older than Ben Jonson was when he died, and my understanding is slowly catching up with his. I understand that poem now as I have never understood it before. And yet, you see, I have had it with me all my life—that and scores of other poems that have sustained me through good times and bad —and that poem is fresher now than when, as a child, I had to get it by heart.

Do I see doubt in the faces of some of you—men and women who have given their best energies to science or engineering and may perhaps look on literature as a "soft course"? My dear friends, science can do many wonderful things, but it cannot comfort the afflicted, or ease a heavy heart, or give expression to the topmost joy of which life is capable. That is what poetry can do. Remember that I told you that.

So—I have done my duty. I have given you advice. I think I have run a little over my ten minutes, and I am not in the least repentant.

18

THE PEELED EYE

"The Peeled Eye" is a curiosity among these pieces. While Davies had his eyes peeled in a literal sense when he had a second cataract operation in 1992, the fiction writer presumably has the upper hand over the historian in this account of a boyish encounter with a penknife-wielding witch. Yet the equally unlikely story of the writhing woman crying "Christian men, come and help me!" occurs elsewhere in his work and is to be believed.

The loose format of this speech perhaps derives from the relaxed after-dinner nature of his talk to the Cosmos Club in Washington on November 11, 1993. As indicated in the text, one part has been excised, a lengthy excerpt from his novel *Leaven of Malice*. Thereafter Davies deals humorously with the vexatious enquiries of "aspiring writers." To demonstrate how best to handle them he wheels in his curmudgeonly alter ego, Samuel Marchbanks, whose correspondence is invariably lively, and ("so with all the fiery planets opposed to Uranus . . .") frequently mischievous.

In the diary he records that in the course of his stay he visited a country estate *not less than 200 years old. Welcomed by our host who seems to be a recluse and lives in this very big house alone; it has a large central section and then additions joined to the main by what he called "hyphens"; one addition is a chapel. He is gentle, charming, wonderful old-style manner. We are joined by his son and daughter-in-law and have lunch in the kitchen, a real 18th century kitchen with a large fireplace, tile floor and superbly scrubbed copper pots hanging everywhere. We tour the house; strong whiff of Edgar Allan Poe about it; unused drawing rooms strike chill even in this beautiful autumn day; portraits of ancestors, stiff as pokers and damned disinheriting countenances. The chapel 18th century. Fine ceramic Stations from Italy; fine furnishings; a pretty little organ, of course out of order; altar bedizened and contains a relic of some sort; war memorial to persons connected with the estate who died. He says he has had to close the chapel to services because if anything fell on anyone, or any mishap occurred, he might meet with ruinous suit as there is a lot of that sort of thing in the U.S. at present. . . . A very remarkable experience for I have never seen anything like this in the U.S. before; material for a novel! . . .*

To begin, I suppose I should tell you why the general title of this evening's affair is "The Peeled Eye."

When I was a very small boy, living in the flatlands of Western Ontario, I was an inattentive child, and an absentminded child. I made a mess of the simplest errand. If I brought a loaf of bread into the house from Johnny Tiffen's bread-wagon, I was likely to drop it in the dust; I was a spiller of milk, a breaker of eggs. Adults kept saying to me, "You must watch what you are doing; you must keep your eyes peeled." The idea seized upon my mind with a force the adults never understood.

So much so, indeed, that I went to see a witch about it. Oh yes, there was a witch; there are always witches where there are children. My witch lived right next door, in a dark house surrounded by fir trees and a high fence, so that it was dark and frightening in there. But I used often to see the witch through a knot hole in her fence, wandering among the trees, her hair flying loose (which was not at all the fashion for old ladies then) and in her bare feet, which surely showed a monstrous lack of decorum. Her name was Patience Minshall.

It took courage, but I sneaked into Old Paishey Minshall's overgrown garden. I was not wholly afraid. My feeling was of awe, and adventure. There she was. I had never seen the bare feet of an adult in my life, and the witch's feet were a caution, let me tell you.

When she came to where I was, the witch fixed me with a red-rimmed green eye, like a gooseberry floating in stewed rhubarb.

"Well boy, what do you want?"

"Please, Mrs. Minshall, I want to have my eyes peeled."

If she had been an ordinary mortal she would have laughed and made some silly remark. In my experience, adults never knew when you were being serious. But she was a witch, right enough. She knew I was in earnest.

"You understand, don't you, that it will probably turn you into another."

"Another what?"

"Not another, stupid! An author."

"Does it hurt much?"

"Being an author? Oh, they all say it does, but just try to persuade one to be anything else."

I knew about authors. My father was one, though at this time he was the editor of a newspaper. He had, in his younger days, written very romantic stories that had even been printed in New York papers. One of them—his best—was called "Dashing Dolly Darrington," or "Manacled at the Major's," which I thought, and still think, a most beautiful and promising title. He had been paid ten dollars for it. There was big money in writing in those days. Authorship had no terrors for me, so I said—

"Please."

Then and there she took a little penknife from her pocket and skilfully peeled my eyes. It hurt—a kind of fierce stinging—but she knew how to deal with that. She did a queer and Biblical thing. She spat into her hand, mixed some garden loam with the spittle, and dressed my eyes with it, and the stinging stopped. Two or three minutes later, when she wiped away the mud, I saw double. I saw a little old woman, crippled and perhaps a little crazy, but I also saw a Witch, possessed of astonishing powers that came from the Great Mother of Us All.

"Be careful what you say about what you see," said the Witch; "not everybody likes to know what's in front of them."

She waved me away, and off I ran, a boy with peeled eyes.

Life was never the same again.

What do I mean by that? Well, when poor Miss MacFarlane, who lived across the street from us and was mad, escaped from the big woman who was her keeper, and threw herself down in the dust of the road, screaming pitifully—

"Christian men! Come and help me!"

—until some men appeared as it seemed from nowhere and carried her back indoors, I saw not only poor Aunt Ellen, but also around her, as she lay screaming in the dust, all the people whose unkindness and want of understanding had brought her to such a pass and some of whom—the ones who were still alive—were waiting for her to die, to get her money.

Nobody else seemed to see them.

When Mr. Harper, who lived next door, threw himself down the well, it was my mother who went to his aid, leaping what seemed to me an incredibly high fence with a bound like an antelope. She rescued him, which was what part of his mind wanted, though the other half was fixed on a different goal. When the men whom my mother had called in—there always seemed to be men around for these jobs—laid him dripping on the grass, he murmured over and over again—

"I want to go to Annie."

Annie was his wife, who had died a few months before. I seemed to be the only one who saw Annie, standing at the edge of the crowd, shaking her head.

I remembered what the Witch had said, and I told nobody, not even my mother. She thought poor old Mr. Harper was astray in his wits, but I knew he had been *come after and fetched,* because a few days later he did die, and at his funeral—I spied it through the fence—I saw Annie, triumphantly leading the horses of the hearse.

I saw lots of things. As I said, we lived in the flatlands—as flat as

Holland—but on the horizon I saw mountains, and I knew they were the mountains of Wales, of which my father had often spoken because that was his native land, and sometimes he missed the mountains terribly. I never saw those mountains in reality until many years later.

When people talk about authors, they often speak of imagination, as if it were a quality that enabled you to invent things. But with peeled eyes, who needs to invent? The reality of what I see and cannot help seeing is enough, and quite often too much, for as the Witch warned me, if I told all I see I should often be in serious trouble. Sometimes it is terrifying, but never, never dull.

Sometimes people have asked me why there is no Sex in my novels. I don't know what they are talking about; my novels are full of Sex. But the kind of sex they mean is the sort of Sex that has been wonderfully romanticised, although the publishers pretend it is fearlessly realistic and sometimes talk about "scenes of explicit sex." What they mean is scenes in which two physically beautiful young people, after a good deal of preliminary sparring, at last find themselves in bed, or on a mossy bank, or on the wet floor of a boathouse, or in an elevator stuck between floors, and there they get to work on what the eager reader has been panting for.

But Sex is an extremely variable experience, and everybody has it, not simply the young and the beautiful. Nor is sex in a novel a substitute for the real thing—unless the novel is pornographic—First Aid for the Wistful. For me, with the Peeled Eye, it is not the act itself which is of chief interest. Everybody knows about that, and they don't need me to instruct them. As an eighteenth-century cynic once said: "The pleasure is fleeting, the posture ridiculous, and the expense damnable." Yet it retains its popularity. What interests me is the people: why do they find themselves in this position? What does it mean in their very special circumstances? Is the prevailing mood simple desire, or joy, or pathos? Is it the sexual act they seek, or rather some human sympathy, some manifestation of intense feeling, some forgetfulness in lives that are dull or even full of pain? In some of my books sex has brought spiritual transfiguration.

In the scene I am going to read you must not suppose that I am laughing at the participants. I am laughing at that incorrigible joker Fate. Because what is important in the scene is that a secret is revealed, and as some of our Members of Parliament have discovered, sex and secrets are very close.

(Here Davies read from Leaven of Malice, "The Frustration of Bevil Higgin.")

The world is full of people who want to write. Of course they *can* write. Everybody in the civilized world, with a tiny group of exceptions, can set down in words what they have seen, or felt, or what they need or think they need. But that is not what they mean. They want to write books. They want to be authors. It is astonishing how this passion rages in so many innocent bosoms.

And of course many of them do write, and even achieve publication, for reasons that have nothing to do with Literature.

Sometimes I wonder what would have happened if, instead of teaching children for the past century or so to use the Roman alphabet, the educational authorities had taught them to use musical notation. Can you imagine what concert-going would be like? A typical symphony concert might begin with a rollicking overture called *Poet and Peasant: I've Had 'Em All,* by some notorious Hollywood harlot. Next would come a Symphonic Poem, called *My Life in Politics: Spilling the Beans,* by an ex-Cabinet Minister. The highlight of the concert would be an immensely long symphony, called simply *Appassionata,* with innumerable sexual climaxes, culminating in a real beauty—a cadenza for solo Big Drum.

It is undoubtedly a mercy that people have been taught to express themselves in words alone.

A very large number of aspiring writers have written to me, asking for advice, and I have always answered, because I was brought up to be polite and never leave a letter unanswered, however difficult the composition of an answer may be. Let me offer you a few examples of my correspondence:

SELECTIONS FROM MARCHBANKS

TO DIONYSUS FISHORN, ESQUIRE

Dear Mr. Fishorn:

No, I will not support your application for a Canada Council grant to enable you to write your novel. I know nothing about you, but I know a good deal about novels, and you are on the wrong track.

You say you want money to be "free of care" for a year, so that you can "create," and you speak of going to Mexico, to live cheaply and avoid distraction. Fishorn, I fear that your fictional abilities have spilled over from your work into your life. You see yourself in some lovely, unspoiled part of Mexico, where you will stroll out of your study onto the patio after a day's "creation," to gaze at the sunset and get into the cheap booze; your wife will admire you extravagantly and marvel that you ever conde-scended to marry such a workaday person as herself; the vil-lagers will speak of you with awe as El Escritor, and will pump your beautiful servant Ramona for news of your wondrous doings; you will go down into the very depths of Hell in your creative frenzies, but you will emerge, scorched and ennobled, in time for publication, translation into all known languages, and the Nobel Prize.

Ah, Fishorn, would that it were so! But take the advice of an old hand: you won't write any better in Mexico than in Tin Cup, B.C., and unless you are wafted into a small, specially favoured group of the insane, you will never be free from care. So get to work, toiling in the bank of wherever it is by day, and serving the Triple Goddess at night and on weekends. Art is long, and grants are but yearly, so forget about them. A writer should not take handouts from anybody, even his country.

Benevolently but uncompromisingly,

Samuel Marchbanks.

TO MERVYN NOSEIGH, M.A.

Dear Mr. Noseigh:

No no; I am not in the least offended by your letter asking about my sex life. I fully realize that no study of any author, living or dead, is of any value without this sort of saucy exploration. And my disenchantment has undoubtedly had more effect on literature than anything since Henry James had his mysterious misadventure.

Like every Canadian of my generation, I picked up my knowledge of Sex in the gutter. I remember the day I did so. There it was, a torn scrap of print, fluttering on the very edge of a manhole. I picked it up, and studied it with care. So far as I could make out, much of it was in foreign languages—squiggly scripts that meant nothing to me; but there was a little left of the English section, and from it I discerned that headaches, a furred tongue, and occasional spots before the eyes were signs of—the fragment was torn at that point, but it was obviously Sex.

From that time forward I made discreet enquiries of every attractive girl I met about her headaches; they never had any. Once I reached a point of intimacy where I was able to ask a marvellous girl to show me her tongue; it was as clean as could be, so obviously I had been misled about her feelings for me, and broke off the affair with a heavy heart.

Years later I discovered that what I had found in the gutter was part of the literature that comes wrapped about bottles of Eno's Fruit Salts.

Such are the tragedies that maim the lives of millions.

Yours in total disillusion,

Samuel Marchbanks.

TO MRS. KEDIJAH SCISSORBILL

Madam:

So you are astonished that a man of my apparent good sense should believe in Astrology, are you? My good woman, if you knew more of my history, you would be astonished that my good sense is still apparent.

You have heard of the Wandering Jew, who roams the earth till Judgement Day? I am his cousin, the Wandering Celt, and my branch of the family is the elder. Therefore I have had a good deal of experience in belief.

In my early days I was invited by learned men to believe in the Triple Goddess, and a very good goddess she was. But when I was Christianized I was commanded to believe in a Trinity that was also a Unity, and a goddess who looked and behaved remarkably like my Triple Goddess, though I was assured she was somebody much more up-to-date and important. Then a man named Calvin demanded that I believe in Strength through Misery, and I did till a man named Wesley told me to believe in Personal Revelation and Ecstasy, and I did. During a brief spell in New England Emerson told me to believe in a Unity that had nothing to do with a Trinity, and was itself of doubtful existence, and I did. But then I was told by people calling themselves scientists to believe in Phrenology, Animal Magnetism, the Germ Theory, Psycho-Analysis, Sociology, Relativity, Atomic Energy, Space Travel, God-is-Dead, Quasars, Spiral Time and so many new faiths that I could not keep up with them, though I tried.

Until I wearied and went back to the Triple Goddess, with Astrology thrown in for fun.

Because as a Celt, you see, I am at once credulous of everything and sceptical of everything, and not a whole-hogger, who rushes from the Mother of God to Mary Baker Eddy, and from her to LSD, expecting some revelation that will settle everything. I don't want everything settled. I enjoy the mess.

So with all the fiery planets opposed to Uranus I am

Yours sincerely,

Samuel Marchbanks.

TO MERVYN NOSEIGH, M.A.

Dear Mr. Noseigh:

Your last question is a humdinger. "When did you first decide to be a humorist; who were your chief humorous influences; how do you define humour?"—you ask, just like that.

I never decided to be a humorist; if I am one, I was born one, but I have never really given the matter much thought. I was once given a medal for humour, but it makes me nervous; I have tried to lose it, but I am too superstitious to throw it away. Men who bother their heads too much about being something particular—a Humorist, or a Philosopher, or a Social Being, or a Scientist, or a Humanist, or whatever—quickly cease to be men and become animated attitudes.

I suppose some of the humorists I have read have influenced me, because I think of them with affection, but never as people to be copied. I have read others, greatly praised as funny-men, who simply disgusted me. If I had to name a favourite, I suppose it would have to be François Rabelais, but I do not give him my whole heart; he had a golden touch with giants and pedants, but he thought ignobly of women.

Don't you know what humour is? Universities re-define wit and satire every few years; surely it is time they nailed down humour for us? I don't know what it is, though I suspect that it is an attribute of everything, and the substance of nothing, so if I had to define a sense of humour I would say it lay in the perception of shadows.

Sorry to be so disappointing,

Samuel Marchbanks.

19

A VIEW IN WINTER:
CREATIVITY IN OLD AGE

A few days after the previous selection, Davies took part in a symposium on old age at Johns Hopkins University. On November 14, 1993, he gave the speech that follows on the subject of creativity late in life. He wrote to a friend: *My news is chiefly concerned with growing old. But does that mean that I am sinking into an armchair, dozing and thinking of times past? It most certainly does not! I do not think I have ever been busier in my life. I am not looking for things to do. They are looking for me. I seem to make a great many speeches, and they all take time to prepare and I do not become less nervous as I grow older. Since last summer it seems almost as if I had never shut up. But the last two ventures were entertaining. I went to Baltimore to the Johns Hopkins Medical Center, where they were having a series of meetings about old age; they asked me to speak about creativity in old age, and as I am now eighty, and still working steadily, I was assumed to know something about it. What I told them was simply that if you have never been creative in your younger days you must not expect to write, or paint, or compose music simply because you have grown old. But if you have done these things when young, you will probably go on till you drop. Who ever heard of a "retired" painter?*

I have been asked to lead off this afternoon's discussion with some remarks on creativity in old age, and while it may appear obvious to you why I was chosen for this task, I assure you it is not so plain to me. It is true that I am old, and it is true that as a writer—primarily a novelist—I continue to work up until the present time, but to me there seems to be nothing extraordinary about it. I simply continue to do what I have done all my life, and I see no reason to stop. I am not tired, I am not wanting in ideas, and for me writing has always been my principal worldly task. Why would I cease?

The answer might be given that I wanted to rest. There is a widespread belief in our western world that after the age of sixty-five *everybody* wants to rest. But I do not want to rest. For me to cease writing would not be a rest, it would be a deprivation. I should become one of those tedious men whom one meets among people who are retired, who is a social nuisance because he has nothing to do. Inactivity and deprivation of all accustomed stimulus is not rest; it is a preparation for the tomb. But I shall not base my remarks entirely on my own opinions, and in preparing to talk to you today I have done quite a lot of research into the matter of creativity in old age, especially as it concerns writers.

I shall not bore you, however, with a recital of all the writers I have found who have continued their work into old age. There are literally scores of them, but many belong to earlier periods of general culture and their names would probably not be resonant to a modern audience. Shall we allow two great names from this century to suffice? Thomas Mann, a towering figure in the world of the novel, died at the age of eighty (1955), having just completed what has been described as Germany's greatest comic novel, *Confessions of the Confidence Trickster Felix Krull.* And in case you do not think a German comic novel an especially thrilling achievement, astonishing though it may be, I refer you to the list of very fine novels, ranging from the ironic to the tragic, which had occupied him since the age of twenty-five. The other figure to whom I call your attention is, of course,

Bernard Shaw (1950), who lived to be ninety-four and was writing up until his final illness. There are critics who point out that Shaw's later work is not on the same level as that of his writing until the age of seventy-six, when he wrote *Too True to Be Good,* a play of remarkable experimental characteristics; what he produced after that time he himself called "Shaw's Dotages." For many years during my life as a university teacher I gave a seminar on the works of Shaw, and every year my students read these last works with astonishment, and agreed that any of us would be happy to have such *dotages.*

You may object that the two examples I have given you are men of genius. But of course. True creativity in old age does not appear in mediocrities.

Here I may be treading on contentious ground. It is an illusion of our modern concept of democracy that virtually everything in life that is good may be attained by virtually everybody. If some people can be creative in old age, obviously everybody can do so, if they can acquire the knack. There must be some secret, some formula, which will open the doors of autumnal creativity to everyone, and for them the Winter View will be a revelation.

This is the point at which we may ask ourselves what we really mean by creativity. My desk dictionary says it is "showing imagination as well as routine skill." That is a very broad definition and not quite what we want. That definition is partly useful in describing the work of children in kindergarten, because what a child does with its crayons is inevitably imaginative because the child does not, for instance, look at a chair, or its mother, or a tree when it draws these things; what it draws is an inner vision. But the child has no routine skill, no technique. It is when it begins to develop these qualities— observation and technique—that it discovers that its symbols for chair or mother or tree do not correspond to what it sees. For our discussion of creativity here I think we might consider the definition that Frank Barron employs in his essay "The Psychology of Creativity," where he says it is "the ability to bring something new into existence." But even that does not cover the ground. When Rembrandt paints an old woman, he does not bring the whole race of old women out of the everywhere into the here; he does not even create the old woman who sits before him in his studio; but he creates the old woman *in the picture* and in so doing he shows us aspects of that particular old woman, and of old women in general, which we had not observed. It is his inner vision and special perception. Creativity is something new brought into existence by someone with a special power to conceive, or describe, or reveal.

Not the most determined social philosopher can pretend that this special power can be aroused in great numbers of people by the acquirement of a knack.

But—*Hope springs eternal in the human breast;/ Man never is, but always to be blest*—as a poet of unquestioned creativity has told us. There are on this continent great numbers of people who optimistically assure others that they too can be creative, even if they are not creative on the highest level. They can paint—not as well as a Renoir, perhaps, but they will never know unless they try. They can write— and although they may not challenge Thomas Mann or Bernard Shaw they may have a very pretty talent which they have not yet employed. It is significant that these optimists never urge their admirers to try their hands at the art of music; they recognize that music requires the discipline of a whole new language of expression, and that there is already as much mediocre music in the world as can be endured. But they urge their listeners to unbridled daubing and word processing, and they assert boldly that what appears is genuinely creative. And they are right in that nothing like what results has ever been seen in the world before and with God's mercy will never be seen again.

Here I must declare a personal prejudice; I am doubtful about the employment of art as a means of therapy for people who are bored and seek something to distract them—as a pastime for the idle. Of course great paintings have come out of asylums for the insane—the astonishing work of Richard Dadd leaps to mind at once—but as a usual thing the doctors and analysts keep the work of their patients for their own inspection. But in the realm of writing the proliferation of sadly mediocre work is the despair of publishers and agents and of authors like myself, who are asked to pass judgement on these undistinguished productions. Somebody—very often a social worker or a healer of some sort—has suggested to these people that they should write, either pieces of fiction, or verse, or personal reminiscence. So far, so good. But human vanity is such that virtually nobody can write anything without feeling impelled to show it to somebody else; the writer is so astonished to find that he or she can indeed fill pages with material that looks like writing that they cannot rest until they have tested it against the taste of somebody who is supposed to know what good writing is. I shall not waste your time with an outburst of personal grievance, but I cannot forbear to say that every week my desk is littered with writing of this kind, sent to me for an opinion by people who do not often enclose an addressed envelope for return, and to whom the concept of return postage is wholly unknown. I have tried to be charitable and understanding about it, but many years as a professor supplied me, in the form of student essays, with all the innocently bad writing that I can cope with in a single lifetime.

What has caused this outburst of yearning for creativity? It is said that after the Second World War the United States became alarmed and discontented because Russian scientists were outstripping them in the field of space exploration. It seemed to me that Bob Hope hit the nail on the head when he said that it was because their Germans were better than our Germans. But the huge world of the educational theorists thought it was because American education was too confined in its syllabus, that too much had to be learned by rote, and that intellectual freedom was not encouraged. Children must be urged to make discoveries for themselves. The belief in the boundless spirit of intellectual adventure in the very young is one of the unchallenged myths of educational theorists. Every tot is thought to be a genius in embryo. Anybody who has ever been a child knows very well how conservative, how dull and intellectually corseted children can be, and one can only conclude that educational theorists have never been children.

The new approach to education was not confined to science; it spread over the whole curriculum. Classics were out; children had to read about people like themselves. This has led to a new school of novel writing called *Teen Tales,* with such titles as *Mary's First Abortion,*

or The Faulty Condom; and *Jimmy's Tough Luck, or the Dirty Needle.*
These cautionary tales have slight literary worth and are valueless in
encouraging literary taste.

Rote learning was abandoned because it stifled the creative spirit.
IQ tests were suspect because they might suggest that one child was in
certain respects superior to another, with supposedly disastrous effects
on the self-confidence of the lesser child. *Out flew the web and floated
wide; The mirror crack'd from side to side*—and the curse was upon us
all, for we in Canada follow American fashions in educational theory
with a deadening faithfulness.

In the world today there are great numbers of people who were children when that educational revolution took place and who are now
in late middle age or in early old age. They have not lived lives distinguished by any special creative zeal, but they can now be persuaded
that creativity lies within their reach, and that it will enlarge and
brighten what some social scientists so hideously call "the twilight
years."

I fear that these trusting souls are doomed to disappointment. You
cannot decide that you are going to be creative at that age. Unless creativity—I don't like the word but there is no precise substitute for it—
has made itself manifest in their lives long ago, they are not going to
discover that they have it now. It is too late. They must not be deceived
by the bombast of Longfellow:

Ah, nothing is too late
Till the tired heart hath ceased to palpitate;
Cato learned Greek at eighty, Sophocles
Wrote his grand Oedipus, and Simonides
Bore off the prize of verse from his compeers
When each had numbered more than four score years.

That is all very well, but Cato had been an intellectual all his life,
Sophocles was a poet of mighty renown, and Simonides had been
writing epitaphs since he was a child. When he wrote those lines
Longfellow set himself on a level with writers in *The Reader's Digest*

and kindred popular publications which urge old people to discover their hidden creativity, just as they urge them not to give up sex, but to keep banging away, however loudly outraged nature cries for rest. The idea of hidden creativity is a delusion, like talk of "mute, inglorious Miltons." If there is any genuine creativity it will assert itself early in life, and if someone is mute and inglorious it is foolish to call him a Milton. If you are prepared to put up with that sort of nonsense, I am a mute inglorious Beethoven.

The trouble, I think, arises because many people confuse creativity with intelligence. They are not at all the same thing. It may very well be that in advanced years many people discover aptitudes and abilities which are related to intelligence of which they had not been conscious before. But creativity is not directly associated with intelligence, and may indeed exist where intelligence is not strong. Artists and poets and musicians are notoriously unskilled in their approach to practical matters, and are disastrous in their handling of money. Sometimes, like Balzac, they acquire great fortunes and then lose them in some hare-brained scheme, or blow them in absurd extravagances; this is not what the intelligent person does. Creative people are often victims of bad habits which they cannot control; intelligence is a safeguard against such folly. I have often declared, to be greeted with incredulity, that it is possible to possess creative power in the highest degree without having intelligence above a modest level.

The intelligence testers come to my assistance. A scientist in this sort of calculation, Catharine Morris Cox, has applied her skill to the work of a great many writers. I am not wholly convinced of her ability to assess their level of intelligence when she has only their published work to go on, and her more exact tests cannot be applied to people long dead; nevertheless, she has made known her findings and seems to have no misgivings about them. And, among authors, who do you suppose she declared to be the most intelligent of all? John Stuart Mill. He was a political economist, and unless you are one of those mocking persons who regards political economy as whimsical, fictional, unfounded vapouring, you will not be likely to think of him as powerfully creative. Out of all his voluminous writings, he has left only one phrase that has crept into common use—and it is "unearned increment." But out of the 200 marks that are possible in intelligence tests, Mill scores a superb 190, five points above Goethe. It is interesting that Lord Byron scores 150, whereas Wordsworth and Keats and Shelley are nowhere. Shakespeare does not even get on the list below the 100 mark. Balzac, of whom I spoke a moment ago as a reckless spendthrift, scores 130. These findings are based on the Terman Intelligence Quotient index.

I confess that I take some comfort in Shakespeare's inadequacy, for many years ago when I was fourteen I was subjected to an intelligence test as I entered a new school. When the results were posted my name was not on the list, and I asked the master in charge why that was so. "I hardly like to tell you," he said. With sinking heart I enquired, "Was my score very bad?" "I won't give you the figure," said he (he was a kindly man), "but I will tell you this. It is a score which, if you were in the army, would mean that you could never rise above the rank of private—not even to corporal." This was bad news indeed, and it affected me for a long time and saddens me still. (But after all these years, I venture to think that if I had spent my life in the army I might have at last risen to be a corporal. Indeed, in a war where men fell like flies and promotion was rapid and haphazard, I might even have become a temporary sergeant.) But as things were I had no choice—it was literature, or starve. So without measurable intelligence I became a writer and, although I have done other things on the side, so to speak—been an actor, edited a daily paper, directed a college for graduate students, lectured as a professor—it was scribble, scribble, scribble all the way. Witless wretch that I was, it was my destiny.

I know that in saying that I am offending those among you to whom the idea of destiny, or fate, is repugnant. You are Americans and your country has prospered in the belief that anybody can do anything if he tries hard enough. And indeed that is, in a measure, true. But common sense must not be snubbed. It is obvious that President Clinton can be the chief executive of your country, and it is possible that he had his eye on that office long before it came within the range of possibility. But it was his fate to be President. If he had set his heart on being a greater tenor than Pavarotti I don't think he would have made it, although it is known that he has some humble musical skill. I do not put forward a dreary doctrine that everybody has his place and cannot rise above it; rather, I say that the place he has attained, and in which for a thousand reasons he is fixed and above which his best efforts will not lift him—that is his destiny. It is a commonplace to say that character is destiny: I think it equally true, but bitterer on the tongue, to say that destiny is also character.

Whose destiny is it then, to be creative and to continue being creative throughout a lifetime? If it is not intelligence, what is it? It gets us nowhere to say it is a gift of nature. How does nature manifest the gift?

Because it is what I know best, I speak principally of writing, and of writing on the level which commands respect above what we are ready to accord to trivial verse, or fiction that is consciously written to pass the time and then be forgotten. But what I am going to say applies also to creative people of other kinds—to musicians, to painters, sculptors, architects, to creators of all sorts who bring something new into existence, or who remind us of something old that has been forgotten or neglected. What sort of people are they?

I hope that the scientists among you do not think that I have forgotten your creativity. By no means. Do we ever forget that it was Einstein who said that the truly creative scientists are those who have access to their dreams? What did he mean by that?

I am certain he did not mean the access to the world of dreams that may be achieved by psychoanalysis. In that mingling of science and art the dreams of the patient are given the most careful consideration and the patient becomes aware of his or her dreams as never before. But to undergo psychoanalysis does not make you creative. Einstein must have meant something else.

What he meant, I think, were not entirely the dreams of sleep but those curious and often startling images and spoken messages, and hints of music, that occur when we are in that state of reverie that lies between sleeping and waking, and in which problems are sometimes solved which have defied the best efforts of the awakened mind.

Scientists are familiar with August Kekulé's famous dream of the snake with its tail in its mouth—the uroboros of myth—which gave him his solution to the problem of the benzene ring. It was in such a state of reverie that Coleridge, assisted perhaps by his accustomed dose of laudanum, composed the poem "Kubla Khan," which he was able to recover and write down after he woke up. It is one of the gems of poetry in English, and as we read it we too are taken into a different world, in which nothing is familiar but in which everything is somehow marvellously clear.

Another instance of a similar sort concerns the composer Richard Wagner. He was composing his opera *Das Rheingold* and he had for some time been searching fruitlessly for the theme of introductory music that would call up the whole splendour and majesty of the river Rhein. One day, very much worn out by the stress of his creative work, he laid himself down for a rest, hoping to sleep. But, as he says, he could not sleep but fell into a somnolent state, a reverie, indeed, and then he became conscious of a chord of music which persisted in the hearing of his mind as other, fantastic variations formed themselves about it. He knew that it was the chord of E-flat major. He wrote: "I awoke in sudden terror from my doze, feeling as though the waves were rushing high above my head. I at once recognized that the orchestral overture to the *Rheingold,* which must have long lain latent within me, though it had been unable to find definite form, had at last been revealed to me. I then quickly realized my own nature; the stream of life was not to flow to me from without, but from within." This is no mere figure of speech; what flowed to him on this occasion were 136 bars of superbly evocative music, rooted in the major triad of E-flat. There was nothing fanciful or vague about it.

This sort of thing is familiar to innumerable creative people, and Wagner puts the matter clearly when he says that the flow is not from without but from within. Every writer knows the experience of having somebody tell him a story or describe a character which is supposed to be exactly what a writer is looking for. But it isn't. Writers can be cantankerous, and any attempt to prime their pump, or insert a story into them, is likely to be met with resistance and sometimes with contempt.

It is of course true that writers pick up hints from what they hear which may in time turn into completed stories. But a hint is all they want; they resist detail. Henry James has written revealingly about this aspect of his art; the hint is all, and too much corroborative detail interferes with the amplification which is the writer's own work. The hint must be absorbed, perhaps forgotten, but somehow "put into the works," so to speak, and in time it may reappear and be used.

The creative process cannot be forced. Sometimes I am visited by very young people, students in high school, whom I have, for one reason or another, agreed to talk to about writing because they study some of my books. It is not a sort of encounter that I meet with enthusiasm, because a book one has written undergoes strange metamorphoses by the time it has been accommodated to a class of students of widely varying capacity by a teacher who may not be a perceptive guide. One of the questions I am most often asked by such visitors is, "Where do you get your ideas from?" My answer is always the same: "I do not get my ideas, they get me." Students think I am being facetious and don't want to tell the secrets of my workshop, but what I say to them is no more than the truth. Unless an idea rises from within, it is of no use to me as the groundwork of a story. It must have some connection, probably indirect but by no means beyond discovery, with me and the inner world where I chiefly live, as do we all. It has been said with truth that virtually all fiction is disguised autobiography, and sometimes the disguise is very thin. But more often it defies the external searcher or the critic, because it is associated with the writer's fantasy life, into which the researcher, the biographer, the critic, cannot intrude.

So I repeat: the creative process cannot be forced. Of course we read exciting stories about Mozart writing the overture to *The Marriage of Figaro* on the day of the first performance, or about Sheridan writing superb pages of comedy almost as the actors are about to go on the stage. But we would be more accurate to say that Mozart and Sheridan are putting on paper the overture, or the scenes of comedy; these things have been in existence before but have not been put in tangible form. Mozart and Sheridan may have been lazy, but they have not been uncreative. Many creative people can tell you of the work that can be done under the pressure of necessity, but the work lies ready to be brought forth; it cannot be dragged into existence from nowhere at all. I suppose psychoanalysts could tell us about the desire to retain something until the precise moment comes for its appearance, but psychoanalysts have not, on the whole, been especially good at explaining the secrets of creativity. I think it is because to them the quality of art is not important, and we all know how ready Freud and Jung and their followers have been to choose second- or third-rate literature as the subject of their investigations on this subject. What is mediocre is more easily dissected and scrutinized than what is first-rate. It is easier to apply psychoanalytical theory to something like *Gradiva* or an adventure tale by Rider Haggard than to go to work on Goethe's *Faust*. When Ernest Jones writes about *Oedipus* or *Hamlet* it is instructive how little his opinions enlarge or increase our pleasure in the plays. It may be that psychoanalysis is hostile to art, which is markedly resistant to systems of analysis.

So, if the creative process cannot be forced, can it be encouraged or assisted? Yes, it can. Elaborate theories in elaborate language can be produced to describe this process, but in the end it comes down pretty much to the artist's ability to get out of his own way. He must not force; he must not strain. In his encounters with the creative process within him he must not dictate, or bully, or make conditions. He must, in fact, give up control and abandon himself to what happens. It is surprisingly difficult to do this in a world where so many of us have been subjected to strenuous education, with its emphasis on the virtues of hard work, and its insistence that virtually anything can be achieved by determined effort. Many people find any such abandonment of control, any non-interference, is impossible.

Artists, if they have the root of the matter in them, know what to do. That is why so many people think of them as idlers, loafers, people without decent ambition and application. The fact is, of course, that they are often working hardest when they seem most idle. They are getting out of their own way and allowing the creative process to take over. Everybody knows how strange it was to see Einstein

standing, sometimes for hours, watching men at work on a construction job, or digging one of their innumerable holes in a busy road.
Watching other people work is, for the creative mind, wonderfully
evocative of all sorts of reflections, some of which are useful. This is
a characteristic of the creative person that can be maddening to those
around him, and is a great source of domestic disquiet.

Knowing that this is true, high-minded institutions have brought
into being places where artists can be creatively idle, living in pretty
little cabins, having everything they need (and much that they merely
want) provided by their kindly patrons, and perhaps appearing only at
dinner time to chew the rag and pass the wassail bowl. But I cannot
find any evidence that these retreats bring forth important artistic work,
and I think that the reason is that they are in their benevolent way urging, expecting, hinting, coaxing. It is in contact with the world at large
that artists—idle lookers-on though they may appear—are most
impelled to do what they do—which is to listen to the inner voices.

Does the artist really do nothing during these periods of apparent
idleness? No. He politely and reverently asks for the help he needs. In
the language of religion, he "waits upon the Lord." Sometimes he
must wait a long time. He must learn patience. Nothing can be forced.
The growth of what is excellent is slow. The mushroom growth of the
third-rate has little to do with real creation.

I have given a good deal of time to talking about how creativity
works, in so far as I understand the matter. I have not said much about
old age. I hope I have made it clear that I do not think creativity makes
a sudden appearance when a man or a woman has laid down the task
that has engaged them for fifty or more years. It you don't have it when
you were young, don't hope for it when you are old. It is a gift, and if
that is élitist and undemocratic, I am not myself responsible.

A gift—yes, but what sort of gift? I have said that the creative person is not necessarily highly intelligent, as the world understands intelligence. On the other hand, the creator, the artist, is not an *idiot
savant*—a simpleton with an inexplicable knack. What is the gift?

I think it has been very well described by a writer of great achievement, the late Vladimir Nabokov. When he was discussing the writing

of André Malraux, he said: "The longer I live the more I become convinced that the only thing that matters in literature is the (more or
less irrational) *shamanstvo* of a book, i.e., that the good writer is first
of all an enchanter." The word *shamanstvo*, a Russian friend tells me,
means "enchanter-quality." Much is contained in that definition. "The
only thing that matters"—this suggests that style, ranging from the
stately prose of Samuel Johnson to the seemingly unstudied prose of
Mark Twain, is a secondary consideration. "More or less irrational"—
this suggests that the writing takes its quality from an inner source
and not from a rigid conscious control. And then, of course—"The
good writer is first of all an enchanter." If you are an enchanter, the
gift may develop and undergo refinement, but it is present from the
beginning; it will not suddenly manifest itself at the age of retirement.
And to be an enchanter—what is that? I shall not attempt to tell you,
because you can meet the quality and fall under its spell, and analyse
and explain it if you can, by reading literature of the first order in
which it is to be found.

Let me give as an example one great poem, which combines
enchantment, art and thought of a superior order, and which concerns
old age. It is truly a View in Winter. Many of you will know it. It is
Robert Browning's "Rabbi Ben Ezra." The first lines are very familiar:

> Grow old along with me!
> The best is yet to be,
> The last of life, for which the first was made:
> Our times are in His hand
> Who saith, "A whole I planned,
> Youth shows but half; trust God, see all, nor be afraid!"

The suggestion that life should be seen as a whole falls heavily on the
ears of many people today, who worship youth and the pleasures of
youth (especially sex) and are determined to prolong youth so far as
possible for as long as possible. After which, who knows what horrors!
The poem praises youth, but not as the best part of life. The poem
tells us to look indulgently on youth and forgive our youthful follies,

but never for a moment pretend that they are not follies and unbecoming the later years of life. Only life seen as a whole reveals any meaning or intention in whatever Power originated the life, and whatever measure of understanding there may be comes with age.

The poem declares that God works as a potter, and man is the pot he fashions. The potter's wheel is the time and circumstances in which man finds himself and the clay is what is man's essence, his spiritual being. Only the totality, the finished work, can be judged if one hopes to find purpose in the work, and that judgement is the work of old age.

The poem has been harshly criticised because it seems to say that man has no free will. Maybe it does say that, and maybe it is right. I do not propose to argue the point, except to point out that Browning is speaking, as he so often does, in the character of another person, in this instance a twelfth-century theologian and philosopher, whose theme is old age. For many years I have made it a point to read "Rabbi Ben Ezra" on my birthday.

These are the reflections of a writer. I make no particular claim for them, except that, for obvious reasons, they are truly "A View in Winter."

20

HONOURING MAVIS GALLANT

For more than twenty years the Harbourfront Literary Festival in Toronto has followed the pleasing practice of publicly honouring the life's work of a senior Canadian writer, on the reasonable grounds that such tributes will tend to mean more to the writer while he or she is still alive.

Davies himself was honoured in this way in 1989. This means that the opening paragraph of the speech, with its wry reference to martyrdom, comes from his own fairly recent and precisely similar experience in the hot seat of adulation.

He was, however, delighted to accept the invitation to be among the speakers praising Mavis Gallant on October 14, 1993. His admiration of her work—which is evident in every line of his speech—was matched by a warm friendship, most obvious when Mavis Gallant deserted her Paris home for Toronto in 1983–1984. During that academic year she was writer-in-residence at the University of Toronto (where she discovered the writing of a student named Rohinton Mistry) and was literally in residence at Massey College. She was most appreciative of the kindness shown her by "Rob and Brenda Davies" during her stay.

Mavis Gallant herself needs little introduction. As a Montrealer who moved to Paris in 1950 to live as a writer, she has earned a brilliant reputation throughout the English-speaking world and beyond. Despite her long exile she has been delighted to receive so many Canadian honours (including the Harbourfront tribute, The Governor General's Award for Fiction for her short-story collection *Home Truths,* and several honorary degrees) because, in her own words, she "can no more stop being Canadian than I can change the colour of my eyes."

One of the last things Robertson Davies wrote, late in 1995, was an appreciative Afterword for Mavis Gallant's most recent collection of stories, *Across the Bridge.*

His diary references are to Windhover, the country home in the Caledon Hills outside Toronto where he and his wife spent most of their week. Oaklands is the mid-town Toronto apartment where the middle of each week was spent, and the problem-solving Jenny is his second daughter, Jennifer Surridge, who helped to produce this book: *... like a great thundering chump, I came away from Windhover this afternoon leaving my Diary and also my type-script copy of my speech about Mavis Gallant for Thursday in my study. Also forgot my watch, which is my god, like Gulliver. This is what comes of relaxing, after having completed my speeches; I thought I would ease my mind for a few days, and this is what comes of it. Total incompetency! Or is it the first signs of Alzheimer's? ... Anyhow I messed about in my study this morn, quite productively thinking about the book. To Oaklands this afternoon, reluctantly for Windhover is trans-portingly beautiful with just a touch of autumn ruin about it ... Discovered what I had forgotten and was very angry with myself; Brenda tries to calm me but I am distraught. But I phone Jenny, who is able to provide me with a copy of the Gallant speech, so the day is saved, but not my amour propre.*

I am honoured to have been asked to join in this assembly which honours Mavis Gallant, for she is a writer whose work I have admired for thirty years and more. But now that I stand before you, I am uncertain what I should say, because on such occasions it is easy to go painfully astray. I know, because I have had some experience myself of being the reason for such a gathering, and of the agonies of embarrassment it can cause. Being praised in public can be deeply embarrassing, though of course it is preferable to being ignored. Those who are doing the praising, and those who have come in a spirit of goodwill to hear the author praised, are having a splendid time and they are filled with kindly feeling. But for the subject of the assembly, the author who is being praised, it is rather like a martyrdom: the martyr is conscious that he is being tortured because he is a saint, and he is delighted by such enthusiastic recognition of his sanctity, but he has strong doubts if his saintliness merits quite such warm attention. The author on these occasions sits wondering "Can this really be me?" At this moment Miss Gallant must banish any doubts she may have: it really is herself that we have come to praise, and we shall do it, come what will, and whatever she may feel about it.

There are some things, however, which I shall avoid. One of these is the biographical information which some speakers cannot refrain from and another is the number of works achieved, listed in chronological order. All I am going to tell you about Mavis Gallant's life is that she was born in Montreal and if you want to know *when* there are plenty of reference books that will satisfy your curiosity. The age of an author is of no consequence; if they are any good, they were born old and wise, and by that standard of measurement, Miss Gallant is already well beyond the century mark. The only other fact about her that I consider relevant on such an occasion as this is that she was educated at seventeen different schools, which suggests either a restless or an unruly temperament, both of which are characteristic of writers as a tribe.

For the greater part of her working life she has been identified as "a *New Yorker* writer" and though that is high praise as far as it goes, it is somewhat too restrictive to be the whole of the truth about Mavis Gallant. *The New Yorker* is unquestionably a distinguished literary magazine—indeed it may very well be the best literary magazine published in English—but in the minds of many readers it is associated with a kind of fiction which is strongly analytical of the vagaries and tribulations of a sensitive, overwrought, and somewhat shallow sort of American; in one way or another the theme is definable as Angst, and if you want an extended definition of Angst it is a pervasive feeling of anxiety or apprehension which induces a sort of depression that is not incapable of being wittily apprehended and lightly expressed. It is unfair to confine *The New Yorker* to the theme of Angst, though at times the spirit of Franz Kafka and Sylvia Plath does seem to hang over its pages like a kitchen smell. It is grossly unfair to Mavis Gallant to associate her with that sort of writing. She is better and deeper than that. She is a Canadian, and as a people we tend to be suspicious of Angst, though we are no strangers to Northern Melancholy.

Angst is the malaise of a single character. It is essentially an egotistical ailment. Mavis Gallant's people do not live under the shadow of anything so trivial as that. When they are unhappy, their unhappiness is related to the unhappiness that is always lurking, in every corner of the globe, for its victim. It is not personal; it is universal and it takes a writer of broad range to make it manifest in a short story without plunging the whole piece of work into a more than Dostoyevskyan misery.

Many of you, I venture to say, know Mavis Gallant's remarkable story called "Up North." It seems to me to display one aspect of her many-sided gift with particular mastery. For those of you who do not know it, it tells of a train journey, taken by an English war-bride and her small son, to join the husband and father in the Canadian north. The woman is doing her best to keep up her courage; she meets a man on the train to whom she talks of her situation, and we sense that he knows much more about where she is going and what she is likely to find there than she can possibly do. The sense of chill that we feel as they talk is painfully increased by the insistence of the little boy that he has seen strange passengers boarding the train during the night. Of course he has seen nothing, and the two adults will not give credence to what he has to say. But we, the readers, know from remarks that have been dropped earlier that what the boy has seen are the ghosts of unhappy settlers who have made this same journey many years before, and that the boy's uncanny experience prefigures what awaits him and his mother when at last they reach their destination. It is a chilling story, about 3,000 words in length, and it is told with perfect art.

How much is packed into that short tale, and what an atmosphere is evoked! The narration is unremarkable, almost flat. No attempt is made to create an uncanny atmosphere or to give the child any quality of second sight. The mother is a commonplace little English girl and one senses that she has not much resource of spirit. But we know that commonplace people suffer in their own way just as do remarkable ones, and that many war-brides faced bitter disillusion when they came to Canada trusting in a splendid new life.

It is all achieved with economy of means, not a word too many and not a word out of key with the commonplace surface of the story. But how much of the sadness of fate is contained in the tale. And how we wonder what the child will meet with when he comes at last to his unknown and undescribed father. It is never suggested that he is an unusual or sensitive child. He is simply at an age when things from more than one world may become mingled in a moment of revelation.

This is an isolated little masterwork. The stories by which Mavis Gallant is more widely known are in a lighter but never in a trivial vein. They are distinguished by a mingling of wit and pathos—the pathos is implied, it is never flatly stated—that is particularly her own. She has written many short stories. My calculation suggests that she has written in this form at least the equivalent of twenty novels. Anybody who has ever attempted to write a short story will realize what this means, in terms of invention, of narrative skill, and of technical command. The short-story writer cannot be profuse, cannot indulge the pursuit of seeming irrelevancies which prove not, in the end, to be irrelevant, as can the novelist. Reading Mavis Gallant we sense in this complexity of structure, this severe economy of means, a delight in the craft of writing which is one of the marks of the superior artist.

If I were asked to name a single characteristic of Mavis Gallant's work which imparts its quality to the whole, I should have to speak of irony. Irony, which is the art of saying one thing while implying the greater truth of its opposite. It is not a device that can be used too generously or it degenerates into facetiousness, but when it is used with complete control it gives unforgettable flavour to a piece of writing.

Every writer uses it in his own way—the right way for him. Mavis Gallant understands it and uses it with total mastery.

It is a commonplace of modern criticism to speak of the influence that film has had on modern writing. We have only to look at the work of some of the great writers of the past to understand what has happened: no longer do writers hold up the action to describe the scene. The long and admittedly splendid set pieces that distinguish the work of Thomas Hardy are not expected in a modern work. We have lost our appetite for them. The scene must be touched in as quickly and as tactfully as possible so that we can get at once to the action and the dialogue. Good dialogue is not something which is at the command of all writers. Dialogue that carries the action forward rapidly but with seeming naturalness—for there is no such thing as "natural" dialogue except in the most naive writing—is extremely difficult to compose. Not only must it move the action: it must reveal the character of the speaker. It is in this that, once again, Mavis Gallant shows her command of her medium. We recall that she spent some time at the National Film Board. Presumably she learned much. Certainly she is now in a position to teach much, if such subtleties as command of dialogue can be taught.

One aspect of life of our extraordinarily diverse Canada Mavis Gallant has made peculiarly her own. Nobody has written so perceptively of the life of the Montreal bourgeoisie, French or English. In her latest collection of short stories, called *Across the Bridge,* she devotes four linked tales to the fortunes of the Carette family. They are not people we should greatly like to meet, but they are people about whom we are delighted to read. There is not an aspect of their confined but complete world which is not explored; there is no social nicety that is not defined, no shade of cheese-paring meanness or squalid avarice that is not brought to light. It seems to be a world without love, and yet we sense deep family loyalty, keen concern for children and parents, and the springings of romance in hearts where it is unlikely to grow to full flowering. The Carettes are fully realized as individuals, but we sense also that they represent hundreds of thousands.

In other stories in the book Miss Gallant writes of the sadness of exile. Not dramatic exile, but just the deprivation of people who are not particularly distinguished but who are sensitive, and have been driven from their homelands by a generalized rather than an individual Fate. In Paris they pursue the sort of life that is open to strangers with some ability but no capital, people who are continually aware that they will always be strangers, people a great portion of whose lives exists only in memory. To write of such lives without obtrusive indignation or easy irony is a notable artistic achievement. Mavis Gallant's eye is not blinded with tears, but it is not unpitying.

Let me repeat what I said when I began. I am honoured to have been asked on this occasion to do honour to a Canadian writer who has added a career of distinguished and individual achievement to our growing literature.

21

AN UNLIKELY MASTERPIECE

When the Pierpont Morgan Library in New York, holder of Charles Dickens's original manuscript of *A Christmas Carol*, wished to celebrate the 150th anniversary of the book's publication, Robertson Davies was a natural choice as speaker. To the task he brought not only a love of Dickens's work but also a deep knowledge of "the theatre of his time," which so greatly influenced the book Davies calls "one of the most powerfully theatrical creations in the whole of English literature." To go through the book with Davies as a guide pointing out stage effects is an extraordinary experience.

His account of the November 1993 event to a friend makes clear how much he relished it: *The other affair, which I enjoyed greatly, was in New York, where the Morgan Library asked me to speak about Dickens's A Christmas Carol. It is a book I have loved since childhood and I was happy to say my say about it. The Morgan Library has Dickens's original manuscript of the book, which was the reason to celebrate the 150th anniversary. I spoke twice, and had large audiences, and loved every minute of it. Part of the fun was a Dickensian Christmas Dinner, at which we ate fried oysters, turkey with chestnut stuffing, and plum pudding with brandy, all washed down with some splendid wines and ending with hot spiced wine—which I avoided as I learned long ago that it is for younger drinkers than I.*

That Dickens's novella *A Christmas Carol* is a masterpiece there can be no doubt. But I have given my address the title "An Unlikely Masterpiece," and you may very well wonder why. It is because the little book offends against every canon of conventional criticism, and if it were to be published today we can imagine the harsh terms with which it would be greeted. "Ill-constructed"; "absurd extravagances of character"; "maudlin sentimentality"; "total failure to find and adhere to a single tone of the authorial voice"; "unmistakable signs of haste in wrapping up the plot"; "vulgarity of diction interspersed with rhetorical wooden thunder"; "total failure to comprehend the economic infrastructure of the modern world"; "an affront equally to labour and management"; "dependent on a world-outlook long abandoned by the majority of readers"; "though rooted in Christmas is chary of Christian forthrightness"; "an absurd and psychologically impossible resolution." And so on. You can hear the heavy newspaper reviewers, the wits of the glossy magazines, and the deep voices of the academic quarterlies—those Rhadamanthine judges of the quick and the dead in the world of literature—searching their hearts for condemnation bitter enough to reflect the greatest possible credit upon themselves.

Nevertheless, the book remains a masterpiece. The latest of Dickens's biographers, Mr. Peter Ackroyd, calls it "this powerful Christmas tale, which has achieved a kind of immortality, born out of the very conditions of the time." Of Dickens's time, and of our time, and of any time, for hardness of heart, avarice, human misery and degradation, are not passing things that can be banished by legislation. Dickens, as so often, seemed to be writing about his own time, but it was one of the splendours of his genius that he wrote for all time, and the abuses he attacked, and the virtues he extolled, have not vanished, but only found new shapes.

The book has been praised extravagantly, and sometimes in terms that quite reasonably arouse the enmity of critics, who are, of course, the most even-handed and moderate of men. Everybody is acquainted with the exuberant judgement of A. Edward Newton who declared that it was "the greatest little book in the world," adding, with generous belligerence, "if you think that rather a large order, name a greater!" A. Edward Newton was not a critic; he was merely a very distinguished collector of books and an ebullient enthusiast for literature of all sorts. Some of the warmest praise has come from contemporaries and fellow-writers who might be expected to be jealous of Dickens. But it was Thackeray who said, with the generosity which was characteristic of him, "It seems to me a national benefit, and to every man or woman who reads it a personal kindness." It is even on record that Carlyle, though a Scot and a philosopher, rushed out after reading it and—bought a turkey!

So, a masterpiece it is. And what is a masterpiece? The production, surely, of a master in his art working at the height of his powers. If it appears to run counter to accepted standards of excellence, may it not be that those standards are not applicable to *A Christmas Carol?* Should we not judge it by other standards, by no means high-flown or contradictory of critical opinion, but simply different from those we have been talking about? That is what I want to talk about tonight.

It is my opinion that in discussing the works of Charles Dickens we should never forget the theatre of his time, to which he was devoted, and in which he first of all hoped to make his career, and whose techniques and characteristics, however he may have seemed from time to time to mock them, determined the form of much of his work and indeed may be discerned even in the later novels, in which his earlier extravagances of plot and character have been moderated.

I come to this opinion as a consequence of sixty years that I have spent in intermittent study of that theatre, and many years in which I have talked to generations of students about it. Much of the popular literature of the nineteenth century leans on this theatrical tradition, but none so plainly or so successfully as Dickens.

It was a theatre, we must remember, that combined in itself all that is shared nowadays among theatre, film, and television. It was popular entertainment ranging between the highest and the lowest taste, incorporating all I have named, and also generous portions of circus and ballet. It was peopled by artists of the highest order, like Dickens's friend Macready, by Edmund Kean (of whom Coleridge said that to see him act was like reading Shakespeare by flashes of lightning), by Samuel Phelps who did the almost impossible task at that time of presenting all but five of Shakespeare's plays, without a penny of subsidy, by the scholarly Charles Kean, and still within Dickens's lifetime, Henry Irving, who compelled the British government to accept the theatre as an art when it knighted him. Below this level were serious artists who brought to the stage qualities of intelligence combined with theatrical insight, who won and held the affection of a huge middle-class audience. And lower still, there were the actors of lesser talent but no less enthusiasm whose rich theatricality delighted Dickens and which he made immortal in Vincent Crummles and his company. Bernard Shaw, who devoted so much of his life to changing this richly emotional theatre into a theatre of ideas and intellect, nevertheless declared that it had been, in its own way, a great theatre, which he had seen when he was a young playgoer, before Dickens died.

The nineteenth century was an age of great acting, and it was Lord Byron—a playwright whose work would be admirably suited to television—who said, "I am acquainted with no immaterial sensuality so delightful as good acting."

We must not think of the nineteenth-century theatre as visually crude or impoverished; at its best it commanded the work of designers and painters of a high order and it had a system of changing scenes which was so rapid that it was done before the eyes of the audience, one scene melting into another with a swiftness that suggests the films rather than the time-consuming scene changes of the early part of this century. It had not our fine versatility of lighting, but it had gaslight which threw upon the scene a magic that was all its own. In those days of painted scenery, many of the effects which are now achieved by lighting were, in fact, painted into the background.

This was the theatre to which Dickens was devoted, and not Dickens alone but such of his contemporaries as George Eliot, Thackeray, Tennyson, and even so stern a critic as Matthew Arnold, who were regular attendants and generous in their praise of what they saw.

What did they see? This is where I have to moderate my enthusiasm for this theatre of the past. There were very few playwrights of even mediocre stature and the repertoire of contemporary plays often makes sad reading. I can speak with knowledge and with feeling, because I have waded through scores of plays which seem to have been written by the same hand, repeating tried-and-true situations and putting in the mouths of the characters such language as has never been uttered elsewhere by human tongue.

If Dickens sometimes makes his theatrical characters speak in this extraordinary language he does not exaggerate. Consider the memoirs of John Ryder, a popular actor of the time who, when he is leaving home as a youth, writes—"I utter valedictory to the author of my being." He means he said good-bye to his mother. There were lots of actors who talked like that. Lines from plays became popular sayings, by no means reverently used. Such a line was "O God, put back thy universe and give me yesterday," from *The Silver King;* another was, "Once aboard the lugger and the girl is mine," from a play called *My Jack and Dorothy.* Many splendid lines are handed down in families where they took on a personal ring; I instance a line from a French Revolution play called *Jacques the Spy,* which became a catchphrase in my wife's family—"She who bathed in milk, and spent a fortune on a single pear." People liked verbal splendour in the nineteenth century, and often I wish it would return. As of course it will; in the theatre, nothing dies.

Nevertheless, verbal splendour divorced from any sort of original thought very soon degenerates into rant, and its intellectual poverty shows through the tinsel. Nineteenth-century theatre delighted in violent incident, improbable confrontations, absurd misunderstandings, and indeed anything at all which provided what was then called "a strong situation." It was the kind of thing we associate with the libretti of operas, but in opera the baldness of the plot and the arbitrary nature of the psychology is disguised, or given another dimension, by the music. Such a popular opera is *Lucia di Lammermoor,* for instance; the musical evocation of the sweetness of youth and the wretchedness of thwarted love conceals from us the violence that the libretto does to

Walter Scott's finely psychological novel. The theatre of the nineteenth century was a theatre of feeling, of strong emotion, and it is not always easy for us, who live in an era where that sort of thing has been given over to the movies and to television, to sympathize with it. Our theatre has become almost a coterie entertainment, where we demand intellectual stress, or some reasonable facsimile thereof, and reject naked passion as improbable unless it is cloaked in some Freudian complexity.

It was an accident that Dickens did not join the vivid, rather brainless theatre of his time as an actor. That was his ambition, but Fate determined otherwise, for when he secured an audition with the influential manager Bartley, he was unable to attend because of a disabling cold in the head and deferred his audition for a year—by which time he was too successfully launched as a shorthand reporter to be able to pursue his earlier goal. What we know about his powers as an actor suggests that he would have had a fine career on the stage as a comedian, for he possessed brilliant comic invention, extraordinary powers of impersonation, and a hawklike eye for detail. He did, of course, take the keenest pleasure in amateur theatricals all his life, and scored successes in such dissimilar roles as Captain Bobadil in Ben Jonson's *Every Man in His Humour* and Justice Shallow in Shakespeare's *Merry Wives of Windsor.* It appears also that he could, at need, play tragedy— or at least pathos—with good effect. When he appeared as Richard Wardour in Wilkie Collins's drama of arctic exploration, *The Frozen Deep,* his death scene brought tears not only from the audience but from the actress who was on the stage with him. But his greatest triumphs as an actor were in the readings from his own work with which he occupied so much of his time during the later years of his life. We know that he gave, in all, 427 of these readings to packed audiences in England and in America and there are abundant records of the effect he produced in both comedy and pathos. *The Trial from Pickwick* was apparently irresistible in its evocation of the sleepy, stupid judge, the garrulous Mrs. Cluppins, the ill-prepared but rhetorically overwhelming Sergeant Buzfuz, the irreverent witness Sam Weller, and the deeply affronted Mr. Pickwick. He filled the stage with people, changing from one to another with the uttermost rapidity, and yet never scamping a characterization or a contrast.

From the descriptions that have survived of his readings we learn much about his technique. He had an astonishing range of voice; he could whisper horribly as the surly Creakle in *David Copperfield*, and he could be light, high, and twittering as Mrs. Nickleby; he could be winningly feminine, he could be shrewish, he could be wondrously drink-sodden as Sairey Gamp and her friend Betsy Prig; he could be sonorous and rhetorical as Mr. Micawber and he could be ignorantly pretentious as Wackford Squeers; as socially pretentious characters he was inimitable in his folly, and he could be ironically derisive as Sam Weller. There was nothing, apparently, that he could not do. In the reading which was his greatest success as a piece of sheer sensation, the murder of the harlot Nancy by the brutal Bill Sikes, his screams as the woman who was being beaten to death alternated with the blasphemous roars of her murderer so rapidly that it seemed almost as if they were heard at the same time. This same extraordinary rapidity and variation in what actors call "picking up his cues" was remarked upon in the scene where the reluctant Nicholas Nickleby is being subjected to the enchantments of Miss Fanny Squeers; people swore that both characters seemed to speak at once, in two wholly different voices.

His brilliance as an actor was not confined to vocal dexterity. As Mr. Pickwick he seemed innocent and portly, when his companion Mr. Nathaniel Winkle was slight and notably weak at the knees. The distinction he drew among the three spirits that visited Scrooge—the silvery Ghost of Christmas Past, the ebullient Ghost of Christmas Present, and the veiled Spectre of Christmas Yet to Come—was one of the many wonders of his always popular reading of the *Carol.* In the *Carol,* too, many among his audience commented on the short but important scene where the reformed Scrooge leans from his bedroom window and orders an incredulous small boy to hasten to the poulterer's and buy the prize turkey. The boy has very little to say, but he appeared as a vivid personality to those who saw and heard that reading. Oh yes, Dickens was a very great actor, but great acting does not come simply. How did he do it?

We know from his letters how hard he worked to perfect all his impersonations. It was nothing to him to rehearse a reading two hundred times, in the privacy of his workroom. If that does not astonish you, I suggest that you might try reading a short passage from one of his books *five* successive times, trying to do it as well as you can, and I think you will discover what taxing, wearisome, tedious work it is. Dickens was a mighty man for detail and among actors whom we have seen he seems to me to resemble most the late Laurence Olivier, who was also a great man for detail, leaving nothing whatever to chance, and regarding no trifle of stage work as too trivial for his understanding and his study. I am not vapourizing about that; my wife worked with Olivier and saw what an insatiably curious artist he was in everything that went to make up the totality of a stage production. That was how Dickens worked, and when he appeared on a public platform to read, without any appurtenances except the book he held—but obviously did not need—and occasionally a paper-knife with which he could extend a very few gestures—wearing only conventional evening dress, he was ready to people the stage with the creations of his own fancy, and to make them palpable to audiences of twenty-five hundred people, some of whom on occasions, sat on the platform at his feet. But never, be it noted, behind him.

What he read was not precisely what appeared in the printed texts of his books. He edited, he deleted, he strengthened a passage now and then, he occasionally wrote in a new joke, or an extension of a particularly telling piece of description. But he was able, at need, to do without description. In the *Carol,* for instance, he comes very early to the description of Scrooge: "Oh, but he was a tight-fisted hand at the grindstone, Scrooge; a squeezing, wrenching, grasping, scraping, clutching covetous old sinner." But in the reading all the latter part of that sentence was omitted. Why? Because, as many people have attested, and his manager Dolby, who heard him read the *Carol* scores of times, makes clear, the squeezing, wrenching, covetous old sinner stood before his audience, and the words were superfluous in comparison with the physical presentment.

He could, as it were, conjure up music. When Scrooge goes after his reformation to the house of his nephew Fred to humbly beg pardon for his earlier bearishness and to ask if he may join in the festivities, we are aware that a dance has been in progress—what the Victorians called a "carpet-hop" when the guests simply danced on the tight-stretched carpet to the music of a single piano-player, who might also be a talented guest. Dickens suggested that music by tapping lightly with his fingers on his reading-desk, and that was all that was wanted to call up the simple, domestic music and the happiness that went with it. To explain how he did this is impossible without employing that now seriously overworked word "charisma"; people use it now to mean a particularly attractive personality, but it really means a gift of God not vouchsafed to everyone; a quality which may be refined and enhanced by indefatigable rehearsal, but which cannot be brought into being by any amount of effort.

The story of Dickens's travels and adventures as a reader are of the greatest interest. Undoubtedly he hastened his death by undertaking such efforts at a time when he was oppressed by fears that his creative powers were waning, by the failure of his marriage and the unsatisfactory nature of his relationship with the young woman who became his mistress, but who seems to have taken uncommonly little pleasure in that capacity; by the demands of his large family who must be launched in the world and in the case of the girls whose future must be assured; and by the anxiety of a man who had reached the top of a very high tree and was fearful of a fall. Those 427 nights of extraordinary exertion, achieved after heroic travel, were dearly bought and there were nights when the faithful manager Dolby feared that Dickens might not be able to complete his announced program. But Dickens always came up to scratch; he rallied magnificently when the time came to perform and there is no record of an audience going away disappointed.

Some of the details of how he did it are in themselves Dickensian, in their extravagance and strangeness. All through the nineteenth century actors seem to have recruited their powers during performances by eating and drinking. I am sure some of you know theatrical people, and are aware of their refusal to eat when a performance is near and, in most cases, to drink anything intoxicating. Not so the great ones of the nineteenth century. Edmund Kean, of course, had recourse to the brandy bottle and was sometimes almost incapable of carrying out his evening's work. Not so Dickens's friend Macready, who took his profession with the uttermost seriousness, and always consumed the lean of a mutton chop just before he went on the stage as he was convinced that it lent mellowness and unction to his voice. Not so Henry Irving, who, late in the century, relied on Bovril laced with brandy. But Dickens—well, in the interval in an evening's reading, he regularly ate a dozen oysters and drank a bottle of champagne, and this at times when otherwise he could hardly bring himself to eat at all. Have you ever eaten a dozen oysters and drunk, let us say, three glasses of champagne? Did it put you in form to do a heavy evening's work? But then, you are not a Victorian. They seem in many ways to have been an heroic race.

On Dickens struggled with the readings. He had his reward. In money, of course, they were very satisfactory. When he died his estate was reckoned at £93,000, of which about half had been gained by the readings. What that estate is worth in modern terms I cannot tell, but in 1820 an English pound sterling was worth seven American dollars, and that would bring it up to substantially more than half a million dollars. What would it be today? Perhaps Miss Jackie Collins could tell us. His readings were packed, and at one Liverpool performance alone over 3,000 people were turned away. One significant fact we must bear in mind, when we think of the effort the readings involved, is that this was long before the era of sound amplification. Yet nobody ever complained that they could not hear, even when he spoke in New York's Carnegie Hall. That demands of an actor a vocal technique in no way inferior to that of a great singer.

A notion of the quality and effect of the readings may have been experienced by some of you when the late Emlyn Williams toured the world, reading, in the character of Dickens, what Dickens had read. He enjoyed great success, and was by no means deficient in ranging from the pathetic weakness of little Paul Dombey to the noisy exuberance of Mr. Bob Sawyer. I saw and heard him several times, and I never failed to be deeply moved when, at the end of his performance, he acknowledged the ample applause of his audience and then turned and bowed in appropriate reverence to his reading-desk, which was an exact replica of that which Dickens used. It was a fine acknowledgement, by an artist of distinguished gifts, of the genius to which those gifts had been applied.

But what, you may ask, has this excursion into the nature of the nineteenth-century theatre to do with the novelist and particularly with *A Christmas Carol?* Quite simply, everything, and I want to talk about that now.

If Dickens was so mad for the theatre, you may say, why did he not write plays? Ah, but he did, and of all the keen Dickensians I know, I am myself the only one who has read them. I claim some credit for it. It is not a pleasure. His farces, *The Strange Gentleman* and *Is She His Wife?,* might have been written by any one of a score of Victorian playwrights who turned out such formula work for theatres which were as demanding of material then as television is today. His dramas, *No Thoroughfare* and *The Battle of Life,* are once again without distinction—without indeed a trace of the Dickens touch. As a young man he wrote the libretto for a little operetta called *The Village Coquettes* and I had the experience of inspiring and assisting at a performance of it—I do not think there have been many performances during this century. The music, by John Pike Hullah, was pleasant, but the libretto was clumsy, and any comedy that emerged was provided by the actors. Why do you suppose a man so keen about the theatre failed so utterly when he tried to write for it?

In part I think it was because Dickens, though an original genius in his deployment of traditional forms, was no innovator. His novels are in the great tradition he inherited from his childhood reading of Defoe, Fielding, and Smollett, and even in his mature work he does not stray far from it, though he richly expands it. Now to be a traditionalist in the theatre in his time was to be committed to a worn-out conception of drama, composed of stock situations and mechanical fun, or else tearful pathos straining to achieve the dignity of tragedy. The successful playwrights were hacks whose names have not survived, except in the antiquarian enthusiasm of theatre historians like myself. Great acting could persuade the public that the plays of Sheridan Knowles or John Westland Marston were worthy of attendance, but there is no dramatic vitality in them and they have not lived.

Until late in the century, and after Dickens's death, the nineteenth-century stage did not attract writers of first-rate ability. The reason was simple: the payment was ridiculous. A playwright sold his play outright to a manager, and thereby relinquished all rights to it. Royalties were unheard of. Douglas Jerrold's immensely popular drama *Black-Eyed Susan* brought the author fifty pounds, but made a fortune for a variety of managers and actors afterward. I do not know what Dickens got for his farces, but as a beginner it was probably twenty pounds. The rewards of authorship lay in the writing of novels and Dickens was strongly aware of it. Writing plays was a luxury he could not afford, and he was too intelligent a man not to realize that he had little talent for it, working under the restrictions of the theatre as it was during his youth.

Restriction—that is the word. He could not work in such fetters as the theatre put on its writers, though he could, and did, find room for his talent in the restrictions that were involved in publishing his works in monthly parts.

This system of publication involved Dickens with theatre in a way which was of considerable interest, but which is rarely discussed. We are so awed, nowadays, by the immensity of Dickens's genius that we are inclined to forget the keen man of business, who was eager to extract the last shilling from his work. He gained little money from the theatre but he was clever enough to exploit it as a tremendous source of advertisement.

As I have said, the theatre of his time was as greedy for material as modern television, and it was the custom of the day to adapt the popular novels which were appearing in monthly parts for stage presentations. These were often of a crudity that we now regard with astonishment, and many of them preyed upon a popular novel that was not yet completed. We know that Dickens's creating of Mr. Micawber offered such a chance for actors that versions of *David*

Copperfield were on the stage before the novel had been finished; indeed, there were versions in which actors who desired to show their versatility "doubled" the roles of Micawber, the richly comic creation, with that of Dan'l Peggotty, the noble and much-wronged uncle of the wayward heroine, Little Emily. It has been recorded that Dickens attended one such version of Copperfield with some friends, and that his anguish at what had been done to his work was so intense that he lay upon the floor of his box and writhed in agony. This was an early, and reversed, version of "rolling in the aisles." But Dickens was a man who could turn misfortune to account during his early days, and that is what he did.

We know now that he made available to playwrights and adapters whom he could trust, advance proofs of his books, revealing the conclusions, so that these favoured adapters could steal an important march on their competitors. Of course it goes without saying that the original author of a novel which had been adapted for the stage received no recompense, but we know that in exchange for these advance proofs money changed hands. And the advertisement value was incalculable.

This was not the case with *A Christmas Carol*, because it was published as a unity. The details of its publishing are, to the modern mind, astonishing: Dickens wrote it in late October and early November of 1843, delivered it to his publishers, Chapman and Hall, by mid-November and by the 19th of December this pretty little book, with its gilt edges and hand-coloured illustrations, was on sale at the price of five shillings, and by December 24 six thousand copies had been sold, and it has sold pretty briskly ever since. The modern author, who thinks himself lucky if his publisher gets his book before the public in six or seven months, is left with his mouth hanging open. As early as possible in 1844 there were four dramatizations on the London stage. One of these, called *The Miser's Warning*, was the work of C.Z. Burnett, and it was advertised as being sanctioned by Dickens; whether he received any money for that sanctioning we do not know, but certainly he did so for later works. Burnett's *Carol*, which is a clumsy and impudently altered version of the book, offered the celebrated actor

O. Smith as Scrooge; Smith was the most famous "villain" of his time, and was the first actor of the Monster in *Frankenstein* when it was adapted for the stage. We have records of his performance, which was criticised as being too gloomy and villainous.

This is interesting. The public has never been ready to accept Scrooge as a villain. He is essentially a comic character, and the exuberance of his avarice is positively refreshing. His cries of "Bah" and "Humbug" sometimes find an echo in our own hearts when we are battered with demands for charities at Christmas. We are repelled by his oppression of his clerk, Bob Cratchit, but we never doubt for an instant that Scrooge is the greater man, and that Bob—decent, good fellow that he is—nevertheless must be reckoned as one of Nature's losers. It takes ghosts and disembodied spirits to get the better of Scrooge; he is in the most powerful sense an active agent in the story, not a passive one, and his conversion is brought about by apparitions that are, when we look at them carefully, elements of himself.

Now we come to my point. We cannot really know the essence of Scrooge, or the magic of his story, unless we meet it in Dickens's book, and that is because the book is in its deepest bones a theatrically conceived, theatrically written story. It is in this and in his other novels that Dickens shows himself to be not only a very great novelist but immeasurably the greatest dramatist of his time, and one might well say the greatest dramatic author in English since Shakespeare.

Drama, yes. But drama is what is left of great theatre when you have drained all the fun out of it. Drama is what serious people are ready to accept as worthy of their distinguished consideration. Theatre is the exuberance, the exaggeration, the invention, the breathtaking, rib-tickling zest of theatrical performance at its peak. There is plenty of theatre in Shakespeare as well as the dramatic essence. There is theatre in all the great playwrights, including even such unlikely figures as Ibsen. When the drama domineers, or drives the theatrical element out altogether you get the plays of Goethe—always excepting *Faust* in which he spoke most truly—and the plays of Schiller, of Racine— plays which we regard with profound respect but which perhaps we do not rush to see when deeply serious companies offer them.

The powerful theatrical element in Dickens's writing has been deplored by critics. Edmund Wilson writes disparagingly of what he calls the ham element in Dickens. But what is ham? May not a great ham still be a great artist? Is it not an element of excess, of—no, not too much, but more than the rest of us are able to rise to in our lives and our creations? My dictionary gives as one definition of excess "over-stepping due limits." But whose due limits? Those of critics, who are always afraid of excess because they are at best classically restrained minds, and on the average crotch-bound, frightened people who fear that if they abandon themselves to the Dionysian excess of a great artist they may never again be able to retreat to their cosy nests? Do they not fear excess because it makes nonsense of their confined world? But the general public loves excess because it feeds upon the energy and invention of the great man, and thus it makes heroes of excessive characters, some worthy and many, it is to be feared, unworthy.

Dickens's excess was an abundance of theatrical device in his writing. His books, and especially the early ones before adulation and misfortune had combined to sadden him, vibrate with his excess. He infects us as readers with his marvellous excess; he even infected his early illustrators, Cruikshank and Leech. Have you ever noticed how theatrical the light is in their illustrations? How it seems to come almost entirely from the front and often from below, as if from footlights? That was how nineteenth-century stage light was. His books— the *Carol* as much as any—are full of effective touches of the kind that actors call "business." Consider the appearance of Marley's face in the knocker of Scrooge's house, illumined with a ghostly radiance like a bad lobster in a dark cellar; have you observed how, when he has opened the door, Scrooge looks to see if Marley's pigtail is sticking backward through the wood? Sheer theatre. Do you recall how, when the Ghost presents himself in Scrooge's chamber, the light flares up in the fire, as if to say "Marley's Ghost!" Now why do you think that was? I think it was because actors of the era of the *Carol* had a trick of stamping on the stage at crucial moments, because the stamp made the gaslights in the footlights flare up, giving a special emphasis, and that is what an actor playing the Ghost—and the actor was Dickens, don't forget—would have done. And when the Ghost retreats toward the window, and at every step the window rises a little higher—what an effective piece of stage management! You can go through the book looking for these stage effects, and you will find plenty of them. And from the nineteenth-century stage derives also the Ghost's elaborate rhetoric—"O captive, bound and double-ironed," it begins in its culminating address to Scrooge, and he, with brilliant comic utterance, undercuts the rhetoric as a great comedian might, saying, "Don't be flowery Jacob, pray." The mingling of pathos and terror is extraordinary, but the interjection of comedy is no less powerful, and it is achieved by means that Dickens had seen in the theatre, given fresh lustre by the splendour of his own invention.

I began by calling *A Christmas Carol* "an unlikely masterpiece." I have shown you, I hope, how unlikely it is as being one of the most powerfully *theatrical* creations in the whole of English literature. It invites us to take part in its nineteenth-century theatricality, becoming ourselves actors, directors, scene painters, gaslight controllers, and also audience as the play unfolds. It is unusual for a book to require this of us; most often a book allows us to sit back, as it were, as the story unfolds, and to judge it by the experience we bring to it. We agree with the new insights the author reveals, and we take pleasure in the characters he describes and the plot in which they are displayed. But how often are we asked so compellingly to be participators in what happens as we are asked to do by Dickens?

I think this is why stage and film versions of Dickens's books are so rarely completely satisfactory. I have seen many of them, ranging from the innocent adaptations of Dickens Fellowship groups to elaborate musical shows in which Dickens's verve and breadth of spirit is supposed to be offered in a musical form—and isn't. Mr. Pickwick singing is not Mr. Pickwick. Films have been more successful, though my gorge rises when I am asked to accept the archetypal con-man W.C. Fields as the high-minded Wilkins Micawber. Many films have been made of *A Christmas Carol,* and one of them, in which the part of Scrooge is played by the great Alistair Sim, comes commendably near to the mark. But to know the *Carol* in its essence you must read it, abandon yourself to it, and personally body it forth with whatever theatrical skill you may command.

That surely is what makes the *Carol* unusual. But—a masterpiece? Why?

In his observations on literature the late Vladimir Nabokov put the matter succinctly. He says: "An original author always invents an original world, and if a character or action fits into the pattern of that world, then we experience the pleasurable shock of artistic truth, no matter how unlikely the person or thing may seem if transferred into what book reviewers, poor hacks, call 'real life.' There is no such thing as real life for the author of genius; he must create it himself and then create the consequences."

The author of genius who brings us artistic truth. Is that not Charles Dickens, and is it not its artistic truth, as opposed to the kind of truth that stands up in a court of law, that makes *A Christmas Carol,* however unlikely, an undoubted masterpiece?

22

A CHRISTMAS CAROL
RE-HARMONIZED

In the early 1980s Davies wrote an updated version of the Christmas Carol story. Bound up in seasonal red binders, signed photocopies were sent out as a Christmas greeting to twenty-five fortunate friends. Since then, its fame has spread. Around Christmas 1982, the *Washington Post* printed the story in its Book World. Later, when the Penguin publishing group in the United Kingdom wanted a story for their sixtieth-anniversary celebration in 1995, Davies was happy to oblige with this tale of Dr. Scrooge, the Great Museum, and another villain named Croucher.

Once upon a time—of all the good days in the year, on Christmas Eve, Dr. Fred Scrooge sat in his office from which, as its Director, he attempted to guide the fortunes of the Great Museum. It was cold, bleak, biting weather outside, but in Scrooge's room and in the adjoining room where his secretary, Miss Cratchit, worked, all was comfort, culture, and amenity. They even had roaring wood fires, a whim of Dr. Scrooge's. It was just upon five o'clock.

"Unless you have something further, I'll go now," said Miss Cratchit; "I've a few details of Christmas shopping to finish."

"A very merry Christmas to you, Roberta," said Dr. Scrooge, rising and pressing upon her an expensive phial of perfume. Where would she wear it? At dinner with her large and loving tribe of

nephews and nieces; no husband, no lover, but Miss Cratchit nevertheless liked being treated as a woman of incalculable allure.

"Oh, Dr. Scrooge, you are always so kind," said Roberta; "how I
wish that all the staff wished you a merry Christmas! But I do! *I* do"—
and she hurried out, in an emotional flutter, for she admired Dr.
Scrooge, in an entirely nice way.

But of course the staff did not wish Dr. Scrooge a merry Christmas,
for they were professional museologists, hard and sharp as flint from
which no steel had ever struck out generous fire and, although, in the
tradition of their profession, they were jealous and intolerant of one
another, they were exceptionally intolerant and jealous of the Director,
who was, by virtue of his office, their enemy.

This was Dr. Scrooge's great sorrow, for he came of a long line of
philanthropists, and wished to love all men and be loved in his turn.
Had not his great-great-grandfather been that very Fred Scrooge,
nephew of the Great Ebenezer Scrooge, from whom the family wealth
and the family disposition toward broad philanthropy descended? Dr.
Scrooge had never quite cursed his wealth, which he had used so well
on behalf of the arts and sciences, but sometimes he had heartily
cursed the family inheritance of benevolence and the desire to be
loved. It was that weakness in his nature which was now driving him
toward crime—or what his colleagues would certainly regard as crime.

He opened a concealed panel in his office wall, revealing an illuminated screen, upon which was a plan to the Great Museum; little
red lights were appearing in every gallery, and as he watched, a pattern was completed, and he knew that all the staff had left the building, and the alarm system was in action—that very expensive system
which was designed to defeat even the remarkably cunning thieves
who made museums their prey. He touched a combination of buttons, and the red lights went off in the foyer, the Medieval Galleries,
the Gallery of Musical Instruments, and the Near Eastern Galleries.

Quite needlessly on tiptoe, Dr. Scrooge ran downstairs, through
the foyer, the Armour Hall, the Gallery of Musical Instruments, and
into the Near Eastern Section, and stopped by showcase Number 333.
Yes, there it was! Of course it was there, for who but himself and the

Curator, Dr. Dagon Croucher, had access to that case? There it was, the thorn in his flesh, the bone of contention!

So small a thing to cause such a mighty row! Just a small flask of smoky glass, with a nicely wrought silver stopper, but unquestionably Persian, unquestionably twelfth-century, and unlike any of the other ancient glass objects in the case. Last summer, during his travels, Dr. Scrooge had found it in the shop of a dealer in Istanbul, and had bought it for a substantial sum of his own money. He had presented it to Dr. Croucher with glee, as an addition to the Great Museum's splendid collection of Near Eastern glass objects, hoping that Croucher would be pleased. But Croucher had been furious, and was furious still.

How dared the Director interfere with Dr. Croucher's careful plan of acquisitions? How dared he buy such an object without consulting Croucher beforehand? Even though he had bought it with his own money, the Director had no right—this was outright abuse of the directorial supervisory mandate—was Croucher to be patronized and taught his job by someone whose own area was Renaissance Carved Gems—a dabbler who wouldn't know a twelfth-century flask from a Coke bottle—Dr. Croucher's rage made him incoherent. He wrote a memo to the Governors, protesting intemperately. He roused his cura-torial colleagues, Drs. Katt, Grout, and Eisel, against the Director, and gained power by so doing, for though Katt, Grout, and Eisel hated Croucher, they hated the Director even more. Dr. Croucher raised hell, and was raising it still.

Of course the Curator put the flask on exhibition, for in his black heart he knew it was a good piece, but he put it in a position of disadvantage, and attached to it a description that knowing readers could tell threw doubt on its authenticity. The description said it was a Gift, but named no Donor. Dr. Croucher had not enjoyed himself so much in years—not, in fact, since he had discredited a book which was the life work of his greatest rival; the rival had died of rage and mortification. Maybe Dr. Croucher could hound the Director out of his job, thereby crowning his own career as a learned malcontent.

Dr. Scrooge, however, was not a man whose soul was entirely

defined by Renaissance Carved Gems, and he suspected something that would never have occurred to Dr. Croucher. He opened the display case with his master key, removed the flask, and looked carefully at the stopper.

Nobody had been able to open it, though if Dr. Croucher had been less malignant and scornful, the preparatorial staff might have found out how to do so. Pulling and twisting had been of no avail, but Dr. Scrooge suspected that the stopper worked like that of one of those modern medicine bottles that are for the protection of children; you pushed it inward, then gave it a quarter turn to the left. The Gallery was as dark as five o'clock on Christmas Eve can be, but the Director had a flashlight, and now he tried his theory. It worked like a charm.

Like a charm indeed, for there was a flash, a roar, a gust of wind that threw Dr. Scrooge back against a neighbouring case, and towering above him stood a huge, naked Jinnee of surpassing ugliness, who roared, "Speak, Master. What is your will? I hear and obey."

Dr. Scrooge had been expecting something of the sort, so although he was startled, he was neither dismayed nor afraid. Aware that his voice was a lyric tenor, as contrasted with the basso roar of the Jinnee, he fluted authoritatively: "First, I must return this bottle to its case, lock the case, and get away as fast as possible. Meet me in my office at once, and I should be glad if you would put on some clothes, and perhaps assume a less extraordinary appearance."

There was a very rapid whirlwind, and Dr. Scrooge was seated in his office, with the transformed Jinnee in the visitor's chair.

"*Inshallah,* you are a cool one," said the Jinnee, smiling broadly. He was now an Oriental gentleman of impeccable elegance; he wore a pearl-grey morning suit, and shoes of patent leather, with pearl-grey buttoned tops. Upon his head was a most beautiful rose turban, his complexion was coppery, and his beard and moustache were splendidly in order. "How do I look?" said he; "quite the modern museum curator, I think. Don't you feel the pearl in the tie inspires confidence?"

Dr. Scrooge, who was himself a good dresser, thought of the terrible garments affected by Croucher, Katt, and Eisel (though not Grout) and did not answer. Instead he came to the point.

"My problem is this," said he, "and I want your most carefully considered advice and help in solving it."

When he had finished his explanation, which took about half an hour and was perhaps rather emotional, the Jinnee, who had never ceased smiling, spoke.

"If I have understood you correctly, O Master, your colleagues detest you for professional reasons, and you wish to sweeten their dispositions, to change their characters, as the character of your great ancestor, Ebenezer Scrooge, was changed in a single Christmas Eve experience. You want them to have a merry Christmas."

"But nothing Dickensian, please," said Dr. Scrooge. "No big turkeys, no dancing Sir Roger de Coverley. These are people of today, you understand."

And Dr. Scrooge looked mistrustfully at the Jinnee's patent-leather shoes with the buttoned cloth tops, which hinted to him that the Jinnee was not fully aware of the modern era. He looked rather pre-First World War. But the Jinnee was full of assurance and spoke laughingly.

"No, no, of course nothing Dickensian," he said. "But human nature does not really change much. Every man has his price, what?"

"Don't forget that Dr. Katt is a woman," said the Director.

"No, of course not. Do they really call her Pussy Katt? How awful! But a Pussy Katt must have a price, too. A nice mousie, do you think?" And the Jinnee laughed merrily.

"Everything is now in your hands," said Dr. Scrooge. "The Museum is closed on Boxing Day, but I shall be here at five o'clock in the evening, and I shall expect your report then."

"Master, I hear and obey," said the Jinnee and vanished, fancy shoes and all.

After a Christmas Day and a Boxing Day in which he vacillated between hope and doubt, Dr. Scrooge was prompt to the minute in his Museum office. A glance at the Jinnee's face confirmed his worst fears. The Jinnee was greenish, rather than a ruddy copper in complexion, and his clothes did not fit so well as before. There was even—could it be?—a splash of salty slush on the toe of one of the splendid shoes, and his expression was almost hangdog.

"Let me know the worst," said Dr. Scrooge.

"Alas, Master, these are such people as I have never met before. My principle is the age-old one of my kind: all men desire Gold, Earthly Power, or the Joys of Sex. But in the past thousand years much has happened to complicate such work as mine. Listen, and you shall hear.

"Dr. Dagon Croucher is obviously a man whose soul yearns for earthly power. What would give such a man a merry Christmas? My device was a subtle one. I discovered that for the past six months he had been intriguing against the scheme that brings thousands of children to visit the Museum. He says they are too young to understand, that they are noisy and disruptive, and that their teachers do it simply in order to spare themselves the trouble of teaching. All these things are true, but they go against the beliefs of the present time. Recently, in a television interview, Dr. Croucher won a brief notoriety by confessing, in answer to a direct question, that he hated children. Surely therein lies the seed of a merry Christmas for Dr. Croucher.

"On the festive day he watches TV for many hours, because it is his pleasure to sneer at the seasonable programmes. So I devised one, visible on his set alone, at which he would not sneer—at which indeed he could rejoice, and be deeply happy. I arranged that the Slaughter of the Innocents should be played before him by the original cast, beginning with Herod the Great himself. Herod, as everybody knows, decreed that all children under two years old should be slain, and there was great lamentation and weeping in consequence. What St. Matthew fails to record is how the slaughter was accomplished, and it has been assumed for centuries that it was done by soldiers. With reprehensible carelessness I had assumed this myself. Alas, what appeared on Dr. Croucher's screen was different.

"It seems that Herod's soldiers had many duties at the time, and only a few could be spared for infanticide. So the palace eunuchs were marshalled, and not being fighting men they devised a rapid, effective, but inglorious means of carrying out their orders. They divided themselves into groups of three, in which one eunuch seized the child, another restrained the mother, and the third and fattest eunuch placed the child beneath a cushion and sat on it as hard as he could. It was lacking in tragic dignity.

"Did it delight Dr. Croucher? It did not. He was soon on the telephone to the president of the broadcasting system which he believed, quite erroneously, to be screening my special programme; the president, when at last he was found, was outraged and he and Dr. Croucher exchanged ugly words. Then Dr. Croucher called the Human Rights people—another frustrating search for anyone in authority—to complain that the programme brought eunuchs into disrepute and derision, and that eunuchs were discriminated against as a minority, and what was going to be done about it?

"I fear it was a day of total frustration for Dr. Croucher. He has a new outrage to deplore—society's indefensible refusal to accept eunuchry as one of the Alternative Lifestyles. He is even more immovably the man he was. Not a merry Christmas at all."

Dr. Scrooge felt sorry for the Jinnee. He said, kindly, "Well, well don't be downhearted. I'm sure you managed beautifully with the others."

"Alas, Master," said the Jinnee, "women have changed greatly since last I left the happy obscurity of my bottle. What was I to do for Dr. Pussy Katt? I knew but one solution to the problem, and on Christmas Eve I placed in her bed a young man of surpassing beauty. His hair hung in ringlets scented with ambergris, his eyes were as pools of cream in which two perfect amethysts float, his teeth were like new ivory, his limbs were like old ivory, his armpits gave out gusts of musk and cinnamon, and his sexual power was inexhaustible. When Dr. Katt returned from her bath he turned to her and cried musically, 'O thou garden of a thousand unexplored delights, hasten to embrace me, my sister, my spouse.'

"At first everything seemed to be going according to plan. Urged by a spirit of inquiry, and three hearty Scotches she had had during the evening, Dr. Katt allowed herself to be drawn into the bed, where my young assistant linked the poetry of speech with the poetry of physical action until Dr. Katt stood—or rather lay—upon the threshold of an experience hitherto unknown to her life. But my young man failed—a poetical failure.

"'O queen among women,' he breathed, 'when has the world seen your like? Your hair—so rich an auburn and yet, like the mystery lying in the heart of a beautiful flower, with a thumb's breadth of dark green at the roots—'

"It was then that Dr. Katt gave a squawk which aroused her companion in life, a lady of much her own stature and sort, who professes Household Science at the University; she appeared with a rolling-pin which she kept always on her bed-side table for just such emergencies, and stunned my young man with a heavy blow. Confusion! A call to the police. My young man, wrapped in an eiderdown, was whisked off to the police station, where I let him undergo interrogation for a bruising half-hour, to teach him a lesson. Then I spirited him away, and the police, who are entirely accustomed to the inexplicable disappearances of people under charge, promptly forgot all about him.

"Not so Dr. Katt and her companion. 'To think what might have happened,' said Pussy, half in awe of herself as an enchantress, half indignant; 'a rapist!' Her companion was half firm in her natural austerity, half jealous; 'Tush, Puss,' said she; 'just a crazy burglar. You were never in the least danger, so don't give yourself airs.'

"The complexity of hurt feelings, jealousy, and unfocused indignation rages still in the dwelling of Dr. Katt and her friend, and I fear it will never be wholly subdued. Not at all a merry Christmas, I fear."

"You must comfort yourself with the reflection that you did your best," said Dr. Scrooge, and immediately regretted it.

"My best belongs to another age, another concept of life," the Jinnee grieved. "The intrusive modern state has made such magic as mine wholly ineffective. Oh, what a mess of things I made with Dr. Ernst Eisel, third on your list, and a man who never stops whining about money, as well you know. So I gave him money.

"You have never been in the Eisels' house—or rather, their stuffy apartment, which might well be in their native Prague, so firmly does it keep the New World outside its door. Twenty-five years here have done nothing to change them in any serious respect. Childless people, they make children of each other, and on Christmas Eve they hang up stockings, and secretly fill them. Pitiable, if they were not so nasty.

"The stockings made my task simple—so I thought. When they were fast asleep, huddled together like withered children, I emptied Ernst's stocking of the candies and cookies and toys that Anna had provided, and instead tucked in one thousand bills each of one thousand dollars' value; it made quite a swollen stocking.

"Christmas morning came, and when Ernst unpacked his stocking he fainted dead away. Anna waited until she had counted the money, then she elected for hysterics instead of a faint. Slowly, I came to understand their problem. How could they possibly present notes of such a denomination in any shop, how deposit them in their bank, how, in fact, conceal what they had? For if it became known that they had a million dollars, how could they explain where it had come from? They had no papers establishing an inheritance, no numbered account in which it could be concealed.

"Their pitiable state slowly became clear to me. There was much talk of a mysterious body called They, to whom such a fortune would have to be explained, and They seemed to be a muddle of tax authorities and public opinion. Their fear went even deeper. I understood, as they chattered in pain, that Ernst and Anna were wedded to what they regarded as their poverty—meaning the by no means trivial salary he received as your Curator of Paleontology and some money he gets from his publications and a handful of widow-and-orphan investments. I had robbed them of their poverty, and they were stricken.

"Where to hide the money—for it was quite out of their moral power to destroy it. It could not be buried, for they had not even a window-box. As I left them, deeply cast down by my failure, Ernst was wrapping the money in small packages and sticking it in the back of their freezer, while Anna peeped from beneath drawn blinds to watch for the approach of the Secret Police, who were Jinn greater even than I in their terrible world. They still sit, trembling, unable even to dress themselves, waiting for something awful to happen. A failure, but not my greatest, Master. O, Master, not my greatest!

"For my greatest, I confess in tears of grief, was with the fourth of your colleagues, Dr. Dirk Grout, your elegant Curator of Fine Art.

"Grout lives, as I am sure you know, with a man younger than himself, an interior decorator ravenous in his yearning to turn their condominium—which Grout paid for but which is now, lock, stock, and barrel, in the name of his young friend—into something so exquisite that even the heart of this inordinate youth could crave nothing finer. So, hopeful of pleasing Grout by appeasing the companion, I hastened on Christmas Eve to cram the condominium with what decorators call 'palace pieces'—boiseries, cloisonné, silken carpets, rare tapestries, Buhl and intarsias, paintings of the quattrocento and tables and chairs of the dixhuitième, all finer than any to be found even in your Great Museum. I took special care to include many articles made of scented woods, so that the condominium smelled like the very Garden of Paradise.

"But—O wretched creature that I am!—when Grout and his companion woke on Christmas morning, what a scene of jealousy and madness! The companion—jealous because Grout seemed to have dared to acquire these things without seeking his approval and the seal of his impeccable taste! Grout—insane because he had invited the Chairman of the Museum Board for dinner on this very day, hoping to poison the Chairman's mind against you, O Master!

"And now—what would the Chairman think? Here there came into the uproar of lamentation and reproach an element utterly unknown to me, called Conflict of Interest. The Chairman, seeing the splendours of Grout's condominium, would at once assume that Grout had been obtaining for himself, at a heavy discount, objects which, as a matter of professional honour, he should have bought on behalf of the Great Museum.

"Grout rushed to the bathroom—now a wonder of gold taps and marble fittings—intent on suicide, but the elegant étagère I had substituted for the medicine cabinet offered nothing more noxious than a roll of Tums. In his distraction he began to rave of a garage sale on a scale of hitherto undreamed-of magnificence. But the companion, having had his fill of insult and affront, began to turn his mind to practicalities, and recalled an uncle who had solved a difficult financial problem with the aid of a fire. He rushed downstairs, siphoned all the gasoline out of the Bugatti Grout had given him last Christmas, and was back in an instant, flinging the stuff hither and thither, like a bishop aspersing his congregation, while Grout heaped any precious thing he could lift into a pile on the living-room floor.

"Alas, they were but children in arson, and they overdid things disastrously. Five minutes after they had left the condominium, flinging a lighted match behind them, the whole building was ablaze, and it was twenty-four hours before the Fire Department could bring it under control.

"Eighty families are now homeless, four firemen are in hospital suffering from smoke inhalation, and the Chief has declared that the blaze must have been caused by a Christmas tree lighted with candles. The companion took an early plane to Florida; Grout is in a padded cell in the psychiatric ward. And I, O Master—if death lay within my power, I would beg to die, but of course I can't. Do with me as you will."

The Jinnee, by this time, had shrunk in stature, his fine Edwardian clothes were rumpled and shabby, his beard was grey, and several buttons had burst from his splendid boots and hung by threads, like doll's eyes. Even his rose turban was dishevelled, and one end hung forward over his blubbered face. Grovelling on the carpet, he whined, over and over—"And you commanded me to give these people a merry Christmas! Another chance, Master, I beg you—another chance. Let me accustom myself to this strange new world, so tangled in rules, restrictions, and complexities of scruple, and then permit your slave to try again. I am sure I can learn."

Dr. Scrooge had no such certainty. He wanted time to reflect, and he gestured the Jinnee to silence.

What was to be done? He reached behind him to the shelf where stood the twenty-four elegantly bound volumes of *Sermons of the Reverend Timothy Cratchit*. Surely Tiny Tim, who had become an enormously popular Victorian evangelist, would have some words of guidance? By chance, however, his hand fell upon a book by a great, but now neglected, American sage and it opened, from long use, at a passage he had forgotten. It began, "Happiness is impossible, and even inconceivable, to a mind without scope and without pause, a mind driven by craving, pleasure or fear." Of course, Santayana knew what he was talking about. What a fool he was to think that Croucher, Katt, Eisel, and Grout could be made happy by anything. But—but—

He was interrupted by the Jinnee, who was capering about the room in a transport of delight. "O Master, it has just come to me! I can make them all happy! Why did I not think of it before! When I looked into their minds—dark caverns filled with serpents as they were—they shared but a single desire. It was that you should resign. O Master, I entreat you to resign! Let me carry you to a castle, East of the Sun and West of the Moon, where a hundred slave-girls, every one with sound teeth and totally free from superfluous hair, await your pleasure! O Master, let me inscribe your resignation in letters of purple on parchment made from the skin of an unborn lamb, and bear it at once to the Chairman of the Board!"

"Shut up, idiot!" said Dr. Scrooge. "Now listen to me—"

"O Prince of the Compassionate Word!" cried the Jinnee. "O fairest child of the Angel of Mercy!"

"Shh! I want to think. Now, see here: no more of this Arabian Nights business, do you hear? And no more tinkering with people to whom happiness is impossible, because inconceivable. You are to do something for me. And this time, if you don't get it right, I shall send you somewhere that you will dislike very much. Are you ready? Are you listening?"

The Jinnee was once more coppery, bright-eyed, and smiling "O Master, I hear and obey," and his voice might have roused envy in Chaliapin.

"You are to give *me* a merry Christmas. To hell with merry Christmas for those who are without faith and therefore without joy. Be very careful because it is with my mind, my personality, indeed with my very soul, that you will be working. I command you, in the name of

Allah, who alone is great, who sits throned in Eternity above the shifts of Time, to give me a mind freed of craving, pleasure, and fear. And watch your step."

The Jinnee resumed his true guise, naked, splendid, and awesome. "I hear and obey," said he.

Dr. Scrooge did not resign, but remained Director until his mandatory retirement, at which he received a handsome pension and left the Great Museum regretted by all, for Croucher, Katt, Eisel, and Grout, unable now to touch him, had become biddable and almost civil.

Why? Because their Director had outsoared the shadow of their malignity. He seemed to want nothing, and yet everything he might have wanted came to him without his bidding. He pursued no satisfactions, and for that very reason he seemed to be fulfilled and happy. He feared no one and nothing, and perhaps because of that he was never forced into situations where he had to display obvious courage. Although his associates could not have known it, this was the most extraordinary transformation of character since his great-great-great-uncle Ebenezer encountered the Three Spirits in a single night.

Above everything else, it was seen even by the most unobservant that he knew how to keep Christmas well, if ever man alive possessed the knowledge. Would that that might be truly said of us, and all of us!

And so, as Tiny Tim would have observed, if he had had the wits to do so, to Hell with those who are in the grip of craving, pleasure, and fear, and being thus without faith, cannot know happiness.

23

FICTION OF THE FUTURE

∽ℰℒ↝

In the Autumn of 1994 in Canada and the winter and spring of 1995 elsewhere, Davies and his wife were engaged in the "Dog and Pony Show"——the tour arranged by the publishers to promote *The Cunning Man*. When a special full-dress lecture was called for, this was the one he chose to give, first as the Duthie Lecture in Vancouver, and later in several other cities.

This, the latest of his full-length lectures, was also one of the most sombre. As it ranges back and forth in time——from Heracleitus to Professor Francis Crick, who helped discover DNA and now suggests that there may be a religion gene——this look at the future is clearly the work of a man who has lived a long and thoughtful life, before returning to the comforting thought that Ecclesiastes was right: "there is no new thing under the sun": *Visit the theatre with Sherry to check lights: seats 2,500 and sold out! Lecture at 7:30: very warm reception and score heavily answering questions, which I did as honestly as I can: they are presented to me written on slips and I choose which to answer, weeding out sillies. Sign a lot of books though I was promised I need not . . .*

I have chosen to talk to you about the Fiction of the Future, and when you hear such a title you have every right to question my capacity to talk of what is still unknown. Am I a clairvoyant or an astrologer? By no means. But I have seen quite a bit of what is now the past, and during my years as a journalist it was my daily job to record it and comment on it; long ago I came to the conclusion that "the thing that hath been, it is that which shall be; and that which is done is that which shall be done; and there is no new thing under the sun." (Ecclesiastes 1:9) But of course the thing that hath been is always presenting itself in new garments, and is always being experienced freshly by new generations, so there is an illusion—a very strong and exciting illusion—of novelty. And that is a good thing, for otherwise we might think that we were all on a treadmill of endless repetition and that life was not worth having. Which of course it is. Life is an ever-renewing pleasure for most of us, and if we are not too spoiled with that pleasure, we recognize it and are grateful for it. If we think about it seriously, just living from moment to moment is an adventure, involving a co-operative effort between our infinitely complex physical and psychological selves and the multifarious universe in which we exist. And although there may be nothing new under the sun, what is old is new to us and so rich and astonishing that we never tire of it. If we do tire of it, if we lose our curiosity, we have lost something of infinite value, because to a high degree it is curiosity that gives meaning and savour to life.

Already, in my introductory words, I have told you two things that underlie everything else that I shall say. I have quoted from the Bible and have told you that I used to be a newspaper man. Why are those two things important, and how are they linked? Many years ago I was reading a biography of one of my literary heroes, the great Norwegian dramatist Henrik Ibsen, and I learned that when he was asked by an admirer—I think it was Edmund Gosse—what he read that underlay his extraordinary perception of life, he replied that he read nothing but the Bible and the newspapers. Gosse saw a well-worn Bible in the great man's workroom, and it was known that every day of his life in Oslo (it was then called Christiania) Ibsen dressed himself impeccably, walked to his favourite restaurant, and sat at his favourite table in a corner; and there all the day's newspapers were brought to him (because in those days restaurants provided newspapers for their customers) and he sat for two hours, drinking aquavit, and reading, and peeping over his paper at the other diners. He read all the papers from end to end, including the advertisements, and he read not only the serious dailies but also the comic papers.

It was here that he gained his profound and wide-ranging insight into human life, it was here that he found his plots, and when he went home he identified what he had read in the daily news with what had been written so long ago by those Hebrew chroniclers, and found the same stories about the three great subjects of all literature—Love, War, and Death.

(As a footnote, I might mention that when Ibsen walked into his restaurant, everyone stood up until he was seated. They knew how to treat authors in those days.)

When I read that, and thought about it, my attitude toward my newspaper work was transformed; I had known that I was a chronicler of my times, and that although the appearance of human experience was perpetually changing its form, the material remained the same. The impress of today was printed in the wax of the ages; the imprint varied, but never the wax.

I was especially interested that Ibsen read the *comic* papers, because all my life I have been a great reader of "the funnies" as they are still called—though God knows they rarely make me laugh—because they give an insight into what people who never philosophize, and who would be astonished if you called them thinkers, imagine the truth of life to be. In *Dagwood and Blondie* a clever woman who seems to be a feather-brain dominates her husband, who really is a feather-brain and who toils under the domination of Mr. Dithers, an unappeasable boss. In *Peanuts* a thoughtful and logical little boy is dominated by a determined, truculent little girl, though he knows that his vision of life is truer than hers. In *Sally Forth* a wife and mother who is also a business woman bears her burdens with stoicism and supplies stability for her husband, who seems to know no care, and her obnoxious child whose demands and criticism are unending. She is the heroine of our time, for millions of readers.

How different these seem to be from the funnies of my youth, when Mutt settled all his arguments with Jeff by hitting him on the head with a spittoon; when the *Katzenjammer Kids* reduced daily life to chaos, and made fierce fun of newcomers to this continent in a way that would outrage the proponents of Political Correctness. And indeed what would Political Correctness make of *Happy Hooligan* who was a cheerful mental defective; or of *Count Screwloose of Toulouse* who was an achrondoplastic dwarf; or of *Barney Google* who was in love with a horse? In the transformation of the funnies we see plainly the change from the comparatively carefree anarchy of feeling during the twenties to the guilt-ridden, apprehensive, Politically Correct spirit of our time, when virtually nothing can be laughed at, when the West is expected to bear all the troubles of the East, and when the retributive justice of the past appears to be giving place to a world where the psychological wounds of the criminal class take precedence over the wrongs of those who suffer from their criminality.

Newspapers have changed their character during my lifetime. They used to be the principal carriers of the world's news, but television holds that position now. Television, however, has serious limitations; it is a visual medium, and it is dominated by the principle that nothing is news unless you can take a picture of it. It is here that the newspapers still hold their own; so much of what goes on in the political world cannot be effectively photographed; statesmen, in their expensive but uninteresting clothes, make very poor TV and their prolonged deliberations are dull when we see them on the box. Politics must be interpreted, and newspapers have become their untiring interpreters. Even MacNeil and Lehrer cannot hold you for too long with a description of what is happening in the world, but at your leisure you can read half a dozen interpretations written by newspaper columnists and draw your own conclusions. That doesn't happen on television; it draws your conclusions for you, and the conclusions it draws are those of people whose primary job it is to see that you do not change your channel. Thus catastrophic wars are seen in terms of starving children, or weary troops of refugees; the reasons for the wars, even when they can be discovered, are too complex for the picture-box. If we knew the reasons, our sympathy might cool. The TV journalists cannot permit your sympathy to cool, for emotion, not intelligence, is what holds you to the small screen.

Intelligence, not perhaps on its highest level but far beyond the sheer emotionalism of TV, has found its refuge in the newspapers. There is discussion there, for even the most modest paper has a few columnists, who may not be profound thinkers or deep students of affairs, but at least you can read what they have to say, and reread it if you wish, and draw conclusions of your own. You can write to the paper and dispute with a columnist, but you most certainly cannot dispute with television. It is significant, is it not, that television now offers printed versions of its educational programs, but not of its programs of opinion.

Another great strength of the newspaper is that you can keep it, or some part of it, for so long as you please. Television cannot be recalled. When I was a very young man I read an excellent book by a French scholar in which he recommended that everybody should keep a dossier of newspaper clippings related to their principal subjects of interest; it was a way, he said, to become a modest expert on any subject you pleased, and also to observe how quickly fashions in ideas changed. I began a personal newspaper file then, and I have it still. It is now very bulky, and from time to time I dip into it to remind myself of the past.

Do you want to know what sort of things I file? Some of the headings are Crime, Psychiatry, Religion, Pornography, Medicine, Art, Music, and other more personal concerns like Grotesqueries and Strange Manifestations of the Holy Ghost. Most of the clippings are serious. Indeed, they were all meant seriously and if I take them somewhat lightly, that is my preference. For instance, I am delighted with the news that in February 1984, Muhammed Aloo, aged 100, married a fourteen-year-old girl in a Muslim ceremony; his best man was eighty-six. I have quite a lot of information about the family of Pierre Plantard de Saint-Clair who claims direct descent from the marriage of Jesus Christ and Mary Magdalen. On a somewhat lower social level I am interested in the murder in which a man killed his brother because he used two rolls of toilet paper in a single day. And of course

I cherish the account of a suit brought by a U.S. Marine against three tough girls who ambushed him and at gunpoint required him to have sexual intercourse with them until he was utterly drained; very properly he sued for rape and the court upheld his suit.

But, you may ask, what has this to do with the fiction of the future? Do you suppose the fiction of the future will radically differ from the fiction of the past? It will seem to do so, because fiction does evolve in manner, if not in matter. Quite often young writers come to me to talk about writing, and many of them are greatly puzzled about how they can keep up with the times. My advice is always to forget about the times, because we all belong to our own time, and there is nothing whatever that we can do to escape from it. Whatever we write will be contemporary, even if we attempt a novel set in a past age, and put on fancy dress, so to speak, in our prose. You can always tell when a novel was written, however the author may toil to place it in an historic past. *Henry Esmond* is unmistakably a Victorian novel, and a fine one, though Thackeray has done his best to clothe it in the prose of Queen Anne. Robert Graves's splendid *I, Claudius* and *Claudius the God* have been given a wonderful Latin clarity of prose, but they cannot disguise the fact that they are post-Freudian novels. So we need not worry about being modern; we cannot escape it.

That is why I tell the young people who want to talk to me about writing that they might profitably cast their minds back to the vendors of fiction in the past. Indeed, to those storytellers many hundreds of years ago who spread a mat in the market-place, sat on it, placed their collection bowl well forward, and cried: "Give me a copper coin, and I will tell you a golden tale." We have some of those tales still— *The Arabian Nights* was composed entirely of them—and they are golden indeed, as are also the folk-tales recorded by the Brothers Grimm. So golden are they, that we can trace their features in many novels that have just fallen from the press. What is astonishing about these old stories is how modern they are in feeling, if not in superficialities.

So we need not worry about modernity. But we do. Oh yes, we do. We are strongly conscious that we stand on the brink of what looks like a great leap in time. It isn't. It is simply one tick of the clock, but it will carry us from the twentieth century into the twenty-first, and for many people this has an almost magical quality.

Indeed, such progressions of time had a deeply magical quality in the past, when many learned people were concerned with the World Astrological Clock, which measured time in Aeons of two thousand years each, every Aeon supposedly being under the domination of one of the signs of the Zodiac. The Aeon we are just winding up is the Aeon of Pisces, the Fishes who are seen swimming in opposite directions. And who can dispute that the past two thousand years have been marked by contrarieties which seem wholly inexplicable but which nevertheless have been historical facts? By the reckoning of the World Clock we are moving into the Aeon of Aquarius, and have been doing so for something like two hundred years. The great astrologers foretell an era of flux, of change, of liquid uncertainties. If you wish to pursue this sort of thinking, you will remember that the age now passing—the Age of Pisces—saw the rise and dominance of Christianity as one of the great world religions, but as the Age of Flux draws nearer, Christianity appears to be losing much of its strength, though it is wholly improbable that its message will be completely lost. But the Age of Flux will require that Christianity and other religions be regarded in a new light, and already we have seen flashes of what that new light may be. A new world for women—because the great religions of the past have never been considerate of women—and a new attitude toward sex, which has not yet declared itself in the nervous shiftings and compromises of the present day. A world, it may be, in which the dominance of what a great poet has called "getting and spending" may be moderated, although we should not build any socialist-utopian dreams on what that moderation may bring. A world perhaps of greater interference in the life of the individual? That might well be, though inevitably in an age of flux such interference would meet with strong resistance. But these waves of change do not happen quickly and some long periods of what looks like certainty may have to be endured by our posterity before they are overthrown by something else. Flux, in world terms, does not mean rapid turbulence and turmoil. It is slow, and we can say with certainty that, although it is slow, it is also sure.

Our posterity will have to make its peace with great new religions. By a religion I mean some body of doctrine that demands acquiescence and conformity by virtually everyone, and which hunts down the non-conformists with righteous fury.

You will not be surprised when I say that one of these new religions, which is already rising to extraordinary power, is Science.

What is Science? The word simply means knowledge but now we use it to signify what experimenters can tell us about the universe in some aspect of its variety. Such knowledge is gained by experiments which confirm hypotheses, and stated very crudely it may be assumed that if an experiment can be carried through a hundred times with the same result, the hypothesis has been shown to be a fact. This of course is totally different from Art, in which nothing is ever precisely the same from one instance to another. The scientific approach to humanity is wholesale; the approach of art, and the art we are talking about here is fiction, is retail. Not masses, but individuals.

I speak of Science as a religion because of the priestlike authority it now assumes in its assertions about many things, and especially about public health. I use the word "priestlike" somewhat sardonically, because we know how brilliantly the priests of past times interpreted history, and especially the history of those who opposed them, to suit their own purposes and support their own doctrines. This was not calculated roguery; all priesthoods are certain that they know the truth and know that it is their duty to protect mankind from error. Instances of this sort of action in the world of Science abound. How weak the voices seem that oppose the evangelical fervour of the scientific opponents of smoking tobacco! We are now assured that not only smokers themselves, but those who are exposed to their exhaled smoke, are in mortal danger, and that unborn children may suffer irreparable damage if somehow tobacco smoke is transmitted to them by expectant mothers who associate with smokers. I am old enough to remember the fervour with which reformers in the past denounced all alcoholic drinks and could prove, with statistics, that a great number of human ills had their origin in the saloon. It is the statistics that bother me because I know a little about how they are achieved. Give a first-rate statistician a supposed fact to prove, and he is a traitor to his craft if he cannot prove it for you. The old saw is true: figures cannot lie, but liars can figure. I do not question the sincerity of the scientists who assure us that tobacco is a deadly poison; but I have lived long enough to have seen how much sincerity can be aroused on behalf of things which in the end proved insubstantial. I often think of the remark of Havelock Ellis who said that the sophistication of a civilization might be measured in terms of its judicious use of poisons. The jocose question, "What's your poison?" is not quite as shallow as it at first seems. Is it coffee? Is it speed—however you interpret the word? Is it alcohol? Is it self-righteousness and determination to save your fellow-man however he may protest that he does not wish to be saved? That last one is a terrible poison indeed, because it is not widely recognized. It was the mainspring of the Christian missionary movement.

Nevertheless, Science must have its day, and a very terrible day it may be because scientists, though superbly trained in their own great mystery, often carry into their work an ethical outlook which may be called primitive. They can do marvels, but they do not care where the marvels may lead. Perhaps that is unjust; many of them do care, but their voices are drowned out by the cries of those whose personal interest is served by something which may not be in the interest of mankind. We know now what doubts were felt by many of the greatest scientists about atomic fission, but they could not be heard above the enthusiastic approbation of lesser men, and many politicians, who saw an immediate advantage in what atomic fission might achieve. But it is fruitless to pursue this theme: the time for the discovery of atomic fission had come, and if it had not been achieved and used immediately as an instrument of power, it would certainly not have lingered much longer in the womb of time.

What has this to do with fiction, you may ask? Here I am on uneasy ground, because the whole world of Science Fiction is closed to me. I simply cannot interest myself in it. But I am aware that it has shown itself prophetic in many instances. The authors propose solutions to scientific problems at which real scientists laugh, but from time to time the laugh is turned against themselves. I think of a movie that was made in 1966, *The Fantastic Voyage,* in which some scientists shrank themselves, and a kind of submarine in which they could travel, to such dimensions that they could be introduced into the bloodstream of an ailing man, and travel through his body to his brain, there to operate on the blood clot that threatened his life. The film was very popular, but it was assumed to be fantasy.

Nevertheless, I read recently in the newspapers of the work of some Australian engineers who are concerned in what is called nano-technology, which is the construction of tiny machines. Already motors less than a millimetre long have been made and Japanese researchers are designing micro-robots small enough to travel through blood vessels and deliver drugs to precisely the right organ in the body; they are powered by a battery a hundredth of the size of the red blood cell and capable of generating twenty millivolts for about forty-five minutes. When we applaud the achievements of these men, I think we should not forget Otto Klement, who wrote the story of *The Fantastic Voyage,* and drape him in a modest prophetic mantle. Scientists are very clever men, but they have no monopoly on imagination.

The great scientific enthusiasm of our time is, of course, the investigation of the genetic code, which has been described as "the greatest discovery of all time" because it is expected to reveal, as one enthusiastic journalist puts it, "the secret of life." You must excuse me from explaining it to you in detail. It is rather complex and would take up a lot of your time, and I suppose that many of you are fully familiar with it already. All I know about it is what I read in the newspapers, and the best I can do for you is to offer a very quick rundown on what a gene is. Now attend very carefully, please, or you may miss something vital. Each of the body's 100 trillion cells has a nucleus: inside the nucleus are forty-six chromosomes, arranged in twenty-three pairs: each chromosome contains genes, which are white areas: each gene is made of the double helix of DNA, which, as I do not need to tell you, is deoxyribonucleic acid, which is the complex molecule that constitutes the genetic material of living organisms:

the cross links between the helices are the bases that form the genetic code. This genetic code is identified by three billion letters, and by the year 2005 the scientists expect to have it all sorted out and after that presumably everything is plain sailing. Are you with me? Good. The secret of life has been unveiled and what will happen next is anybody's guess.

The greatest part of the work on this extraordinary leap forward in the understanding of life has been done, and is still being done, at Cambridge in the Cavendish Laboratory by James Watson and Francis Crick. Of course work is being done in every advanced country under the aegis of something called the Human Genome Organization, popularly known as HUGO. Overwrought journalists say that this work compares in scale with the Apollo moon landing and the Manhattan Project to build the atomic bomb. By scale I suppose they mean the number of people involved and the money spent, because the moon landing has not told us much we didn't know before. A celebrated modern historian, A.J.P. Taylor, described it as "the biggest non-event of my life" and there are many who agree. The atomic venture has certainly not proved, in ordinary use, the great boon that was promised, though it is still a terror when threatened for use in war. In peace it has proved to be dangerous, in spite of great precautions.

When the three billion letters that make up the genetic code have at last been arranged in the right order it will apparently be possible to identify in the foetus of the unborn child the gene which disposes toward breast cancer, heart disease, diabetes, and a number of other serious human ills. Then what do you do? Abort the foetus or take a chance? A nice theme for fictional treatment, that one. What if the genetic prediction shows the unborn child to be prone to accumulation of cholesterol, or of becoming a psychotic, or being gay? The opportunity to develop a humanity free from all its ills, perfect in health, with no leaning toward crime and no ethical problems, is a great temptation to a certain type of mind. It would be extraordinary if, under such circumstances, governments did not decide to take a hand in the decision. And we all know how clever governments are about ethical problems. Genetic engineering is said to be the coming thing. And tinkering on behalf of some idea of human betterment would be an irresistible temptation.

Professor Francis Crick has even suggested that there is a religion gene, which determines whether its carrier will become a believer. Now *there* is a chance to rid the world of what Sigmund Freud described as an illusion, and have a human race with no sense of awe or obedience to inherited moral codes. If God is not already dead, as many people insist He is, the chance is coming to kill Him.

Who would take God's place? God—the Christian and Hebrew God, and the gods of Olympus and of the past, were open to appeals for mercy. The Gene is implacable. The discovery that so many of our activities are the result of our genetic make-up ushers in a new fatalism.

God—you understand that I use the word very generally and not with special reference to the Jehovah of the Old Testament—allows you to discover and experience your destiny slowly, as it happens. But when your genetic code can be read by your doctor, you and he, and your government, can know a great deal about yourself long before it happens. This is the new astrology. The old astrology is notoriously open to error and misunderstanding. But the genetic forecast cannot go wrong. What kind of life does that promise? Let me read you something in which two modern writers foresee the future of a family.

"Hugo wakes and checks his bedside clock. It is 8 a.m., May 2 in the year 2044 and he has 306,600 hours, or 35 years, to enjoy before he can expect the onset of Alzheimer's disease his genetic profile predicts. Above the bed hangs a colourful computer-generated chart that baldly presents the stuff of his life: his genetic strengths and weaknesses and their implications for his health, finances and his fitness to be a parent. The morning begins with a breakfast of hi-bran cereal and soya milk to which Hugo must limit himself in the sombre knowledge that he has an inherited predisposition to heart disease. Into the kitchen runs his three-year-old daughter Anna. She is proving more precocious than he and his wife Jean had been led to expect during their sessions with a counsellor in the genetic planning clinic. But will her parents regret the choice of bright red hair, green eyes and a dusky complexion which turns out to be more arresting than attractive in the child? . . . Though a natural City type, Jean works from home as a consultant. Her genetic profile, for which she was first tested ten years ago, recommended a swift departure from the frenetic world of the dealing room after an extra copy of chromosome 8 was detected and indicated a risk of leukemia. Her session with a Harley Street cell-formation expert was definitely worth the investment, although it doubled the family's annual insurance premium . . . In spite of strict legislation governing the use of such personal information, Hugo and his wife are concerned by press stories that employers are paying shadowy agencies to provide black-market genetic profiles of prospective employees. Lobby groups representing the 'genetically challenged' claim that a single hair is enough to ruin a person's career. But such legitimate anxieties are out-weighed by the control Hugo and Jean feel they exercise over their lives."

I think that Hugo and Jean are dreamers if they believe that in their world they will have control over their lives for long. In a civilization where the genetic code may be determined at birth what government is going to waste time and money educating the genetically inferior? They will become a slave group, inexorably directed toward the kind of work they are best fitted to do. The genetically superior will at birth have passed the examination that directs them toward the ruling caste. When we think how many of the world's geniuses have come from disastrous genetic backgrounds, endowed, we know not how, with gifts that have built and extended our civilization, we wonder what genetic engineering will be able to do that works better than chance? Why did Beethoven emerge from physical and moral squalor? Why did Goethe emerge from a long line of intellectual nobodies? Can genetic engineers tell us? Can they, by their art, replicate genius? And who are the genetic engineers? Persons of high intellect, perfect physique, and numbing normality, one presumes; persons heavily weighted on the scientific side and thus, while not hostile to arts and learning, have the attitude toward such things that is dictated by their highly logical minds. Such a world has many advantages.

Oh, has it, you say; but you have been painting a bleak picture of what it might bring. Oh yes, there are advantages in a genetically managed world. Better therapies for such diseases as cannot be stamped out. And of course commercial benefit, to which the world of the geneticists is not unheeding. The Centre for the Exploitation of Science and Technology has estimated that drugs derived from genome research will be worth $60 billion a year by the year 2010. And won't that be delightful for those who provide the drugs? And those who invest in them, getting in on the ground floor.

Improved health screening is a decided benefit, warning those who are likely to develop certain ailments to go on diets or do other appropriate things, to keep heart disease or cancer at bay. And think what a blessing it would be to employers, banks, and insurance companies to estimate whether or not they should become involved with people whose genetic pattern was likely to cause trouble. Beneath a benevolent front, banks and insurance companies are, to put it as kindly as possible, very canny.

Genetic engineering could improve food plants, making them resistant to drought, or plant diseases. This is already in progress, and has already discovered that there are problems, unsuspected, in feeding such plants to animals who respond unexpectedly—having, of course, no understanding of the marvel that is being tested on them.

(Or have they, and being without speech, are unable to tell us about it? The geneticists assure us that the genetic make-up of a human being is 98.4 per cent the same as that of a chimpanzee. What a pity that our brother the chimp is unable to share his thoughts with us. What a lot that difference of 1.6 per cent appears to make! Almost as great, may we say, as the difference between Einstein and—I had better not say?)

And we are assured that under genetic engineering, animals could produce organs that could be transplanted into humans without being rejected. Surely this will greatly increase the number of neighbourhood zoos, to which appeal can be made whenever somebody is seriously injured in a motor accident. How close we shall grow to Nature in the coming world! And of course psychoanalysts will have to cope not only with the inner child, but also the inner dog, monkey, or perhaps hen. There's a theme for fiction!

There are of course things—not organs but entities which in the past we were assumed to have—with which we shall no longer have to bother. Dr. Francis Crick thinks that what we have been accustomed to call the soul is simply grey matter and of little consequence. Dr. Crick is a Nobel Laureate. So are they all, these mighty scientists—all Nobel Laureates, and not to be cheeked by the likes of you and me.

When am I going to begin talking about the Fiction of the Future? But I have been talking all the time of the rich soil in which it will grow. Genetic engineering—what could open up a greater prospect to the writer of best-sellers? The Great Gene Scandal in Big Business, when it is discovered that the Chairman of the Board is genetically inferior, and that the jealous mockery of those who have always said that he was no better than a chimp has proved to be dreadful truth? There's a plot for you! And here's another: Hugo and Jean marry, or decide to cohabit, and have a child. They put in their order with the gene scientist and in due course their ideal child is born, genetically suited to the parents and they to it. But something goes wrong: Hugo has, somewhere in his make-up, a recessive gene which leads him to have an affair with a girl at the office, who has a particularly strong combination of sexually attractive genes. Do Hugo and Jean fight? Of course not. They agree to part amicably. But what about the tailor-made child? What happens to it? Which of the new unions will it fit? There's a *New Yorker* story for you. And of course all stories written on such themes must have happy endings. Nobody may blaspheme against the gene world, any more than in Queen Victoria's reign they could hope for popular success if they blasphemed against the Christian God.

Of course there will be darker tales, written by authors who value their inner vision above popular success. It requires no great feat of imagination to see what desolation of the spirit—if an author is still so courageous as to suggest the existence of such a thing—could arise in a world where so much can be controlled and scientifically determined. Can we suppose that in the future there will no longer be that group—call it ten per cent of society—which cannot accommodate to the civilization of their time, because they seem to be living in a different time? Their fate in a world where so much could be controlled by a variety of agencies and by governments composed of genetically sound people, and under the domination of Presidents and other rulers whose election had depended on the widest possible dissemination and public study of their genetic pattern—their fate, I fear, would not be as endurable as it is even now. And a wretched fate has always made good material for fiction.

There will be fiction of a finer sort, warning against the horrors that await a world which has gone—in the biblical phrase—whoring after unbridled science. We have already had some examples of this. So long ago as 1932 Aldous Huxley published *Brave New World,* about a future in which everything is controlled, and everybody happy—or as happy as people can be who have never known any other mental state. It is not perhaps a very good novel, for in it rather more than in most of Huxley's fiction, his ideas are vastly more interesting than his characters, and fiction at its best is an art devoted to the exploration of character. It is a world where no art exists, because people with no gamut of feeling need no art, and art may be disruptive. I reread it last summer, and in the heat of July it chilled my bones.

But did it fill me with fear? No, it did not. Nor do the newspaper reports of new triumphs in genetic study make me tremble for a future in which all of mankind will be guided and conditioned by what scientists believe is good for it. It certainly did not make me fearful of the end of all art, and fiction among the rest. As an experienced and careful newspaper reader I know better than that, and I have seen too many scientific marvels subside quietly into something less than was foreseen for them by the Henny-Pennys of the media who rush as often as possible to tell the King that the sky is falling.

Genes may explain much, but I do not think they can explain the inveterate hatred between the Serbs and the Croats, or the destructive ill will of the Hutus and the Tutsis. They cannot repeat Nature's splendid jokes, like Mozart and Shakespeare. They can do much for mankind, just as Pasteur's germ theory has done, but like Pasteur's germ theory they will become accepted as one of the miracles of science which the greater part of mankind is aware of, does not understand, and benefits from without quite knowing how. But the great gods of Chance and of Necessity, which the Greeks called *Anángke,* will continue to rule mankind as they always have, and in their cruel compulsions and sly jokes the writers of fiction—the real writers and not simply the followers of fashion—will find their themes.

Perhaps at this point I should interject that a new universal language is in the womb of time, but will not come to birth right away. It is the language of mathematics. My authority is the great philosopher, Alfred North Whitehead, who predicted, in 1941:

> Mathematics is the most powerful technique for the understanding of pattern, and for the analysis of the relation of patterns ... Having regard to the immensity of its subject matter, mathematics, even modern mathematics, is a science in its babyhood. If civilization continues to advance in the next two thousand years, the overwhelming novelty in human thought will be the dominance of mathematical understanding.

What might that mean to fiction? I cannot tell, but unless the entire structure of the human mind and spirit changes, I think that fiction will have a continuance for those who are impatient of the insistence of mathematics on certainties as opposed to probabilities, and even if mathematics develops to encompass the ambiguities of human experience, one wonders if it will ever have anything whatever to do with one of the greatest developments of the human spirit. I mean humour, the true deep humour, and not simply the humour of jokes. Not wisecracks among mathematicians about the Reciprocal of Pi.

One of the very great sages of the past, to whom I have always paid particular attention, was called Heracleitus; he lived about 2,500 years ago, and his ideas still seem to me to be fresh and widely applicable. He thought that the first principle of the universe was flux, a sequence of becoming and perishing. The world neglects him, and he is called The Weeping Philosopher, because people of sunny nature cannot bear his notion of the eternal ebb and flow; they think it pessimistic, because they are wedded to the idea that the history of mankind is unquestioningly progressive, and that every day in every way things are getting better and better. This notion of serial progress is particularly popular in the New World. But in spite of our nervous optimism, we seem always to need a bugbear ruler somewhere upon which we can fasten the fears without which civilized man seems unable to live. The bugbear used to be God; now it seems to be Science.

Heracleitus is not gloomy; he is just long-sighted. His most famous principle was that of regulating opposites; that is, in a terribly tight nutshell, the principle that positive and negative, struggling for supremacy, bring about equilibrium, or harmony. The grand name for this idea is dynamic monism, and we can catch glimpses of it out of the corner of an eye, though we cannot command the whole scheme unless we make an intensive study of history.

These warring opposites, like the fishes going different ways which are the symbol of the astrological sign of Pisces—can we see anything of them in the modern world? Well, as a determined newspaper reader I can inform myself every day about the latest developments in tolerance, political correctitude, and scientific advance and I can contrast them, sometimes on the same page, with the news that in the rural districts of South Africa, where a new freedom has just asserted itself, there is also a sharp rise in the number of witch-burnings; by mid-summer of 1994 there were records of seventy-one such burnings, which is greater than the total for all of the previous year. And where freedom of speech is loudly proclaimed in our part of the world, Muslim fundamentalists have now declared the death of two authors to be imperative, because they have contradicted the Koran. Can these opposites run together and form a balance? Heracleitus would probably say that as they exist side by side in what we triumphantly proclaim to be a global village, they are already doing so. The witch-burners are our neighbours.

I assure you that I am not straying from my theme, which was the Future of Fiction. The field for fictional exploration is broader perhaps than it has ever been, because the world reads more. Nothing that concerns mankind is alien to the teller of tales, whether he is the one who unfolds a mat in the market-place, or the one who works in her solitary room with her word processor. The writer looks with satisfaction toward our official entry into the Era of Flux, because if he pays heed to his daily paper, he has daily and almost hourly assurances that flux and the compensating dynamism of opposites is boldly at work.

He does not imagine—unless he writes Science Fiction and wants to make your flesh creep—that genetic engineering is going to reduce mankind's variety. Nor does he believe that good genes alone will produce a good human creature with a good destiny. If he should momentarily be tempted to think any such thing he has but to turn to his Bible for the ancient assurance that *Anángke* is still the ruler of all. He reads: "I returned, and saw under the sun, that the race is not to the swift, nor the battle to the strong, neither yet bread to the wise, nor yet riches to men of understanding, nor yet favour to men of skill; *but time and chance happeneth to them all.*" (Ecclesiastes 9:11)

In those words he knows that whether its form is the film or television, or simply the unfailing, reliable printed book, the Future of Fiction is safe. It is a necessity of life. For as Socrates assured us so long ago, the unexamined life is not worth living.

24

A GHOST STORY

From 1963 to 1981 Davies was the Master of Massey College, the graduate residential college at the University of Toronto. For most people, to conjure a university community out of thin air and to leave it with its traditions proudly established would mark the culmination of a life's work. Though not without achievements in other fields, Davies was justifiably proud of what he had done, and of the legacy left to later generations of scholars.

One of the happiest traditions established in these early years was Gaudy Night, a concert staged by the College community for its friends shortly before Christmas. The Gaudy incorporated another tradition, the annual ghost story told by Davies. (These stories have been collected and published under the title *High Spirits*.)

On December 10, 1988, in the Gaudy that celebrated the twenty-fifth anniversary of the College, Davies took the opportunity to pay tribute not only to the college, but to Vincent Massey, the remote, rather distant figure whose family fortune established it. The former Canadian diplomat, for many years Canada's High Commissioner in London, was reputed to be so urbane and polished that a British peer once complained that Massey made him "feel like a bit of a savage." Here Davies shows a different, more relaxed side of the man. Appropriately in this closing piece in the collection we find Davies remembering, at the end, his laughter.

His diary records the events of the Gaudy: College Gaudy Night *and a considerable success, for the Hall was full and the audience appeared to enjoy themselves. The student choir sang a few carols; LePan read several poems. Robert Finch read some occasional verse about the College; read well, verse admirably suited to the evening, witty and accomplished; warm applause. My Ghost Story went well, and afterward several people said how much they liked hearing some-body speak well of Vincent. After spiced wine and cake a group did Lister Sinclair's* We All Hate Toronto *very well, to deserved applause.*

When I was master of this College it was haunted, not just by a single apparition, but by a new ghost, or group of ghosts, at least once a year. I do not attribute this fact in any way to my own presence here; I have never had any reason to think myself particularly attractive to ghosts. Therefore I assumed that when I had retired the hauntings would continue, and I presume they did so, though I heard nothing of it. My successor was a scientist, and scientists do not hold with ghosts. I had not expected ever to meet with a Massey College Ghost again. But this is the twenty-fifth anniversary of the founding of the College, and it was my luck to be the one, in this special year, to see the ghost.

No, I should say, the ghosts, for there were two of them. Were they ghosts? Not precisely, but—let me explain. It happened one night in the late autumn—the Eve of All Souls, to be precise. I had been dining with the Master, and any of you who have had that splendid experience know that the Master not only provides an excellent dinner, but rather a lot to drink. I have frequently observed this in women who occupy official and ceremonial positions; they are astonishingly brisk and generous with the decanter—much more so than their male counterparts. Thus it was that, midnight having struck, and having dined very well, I picked up my coat in my own room, at the end of the quadrangle, and was making my way toward the gate, when I observed an extraordinary figure standing beside the pool. It was a young woman, stark naked, and so far as I could judge in the darkness and seeing only her back, of remarkable beauty. She seemed to be dipping a toe in the water, as if to test the temperature.

Who could she be? Since the College decided to include women among its Junior Fellows such apparitions are not utterly unheard of, but there was something about this young woman—rather a lot about her, in fact—which made it unlikely that she was a female academic. Some member of the Toronto Polar Bear Club, I wondered, training for the New Year's Day swim in Lake Ontario? But no. I do not know how to phrase this without seeming ungallant, but about the Female Polar Bears there is a want of spiritual quality, which this young woman evinced very strongly. She was no mere pretty girl, nor even a very beautiful girl; she was goddesslike, and I felt a strong sense of awe as I approached her. Because, you see, I had to pass her quite closely to reach the gate, and what with the stillness of the night, and the late autumn chill which had raised a slight mist, and it must be confessed the Master's generous drinks, I was not sure how I could do so without seeming to brush past her.

I had an unhappy inspiration: I would sing, or rather hum, thus displaying goodwill combined with nonchalance, and she might move out of my path. So I hummed the first thing that came into my head, and as it proved I could not have made a worse choice.

What I hummed was a round, the sort of round one learns as a child, and in which one takes an innocent delight because it is such an easy way of producing what sounds like fairly complicated harmony.

Youth is brief;
Hours of glee,
Time's a thief
And steals from me.

That was what I hummed, in a rollicking, carefree, but very musical manner.

The girl snatched her foot out of the water, and rounded on me. Her eyes were blazing, her nostrils dilated and contracted rapidly, and fierce indignation seemed to well out of her like heat from a fire.

"What did you say?" she demanded, in a voice that was indeed goddesslike, imperious and terrible.

Taken aback I hummed again:

Youth is brief;
Hours of glee,
Time's a thief—

"You wretch!" she said in low thrilling tones. "How dare you speak so? You shall be punished for your presumption. Into the pool with you!"

She seized me and began to push me toward the edge. I struggled, but I am no wrestler, and in any case she was a good fifty years younger than I, and in the pink of condition. I, after all, am no chicken—and I *had* been dining with the Master.

I was a gone goose, it seemed. Within seconds I would have been floundering in the icy water, but from behind me came a protesting voice.

"No, no, Verry! He meant no harm! Let the poor old soul alone. He might catch a dreadful cold."

"Didn't you hear what he said, Daddy?" cried the girl, or the goddess, or whatever she was. "'Time's a thief,' he sang. Am I to stand by and hear you spoken of in that way? Let me give him a good dowsing! Teach him a lesson."

I had escaped her clutch, but my umbrella was now floating in the pool, and I was astonished and frightened. My days of wrestling with girls, even clothed girls, are long past. But now the source of the protesting voice came within my view.

He seemed to be very old indeed, but he was a muscular, robust old man, to judge from the one bronzed arm with which he steadied me on my feet.

"Now, now, Verry. How often have I urged you not to make hasty judgements. You must excuse my daughter, sir," he said, very courteously. "She means well but she is dreadfully impulsive. Allow me to introduce myself: I am Time, as you may see from my hourglass and scythe, and this is my daughter Veritas. I call her Verry, for reasons of affection. Truth, the Daughter of Time. You fetch the gentleman's umbrella, Verry, and mind your manners."

"Shan't," said Veritas, pouting.

"Verry," said Time sternly, "just you do what Daddy tells you, and none of your nonsense."

Still pouting, but cowed, Truth stepped into the pool, and after a good deal of splashing about she found my umbrella, which had sunk to the bottom. She clambered wetly ashore, and thrust it at me. It was soaking.

I was greatly surprised. I shall go further, I was amazed, taken aback, flabbergasted, and totally overthrown. These were not *ghosts,* of which I have considerable experience, but mythological figures, whom I have never met before except in the pages of books, or represented in ormolu on the tops of those old-fashioned French clocks which insensitive relatives thought suitable as wedding presents. I accepted my dripping umbrella with a slight bow.

"I am much obliged," said I.

"No you're not. You're as mad as a wet hen, and so am I," said Truth, crossly.

"Verry, where are your manners?" said Time.

"But Daddy, he spoke an Untruth, and you know that if there is one thing I can't stand, it is an Untruth," said the girl.

"Don't tempt me, my daughter, to teach you that Truth is relative," said Time, looking threateningly at her.

I attempted to be a peacemaker in this family spat. "And a splendid young relative she is, sir," I said. "You have obviously given her a truly moral upbringing, and you may be proud of her. A fine figure of a goddess," I said, looking at her admiringly.

Mythological manners are not ordinary manners. Truth, who was still wet from the pool, shook herself like a large dog, and drenched me with water.

"Do you mind if we walk?" said Time. "You know, no doubt, that I never stand still. Let us promenade gently around this handsome quadrangle." And, taking me by the arm, he set out on what proved to be rather a long trek around our paths.

"Better put on your robe, Verry," said he; "we all know that truth is naked and unashamed, but Truth can also be embarrassing, and you may attract the wrong sort of attention. Not everybody recognizes mythology when they see it."

Truth picked up a splendid robe which I had not noticed at the poolside, and threw it about herself in a classical but not totally concealing manner.

We walked. Oh, how we walked! I have often walked around our College quadrangle, happy in its peace and retirement, but this was walking of a different sort. This was walking with Time. There was a disturbing inevitability about it, a lack of any occasional pause or stepping backward. I know that some poets and philosophers talk about Man being the prisoner of Time, but I had never understood the sinister overtone of the expression until now. But I tried to be agreeable.

"You are a formidable walker, sir," said I. "And I quite understand that you have to keep on the move. But did we not stand still for a moment or two beside the pool while your daughter was recovering my umbrella?"

Time laughed, a quiet, old man's laugh like the rustling of leaves. "That's because of your College clock," he said.

"You mean it's stopped? My dear Father Time, it would be more correct to say that it has never gone. It's a very modern clock, you see. The very latest thing—state of the art, and all that. So it's always been out of order. Sorry."

"You disappoint me," he said, chuckling deeper than ever. "I thought you kept it like that to signify that learning is eternal and outside time. I love stopped clocks, and wrong clocks, and clocks that have lost their hands; they give me a fleeting sensation of choice—as if I might stop for a bit and rest myself. That's part of the reason why I came here tonight; to refresh myself with a peep at your wonderful, computerized, solenoid-controlled, ineffectual modern clock."

"Indeed?" said I. "I had ventured to hope you were adding a little something special to our twenty-fifth anniversary. Not that twenty-five years means much in university life. Nevertheless, it has seen great changes in this place."

"Massey College looks as if it had been here much longer than a quarter of a century," said Time.

"Yes, but you know how fast Time flies in universities," said I. "Three years is a student generation. Twenty-five years ago, when this College was brand-new, everybody hated it: the architecture was ugly, the concept of the place was an insult to democracy, the peaceful structure of the life within these walls was an absurdity in the feverish modern world. But now, eight student generations later, it seems to the freshmen to have been here forever. They peep reverentially through the gate, hoping to catch a glimpse of Northrop Frye. As for the second- and third-year students, they have new buildings to hate, and new insults to deplore. You spoke a moment ago as if Time stood still in the world of learning, and, although that may be true, it is also a fact that Time flies here, as well." And carried away by the situation, I began to sing—

Youth is sweet;
Hours of glee—

"That's enough of that," said Truth, nudging me rudely and painfully in the ribs. "You keep a civil tongue in your head."

"Don't be intolerant, Verry," said Father Time. "He means no harm. He is a musical person, you see, and musical people never pay any attention to the words they are singing. They just like the noise. He doesn't really mean that I am a thief. Of course, I am a collector, but that is quite another thing. For instance, I have collected quite a lot of the past of this College."

"The best of it, I hope," said I.

"The most interesting," said Time. "Which is not the same thing. I have a fine collection relating to the Student Revolt of the sixties, when this College came into being. What lively times they were!"

"Pretty well forgotten, now," said I. "Modern students are very placid, on the whole."

"Yes, the revolutionary group have moved on," said Time. "Several who once were student leaders are now in politics. What nostalgia it arouses to see them in Opposition in the Legislature as they wave their accusing fingers across the House at the Government benches, uttering the same old cries, denouncing the same old enormities, and threatening the same old vengeances. Dear, good souls, they are growing grey in the cause of Reform, which is a very durable cause, but demands terrible personal sacrifices. The pickings are very poor in the Reform parties, so they have to find their satisfaction in virtue."

"You are a cynic, Father Time," said I.

"Not in the least. I think of myself as a realist because, placed as I am, I am able to see behind things, and know significant facts that escape the historians. For instance, you didn't have much trouble with student revolt here, did you?"

"Some slight protests," said I, "but nothing to speak of. I put it down to the fact that our Junior Fellows were graduate students, and had more serious things to do than raise Cain."

"Oh, but some of the most ensanguined student revolutionaries were graduate students," said Time. "No: what saved you from trouble here is a simple but powerful truth. It was regular meals."

"And that's a *very* powerful truth," said Truth.

"You were wise when this College was founded to establish a series of regular mealtimes. Sit-down meals nicely served are irresistible arguments against disorder," said Time. "The keenest revolutionary fervour has to pause when the bell rings for dinner. Consider the history of all revolutions: they are implemented by hungry crowds raging through the streets, and without any idea where or when their next meal is going to appear. Think of the French Revolution: people who were angry because they were hungry. Think of the American Revolution, begun by a people eager to initiate the Age of Fast Food. But here in Massey College dinner was always a certainty. Though the sky fell, dinner would be on the table. It is very hard to eat and feel indignant at the same time."

"And wine on guest nights," said Truth. "That was a clincher. Revolutions have been floated on gin, but never on good wine."

"How true all that is," said I. "It reminds me of one of my favourite Massey stories. In our very first month we were picketed by a group of girls carrying placards, demanding that they should be admitted to the College as Junior Fellows. They stalked up and down outside the gate, shrieking with fury. I had no idea what to do. But my wife and I were at lunch, and she said, 'Let me deal with this,' and she picked up a large loaf of gingerbread from the table and walked out to the protesting mob. 'Have you girls had any lunch?' she asked. The noise of the protest abated; indeed, it became almost pathetic. 'No,' said the girls. 'We haven't had a bite since breakfast and we won't get anything now. The seniors said we had to picket Massey for an hour, and when the hour has gone the seniors will have eaten everything. It's because we're freshies, you see.' Thereupon my wife, with Napoleonic éclat, unveiled and divided the gingerbread among them, and the atmosphere became positively genial. It was a lesson to me, I can tell you."

"I don't suppose you are going to pretend that you bought off all the ill will toward the College with gingerbread, are you?" said Truth. She was a disagreeable girl; always bringing everything down to rockbottom.

"No," I hastened to assure her. "Gingerbread would have been powerless against the students at Devonshire House, who were great wits, and thought it wildly funny to poison the goldfish in our ponds. Nor would gingerbread have prevented the cunning thieves who stole one of our bells right out of the tower, which must have been a dangerous and difficult thing to do. I often wonder where that bell is," I mused.

"I know where it is," said Truth; "and it has not brought much happiness to the people who took it. A bell is a noisy, embarrassing piece of booty. Hard to dispose of a hot bell."

"But aren't we becoming rather solemn?" I said. "You are visitors to the College. As one of its oldest members I should not like to think that we had dwelt too much on unhappy memories. We had some first-rate jokes. Of course you remember the lamb and the rabbits that appeared in the Quad our first Easter Sunday? Our College chronicle is really rather a happy one. You, Father Time, the great chronicler, know that very well."

"Oh, indeed, I do," said Time. "But it is beginning to rain quite heavily and you seem rather wet. Wouldn't you like to come under my mantle? You'll be very snug there."

I was tempted, for I was indeed very wet. That miserable girl Truth, who had shaken a lot of pool-water over me, had wetted me thoroughly, and the sleety downpour of the November night—All Souls' Eve, as I told you—had completed a terrible drenching. Could I avoid a cold by huddling under Father Time's ample blue cloak?

He lifted his arm invitingly, and I stepped forward—but only to recoil at once, in horror. For under Time's cloak I saw the faces of all the Massey people who were no longer with us: my dear friend Bill Broughall, the college lawyer; Austin Thompson, who was the most genial of financial advisers; Lionel Massey, who took such delight in the College and who died so early in its history; Vincent Bladen, dean of arts and sciences and a strong College friend; Gordon Wry, who used to arrange delightful music for us on such occasions as this; Ron Thom, our architect, who believed so devoutly and so truly that architectural surroundings influenced the people who lived in his buildings, either for good or evil, and who built so strongly for the good. There was Peter Lapajne, one of our best Porters, with a squirrel perched on his shoulder. And several faces I saw there, of Junior Fellows who had died untimely; there were young Africans there, who had been killed in the bloody disputes of Nigeria, and whom I remembered with respect and affection; some who had died of what are so strangely called natural causes, but which seem so unnatural in the young; and there was one who had died, unhappily, by his own hand. Many others; too many.

"Come along," said Time. "I have them all safely in my cloak, and there is plenty of room for you."

"Not yet," said I. "The wet and the cold are not so bad as I had thought."

"You never spoke a truer word than that," said his daughter. "And never forget it when you think you have cause to complain."

"Have it your own way," said all-devouring Time, and dropped his cloak.

"But Father Time," said I: "There was one face I missed, which I should dearly like to see again. Wasn't Vincent Massey somewhere beneath your cloak?"

"Indeed he was," said Time. "Didn't you see him?"

"I did not," said I. "But—no, no, the request is too bold—still, let me ask: could you, do you think, allow him to revisit this College that meant so much to him? It was here, I think, that he was most truly himself. It would give him so much pleasure to walk these paths again."

"What a fool you are," said Truth. "Do you suppose he is ever absent from it?"

"You mean that?" said I.

"Of course I mean it," said she; "I mean every word I say. Don't you remember that he used to talk about the *Genius Loci* of the College?"

"Indeed I do," I said. "The Genius Loci: the guardian of the Place."

"The atmosphere, the presiding spirit," said Time.

"That is what Vincent Massey is here," said Truth. "And so long as he is remembered by the College, it will continue to be so."

"How do you remember him?" said Time.

"Ah, well," said I; "I remember him as few people do, I think, because I knew him in a very special way. You see, he was not a man to whom everybody warmed, when they met him. They said he was austere, and forbidding, and he made them feel inferior. That wasn't what he wanted, of course, but he aroused that feeling in many people who are unsure of themselves. Canadians are like photographers: they think everybody smiles all the time. They knew that he was a friend of royalty, that he had known great statesmen and world figures intimately, that he was impatient of fools and people who took refuge in what was second best so that they could not be accused of élitism. Jealous people told rather derogatory stories about him. They said that he had built this College as a monument to himself. But he was a wise, shrewd, and ironic man; he used to laugh when high schools were named after him, and he cherished a headline about a high school hockey game that read: 'Vincent Massey Lambastes Sacred

Heart.' If perpetuating the ideals that were dearest to him makes this College his monument, let it be so."

"You do not paint an especially endearing picture," said Time.

"But I haven't finished," said I, "and I want your daughter, Truth, to understand that in what I am going to say I am very much aware of the quality she exemplifies and desires in others. His outward man could be chilling, but the inner man was a romantic and an artist, and he desired fiercely that romance and art should touch as many lives as possible. I understood that he was, in his heart, an artist, and I treated him like one."

"Being rather in that line yourself," said Time.

"Pooh! A concocter of complicated lies to amuse idle people," said Truth.

"You must excuse Verry," said Time. "I can never get it through her head that Art and Truth are not enemies but near relations."

"Exactly what Vincent Massey thought!" said I. "And so he found an artist to design and build this College for him, and he hoped earnestly that it would touch the lives of all who were associated with it in a special way, and give their lives an enduring truth. Because that is what colleges can do, you know. And whatever political and diplomatic concerns may have occupied a part of his life, he was first, last, and always a university man, and he believed in universities as places that could touch their children with fire, and light a flame that they would carry with them through the whole of their lives. You have seen the flames on the bordure that surrounds the College Arms. If, as you tell me, he is truly the Genius Loci of this place, he must be a very happy man, infusing the place that was dearest to his heart."

"What do you remember most clearly about him?" said Truth.

"I must say, his laughter," said I. "I always remember him as laughing, not because it was frequent but because it was so characteristic. He loved a joke—a real joke and not simply a wisecrack or a silly anecdote; he loved a real joke, that echoed and recurred and fed the fire I spoke of. He never forgot that one of the principal values of a college to the world around it is that it creates and fosters such jokes.

Sometimes the jokes raise a laugh; sometimes they provoke a smile that is a signal of quiet enjoyment; sometimes they do not show themselves outwardly at all, but sink down into the heart, and nourish it. I have heard him, in the Common Room here, yes, and in the Master's Lodging, produce jokes of all three kinds, and the students and the Seniors who heard him were enlarged and enriched, and were encouraged to seek jokes of their own, so that a splendid spirit of Humour was created. A spirit which never wholly dies, and which can be evoked and enlarged at any time when the Genius Loci is felt to be at work."

"If that is what you feel about him, why do you ask to see him?" said Truth. "What is deeply felt does not need to be seen, surely?"

"Quite true, Verry," said Father Time. "She has you there. But you know, we must be going. Time marches on, as people say, and time flies, and time hangs heavy, and all that nonsense. But Time must move. We have rested long enough under your ineffective clock—there's a joke for you. We shall say goodnight, sir, and ask you to present our compliments to the Master of this College, and beg her never to forget the Genius Loci, for without it your College is no more than a heap of brick, inhabited by students who are no more than lodgers, untouched by the hopes of the Founder."

Time shouldered his scythe, took a firmer grip of his hourglass, and began his walk to the gate. And much to my astonishment, as he walked he sang, and what he sang was a different version of the round by the singing of which I had fallen foul of Truth.

Youth is brief;
Hours of glee;
But no happy hour
Is lost to me.

Thus he sang, and Truth took up the second voice, and I the third, and so we carolled happily until Time and Truth reached the gate and—as one would expect of mythological creatures—walked right through the iron bars and into Devonshire Place, where they vanished.

I did not leave the College at once. I looked about at the quadrangle, which was still wet, though the rain had ceased, and a shy moon was peeping tentatively through some ragged cloud. The College looked very fine, I thought. All set for another twenty-five years of doing what, from the beginning, it had been meant to do. And as I left I thought I heard, faintly but clearly, a well-remembered laugh.